The Posh Pescatarian

Stephanie Harris-Uyidi

Going Coastal

200+ Coastally Inspired Seafood Recipes
from Around the Globe

Posh One Media

1st Edition
Graphic Design and Illustrations by Oriana Bonato
Edited by Kelly Greenwood
Photography by Stephanie Harris-Uyidi, Juan Bautista, Chantal Lim,
Meritt Thomas, Rachel Martin, Pietro Izzo, Red's Best
Photo Editing by Anastasiya Murachova
Library of Congress Cataloging-in-Publication Data
Publication Data
Names: Harris-Uyidi, Stephanie
Title: The Posh Pescatarian: Going Coastal – 200+ Coastally Inspired Seafood Recipes
ISBN- 13:978-1468144444
Description: Posh One Media (2022)
Subject: Pescatarian cooking, seafood cookery, cuisine, food travel, cookbooks, sustainable cooking, international gastronomy, home cooking

Catfish, Cod, Halibut, Sea Bass, Tilapia and More

Mahi Mahi, Opah, Swordfish, Tuna, Yellowtail, Wahoo & Other Large Game Fish Recipes

Shark & Skate Recipes

Salt Cod

Arctic Char, Salmon, Trout & Other Oily Fish Recipes

Whole Fish

Raw Seafood Recipes

Brunch, Sandwiches and Salads

Soups, Chowders and Broths

Tinned Fish Recipes

Sauces, Salsas and Spice Blends

DEDICATION

This book is dedicated to all of the spectacular coastal cities around the world that I have had the pleasure of visiting and the communities of people that were kind enough to share the wonders of their cultures, traditions and food. You kept me safe, well-fed and inspired. To the waterfront places that I have yet to set foot in, rest assured, I'm coming your way soon.

ACKNOWLEDGEMENTS

Creating this book would have proven impossible were it not for the support of an entire network of people.

Mom and Dad, thank you for bringing me into this world, for teaching me that there are no limits in life, and for encouraging me to actively seek out new adventures.

To my sisters, Natalie, Leslie, Kimberli and all of my nieces, nephews, aunts, uncles, cousins and friends —thank you for providing me with an endless supply of encouragement, good vibes, and for being some of the best food critics a girl could ask for.

A special thanks to my husband, Alain, for rolling with me during all of our vacations-turned-food-tours, random trips to the market, and displaying an incredible amount of patience as I turned our kitchen into "The Lab."

To my creative, eagle-eyed editor Kelly Greenwood, thank you for pushing me to level up the manuscript.

I would also be remiss not to mention my incredible supporters, PR team, creative minds, and travel partners who continue to keep me motivated, challenged and inspired.

Finally, thanks to my Creator, who made all of this possible.

Introduction

Can you hear the waves crashing around you? From the big, beautiful breakers of the California coast and the bold and boisterous sands of Rio de Janeiro to the cool, rocky beaches of Ireland—sea swells and shores around the world abound with a vivid array of captivating seafood species. Smell the salty sea air and prepare to Go Coastal!

In this collection of globally inspired seafood recipes, I have thoughtfully curated dishes inspired by my travels and food tours to coastal regions. You'll find recipes shared by families along the seaboard who opened their homes to me for private cooking lessons; seaside chefs who shared their secrets for creating restaurant-quality seafood meals; and seafaring friends who have gladly shared their cooking traditions and favorite family recipes with me.

I believe that we are all looking to connect. What better way to bring people together than to prepare a meal from a different part of the world and experience its unique, exciting flavors? Within these pages, you'll find a balance of recipes with a pinch of posh and a dash of down-to-earth and practical. Those looking to dive into more complex recipes will devour chic recipes like West

African Fish Stew and Scandinavian Gravlax or Caribbean Salt Cod Fritters. On the other hand, if you are looking to sink your teeth into simple, straightforward seafood dishes, you'll enjoy whipping up a 'Best Coast' Salmon Caprese Sandwich or a big bowl of Isle of Capri Lemon Garlic Scampi Pasta. If you are new to seafood or have only dabbled a bit, don't worry—there's plenty here for you, too. Mouthwatering Aleutian Islands Fish & Chips and Baja Fish Tacos will have you looking forward to fish night every week! No matter your cooking skills, you'll be able to dive right into all kinds of fun, flavorful seafood recipes.

Rest assured that you will not have to search to the ends of the earth for any of the ingredients called for in this book, but on occasion, you may need to place a special request with your local fishmonger for an item like fish bones or collars, or order something online like salt cod or sambal oelek. I think you'll find it's well worth it!

In these pages, you'll find that I often attribute recipes to a specific location; in other instances, I mark them as regional since some culinary traditions, cooking styles and ingredients ring true for miles in many parts of the world. This is especially true in the Mediterranean, West

Africa, Scandinavia and the Balkan Peninsula. I did my best to represent as many coastal regions as possible and was admittedly a little heavy-handed with the West Coast of the United States—it's where I am from and it is a region that boasts some of the best seafood on the planet. This is why you'll see me affectionately refer to the West Coast as the 'Best Coast' in some recipes.

You'll find seafood varieties that are familiar and available in almost every part of the world due to the advent of aquaculture and popular delivery services, as well as to me species that are local and native to specific regions. I did this in case, you have the opportunity to travel to a recipe's destination and want to use truly authentic ingredients; however, in most of these cases I have provided alternative options and substitutes, just in case.

Throughout this book, you will find tips, cooking advice and my notes in sections affectionately called "Posh Pointers." These pages are designed to provide how-to tips, detailed info on species, and fun facts. They will help you get unstuck when faced with a new food challenge, like selecting shellfish or cleaning squid. Topics like purging clams and removing the bloodline from fish are also included.

Most of the food photos you'll find throughout the book have been styled and photographed by yours truly, along with snapshots on loan from friends. Aside from being a practical decision (I was free to cook and snap away any time of day!), I wanted you to know what the food would actually look like once made. In this era of social media, I've learned that overly produced images can lead to confusion and disappointment. Naturally, I did fancy things up a bit with styling and color correction, but nothing out of reach or over the top.

Use this book like a good friend (me!) who is hanging out with you in your kitchen, planning your next culinary trip to the coast. Thumb through the pages, find the recipes and flavors that resonate with you, and start cooking! After you make the recipe my way for the first time, I encourage you to start experimenting and make the dish with your own spin. The beauty of cooking at home is that you are in charge.

So from my kitchen to yours, **bon appétit!**

Stephanie

About this book

~~~~~~~~~~

This book is meant to transport you to different parts of the world through sustainable, approachable seafood recipes that feature a host of lively ingredients. It's a celebration of the coastal regions around the globe. I aimed to cover as much territory and reference as many places as possible.

To make searching easy, I've broken the recipes up into seven main sections. My reasoning is a bit unconventional, but hear me out. I start with the end in mind with entrées—from there, you can build your meal. This is how I typically plan for entertaining; I decide on the main dish and build my menu from there.

- **Entrées**
- **Side Dishes and Legumes**
- **Soups & Chowders**
- **Appetizers and Small Bites**
- **Raw Seafood**
- **Brunch, Sandwiches and Salads**
- **Sauces, Salsas and Spice Blends**

You will enjoy the recipes in the **Entrées** section, which makes up the bulk of the book and is further broken down into seafood types to help you navigate and find what speaks to you! There are boatloads of delectable dishes in this section, like Isle of Capri Lemon Garlic Scampi Pasta, Trinidad & Tobago Curried Shrimp, Galician Navajas (Razor Clams) with Saffron Rice, Icelandic Sea Scallops with Basil Lemon Butter, Cambridge Bay Arctic Char with Creamy Dill Sauce, and about 80 more.

The Side Dishes and Legumes chapter is designed to satisfy all kinds of palates; some recipes are even hearty enough to work as a vegetarian meal and most are kid-friendly. Brazilian Feijão, Crispy St. Petersburg Potatoes, Cuban Accaras and Tunisian Vegetable Couscous are a few to look forward to.

You will find the Soups and Chowders in this book to be incredibly flexible and forgiving. I encourage you to get playful and tweak the portions and ingredients when appropriate. Get creative with recipes like Central Coast Wild Salmon & Fresh Corn Chowder, Louisiana Seafood Gumbo and Mexican Halibut Pozole—an extra dash of this or a heavier pinch of that will help make these recipes your own.

The Appetizers and Small Bites section includes dishes that require a little preparation and some that are pretty much effortless. You'll relish recipes like English Whelks with Garlic and Basil Lemon Butter, Texas Gulf Shrimp,

Queso Fundido (Cheese Sauce), Loch Etive Scottish Smoked Trout Pâté, and Tinned Fish recipes like Italian Smoked Clams and White Beans on Toast.

I carved out a **Raw Seafood** section because this style of cooking has started to gain traction and is one of my favorite ways to enjoy seafood. You'll find dishes that make great starter options, like Peruvian Shrimp Ceviche and Wild Alaskan Halibut Ceviche with Mango, and more exotic options like Hokkaido Opah Tataki, Tahitian Poisson Cru and Spicy Tuna Poke.

Starting the day with fish is common in places like the American South, Israel, Norway and throughout the Caribbean. Tasty meals like Blackened Snapper & Grits and the Big Sur Dungeness Crab & Avocado Benedict can be found in the Brunch, Sandwich and Salads section, along with approachable sandwiches and exotic salads. Tillamook Bay Wild Sockeye Salmon Grilled Cheese and NOLA Oyster 'Po Boy are coastally inspired comfort foods for the soul.

Sauces, Salsas and Spice Blends range from simple dressings to exotic, chunky salsas. They add flavorful panache to baked, broiled and roasted fish and vegetables. Caribbean Pineapple Chow, Carpinteria Avocado Salsa and Hopkins Village Mango-Avocado Salsa will take you to another world.

Meander through the pages as if you are walking along your favorite beach, or better yet, stick your toes in the sand, thumb through the recipes, and discover your next vacation on a plate.

CONSCIOUS CUISINE:

Sustainable Seafood

This book focuses on global seafood recipes, but I would be remiss not to mention a topic that is close to my heart, and that may explain why some species have been left out of these pages (orange roughy, for example)—the issue is sustainable seafood.

Over the years, my focus has been on preparing sustainably harvested seafood. I quickly became an advocate when I learned that I could be responsible for eating the very last red snapper on earth. I soon changed the way that I shopped for fish and started asking questions.

You have certainly heard the term "sustainable seafood" but may not know its significance. Sustainable seafood is seafood that is caught or cultivated in a manner that has minimal environmental and social impact.

Here's the deal: seafood is so delicious that wild fish have been extracted from the ocean faster than they can replenish. It's called overfishing, and it's one of the biggest threats facing our oceans. Overfishing, combined with the steady demand for fish, has put the availability of wild seafood on the decline and has placed aquaculture front and center. Farmed fish, which is also referred to as cultivated seafood, is the answer to our current state of affairs, although sustainable wild-capture fisheries are active in some places like Alaska. Sustainable seafood can limit the impact on our oceans, protect essential habitats and reduce the social and economic impact on communities.

The U.S. is a recognizable leader in both farmed and wild-capture sustainable seafood. Since I am an American, most of my sources and experts are U.S.-based. One of my go-to sources is the U.S. National Oceanographic and Atmospheric Administration (NOAA) Fisheries. NOAA Fisheries supports U.S. participation in a number of international fisheries agreements and takes steps to address global illegal, unreported, and unregulated (IUU) fishing, and provides assistance to other countries. Through sustainable seafood practices, fish populations are managed in a way that provides for today's needs while allowing the species to reproduce and be available for future generations.

How do you know if your fish is sustainable?

Start by identifying the source—where the fish was harvested is a good starting point, and most markets will have this info noted on the tag. The other thing to look for is the method of harvesting. Fishers use a variety of methods to land their catch, and the most common are listed here. Visit **montereybayaquarium.org** for more details.

Fishing Methods

- Beach and Boat Seines
  (long nets with ropes on each end)
- Bottom Trawls
- Dredges
- Gillnets
- Hardlines and Gills
- Harpoons
- Longlines
- Midwater Trawls
- Pole-and-Line or Rod-and-Reel
- Pots
- Purse Seines
- Trolling Lines

Farming Methods

- Bottom Culture
- Off-Bottom Culture
- Pens
- Ponds
- Raceways
- Recirculating Tanks

Each type has its own effect on the environment. Organizations around the world are dedicated to promoting sustainable fisheries and have made the selection process simple by offering seafood guides and labels that help to easily identify sustainable seafood. Some restaurants even advertise that their products fall in line with sustainable practices.

The list of seafood considered 'sustainable' can change at any given time. To stay informed, be sure to check with reliable sources. I have included a list on my website www.poshpescatarian. com with organizations like the EDF Seafood Selector, Monterey Bay Aquarium Seafood Watch, Ocean Wise and WWF Seafood Guides.

Kitchen
Favorites

〰〰〰

This book is a celebration of the coastal kitchen. Just like traveling to another part of the world where you learn to say "hello," "thank you," and "which way to the beach" in the native tongue, there is also a kitchen language that you'll soon learn to navigate. It's easy to learn and worth exploring!

Coastal cooking is all about flavorful, high-quality ingredients. It starts with the seafood, but the supporting cast of pantry staples and refrigerator essentials helps bring personality and cultural significance to each dish.

Specialty ingredients are rare in this book, but they will pop up on occasion. Fortunately, we live in an age where almost anything is accessible via the internet. In some cases, you can ask your local market or grocery store to place an order for you at no cost.

A few of my favorite coastal ingredients you'll find throughout the book:

- **Avocado oil**
- **Butter: European, American**
- **Ghee or clarified butter**
- **Freshly ground black pepper**
- **Salt:** Kosher salt, sea salt, fleur de sel and specialty salts made from scratch

- **Seaweed**
- **Red pepper flake**
- **Fresh herbs**
- **Olive oil**
- **Citrus fruit:** Lemon, lime, orange

Equipment:

- Dutch oven
- Cast iron skillet
- Fish grate
- Bowls and ramekins
- Mandoline
- Sharp knife
- Microplane for grating citrus and hard cheeses
- Vegetable peeler
- Fine mesh colander or strainer
- Silicone or rubber spatula
- Seafood cracker and pick
- Fish spatula
- Metal spatula
- Tongs
- Parchment paper
- Grill pan
- Sheet pan
- Food processor
- Immersion (stick) blender
- Cutting board
- Lump charcoal
- Salad spinner
- Pressure cooker

Pantry basics:

- **Rice:** Carolina Gold, jasmine, basmati, brown, short-grain white
- **Panko breadcrumbs**
- **Canned tomatoes:** Crushed, diced and sauce
- **Legumes:** Cooked and dried
- **Tinned fish**
- **Pasta:** Dried and fresh
- **Capers in brine**
- **Mustard:** Yellow and whole grain
- **Jam and jelly**
- **High-quality prepared bouillon such as clam base, seafood stock, vegetable broth**
- **Tortillas:** Flour and corn

❄ Freezer:

- **Fish and shellfish of all sorts**
- **Rice of all kinds**
- **Legumes:** Black-eyed peas, fava beans, lima beans
- **Flatbread:** Chapati, naan, padinia, paratha, roti, tortillas
- **Vegetables:** Bell pepper, spinach, mushrooms, pumpkin

SEAFOOD BENEFITS:

Fish is Brain Food!

As Mark Bittman says in his cookbook Fish:

"... in the best of times people believe that a serving of fish a day guarantees a long life. In the worst of times, they believe that each serving shortens their lifespan."

In this part of the book, I aim to arm you with the basics of the benefits of seafood and to encourage further exploration.

There is no doubt that fish is healthy and an important part of our overall diets. In addition to being delicious, eating at least two servings of seafood per week offers numerous health benefits. A routine of 4 ounces of non-fried fish every week may also lower your risk of heart disease and reduce the onset of Alzheimer's, dementia and more. According to one Harvard study, seafood can prevent heart disease, stroke and congestive heart failure.

Fish-derived omega-3 fatty acids known as eicosapentaenoic acid (EPA) and docosahexaenoic acid (DHA), also referred to as marine-derived omega-3s, are types of fat that our bodies cannot make on their own, yet are essential to our survival. We can only get omega-3s from the foods that we eat, and fish are one of the most excellent sources. Catfish, cod, oysters, shrimp and tilapia contain some of this essential nutrient, but oily fish like herring, mackerel, trout, tuna, salmon and sardines are the best options. For

vegetarians or occasional fish-eaters, plant-based sources like chia seeds, flaxseeds, pumpkin seeds and walnuts are great omega-3 sources.

Oily fish are those with oil permeated throughout their flesh and belly cavity, rather than just their organs as in most white fish. They are predators that typically swim near the surface, or pelagic zone. They are rich in omega-3 fatty acids and vitamins A and B.

The benefits of omega-3s were first discovered in the 1970s when Danish researchers studying Inuit communities in Greenland observed a lower rate of death from coronary disease among local Inuit people versus the Danish people living in the area, as reported by ACSM's Health & Fitness Journal.

The lower incidence of coronary disease was thought to be caused by a difference in diet. Inuits consumed high amounts of whale, seal, fish and marine life, while the Danish ate a traditional diet of meat and full-fat dairy products. This natural experiment demonstrated the benefits of eating a diet rich in omega-3s. This research had a profound effect on cardiovascular research since it showed that some fats can be good for your heart.

The Nutritional Studies Research Group at Stanford University writes that omega-3 fatty acids have been shown to lower blood triglyceride levels and inflammatory markers. Check with your health care provider for information and specific guidance. Here are a few of my favorite factoids:

✳ Researchers from the Ronald Reagan UCLA Medical Center have found that consuming fish that is prepared in a healthful way—broiled, baked or steamed—on a regular basis is linked to higher functionality in areas of the brain that are responsible for comprehension and recollection in adults. Other studies reveal that a diet that includes fish helps prevent plaque build-up in the brain, which is believed to be one of the causes of Alzheimer's disease and dementia.

✳ Enjoying fatty or oily fish such as salmon, mackerel and sardines, which contain selenium and omega-3 fatty acids, can help balance mood and lower the risk of depression.

✳ Eating more fish and seafood regularly can reduce the risk of obesity since it is low in calories and saturated fat and high in healthy fats. White-fleshed fish in particular are lower in fat than 27 any other source of animal protein, while oily fish are high in omega-3 fatty acids, or the "good" fats. Since the human body can't make significant amounts of these essential nutrients, oily fish are an important part of the diet. Fish is also low in the "bad" fats (commonly found in red meat), known as omega-6 fatty acids.

✳ Fish is a high-protein, low-fat food that provides a range of health benefits. According to contemporary guidelines, eating two 3–4-ounce servings of non-fried seafood per week benefits the cardiovascular system and can help reduce the risk of heart disease, stroke, Alzheimer's and dementia.

There are countless organizations, studies and research efforts that explore the benefits of seafood in great detail. Note that it is important to mix up the variety of seafood that you eat on a regular basis—sticking to one variety is not only unexciting but has an effect on the sustainability of seafood and exposure to contaminants. I encourage you to speak with your doctor and do a little research on your own.

Navigating Seafood Counter Terminology

No doubt you have visited a seafood counter or fish market and been faced with some confusing terminology. Labels are great if you know how to interpret them, but *what if you don't?*

How long has your seafood been out of the water? How was it caught and what has happened to it since? These are the questions that I'll address in this section.

Let's start with the debate over fresh vs. frozen fish, which has often been an argument about nutrition and quality. Rumor has it that frozen fish is less nutritious than fresh fish, but that is not necessarily the case. Fish frozen within hours of harvesting maintains as many of its nutrients as fresh, depending on the time between harvest and freezing. Crab is a good example.

The terms outlined below hold true for most parts of the world. Because I'm based in the United States, my expert sources are predominantly U.S.-based; however, there is no universal labeling system for fresh and frozen food.

FISH OUT OF WATER: SEAFOOD PRESERVATION AND PROCESSING

[FRESH]

This term generally implies that the fish is in its raw state and has never been frozen. However, the term is not regulated in most countries and is not an indication of quality. When you see this label, ask the fishmonger how long the fish has been there.

[FRESHLY FROZEN, FRESH FROZEN, FROZEN FRESH, OR FROZEN AT SEA (FAS)]

Seafood described by any of these terms generally implies that the seafood has been quickly frozen while fresh, either on the fishing vessel or within hours of harvesting at a processing plant. Fish frozen at sea can mean that the fish was frozen whole for later processing or that it was landed, filleted and processed. Groundfish, which live near the bottom of the sea, are highly perishable and are typically FAS.

[INDIVIDUALLY QUICK FROZEN (IQF) AND GLAZED]

This describes fish pieces that are individually flash-frozen and glazed, bagged, and boxed for shipping to stores. Fish that have been glazed have been sprayed with or dipped in icy water, which freezes them instantly in a protective coating that helps prevent freezer burn.

[FLASH-FROZEN OR BLAST FREEZING]

When seafood is quickly blast-frozen at a sub-zero temperature, it's considered to have been flash frozen. This blast freezing process is a technologically advanced preservation method that ensures that the fish is fully frozen at the peak of freshness. Under ideal conditions, this process prevents the formation of ice crystals, which helps maintain flavor, texture and quality.

[PREVIOUSLY FROZEN, DEFROSTED OR REFRESHED]

These terms can be used interchangeably and mean that seafood has been defrosted after being frozen. Note that previously frozen fish that is fully defrosted should never be added back to the freezer or the quality and flavor will be compromised. Fish that has been 'refreshed' typically refers to fish that was frozen in blocks and then thawed for resale. The quality of refreshed fish can be high, but it depends on how it has been handled.

[1X AND 2X FROZEN]

Seafood that has been frozen one time, typically at sea is considered 1X frozen. Fish that is first frozen at sea, then brought back on shore, thawed and processed into steaks, fillets and portions then refrozen are considered 2X frozen.

Country of Origin, sometimes abbreviated as COO or COOL, is a labeling standard in the United States that requires retailers to provide customers with information about the source of the seafood and indicate where the fish was significantly modified, e.g., skinned or filleted. This holds true for other products like produce, nuts, seeds and ginseng.

[SUSHI GRADE]

The term "sushi grade" is a pure marketing term. The truth about sushi-worthy fish is that the U.S. Food and Drug Administration (FDA), the European Food Safety Authority and other government agencies require that all seafood used for sushi be processed in what is referred to as a "parasite destruction guarantee." This process requires freezing at certain temperatures for several days.

The effectiveness of freezing depends on the temperature, the length of time, the species and the source of the fish. Critical limits, according to the FDA, are freezing and storing at an ambient temperature of -4°F (-20°C) or below for seven days or freezing at -30°F (-35°C) or below until frozen solid or storing at an ambient temperature of -31°F (-35°C) or below for 15 hours.

All living organisms can have parasites, including fruit, vegetables and seafood. Cooking or freezing can help prevent health concerns.

[CATCH OF THE DAY: SEAFOOD HABITAT & CATCHING METHODS]

The Marine Stewardship Council (MSC), Monterey Bay Aquarium Seafood Watch Program, the Sustainable Seafood Coalition and other organizations provide a wealth of information on all things fisheries. It's important to know that fisheries are defined by the way they catch fish and the type of equipment used.

[WILD CAUGHT]

Caught in their natural environment, wild fish are considered higher in quality because they enjoy a diet that is more diverse than cultivated fish. Wild fish will always cost more than farmed fish and are in decline due to overfishing, which has resulted in the rise of aquaculture.

[CULTIVATED OR FARMED (AQUACULTURE)]

Used interchangeably to describe farmed fish or aquaculture, cultivated fish are commercially raised in pens that float in lakes, rivers and oceans (controlled water environments). Fish and shellfish are raised in this way due to our global appetite for seafood. Barramundi, clams, oyster, halibut, mussels, salmon, tilapia and other varieties of seafood are farmed these days. The Marine Stewardship Council notes that responsibly raised seafood is produced in a way that minimizes environmental impact and protects workers' rights and local communities.

[FRESHWATER VS. SALTWATER]

Aside from the actual water that they swim in, saltwater fish have a brinier taste, and despite their habitat, are not high in sodium. Freshwater fish are mild in flavor and the flesh has small flakes and bones.

Shopping for Seafood

Fishmongers are the boulangères, fromagers and sommeliers of the seafood world.

The same way you'd query a fromager about the best cheese options for your charcuterie platter or a sommelier for guidance on the best wine to serve with supper, consulting fishmongers about your seafood purchase can make all the difference in your shopping experience. Find a good one, and shopping for seafood will be easy, enjoyable, and if you're lucky, adventurous—most fishmongers love to introduce customers to new varieties and cuts of seafood like bones, cheeks and wings.

If your local market does not have a designated fishmonger or knowledgeable seafood counter staff, no worries! I will provide you with some shopping tips to help you buy quality seafood that will fit your budget, recipe type and lifestyle.

I'm stating the obvious here, but a good seafood meal starts with good fish! Don't be afraid to chat up your fishmonger. Tell them what you have on the menu and your budget and they can help guide your selection, often helping the novice cook avoid making bad choices like catfish ceviche.

ASK QUES- TIONS

Fishmongers know all about the fish that they have available—when it arrives, whether it's wild or cultivated (farmed), and so on. Most fishmongers should be able to offer recipe ideas and serving tips.

Don't be afraid to ask questions at the fish counter. In the same way that a proper restaurant server is required to know about the establishment's menu, the folks behind the fish counter are inclined to do the same.

"WHERE IS THE FISH FROM? HOW WAS IT CAUGHT?"

This will give you the first clue about the sustainability of the fish. There should be signage available that spells out important details about the fish's identity, but sadly not every shop follows this policy.

"HAVE YOU TRIED THE ____?"

Asking this question will reveal whether your fishmonger has actually cooked with or eaten the fish you are eyeing in the case. This is important because it will tell you if you can rely on them for recipes.

"WHICH OYSTERS ARE YOUR FAVORITES?"

You will either get a direct and specific answer or a total diversion. If your fishmonger does not like oysters, it's ok—what you want to hear is something like, "My customers who love oysters enjoy these ____." Or "I'm not a big fan, but my oyster-loving customers like these ____ for barbecuing and these ____ for eating raw."

"I HAVE 30 DOLLARS AND NEED TO FEED FIVE PEOPLE! WHAT SHOULD I BUY?"

This question may get you a good deal per pound on fresh seafood or sent to the frozen section for bulk seafood packages. Nothing wrong with this—frozen seafood is often a great option.

NO FISHMONGER? - NO PROBLEM!

With a little foresight and direction, anyone can learn to shop for seafood on their own with a little help from an expert. It can be a straightforward experience if you follow a few basic guidelines. Here are some tips from a few expert sources like the U.S. FDA, the Environmental Defense Fund and good old common sense.

Tips for buying fresh fish:

• The seafood section or market should look inviting and smell clean. If you happen to be shopping at a store that processes and sells fish (my preference), then the shop will likely smell like fish but not fishy.

• Out-of-package seafood located behind the fish counter case should be refrigerated or packed on ice and the display should look appealing, demonstrating the store's commitment to excellence. Neatness counts!

• Product behind the case should be labeled appropriately. Depending on where you live, the amount of detail on the label will vary. Basic information will include descriptions like: wild, cultivated/farmed, line-caught, country of origin and sustainability qualifiers like the Marine Stewardship Council (MSC) and the Aquaculture Stewardship Council (ASC).

- Use your senses.

Look for seafood that smells fresh and mild, not fishy, sour or ammonia-like.

When buying whole fish, look for eyes that are clear and that bulge a little (except for a few naturally cloudy-eyed fish types, such as walleye pike).

Whole fish and fillets should have firm, shiny flesh, bright red gills free of slime, and the flesh should spring back when pressed.

Fish fillets that have been previously frozen may have lost some of their shine, but they are fine to eat; however, they should display no darkening or drying around the edges.

BUYING FROZEN FISH:

Frozen fish is a good and sometimes economical option that will allow you to enjoy seafood year-round, even when a particular species is out of season. I keep frozen seafood and various cuts of fish in my freezer as a rule and make sure to note the date of purchase so that I can rotate it as needed—the fish with the older date gets used first.

Quality frozen fish is readily available in most markets. Thanks to modern technology, commercially caught fish can be processed and frozen immediately on the fishing vessel, which means that frozen fish can be "fresher" than fresh fish since it is immediately preserved. The level of freshness of seafood depends on where you shop and if the store is following all of the best practices I mentioned in the previous section on buying fresh fish.

Follow these shopping tips to catch the best frozen seafood:

- The freezer section of the store should be clean, orderly and look appealing. This is a sign that the store cares and that this section of the store is not neglected.

- Bypass packages that are positioned above the "frost line" or at the top of the market's freezer case because the temperature at the frost line is different from the temperature below the line, and this can affect the quality of the fish. Avoid purchasing seafood with packages that are open, torn or crushed on the edges.

- Don't bother with packages that contain ice crystals—this usually means that the fish has been stored for a long time or has thawed and been refrozen, which is a no-no. Poor handling of fish results in low-quality, freezer-bitten flesh.

- Do not refreeze fish once it has been defrosted.

FAUX FISH: BEWARE OF FISH FRAUD

When a less expensive fish is substituted and sold for a more expensive variety, it's called fish fraud. I have actually been a victim of this and learned my lesson fast! I wasn't confused, I knew what I ordered, but suffered the old bait and switch—I ordered and paid $32 for two pounds of sea bass, and when I got home I had about $6 worth of another fish called basa.

Getting familiar with the look and feel for specific fish in their whole, filleted and steak versions will help you identify this issue, which happens at restaurants and markets all over the world.

Other forms of fish fraud include dishonest labeling. If you have seen seafood labeled as "organic," this is a red flag. Another one is "wild" Atlantic salmon—as a reminder, Atlantic salmon are only cultivated these days.

If you think you have experienced fish fraud, raise the issue with the market or seller.

Seafood Safety and Storing Fish

It happens to all of us—you buy a few pounds of seafood and you end up having to push pause on cooking it for one reason or another. Don't sweat it; as long as you store it properly and keep it safe, you will be fine and the quality will be maintained.

Keep these tips in mind for "fresh" or "refreshed" (thawed) finned fish:

• For finned fish that you purchase and plan to use within two days, place fillets, whole fish, steaks or parts on ice in the refrigerator in a covered container that drains so that melted ice does not touch the fish. Or, securely wrap and place the fish in the back of the refrigerator, which tends to be the coldest area.

• For fish that you plan to cook further out, wrap it tightly in moisture-proof freezer paper or better yet, vacuum-seal the wrapping to prevent air leaks and store it in the freezer.

• Do yourself a favor and freeze fish on the first day of purchase instead of a few days later when the fish has started to spoil. When in doubt, freeze it.

• The freezer is not a "forever home" for your catch. Truth be told, frozen fish and shellfish can remain technically safe in your freezer indefinitely, but the flavor and texture will be compromised dramatically if held too long. The general guidance for holding frozen finned fish is 3 to 8 months, but I never keep it that long (guidance for shellfish is in the next section). The U.S. FDA recommends maintaining a freezer temperature of 0°F (-18°C) or less.

Storing Shellfish

Shellfish fall into two categories: crustaceans like lobster, crab, crawfish and shrimp, and mollusks such as clams, squid, octopus and scallops. They have slightly different storage needs than finned fish.

The Washington State Department of Health recommends keeping your live shellfish in an open container covered with a damp towel or cloth to provide the live seafood with much-needed moisture until ready to use. This is important because if the temperature of shellfish rises, bacteria begin to form, making the seafood unsafe to eat. Shrimp, oysters and clams often get a bad rap due to no fault of their own; it's usually unintentional poor temperature handling by the customer or restaurant.

Storage guidance for shellfish:

• Live mollusks that can fully close their shell, like oysters and littleneck clams, can be stored for up to a week in ideal conditions. My preference is a 3-day window since you don't always know how long the market has held the seafood. To store, place these fruits of the sea in a bowl and cover with a damp cloth to keep them moist for up to 7 days. The one exception is mussels: they have a shelf life of 3–4 days.

• Varieties of shellfish that do not close their shells fully, like Atlantic and Pacific razor clams and geoducks, can remain fresh in the fridge for up to 3–4 days when stored properly. Place them in a bowl covered with a damp cloth to maintain humidity.

• Although it is rare to find live mollusks like squid and octopus at the market, it is possible in some parts of the world, or even possible to catch your own. These types of shellfish do well in the refrigerator for up to 2–3 days when covered with a damp cloth and stored in the coldest part. My preference is to keep these for 1–2 days max; outside of that, into the freezer they go!

- Live crustaceans like crab, lobster and shrimp have a very brief shelf life. Other than lobster, it's rare to find crab live in most markets, if you are lucky enough to find them live, keep them cool and moist, but not wet.

- Fresh-shucked shellfish like oysters, crab and clams will be fine in the refrigerator for 2–3 days.

- Thawed (refreshed) crustaceans and mollusks have a solid shelf life of 2 days when stored properly. Keep in mind that once you thaw it, you should be committed to cooking it, so plan accordingly.
  - **If you get stuck in an "OMG" moment (it happens), you can always quickly cook the shellfish—boil, steam or broil are good options—and refrigerate for use the next day for tacos, soup or stir fry.**

- Cooked shellfish like steamed clams, fried oysters or grilled shrimp can safely last for up to 2 days in the refrigerator.
  - **This includes takeout and "doggie bags" from restaurant meals.**

THAW IT SAFELY

Some frozen fish can defrost in as little as 30 minutes—pollock, cod, sablefish and shrimp come to mind. Other varieties and cuts, like steaks or whole fish depending on thickness, can take an hour or more.

If you are in a hurry to thaw seafood, I have two favorite options: either seal it in a plastic bag and immerse it in cold water, or use the microwave on the defrost setting and stop the defrost cycle while the fish is still icy but pliable. If you have more time, thaw frozen seafood gradually by placing it in the refrigerator or in the sink covered with a cold, damp cloth.

COOK IT PROPERLY

Some seafood varieties taste great raw—tuna, halibut, opah, oysters and salmon are some of my favorites—but others need to be cooked for their true quality to shine through. This is especially true for freshwater fish like bluegill, catfish, striped bass and walleye.

Fish harvested from freshwater—water with less than 0.05% salinity—tend to be more mild in flavor due to their diet (often described as muddy) and have smaller bones than saltwater fish, which are bold and briny in flavor with larger bones that are easier to work with.

The basic goal of cooking is to alter the texture and flavor of the fish and to kill any bacteria or parasites that may be present. As Jay Harlow notes in his book West Coast Seafood, the goal of cooking seafood is to provide a dish that is both safe and a pleasure to eat.

Most seafood should be cooked to an internal temperature of 145°F. But if you don't have a food thermometer, there are other ways to determine whether seafood is done.

- Slip the point of a sharp knife into the flesh and pull it aside. The flesh should be opaque and separate easily.

- Shrimp and lobster become pearly-opaque when cooked.

- Scallop flesh turns milky white or opaque and firm.

- For clams, mussels and oysters, watch for the point at which their shells open—this means they're done. In most cases, these shellfish only need a kiss of heat to cook.

TEMPERATURE COUNTS

If you are headed outdoors with your seafood, **keep the following tips in mind once your seafood is cooked and ready to be enjoyed:**

- Never leave seafood or other perishable food out of the refrigerator for more than 2 hours or for more than 1 hour when temperatures are above 90°F. Bacteria can cause illness to grow quickly at warm temperatures (between 40°F and 140°F).

- If you are heading out to the beach or park with your fish, pack it in a cooler with cold packs or ice. When possible, put the cooler in the shade. Keep the lid closed as much of the time as you can.

- Keep hot seafood hot and cold seafood cold. This is fairly straightforward and only requires that you invest in two separate coolers.

For Moms, Kids, the Elderly and those with Compromised Immune Systems

Food safety is important for everyone, but even more so for moms and moms-to-be, children under 5, the elderly and those with compromised immune systems.

This population is among the most vulnerable to foodborne illness and should be mindful of eating smoked seafood, raw fish such as sushi, poke, crudo or oysters on the half shell and large predatory species such as shark, swordfish, tilefish, king mackerel and bigeye tuna to prevent complications from the mercury levels that may be present.

GOOD NEWS

Although there are a few things to keep in mind for this special group, seafood remains a healthy option. Here are some things to note:

1. Consume 8–12 ounces of fish twice per week.
2. Avoid eating seafood that is high in environmental pollutants such as mercury or PCBs.
   a. The varieties of seafood with the lowest levels of toxins include anchovies, butterfish, clams, cod, Dungeness crab, king crab, snow crab, crawfish, haddock, Atlantic herring, Maine lobster, Atlantic mackerel, blue mussels, oysters, salmon, sardines, bay scallops, shrimp, pink squid and tilapia.
3. Consume fish that provide healthy omega-3 fatty acids (e.g., EPA and DHA).
   a. Sardines, salmon and trout are excellent choices.
4. Avoid eating raw fish when pregnant and avoid serving raw fish to infants or young children.
   a. This includes ceviche, poke and sushi.
5. Use caution when eating locally caught seafood (i.e., seafood not purchased in a grocery store or restaurant).
   a. Check out your state's fish advisory program to determine any possible health risks associated with eating fish that may have been subjected to contaminated waters.

To provide deeper insight on the topics of seafood sustainability and safety, experts from around the world have established websites and mobile apps to help. The American Academy of Pediatrics, the Monterey Bay Aquarium Seafood Watch Program and Marine Conservancy Society are among the best.

Catching
Your Own

If the idea of spending a relaxing day casting a line to catch your supper sounds like fun, you would be enthusiastically welcomed by my family!

I grew up in a rambunctious community of piscators and have fond memories of fishing with my grandfather and catching crawdads with my sisters along the canal banks in Central California. I learned early on that sharing the locale of a favorite fishing spot was a no-no but sharing information about where NOT to fish was commonplace. This info was shared in the spirit of keeping everyone safe and aware of any spoiled waters in the area due to environmental runoff, commonly referred to as mercury (methylmercury), and PCBs (polychlorinated biphenyls). Fortunately, this was rare.

When catching your own, check for caution signs around lakes, ponds, rivers and coastal areas that indicate public health advisories such as "No fishing allowed," "Only eat one fish per week from this water source due to high mercury & PCB content," or "Warning: do not eat fish caught in these waters." These signs actually exist and should be taken seriously. Honestly, if I saw any of these signs while fishing, I'd run as fast as possible and encourage you to do the same.

Murky
Waters

Seafood taken from polluted waters not only tastes terrible but can be harmful to your health. Chemical pollutants in water come from factories, sewage and runoff from city streets. According to the United States Environmental Protection Agency (EPA), pollutants are also carried long distances in the air and settle in bodies of water, so the bad stuff travels. As a result, some fish are exposed to pollutants that get trapped in the water they swim in and in the food they eat. Pollutants can be found in the skin, fat, internal organs, and sometimes the muscle tissues of fish.

As a matter of everyday life, most of us have no need to fret over the possibility of consuming contaminated fish, especially when it's purchased at a reputable market. Nevertheless, as much as I enjoy highlighting the benefits of seafood, I would be remiss not to inform you of some of the possible risks.

According to expert sources, there are some types of fish that we should eat infrequently. The shortlist includes:

- **King mackerel**
- **Shark**
- **Swordfish**
- **Tilefish**
- **Tuna**

The reason these fish are highlighted is that they are large predators that eat smaller fish that may have trace amounts of mercury. Through the years, the accumulation of mercury can lead to higher-than-normal levels of toxins.

The good news is that the risk of mercury poisoning from eating fish is not a major health concern for most adults, according to the U.S. FDA. The risks depend on the amounts of seafood eaten and the levels of mercury found within. Pregnant or nursing women, children, the elderly, and those with weakened immune systems should take extra precautions when consuming fish.

Preparing
Perfect Fish

When cooking seafood, always err on the side of undercooking the fish. It only takes a minute or two for the flesh to shrink and push all of the moisture out, leaving the fish dry and tough.

Whether you've grilled it whole or cooked it en papillote, there is nothing worse than sitting down to an alluring fish dinner only to discover that you have a little slice of the Mojave Desert sitting on your plate. Dry, overcooked fish makes for a terrible dining experience and is unfortunately, something most of us experience at some point in life.

How can you tell when you have overcooked your fish, or better yet, how can you avoid the problem altogether? If your fish looks done in the pan, then it will likely be overcooked by the time it gets to your plate. Residual heat is the primary culprit. After your fish leaves the pan or grill, it will continue to cook for about 2–3 minutes. This is twice as long as it should be heated in some cases.

In an article on Food52, writer Harold McGee came up with the slogan **"Fish should be fast,"** and I couldn't agree more. The protein structure and tissue of fish is very delicate and should generally be cooked as quickly and as little as possible.

In the case of shellfish like lobster, shrimp and sea scallops, the quintessential sign of overcooking is tight, super-firm, rubbery flesh. The flavor becomes flat and the usual sweet, earthy flavor is lost. They won't taste true to form and will likely require a knife or at least a heavy-handed fork to cut through. The key to succulent shrimp and sea scallops is to remove them from the heat once you have a nice uniform color on both sides. It only takes 3–4 minutes to cook these beauties to perfection.

When it comes to salmon, overcooking results in super-firm flesh that has opaque orange flesh all the way through. It will be dry, flaky and practically flavorless. Ideally, salmon will be moist and a little pink in the middle.

Whitefish, such as cod, halibut, pollock and mahi-mahi have the least amount of fat and can be practically inedible when overcooked. The flesh becomes super firm, dry, rubbery and lackluster in flavor. Whitefish should be moist, tender and slightly firm.

Keep in mind that you can always cook your fish a little more if needed, but it's impossible to go backward, as the texture will never be the same.

If you have a tendency to overcook seafood, do yourself a favor and use cooking techniques that impart moisture, like en papillote, sautéing and steaming.

Recipe Review

(DON'T SKIP THIS PART!)

You are probably pretty excited about diving into these recipes—I'm right there with you! However, I ask that you please take the time to read through the whole recipe before diving in. Some of the dishes have a few steps to them and include ingredients that can take up to two days to prepare (salt cod, for example). Spending time reading through the instructions before you start cooking will allow you to pace yourself and avoid frustration.

MISE EN PLACE, PLEASE!

Just as reading through a recipe prior to cooking will benefit you greatly, so will organizing your ingredients in advance.

Mise en place is a French phrase that loosely translates into "everything in its place."

This method of preparing and organizing ingredients is designed to maximize the efficiency of a recipe and save time. Having all of your ingredients cut, diced, deveined and peeled will help your cooking process go swimmingly.

I have discovered that a lot of people do not enjoy cooking because they find themselves fumbling around the kitchen or discovering in the middle of a recipe that they are missing ingredients. Lack of kitchen organization can lead to mistakes like adding sugar to a recipe instead of salt (ever happen to you?) or misreading a measurement and adding tablespoons instead of teaspoons. **Mise en place is the secret ingredient to success in the kitchen!**

When a list of ingredients is long, having your mise en place will give you kitchen confidence and reduce any anxiety you might have before diving in.

MAIN
DISHES
/ENTRÉES

SHELLFISH RECIPES

The Scoop on Shellfish

Shellfish are one of my favorite types of seafood, with clams, conches, mussels, shrimp and oysters as some of my top choices. As a reminder, shellfish fall into two categories: crustaceans like lobster, crab, crawfish and shrimp, and mollusks such as clams, squid, octopus and scallops.

In the United States, shellfish are regulated through a federal-state-industry cooperative program that helps make them safe to eat year-round. The program is known as the National Shellfish Sanitation Program (NSSP). Through this cooperative, the U.S. FDA, state regulatory agencies, and the shellfish industry work together to keep molluscan shellfish (such as oysters, clams and mussels) safe for consumption by adhering to strict controls on their growing, harvesting, processing, packaging and transport.

This program requires shellfish harvesters and processors to tag sacks or containers of live shellfish and label the containers or packages of shucked shellfish. These tags and labels contain specifics about the seafood, including a certification number for the processor, which means that the shellfish were harvested and processed in accordance with national shellfish safety controls. Just for kicks, ask to see the tag or check the label when making a purchase.

SELECTING SHELLFISH

When shopping for shellfish, keep thes tips in mind:

1. Throw away clams, oysters and musse if their shells are clearly cracked, broken or damaged.

2. Perform the "tap test" on live clams, oysters and mussels to make sure they are still alive. On occasion, bivalves will relax with their mouths agape. To ensure that they are safe to eat, gently tap on the shell. If they don't close when tapped, they have expired—toss them into the trash.

3. Purge fresh live clams to remove sand and silt. See page 49 for details on how to accomplish this.

4. Live crabs and lobsters should show some leg movement. They expire quickly after harvest, and a good way to determine signs of life and freshness is if they are kicking! Only live crabs and lobsters should be selected and prepared.

5. Live lobsters should have a curled tail A healthy lobster will curl its tail tightly when held; this is a good sign of life and vitality.

6. When buying shucked shellfish, know that the seafood should be plump and surrounded by clear, fresh, opalescent-looking liquid.

Clam Recipes

- Mexican Almejas Chocolatas (Chocolate Clams) Escabeche-Style

- 'Best Coast' Steamed Littleneck Clams

- Vancouver Ale Steamed Clams with Garlic Thyme Butter

- Mediterranean Fabes con Almejas (White Beans and Clams)

- Algarve Clams with Meyer Lemon Rice

- Galician Navajas (Razor Clams) with Saffron Rice

- Pacific Rim Razor Clams

- Pacific Northwest Pan-Fried Razor Clams

- Cape Disappointment Razor Clams

Digging into Clams

~~~~~~~~~~~~~~~~~~~

Clams are a hard-working shellfish! They get tucked into chowders, soups, and pasta dishes, and are even served on the half shell. There are three primary species of clams that are harvested commercially: hard-shell, soft-shell and sea clam.

Hard-shell clams are highly valued and are named for their location and size.

- Small hard-shell clams called littlenecks are typically sold raw on the half shell.

- Medium-sized cherrystone clams are mostly steamed or baked and are sometimes sold on the half shell.

- The biggest of the bunch, quahogs—also known as chowder clams or chowder quahogs—have a tough texture and a rich flavor. They are typically chopped and used for chowders and soups.

- Manila clams are a common Pacific coast hard-shell clam that are mostly farmed.

- Chocolate clams are a brown-hued hard-shell clam found along the coast of Mexico. They are mostly served raw or quickly cooked.

Soft-shell clams are thin and brittle and cannot close their shells tightly because of their long necks, or siphons, which extend beyond the shell.

- Examples of soft-shell clams include steamer, belly and mud clams. Rarely eaten raw, they are mostly enjoyed fried or steamed.

- Geoducks are included in this bunch. They weigh about 3 pounds, half of which is edible.

Sea clams also go by the name of beach, skimmer or surf clams. They comprise the largest group of harvested clams and are minced and chopped for packaging, prepared products and restaurants.

Clams are sold live in shell, tinned, jarred, precooked and frozen in shell, or as fresh or frozen shucked meat. Clam liquor, juice and nectar are available in cans or bottles.

When buying hard-shell clams, make sure the shell is closed. If the shell is slightly open, tap it to see that it closes. Discard any that don't close. In the case of a soft-shell clam that can't close its shell, touch the neck to see if it twitches; if it does, it's good. Otherwise, toss it.

It's okay to refrigerate clams wrapped in moist wrapping. Do not store them in freshwater.

PURGING FRESH CLAMS

Live clams are among the easiest shellfish to cook, but they do require a little prep work to remove any residual sand that they naturally acquire through feeding.

Purging—the process of removing sand from clams—is an important step that should not be overlooked. There is nothing worse than tucking into a delicious-looking clam dish, only to end up with a gritty mouthful.

Clams, like mussels, oysters and scallops, are bivalves—invertebrates with shells that consist of two parts or "valves" held together by a hinge.

To feed, clams raise their "siphons" or necks to take in water, which traps tiny food particles and nutrients present in the water that flows over them. Once trapped, the water is exhaled through the 47 siphon, which strains the plankton and provides sustenance for the clam while leaving a bit of sand behind. The University of Florida reports that a clam can filter more than 4 gallons of seawater per day.

In some cases, the clams that are sold in markets have been cleaned and purged of sand, but I encourage you to go through the process on your own to be sure.
Trust, but verify!

Simple steps for purging clams:

- Rinse the clams under cool water and weed out any that are open or have cracked shells. See page 35 for tips on storing shellfish.

- In a sink or large container, add enough cool water and sea salt to cover the clams. Actual seawater is best if you can get it, but otherwise 2 ounces of sea salt per liter of water should do the trick. Keep in mind that using freshwater will kill clams.

- Purge—or soak—the clams for 45 minutes to 1 hour. If you leave them for longer than 1 hour, be sure to check on them and change out the water so the clams have a good source of oxygen. Any sand that the clams are holding onto will sink to the bottom of the container.

- When the time is up, remove the clams from the water by hand or with a large spoon, taking care not to disrupt the clams too much and to prevent any sand from reentering the shellfish.

One alternative to cooking with fresh clams is to use the frozen in shell variety. These are precooked, thoroughly purged clams that are available year-round. Since they are precooked, they can be added to soups and sauces toward the end of the cooking process, oftentimes only partially defrosted.

OPENING CLAMS

To open a clam, insert a thin paring knife or clam knife between the shells. Run the knife blade around the shell halves to sever the muscles holding them together. Cut the clam free of the bottom shell and remove any grit or shell debris from the side. Strain the clam liquor into a bowl. In most cases, opening clams is only necessary when eating them on the half shell or if you plan to use them in soups and stews.

RAZOR CLAMS

I'm discussing razor clams separately because they are handled slightly differently than other clams. There are two main varieties of razors: Atlantic and Pacific.

Atlantic razor clams are long and narrow and resemble an old-school razor, which is how they got their name. They are harvested all over the Atlantic and have a delicate, briny flavor. They don't require much work to cook; they just need a rinse.

Pacific razor clams are large and oblong delicacies that are a major part of the gastronomy of the Pacific Northwest. They are harvested primarily in Washington State's southern coast and Northern Oregon. They are collected at low tide and have a tender, pleasantly chewy texture. Cleaning them is fairly straightforward:

• Rinse the clams and place them on a clean surface with a damp towel over the top.

• Using a sharp knife, remove the clam from the shell by sliding the blade down the side.

• Cut the tip off the siphon and use a pair of kitchen shears to cut open the zipper-like line.

• Rinse well to remove the sand and dirt that may be trapped.

Mexican Almejas Chocolatas

(CHOCOLATE CLAMS) ESCABECHE-STYLE

Along the Pacific Coast of the Baja Peninsula, you'll find anglers and small beachside restaurants selling some of my favorite beach eats—ceviche, fish tacos, grilled shrimp and almejas chocolatas escabeche.

Almejas chocolatas, or chocolate clams, are named for their beautiful uniformly dark shell color. As one of the West Coast's largest bivalves, they can grow up to 5–6 inches across. They are often cracked open right on the beach and served escabeche-style with fresh lime and chilis, which is how I first experienced them. I could eat dozens of these meaty, briny and flavorful clams and never tire. Like most shellfish, they are best when prepared simply.

INGREDIENTS

{ Makes
24 clams }

- **24 chocolate clams or large cherrystone clams**, sorted, rinsed and purged (see page 49)

- **6 large limes**, halved

- **¼ cup chopped fresh cilantro leaves**

- **2 large serrano chilis**, minced

- **1 medium red onion**, minced

- **Sea salt**, as needed

SERVING SUGGESTIONS: HOT SAUCE, TAJÍN SPICE BLEND, FRESH LIME JUICE

DIRECTIONS

1. Over a large bowl, shuck or open the purged clams (see page 49) using a thin knife or a clam knife; the bowl will help collect the precious liquor. Remove the brown, sandy innards from the clam and discard.

2. Separate the clam from the shell and add to the bowl. Save the shells for presentation.

3. Use a pair of kitchen shears to chop the clams into small, bite-sized pieces and add back to the bowl. Squeeze the juice of two limes over the clams along with 1 tablespoon of cilantro, the serrano chili and red onion. Taste for flavor and add sea salt as needed. Let the clams and aromatics marinate for 10 minutes.

4. Once the clams have marinated, artfully place the clam shells on a platter and fill them with equal portions of the clam mixture. Garnish with cilantro and serve immediately with hot sauce, the remaining lime and Tajín as desired.

'Best Coast' Steamed Littleneck Clams

This recipe is based off of a dish I enjoyed at a restaurant along the Oregon coast. It's a bit unusual, but in a good way; instead of the addition of clam broth, I call for vegetable broth and cream, which gives the broth a more robust flavor.

Served with rustic sourdough bread, these littleneck clams are hard to beat. Made with simple, easily accessible ingredients, this dish is 'Best Coast' inspired—my affectionate way of showing love to my part of the world, the West Coast of the United States.

Fresh live littlenecks or cockles work best for this recipe. If you can't find live clams, the whole frozen, cooked variety can be substituted.

INGREDIENTS

{ Serves 4 }

- **2 tablespoons ghee**

- **2 tablespoons granulated garlic**

- **3 large scallions**, sliced

- **3 tablespoons unsalted butter**

- **1 cup vegetable broth**

- **Sea salt**, as needed

- **1 large lemon**, juice and zest

- **1 cup white wine**

- **5 pounds live hard-shell clams**, sorted, rinsed and purged (see page 47)

- **¼ cup half-and-half**

- **½ cup chopped fresh parsley**, 1 tablespoon reserved for garnish

- **Sea salt and freshly ground black pepper** to taste

OPTIONAL: RUSTIC SOURDOUGH OR YOUR FAVORITE BREAD

DIRECTIONS

1. In a large Dutch oven or heavy-bottomed pot, heat the ghee over medium heat. Add the garlic and scallions and sauté until fragrant but not brown.

2. Add the butter, vegetable broth, lemon juice, lemon zest and white wine and bring to a simmer. Add the clams and close the pot with a tight-fitting lid. Gently shake the pot to help the clams settle. Cook the clams until they have opened, about 6 minutes, then turn off the heat and do not open the pot—this will give any unopened clams time to open and will allow the flavors to meld.

3. After 3 minutes, remove the lid, add the half-and-half and toss in the chopped parsley. To serve, divide the clams equally among 4 bowls, or serve family-style in a large, deep platter. Garnish with fresh parsley and serve with fresh bread as desired.

Vancouver Ale Steamed Clams

WITH GARLIC THYME BUTTER

British Columbia, Canada is framed by the Pacific Ocean and the Rocky Mountains. The province is home to the beautiful city of Vancouver, a bustling West Coast seaport and one of the most populous and culturally diverse cities in the region. Did I mention that it has a fabulous food scene?

Seafood dishes from every persuasion can be found in this maritime metropolis, which leans heavily toward Chinese cuisine. Everything from mussels and oysters to halibut, salmon and clams thrives in the waters surrounding Vancouver. All of this lovely seafood gets washed down by the refreshing craft beer options produced by the dozens of local brewers.

If ale is not your thing, feel free to substitute it with another beer variety or water.

INGREDIENTS

{ Serves 4 }

- **1 tablespoon olive oil**

- **3 tablespoons garlic thyme butter** (see page 542)

- **2 shallots,** peeled and minced

- **1 bottle dark brown ale**

- **1 cup water**

- **3 sprigs fresh thyme, whole**

- **5 pounds live littleneck clams, sorted, rinsed and purged** (see page 49)

- **2 teaspoons red pepper flake**

- **2 large lemons,** divided

- **Sea salt and freshly ground black pepper**

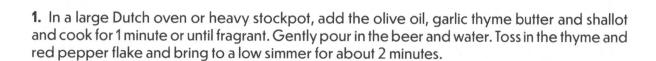

SERVING SUGGESTIONS: CRUSTY FRENCH BREAD

DIRECTIONS

1. In a large Dutch oven or heavy stockpot, add the olive oil, garlic thyme butter and shallot and cook for 1 minute or until fragrant. Gently pour in the beer and water. Toss in the thyme and red pepper flake and bring to a low simmer for about 2 minutes.

2. Add the clams to the pot and squeeze in the juice of half a lemon. Cover the pot with the lid slightly ajar, reduce the heat to medium and steam the clams until they have opened, about 6–8 minutes. Taste the broth and season with sea salt and freshly ground black pepper to taste.

3. Turn off the heat and let the pot rest for 5 minutes; this will give the clams time to absorb the flavors from the liquid. While the clams rest, slice the remaining lemon into wedges for serving.

4. To serve, remove the thyme sprigs from the pot and discard. Ladle out even portions of clams and broth into large bowls or serve in a generous family-style bowl. Garnish with lemon wedges and serve immediately with crusty French bread or Belgian frites as desired.

Mediterranean Fabes con Almejas

(WHITE BEANS AND CLAMS)

This flavorful Mediterranean-inspired dish leans heavily toward Spain, where seafood and beans are a popular combination. Judión beans are a favorite in Spanish kitchens. They are a large, thin-skinned bean with mild flavor and smooth texture. I typically make a large batch from which I create several hearty dishes, including this recipe for fabes con almejas. If live clams are not available, you can replace them with shucked or tinned clams. If Judión beans prove challenging to find, cannellini or most other white beans can be substituted.

INGREDIENTS

- **2 cups dried white beans such as Judión, cannellini, navy or giant beans,** sorted and soaked overnight

- **1 bay leaf**

- **1 large carrot**, chopped

- **2 stalks celery**, chopped

- **1 tablespoon finely chopped fresh mixed herbs** (oregano, tarragon and thyme)

- **1 small Spanish onion**, finely chopped

- **2 ounces sun-dried tomatoes**, chopped

- **3 cups low-sodium vegetable broth**

- **2 tablespoons Spanish olive oil**

- **2 cups water**

- **1 cup clam juice**

- **1 teaspoon sea salt**, more as needed

- **1 teaspoon freshly ground black pepper,** more as needed

- **4 pounds small live clams**, such as littlenecks, sorted, rinsed and purged (see page 49)

- **¼ cup coarsely chopped flat-leaf parsley**

DIRECTIONS

1. In a large heavy-bottomed pot or Dutch oven, add the soaked beans, bay leaf, carrot, celery, mixed herbs, onion, sun-dried tomatoes, vegetable broth, olive oil and water and bring to a boil for 10 minutes. Cover with the lid slightly ajar and simmer for 90 minutes.

2. Add the clam juice, sea salt and black pepper and stir. Taste for seasoning and doneness; the beans should be tender. Add additional cooking time and liquid as needed; the beans should be completely covered in liquid.

3. When the beans are done, add the clams and cover the pan tightly. Cook over moderate heat until the clams have opened—about 8 minutes. Ladle the beans and clams into bowls, garnish with parsley and serve.

Algarve Clams

WITH MEYER LEMON RICE

The region of Portugal known as the Algarve is located in the country's southernmost district. It is a stunningly beautiful location filled with craggy cliffs, jaw-dropping views of the Atlantic Ocean, and fresh local seafood.

My husband and I had a chance to visit the Algarve while food-touring Lisbon. We rented a car, grabbed a few snacks and headed south. The drive was memorable, as we stopped for coffee and pastéis de nata, a nationally recognized custard tart, and happened upon groves of decades-old cork oak trees and rolling vineyards.

This dish reminds me of the warm summer evening that we spent dining al fresco enjoying cataplana, or a seafood stew made in a pan by the same name.

Soft-shell clams like steamers work great for this. Meyer lemons, which are a cross between a lemon and mandarin orange, have a more delicate flavor than the tart and acidic Lisbon or Eureka varieties that are more common. I like long-grain Jasmine rice for this dish because the grains remain firm and fluffy after cooking. Medium-grain rice like Arborio or Valencia will also work, resulting in a texture similar to paella or risotto.

Turmeric is a warm yellow spice that is used in all types of cuisine and is often used as a food coloring for cheese, mustard and curries. I'm using it here for its earthy flavor and to add visual interest to the dish with its light lemon-yellow color. Visual stimuli have been shown to alter our sense of taste, smell and flavor.

INGREDIENTS

{ Serves 4 }

- **1 tablespoon unsalted butter**
- **1 tablespoon olive oil**
- **½ teaspoon ground turmeric**
- **1 tablespoon garlic powder**
- **½ teaspoon sea salt**
- **½ medium shallot**, minced

- **1 cup white Jasmine rice**
- **1½ cups water**
- **1 Meyer lemon**, juice and ½-inch piece of peel
- **¼ cup chopped fresh parsley**
- **1 pound whole live clams**, sorted, rinsed and purged (see page 49)
- **Freshly ground black pepper to taste**

DIRECTIONS

1. In a large heavy-bottomed skillet, melt the butter with the olive oil. Add the turmeric, garlic powder, sea salt and shallot to the pan and sauté over medium heat until fragrant. Add the rice and cook for 3 minutes until the rice smells toasty.

2. Add the water, lemon juice, lemon peel and parsley. Cook uncovered for 6 minutes, then check the water level—the rice should be covered in liquid. Stir the pot occasionally and add water if needed. Stir, then cover and cook for 3 minutes. Add the clams, stir, then cover and cook for 2 minutes. Turn off the heat and allow the pot to rest for a few minutes before serving.

Galician Navajas

RAZOR CLAMS WITH SAFFRON RICE

During a recent trip to Barcelona, I carved out time to visit La Boqueria Market, one of the most popular foodie destinations in Spain. Located in the heart of the city, Las Ramblas, the market has been around since 1836 and boasts more than 200 shops, including dozens of spice vendors and extravagant seafood stalls.

La Boqueria is by far, one of the most beautiful markets that I have had the pleasure of visiting. Among the baskets of live langoustine, lobster, crab, oysters and octopus, I found gorgeous Atlantic razor clams. I bought two dozen (among a bunch of other seafood) and brought them back to my rental loft to cook them up for supper. The Galician coast of Spain is famous for its seafood, and the razor clams from the area are some of the best. Combined with a little saffron and short-grain rice, they make for an incredible meal.

The Atlantic variety of razor clams is the smaller and leaner counterpart to the supple and more robust Pacific razor clams. This recipe also works with littleneck clams or most shellfish like shrimp and mussels.

INGREDIENTS

{ Serves 2 }

- **2 tablespoons olive oil**

- **1 clove garlic**, minced

- **1 medium shallot**, minced

- **1 dozen Atlantic razor clams**, cleaned (see page 49)

- **1 large lemon, juice only**

- **Saffron rice** (see page 412)
  ½ teaspoon smoked paprika sea salt (see page 548), for garnish

- **¼ cup chopped fresh parsley**

DIRECTIONS

1. In a medium-sized pan, heat the olive oil over medium heat. Add the garlic and shallot and sauté for 2 minutes. Add the razor clams and sauté for 3–4 minutes. Be careful not to overcook. Squeeze the lemon juice over the clams, then shake the pan to coat the clams in the sauce. Remove from the heat and set aside.

2. To serve the clams, place the saffron rice in a serving dish and pour the clams and the sauce over the top. Sprinkle with a little smoked paprika sea salt and garnish with fresh parsley. Serve immediately.

Pacific Rim Razor Clams

Long Beach, Washington is famous for its Pacific razor clams, which are plump and juicy and more robust than the thin, lithe Atlantic razor clam. I love both varieties and appreciate Pacifics for their meaty texture and briny flavor.

While visiting the Washington coast over a winter holiday, my husband and I had a chance to experience the annual clam harvest, where dozens of people lined the beach armed with their shovels and clam guns prepared to dig in the sand to uncover their share of the bounty, or roughly 15 clams per person.

Like most clams, Pacific razor clams are best enjoyed simply and quickly prepared. I adapted this recipe from one provided by the Washington Department of Fish & Wildlife.

INGREDIENTS

{ Serves 4 }

- **2 dozen razor clams,** cleaned (see page 49)

- **2 small stalks fresh lemongrass,** sliced

- **1 1-inch thumb fresh ginger,** sliced

- **½ bunch fresh cilantro,** with a few leaves reserved for garnish

- **3 large scallions,** sliced

- **1 tablespoon sambal oelek,** or another red chili paste

- **2 tablespoons ghee**

- **½ cup coconut milk**

- **Sea salt and freshly ground black pepper to taste**

- **Fresh cilantro leaves,** for garnish

SERVING SUGGESTIONS: STEAMED COCONUT RICE (SEE PAGE 418), COOKED PASTA, TOASTED BREAD

DIRECTIONS

1. Clean the clams and cut them into strips. Set aside.

2. Using a food processor or large mortar and pestle, combine the lemongrass, ginger, cilantro and scallions to create a paste. Set aside.

3. In a medium-sized bowl, stir together the razor clams, red chili paste and the lemongrass paste. Place in the refrigerator and marinate for 10 minutes.

4. Once the clams have marinated, melt the ghee in a large skillet over high heat and add the clams along with the sauce. Sauté for 4 minutes. Pour in the coconut milk and simmer for 3 minutes. Taste for seasoning and add salt and freshly ground black pepper as needed. Divide the clams among two bowls, garnish with fresh cilantro leaves, and serve immediately with steamed coconut rice, pasta or toasted bread as desired.

Pacific Northwest Pan-Fried Razor Clams

One of the best parts about clam digging is clam eating! It's seriously one of my favorite culinary sports. Harvesting my own seafood is a fun way to connect to nature and gain an appreciation for the food that I'm consuming—farm-to-table cooking at its best.

If you are new to clam digging, it is a seasonal recreational activity popular in the Pacific Northwest, California and the U.K. My first experience with clam digging was in Coos Bay, Oregon. Donning a pair of wading boots and with a clam "gun" in tow, I set out with my guide for a few fun hours of digging. By the end of the day, we had enough for a nice supper.

This simple pan-fried Pacific razor clam dish is one of the most popular and delectable ways to enjoy shellfish. Things go really fast once you have everything in place, so prepare for a quick and delicious meal.

INGREDIENTS

{ Serves 4 }

- **3 pounds or 12 large Pacific razor clams,** shelled and cleaned (see page 49)

- **Sea salt and freshly ground black pepper to taste**

- **1 teaspoon paprika**

- **1 teaspoon garlic powder**

- **2 cups all-purpose flour**

- **1 cup breadcrumbs**

- **2 large eggs**

- **1 tablespoon water**

- **2 tablespoons ghee**

- **Vegetable oil,** for frying

SERVING SUGGESTIONS: FRESH CHOPPED PARSLEY, LEMON SLICES

DIRECTIONS

1. Place the clams on a clean surface and add a dash of sea salt and freshly ground black pepper. Set aside.

2. In a medium-sized bowl, combine the paprika, garlic powder, flour and breadcrumbs. Set aside.

3. In a small bowl, whisk together the eggs and water. Set aside.

4. In a large skillet, heat the ghee and about ¼ cup of vegetable oil over medium-high heat. While the oil is heating, dip each clam in the egg wash, then dredge in the flour mixture and set aside. Repeat with all of the clams.

5. Once the oil is hot, add the clams and cook on one side until golden brown, then turn and cook on the other side. Remove and drain on a bed of paper towels. You may need to do this in batches. Repeat until all of the clams are cooked.

4. Garnish with fresh parsley and lemon slices if desired and serve immediately.

Cape Disappointment Razor Clams

Cape Disappointment, located on the extreme southernmost point of Washington state's Long Beach Peninsula, does not live up to its name, thank goodness! Quite the opposite, in fact. The state park offers gorgeous views of the Pacific Ocean, mind-clearing hiking trails, a historic lighthouse, and of course, amazing Pacific razor clam digging sites.

Clamming is one of the most exciting winter sports around. With a short season lasting only a few weeks (or sometimes a bit longer depending on local updates), there are dozens of people dotted along the beach in hopes of foraging their share of the famously fat shellfish.

This version of pan-fried razor clams is a simple recipe that is a local favorite on the peninsula and allows the flavor of this delectable shellfish to shine through.

INGREDIENTS

{ Serves 4 }

- **3 pounds or 12 large Pacific razor clams, shelled and cleaned** (see page 47)

- **Sea salt and freshly ground black pepper to taste**

- **1 teaspoon hot sauce**

- **1 teaspoon garlic powder**

- **2 cups all-purpose flour**

- **1 cup breadcrumbs**

- **2 large eggs**

- **1 12-ounce beer or seltzer**

- **2 tablespoons ghee**

- **Vegetable oil**, for frying

SERVING SUGGESTIONS: FRESH CHOPPED PARSLEY, LEMON SLICES

DIRECTIONS

1. Place the clams on a clean surface and add a dash of sea salt and freshly ground black pepper. Set aside.

2. In a medium-sized bowl, combine the hot sauce, garlic powder, flour, eggs and the beer or seltzer. Whisk together and set aside.

3. In a large skillet, heat the ghee and about ¼ cup of vegetable oil over medium-high heat. While the oil is heating, dip each clam in the flour mix and add to the hot oil.

4. Cook on each side until golden brown. Remove and rest on a bed of paper towels. Repeat until all of the clams are cooked.

Serve immediately and garnish with fresh parsley and with lemon slices if desired

Crab
Recipes

- California Maki (Crab and Avocado Roll)

- Half Moon Bay Dungeness Crab Quesadillas

- Hispaniola Curried Crab in Avocado Cups

- Vietnamese Crab Fried Rice

- Pribilof Islands King Crab Legs with Garlic Thyme Butter

- San José del Cabo Crab & Shrimp Enchiladas

Cracking into Crab

~~~~~~~~

It always breaks my heart a little when I hear people say that they boil whole crab or crab legs to "cook" them. Little-known fact—this is totally not necessary! Ninety-nine percent of the time, the crab you buy at the market is already cooked and just needs to be heated through.

Crabs live all over the world! There are more than 4,000 species in existence, with a handful that are suitable for dinner tables and restaurant menus. Blue, Dungeness, Florida stone, Jonah, king and red (Alaskan) king crab are some of the most popular varieties of this tasty crustacean.

They follow the same seasonality as lobster in most cases and fare well in cold water, which makes their meat a little sweet. Underneath that hard, often spiny shell is a delicate and delicious creature.

Crabs are quite a catch, flavor-wise and literally speaking. Commercial crab fishers and women, specifically those of the Alaskan king crab persuasion, live at sea for long periods of time, up to 3–4 weeks, performing some of the hardest and most dangerous workarounds.

On boats ranging in size from 50 to 300 feet in length, harvesters float along the Bering Sea with high hopes of catching crabs in large 600-pound pots that are designed to withstand the freezing Alaskan weather. Because of the long days out at sea, once the crab is caught, it is cooked and flash-frozen right on the vessel.

A lucky few of us have the ability to buy fresh blue, Dungeness, and Jonah crab right off the boat when they are in season. Some seafood harvesters even offer live crab shipping, which can be a fun kitchen experience. But for the most part, crab purchased at the market is cooked and does not need to be boiled or steamed—doing so can risk flavor or texture, so make sure to ask your fishmonger what you're buying.

Once thawed, you can serve crab chilled or warm if so inclined. If you'd like to serve it warm, moist heat is the best option.

- Steam – Add water to your steamer and bring to a boil. Add your crab and steam for a couple of minutes until warm, about 5–7 minutes.

- Microwave – Wrap the crab in moist paper towels covered with plastic wrap and microwave for 3–5 minutes or until heated through.

- Oven prep – This is an option that does not use moist heat, but it will get the job done. Wrap the thawed crab in foil and place it in a 375-degree oven for 7–10 minutes or until heated through.

You will also find crab meat cooked and out of the shell in a few different forms, such as canned, canned and refrigerated, frozen, and fresh (refrigerated). Shelf-stable canned crab has been heavily pasteurized and is best suited for other recipes. If you must use canned crab, go for the refrigerated version that has been less pasteurized, which is why it is located in the cold section of the store.

JUMBO LUMP

This type of crab meat is off-white in color and comes from the crab's swimmer fin muscles. Crabs have just two of these muscles, so a lot of crabs are needed to make one serving of jumbo lump crab, which makes it more expensive than the other varieties. It's a succulent and sturdy crab meat and holds up well when cooked.

BACKFIN

Backfin crab meat, also known as flake crab meat, comes from the body of the crab and includes the broken pieces of lump crab meat. It is flakier than jumbo and lump. Backfin crab meat is great for seafood stuffing, crab cakes and gravy.

LUMP

Lump crab meat is off-white in color and is smaller than jumbo lump. It's equally as sturdy and flavorful and comes from the body of the crab. It is ideal for those delicious, chunky crab cakes!

CLAW

Claw meat is exactly what it sounds like! It is darker in color, less sweet, and stronger in flavor than the other types of crab meat. It is the least expensive variety and is often used for dips and stews.

California Maki

CRAB AND AVOCADO ROLL

According to the website Eat Japan, sushi loosely translates into "sour taste." Centuries ago, the dish started as a way to preserve seafood using rice and vinegar and sometimes sake. Once cured, the rice was thrown out, while the fish was enjoyed. Later, in Japan's capital city of Edo (modern-day Tokyo) sushi as we know it today was created—vinegared rice served with raw fish.

There are five basic types of sushi that you'll find in restaurants: nigiri, sashimi, uramaki, temaki and maki, which is how the California Roll is classified. My nephew Justin is a huge fan of maki, which is essentially a seaweed wrapper called nori lined with seasoned rice and stuffed with savory filling, in most cases seafood, and served with a side of wasabi, pickled ginger and soy sauce. Sushi rolls is how they are often described.

The California Roll, a 1970s classic, was created in Vancouver by Japanese sushi chef Hidekazu Tojo, although other chefs are attributed with having invented it including Chef Ichiro Mashita, a sushi chef from Los Angeles' Little Tokyo and Chef Ken Seusa, also from Los Angeles.

I find Chef Tojo's story interesting. After emigrating to Canada, he was looking for a dish that would excite West Coast diners and encourage them to try raw fish. He was met with a lukewarm response yet continued to experiment. In an interview for Insider magazine, Tojo explains that Canadians were interested in trying Japanese food, but without the seaweed.

He soon found the magic combination by using ingredients that were available and easily accessible—local boiled Dungeness crab, avocado and cucumber. The seaweed wrapper that most customers found peculiar was hidden by a layer of sushi rice, masking the green sea vegetable. He coined the term 'inside out roll."

Surimi, or imitation crab, is often used for this dish, but my preference is to use lump crab meat. Use what you can find. If there was ever a reason to use surimi, this is it. Surimi is a fish paste flavored with crab, lobster and shrimp that is popular in Asia. It's mostly made from wild Alaskan pollock.

Mise en place is key for this recipe. Take the time to get all of your ingredients in order and you will be rewarded with a smooth maki-making process.

INGREDIENTS

{ Makes 6 maki rolls }

- **4 cups sushi rice** (see page 416), plus more as needed

- **1 cup lump crab meat or 5 surimi crab sticks**, sliced

- **1 medium ripe avocado**, peeled, seeded and sliced

- **1 English cucumber**, thinly sliced

- **6 toasted nori sheets**

SERVING SUGGESTIONS: SOY SAUCE, PICKLED GINGER, WASABI PASTE, SESAME SEEDS

DIRECTIONS

SPECIAL EQUIPMENT: BAMBOO SUSHI ROLL MAT, PLASTIC WRAP

1. Place the sushi mat on a flat surface and cover with a piece of plastic wrap. Add a piece of nori and about ¼ cup of sushi rice, plus more if needed. With slightly moistened hands, spread the rice over the entirety of the nori. Add 2 tablespoons of crab or a few slices of surimi, 2 slices of cucumber and 2 slices of avocado. Alternatively, you can make an inside-out roll by flipping the nori roll prior to filling so that the rice is on the outside.

2. Start to roll with your hands to get started, then use the mat to roll and squeeze the maki. Continue with the remaining nori and rice.

3. Use a sharp knife to cut the rolls into pieces and serve with soy sauce, pickled ginger and wasabi paste. Garnish with sesame seeds.

Half Moon Bay Dungeness

CRAB QUESADILLAS

South of San Francisco lies a coastal farming town called Half Moon Bay, which bills itself as the "World's Pumpkin Capital." The area also boasts impressive amounts of Dungeness crab. At the Pillar Point Harbor, a small bare-bones facility at the north end of town, you can fish for your supper on the pier or purchase fresh wild seafood right off of the bay boats, which usually sell salmon, rockfish, sand sole, sardines and Dungeness crab.

Half Moon Bay has some of the highest concentrations of Dungeness crab in California with more than 50 commercial boats fishing off Pillar Pier around November. The crustaceans are highly sought after by locals and visitors alike. These large, sweet, hard-shell crabs are one of my favorite varieties.

This quesadilla recipe is a fun way to incorporate crab into an everyday kind of meal. Stuffed with some of my favorite veggies, this dish can easily be customized with your top choices.

INGREDIENTS

{ Serves 5 }

- **2 tablespoons olive oil**, divided

- **1 medium Spanish onion**, diced

- **2 medium zucchini**, diced small

- **Sea salt and freshly ground black pepper to taste**

- **1 cup baby spinach**, stems removed

- **5 6-inch flour tortillas**

- **1 ½ cups Mexican cheese blend**, shredded

- **2 pounds cooked crab meat**, picked through for shells

SERVING SUGGESTIONS: GUACAMOLE, PICKLED JALAPEÑOS, SOUR CREAM AND SALSA

DIRECTIONS

1. In a large skillet, add enough olive oil to coat the bottom of the pan (about 2 teaspoons) and heat over medium-high heat. Add the onion and sauté for 1 minute or until fragrant. Toss in the zucchini and a pinch of salt and pepper and cook for another 30 to 40 seconds. Add the spinach and stir; when it begins to wilt, turn off the heat. Set aside and prepare the quesadillas.

2. In a large skillet, heat 2 teaspoons of olive oil over medium-high heat. Add a flour tortilla and flip intermittently, cooking on both sides until soft and lightly toasted. Once lightly toasted, lay one tortilla flat in the pan and on one half add 2 tablespoons of cheese, a small scoop of the veggie mix and two tablespoons of crab meat—feel free to tailor the portions to suit your taste. Fold the tortilla over to close and continue to cook until golden brown on one side, then flip and cook until brown on the other. Repeat with remaining ingredients. Serve with guacamole, pickled jalapeños, sour cream and salsa as desired.

Hispaniola Curried Crab

IN AVOCADO CUPS

The Republic of Haiti and the Dominican Republic make up the island known as Hispaniola, which is part of the Greater Antilles archipelago that also includes Cuba, Jamaica, Puerto Rico and the Cayman Islands.

Dominican fare is similar to the cuisine that you'll find in Latin-influenced countries like Cuba and Puerto Rico, and you'll find ingredients like onion and cilantro. Haitian food is heavily influenced by West African, French and Arab cultures. With its proximity to the ocean, the region counts seafood as an important part of its gastronomy. Conch, lobster and blue crab are popular on the island, and in fact, there are more than 30 native species of crab on the island. A major export for Haiti, avocados are important to Hispaniola's gastronomy as well.

I am partial to using lump crab meat in this recipe for its sweet flavor and firm texture. It also presents beautifully. Check out my Posh Pointers on page 46 for tips on selecting crab.

INGREDIENTS

{ Serves 4 }

- **1 tablespoon avocado oil**

- **1 tablespoon curry powder** (see page 538)

- **1 small white onion,** diced small

- **1 small clove garlic,** minced

- **2 scallions,** green part only, thinly sliced

- **2 pounds lump crab meat,** cooked and picked over for shells

- **1 teaspoon habañero pepper sauce** or ½ teaspoon chopped habañero pepper

- 1 small bunch fresh cilantro, leaves only, chopped, 1 tablespoon reserved for garnish

- **1 teaspoon soy sauce**

- **1/3 cup coconut milk**

- **Salt and freshly ground black pepper to taste**

- **2 large ripe avocados**

- **Lime juice,** as needed

- **1 large lime,** sliced into wedges

DIRECTIONS

1. Heat a large skillet over medium-high heat. When the pan is hot, add the avocado oil and the curry powder. Stir to prevent the spice from burning and cook until fragrant, about 1 minute. Add the white onion, garlic and scallions and cook until the onion is translucent.

2. Add the crab, habañero pepper sauce (or chopped pepper if using), cilantro, soy sauce and coconut milk and gently fold to combine. Taste for seasoning and add salt and freshly ground black pepper as needed. Cover and set aside.

3. Slice the avocados in half and remove the pits, creating 4 cups. Sprinkle each half with a little sea salt and freshly ground black pepper if desired. Drizzle with lime juice to prevent avocados from browning.

4. To serve, add equal portions of the warm curried crab to the avocado cups. Garnish with cilantro and lime wedges. Serve immediately.

Vietnamese Crab Fried Rice

Located in Southeast Asia, Vietnam is home to more than 2,000 miles of coastline. The country boasts the UNESCO-designated site of Ha Long Bay and the beautiful islands of Côn Son and Phú Qu, which have some of the most gorgeous resort destinations in the country.

Outside of its bustling cities and gorgeous landscapes, Vietnam is one of the largest rice-producing regions in the world and has an incredible food scene. Exotic dishes are not uncommon in the region, but this crab fried rice recipe is very approachable and is an excellent way to easily bring some of the country's enticing flavors into your kitchen.

Day-old rice is mandatory. Making the rice the day before will allow the grains to dry out a bit and will give the dish better texture; using rice cooked on the same day will result in a mushy dish. Feel free to add more or less of the listed ingredients based on your preferences.

INGREDIENTS

- **2 tablespoons sesame oil,** separated

- **1 small red onion,** thinly sliced

- **2 cloves garlic,** minced

- **1 thumb fresh ginger,** grated

- **1 large carrot,** diced small

- **2 teaspoons red pepper flake**

- **4 ounces firm tofu or tempeh,** diced into ½-inch pieces

- **2 cups steamed white or brown day-old rice**

- **2 tablespoons fish sauce**

- **1 tablespoon tamari soy sauce,** more if desired

- **2 eggs, beaten**

- **½ cup bean sprouts**

- **2 scallions,** green part only, sliced

- **1 cup cooked lump crab meat,** picked through for shells

- **Sea salt to taste**

- **½ bunch fresh cilantro,** leaves only

DIRECTIONS

1. In a large skillet or well-seasoned wok, heat 1 tablespoon of sesame oil over medium-high heat. Add the onion, garlic, ginger and carrot, and cook until fragrant, about 3 minutes. Remove from heat and place in a container; set aside.

2. In the same skillet or wok, add the remaining tablespoon of sesame oil, the red pepper flake, and the diced tofu or tempeh. Cook and stir occasionally, lightly browning on all sides. Remove from heat and place mixture in a container; set aside.

3. Add the cooked rice to the same skillet or wok and stir constantly over medium-high heat. Add the fish sauce and tamari soy sauce and fold to combine, taking care not to break up the rice. Continue cooking for 3 minutes or so until the rice and sauces combine and the mixture heats through.

4. Add the reserved vegetable mixture along with the eggs, bean sprouts, scallions and crab to the rice and fold together, taking care not to break up the crab. When the egg starts to cook, turn off the heat and taste for seasoning. Add salt or tamari soy sauce as needed.

5. To serve, divide equal portions of the crab fried rice among 4 plates and garnish with cilantro leaves. Enjoy immediately.

Pribilof Islands King Crab Legs

~~~~~~~~~~

WITH GARLIC THYME BUTTER

Located in the Bering Sea 300 miles off the coast of Alaska are a set of four beautiful, wild and exotic islands called the Pribilofs. St. George and St. Paul are the two main islands of this stunning volcanic island group. Windy and covered in fog most of the year, they are an unlikely destination for visitors, but despite the conditions, the Pribilofs have a thriving tourist industry.

Red king crab (aka: Alaskan king crab) inhabit the waters near St. George and St. Paul. They are also found in Japanese and Russian waters. Commercial crabbing season is carried out in the fall months in Alaska and around the Aleutian Islands. The guys and gals who brave the rough waters of the Bering Sea to bring this succulent crustacean to our tables should be applauded.

Once captured, crab is cooked on the boat or immediately upon landfall and blast frozen, according to the Salty Dog Boating News website. This process helps maintain the freshness of this highly perishable shellfish.

Unless you live around a crabbing village, the king crab you'll find at the market will be pre-cooked and only needs to be slightly heated. See page 73 for more info.

If using frozen crab, you will need to thaw your king crab legs overnight. My preferred method of heating crab is in the oven. The meat stays moist and the shell firms up and is easy to crack, which is all part of the experience.

King crab is one of those seafood ingredients that should be eaten as close to its natural state as possible. A little herb butter and lemon are as far as you should go, in my opinion. I like to average about 1 pound per person.

INGREDIENTS

{ Serves 2 }

- **4 large king crab legs,** defrosted if using frozen

- **Garlic thyme butter (see page 542)**

- **4 cloves garlic,** peeled and minced

- **1 large lemon,** quartered

SERVING SUGGESTIONS: CRUSTY BREAD, GREEN SALAD

DIRECTIONS

1. Preheat oven to 400°F.

2. Wrap the defrosted crab legs in foil, place them on a baking sheet and cook for 8–10 minutes. Remove the crab from the oven and set aside.

3. In a small pan or microwave, heat the garlic thyme butter for about 2 minutes or until it has melted. Add the warm butter to serving ramekins.

4. To serve, place the crab on a platter and serve alongside the garlic & herb butter, lemon wedges, crusty bread and salad as desired. Enjoy immediately.

San José del Cabo Crab & Shrimp Enchiladas

With its proximity to the ocean, Baja California is home to many delicious and approachable seafood dishes—some more traditional than others. As a major tourist destination, the local restaurants and markets are primed to accommodate the taste buds of people the world over. Tacos and burritos are popular fare, but seafood-stuffed enchiladas are the stuff of dreams.

If you are new to this Mexican or Tex-Mex delicacy, enchiladas are composed of a corn or flour tortilla stuffed with savory filling and shredded cheese then rolled, drenched in spicy sauce, and baked until bubbling and lightly golden brown.

This seafood enchilada recipe is my version of the dish that I enjoyed while visiting San José del Cabo, Mexico. Green sauce, instead of the traditional red variety, is ideal and balances well with the flavors of crab and shrimp. There are many high-quality canned and jarred green sauces on the market. I rarely make my own sauce unless I'm gifted a few pounds of tomatillos. I recommend Hatch, Las Palmas or La Victoria brands.

INGREDIENTS

- **½ cup avocado or vegetable oil,** separated

- **½ large onion,** diced

- **1 pound Mexican white shrimp,** peeled, deveined and sliced lengthwise

- **1 teaspoon Mexican chili powder** or **Hatch green chile powder**

- **1 teaspoon garlic powder**

- **1 teaspoon Mexican oregano**

- **1 28-ounce can green enchilada sauce,** separated

- **½ pound or 1 cup crab meat**

- **Sea salt and freshly ground black pepper to taste**

- **1 cup cooked black beans,** drained

- **2 cups shredded Mexican cheese blend**

- **12 6-inch corn tortillas**

SERVING SUGGESTIONS: AVOCADO CREMA (SEE PAGE 546), MOROS Y CRISTIANOS (SEE PAGE 370), FRESH CILANTRO

DIRECTIONS

1. Preheat oven to 375°F.

2. Heat 1 tablespoon of the avocado oil in a large skillet over medium-high heat. Add the onion and sauté until fragrant and slightly brown. Next, add the shrimp, chili powder, garlic powder and oregano and sauté for 3 minutes. Pour in ½ cup of the green enchilada sauce and the crab and stir to combine.

3. Taste for flavor and season with salt and pepper as needed. Turn off the heat, add the mixture to a clean bowl, and set aside to cool slightly.

4. Rinse and dry the skillet and place it back on the stove over medium-high heat. With the remaining avocado oil, use a pastry brush to grease the bottom of the pan or use an oil sprayer. Place a tortilla in the skillet and cook for 3–5 seconds on both sides to warm through and set it aside—the result should be a soft, pliable tortilla. Continue with the remaining tortillas.

5. Coat the bottom of the baking dish with about ½ cup of the green enchilada sauce and set aside.

6. This is the fun part where you get to use your instincts and preferences to create your ideal enchilada. Lay one tortilla flat on a clean surface and add about 1½ tablespoons of the crab and shrimp mixture, about 2 teaspoons of black beans, and about 2 tablespoons of cheese to the top third of the tortilla. Wrap the tortilla tightly around the filling and place in the baking dish. Repeat until all of the tortillas are used, lining them up in a tight row. Add any remaining crab and shrimp filling and cheese to the top of the dish and pour on the remaining green sauce.

7. Cover with dish foil and bake for 10 minutes, then remove the foil and cook for another 5 minutes or until the cheese is hot and bubbly. Let stand for 5 minutes, then serve with your suggested toppings as desired.

Crawfish Recipes

~~~~~~~~~~

Celebrating Crawfish

Crawfish are also known as crawdads, mudbugs and baby lobsters. They are small shellfish naturally found in rivers and estuaries where the river meets the sea. If the water is clean and well- oxygenated, then you will likely find crawfish hiding under rocks and crawling in the mud.

In the United States, crawfish have been harvested in fresh natural waters and consumed by Native Americans and some Europeans for centuries, according to the Louisiana State University Agricultural Center (LSU AgCenter). They are predominantly found throughout the warm waters of all Southern American states, with Louisiana being responsible for more than 90 percent of the crustaceans harvested in the U.S. The high season runs from November through May.

Growing up as a child in California, my sisters and I would find these creatures along the aqueducts while fishing with my grandpa. It can be fun to harvest your own while out in the wild, but I'd advise against it unless you are certain that the waters are safe (see page 41).

Around the 1950s, the cultivation of these crustaceans got underway in Southern Louisiana through the flooding of fallow rice fields. Harvested in bait traps like lobster and crab, crawfish can grow up to 8 inches in length. Most of the meat is found in the tail although the bodies are also embraced. Production is labor-intensive, which helps explain the premium price point.

As the mecca of crawfish production, Louisiana is famous for its crawfish bisque and étouffée and most notably, its grand, communally minded crawfish boils, a time-honored tradition. This event is an impressive and often dramatic display of crawfish boiled with herbs, spices, citrus fruit, potatoes and corn and served family-style. Every family and restaurant has its own recipe, and I'm no exception! See page 92 for my take on the classic dish.

Once used as pets or pet food in the region, crawfish are also popular in China. According to Shunsuke Tabeta, a writer for Nikkei Asia, restaurants are now featuring steaming plates of crawfish bathed in garlic and chilis. Guests enjoy the spicy "little lobsters" while donning plastic gloves and bibs. The Japanese are thought to have introduced crawfish to China in the 1920s.

If you can't find them in your local market, you can have bags of fresh or frozen crawfish shipped to you from a host of reputable U.S.-based farmers and grocers. In my opinion, the best quality crawfish come from the United States. The flavor and texture is hard to match!

NOLA Crawfish Flatbread

New Orleans, Louisiana is a melting pot of cultures, and this flatbread dish is a nice way to combine local flavors with an Italian twist. When combined with flatbreads like Indian naan, Greek pita or Italian piadina, crawfish make for a succulent, easy homemade flatbread seafood pizza.

I use previously frozen crawfish tails for this recipe since it's all about convenience. Because of the limited crawfish season, you can find an abundance of American southern harvesters that sell frozen whole shellfish and tails. Use more or less of the suggested ingredients to suit your palate. In a pinch, the crawfish can easily be swapped out for cooked Gulf shrimp.

INGREDIENTS

- **¼ cup tomato sauce**

- **1 teaspoon blackening seasoning** (see page 530)

- **2 teaspoons olive oil**

- **1 clove garlic,** halved

- **2 flatbreads of your choice, such as naan, piadina, pita or premade pizza crust**

- **½ cup grated mozzarella or slices from a mozzarella cheese ball**

- **1 large fresh tomato,** thinly sliced

- **1 large zucchini,** thinly sliced

- **½ cup thinly sliced bell pepper**

- **1 small scallion,** green part only, sliced

- **½ cup thinly sliced red** or **yellow onion**

- **½ cup cooked crawfish,** more if desired

DIRECTIONS

1. Preheat oven to 450°F.

2. In a small bowl, combine the tomato sauce and blackening seasoning and set aside.

3. Using a pastry brush, spread one teaspoon of olive oil onto each piece of flatbread and rub with the sliced side of the garlic. Use the pastry brush to spread equal portions of the tomato sauce mix on the flatbread, then layer on the mozzarella cheese, tomato, zucchini, bell pepper, scallion, red onion and crawfish.

4. Place the flatbread on a baking sheet and cook for 6–8 minutes until the cheese is melted and the flatbread lightly toasted. For a crispier crust, place the flatbread directly on the oven rack; just make sure to place a sheet of foil or a baking sheet on the rack below to catch spillage. Remove from the oven and serve immediately.

Louisiana Crawfish Boil

A delicacy enjoyed by many, crawfish holds a special place in the gastronomy of coastal Louisiana, where the majority of the world's crawfish are produced. I once had the great fortune of spending a couple of weeks in the Deep South during crawfish season and had the chance to experience a traditional crawfish boil served up by a local. It was a remarkable and messy experience, since you handle the mudbugs and eat them using your hands. I use previously frozen crawfish tails for this recipe since it's all about convenience. Because of the limited crawfish season, you can find an abundance of American southern harvesters that sell frozen whole shellfish and tails. Use more or less of the suggested ingredients to suit your palate. In a pinch, the crawfish can easily be swapped out for cooked Gulf shrimp.

Most boils are considered a social event as much as they are a dining experience. Typically cooked outdoors in large stockpots, this is a meal designed to serve a large crowd.

My recipe is built for a much smaller group and includes Gulf shrimp, which I think adds flavor and variety to the meal. The recipe easily doubles or triples, and you can make it your own by adding optional ingredients like fresh artichokes.

It is important to give the dish time to steep, so don't skip this step. Steeping gives the shellfish time to absorb the flavor from the bouillon.

INGREDIENTS

{ Serves 4 }

- **4 quarts water**

- **2 bay leaves**

- **1 large bunch fresh thyme**

- **2 tablespoons black peppercorns**

- **1 large white onion**, halved

- **4 cloves garlic**, whole

- **2 oranges**, halved

- **2 lemons**, halved

- **1 tablespoon whole cloves**

- **2 tablespoons cayenne pepper** (less if desired)

- **3 tablespoons smoked paprika sea salt** (see page 548)

- **2 pounds baby red potatoes**

- **5 ears fresh corn**, shucked and cut in half

- **2 pounds gulf shrimp**

- **6 pounds whole crawfish**

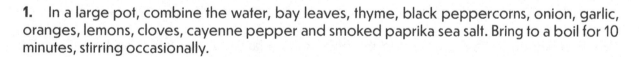

SERVING SUGGESTIONS: PEPPER SAUCE, LEMON WEDGES

DIRECTIONS

1. In a large pot, combine the water, bay leaves, thyme, black peppercorns, onion, garlic, oranges, lemons, cloves, cayenne pepper and smoked paprika sea salt. Bring to a boil for 10 minutes, stirring occasionally.

2. Add the baby red potatoes, corn, shrimp and crawfish, and cook for another 10 minutes with the lid on and slightly ajar. Turn off the heat, place the lid on fully, and allow the liquid to cool.

3. To serve, ladle equal portions into large bowls. Serve with pepper sauce and lemon wedges as desired.

Breaux Bridge Crawfish Étouffée

Étouffée is a classic southern dish that hails from Breaux Bridge, Louisiana, a small town that is a hop, skip and a jump from the Gulf of Mexico. Located in St. Martin Parish, this area is known as Cajun Country where most of the world's crawfish are produced. The word étouffée means "stewed" or "smothered" and is a favored cooking technique in this part of the world.

When exploring this area, you'll find this dish both on family dinner tables and on menus of fancy restaurants. This recipe is an approachable way to bring the flavors of Louisiana home, and it beautifully showcases the flavor and texture of local crawfish. If crawfish is hard to find, shrimp can easily be substituted.

INGREDIENTS

- **1/3 cup all-purpose flour**

- **¼ cup (½ stick) unsalted butter**

- **1 cup finely diced celery** (about 3 stalks)

- **1 cup finely diced white onion** (1 small onion)

- **1 cup diced bell pepper**, any color (1 small pepper)

- **2 large scallions**, green and white parts, **with 2 tablespoons reserved for garnish**

- **2 cloves garlic**, minced

- **2 cups lobster stock** (see page 492), vegetable broth or water

- **2 large Creole tomatoes, diced, or 1 cup canned tomatoes**

- **1 teaspoon blackening seasoning (see page 530)**

- **Sea salt and freshly ground black pepper to taste**

- **1 pound cooked, shelled Louisiana crawfish tails**

- **4–6 cups warm cooked white rice as desired**

- **Hot sauce, optional**

DIRECTIONS

1. In a Dutch oven or medium-sized heavy-bottomed pot, whisk the flour and butter together over medium heat to make a light blonde-colored roux. Stir constantly to avoid burning.

2. Add the celery, white onion, bell pepper, scallions and garlic. Stir to combine and cook for 6–8 minutes or until the vegetables have softened. Turn the heat to low and pour in the seafood stock, vegetable broth or water. Use a small whisk to remove any lumps. The roux should be smooth and slightly thick. Add a little more liquid if needed to thin it out. Add the tomatoes, blackening seasoning and a pinch of salt and freshly ground black pepper. Stir, cooking for 3–4 minutes.

3. Add the crawfish tails and gently fold them into the sauce, taking care not to break them up too much. Cook for another 1½ minutes, just enough to heat the crawfish through. Taste for seasoning and adjust as needed.

4. To serve, add equal portions of white rice to bowls and top with portions of the étouffée. Top with remaining scallions and serve immediately. Add hot sauce as desired.

Gulf Coast Crawfish Quesadillas

The Gulf Coast of the United States is made up of five states: Alabama, Florida, Louisiana, Mississippi and Texas. Crawfish are cherished in this part of the world, with Louisiana producing the lion's share of the beloved shellfish.

Sharing a border with Mexico, Texas has a unique gastronomy scene referred to as Tex-Mex. As the name implies, this style of cooking is a mashup of the cuisines of Texas and Mexico. It was developed by the Tejano community—Texans of Spanish or Mexican heritage who lived in Texas before it became a state. This quesadilla recipe brings even more to the table by adding southern flair with the addition of crawfish!

Quesadillas are an easy meal that only takes a few minutes to go from pan to table. The key to a perfect, crispy version is to lightly oil the tortilla and cook it until slightly golden brown. Undercooking will result in a soggy, undesirable meal. If you have an oil spritzer or a pastry brush, these tools will come in handy. Alternatively, you can use a commercial cooking spray, but make sure the oil is good quality, as it imparts flavor. A stick of butter will work in a pinch—just peel back the paper and use it like a marker to lightly oil your pan.

INGREDIENTS

- 2 tablespoons avocado oil, separated, more as needed

- 1 tablespoon butter

- ½ cup thinly sliced onion

- 1 small bell pepper, any color, thinly sliced

- 1 cup cooked crawfish tails, roughly chopped (defrosted and drained if using frozen)

- 1 teaspoon garlic powder

- Sea salt and black pepper, as needed

- 4 8-inch flour tortillas

- ¾ cup shredded Mexican cheese blend (Monterey Jack, mild cheddar, asadero & queso quesadilla)

SERVING SUGGESTIONS:

AVOCADO SLICES, GUACAMOLE, CHOPPED CILANTRO, DICED TOMATO, SALSA

DIRECTIONS

{ Makes 4 quesadillas }

1. Heat 1 tablespoon of the avocado oil and butter in a large skillet over medium-high heat. Add the onion and bell pepper and sauté until fragrant and slightly brown. Add the crawfish and garlic powder and cook until warmed through. Taste for flavor and season with salt and pepper as needed. Turn off the heat, add the mixture to a clean bowl, and set aside to cool slightly.

2. Rinse and dry the skillet and add it back to the stove over medium-high heat. With the remaining avocado oil, use a pastry brush to grease the bottom of the pan. Alternately, you can use an oil sprayer or the open end of a stick of butter to oil the pan. Place a tortilla in the skillet and cook for 5 seconds on both sides to warm through.

3. This is the fun part where you get to use your instincts and preferences to create your ideal quesadilla. With the tortilla lying flat in the skillet, add enough of the Mexican cheese blend to cover one half of the tortilla (about 1½ tablespoons), along with a portion of the crawfish mixture. Fold the tortilla over to make a half-moon shape.

4. Cook for 2–3 minutes on each side, allowing time for the cheese to melt and the tortilla to brown. When the cheese has melted and the outside of the tortilla is crispy, remove from the heat. Cover with a tea towel or place in the warmer tray of your oven to keep warm. Repeat with the remaining tortillas and ingredients.

5. Cut each quesadilla into 3 pieces and serve with your choice of toppings.

Tex-Mex Crawfish Enchiladas

Enchiladas have roots in royal Aztec feasts. Centuries later, they found their way into modern Tex-Mex cuisine, according to the publication History Today, and continue to evolve in the modern-day.

One of the main ingredients that makes enchiladas special is the sauce. Seafood enchiladas are best prepared with green sauce, the fresh and vibrant cousin to the spicy, traditional red sauce commonly associated with this dish. There are many excellent green enchilada sauce brands on the market—two of my favorites are Las Palmas Green Chile Enchilada Sauce and Hatch Green Chile Enchilada Sauce. Both have well-balanced, deep, rich flavor. There are many other brands you can explore based on your preferences.

INGREDIENTS

2 tablespoons avocado oil, **separated**, more as needed

1 tablespoon butter

½ cup diced onion

1 small bell pepper (any color), diced

1 cup cooked crawfish tails, roughly chopped (defrosted and drained if using frozen)

1 teaspoon garlic powder

1 teaspoon cayenne pepper

1 28-ounce can green enchilada sauce, separated

12 8-inch flour tortillas

2 cups shredded Mexican cheese blend (Monterey Jack, mild cheddar, asadero & queso quesadilla)

Sea salt and black pepper, as needed

SERVING SUGGESTIONS:

AVOCADO SLICES, GUACAMOLE, CHOPPED CILANTRO, DICED TOMATO, SALSA

DIRECTIONS

{ Makes 12 enchiladas }

1. Preheat oven to 375°F.

2. Heat 1 tablespoon of the avocado oil and butter in a large skillet over medium-high heat. Add the onion and bell pepper and sauté until fragrant and slightly brown. Add the crawfish, garlic powder, cayenne pepper and half of the green enchilada sauce and stir to combine. Taste for flavor and season with salt and pepper as needed. Turn off the heat, add the mixture to a clean bowl, and set aside to cool slightly.

3. Rinse and dry the skillet and place it back on the stove over medium-high heat. With the remaining avocado oil, grease the bottom of the pan using a pastry brush (alternately, you can use an oil sprayer). Place a tortilla in the skillet and cook for 3–5 seconds on both sides to warm through, then set it aside—the result should be a soft, pliable tortilla. Continue with the remaining tortillas.

4. Coat the bottom of the baking dish with about ½ cup of green enchilada sauce and set aside.

5. Lay one tortilla flat on a clean surface and add about 1½ tablespoons of the crawfish mix to the top third of the tortilla along with 2 tablespoons of cheese. Wrap the tortilla tightly around the filling and place in the baking dish. Repeat until all of the tortillas are used, lining them up in a tight row. Add any remaining crawfish filling and cheese to the top of the dish and pour on the remaining green sauce.

6. Cover with foil and bake for 10 minutes, then remove the foil and cook for another 5 minutes or until the cheese is hot and bubbly. Let stand for 5 minutes, then serve with your favorite toppings.

Lobster Recipes

The Lowdown on Lobster

Few creatures from the ocean's depths are as celebrated as the lobster. The classic images of lobster are that of the clawed, New England or Maine varieties, but there are a few others to keep an eye out for while shopping at your local market or while traveling internationally.

According to the Marine Education Society of Australia, lobsters fall into two main varieties: clawed lobster (30 species) and spiny or rock lobster (45 species). In simple terms, any lobster with defined front claws is a cold water lobster, and any lobster with five sets of appendages but no front claws is considered a warm water lobster.

On one of my SCUBA diving adventures in Mexico, I observed spiny lobsters in the wild. It was a very cool experience. As nocturnal animals, lobsters hide in and around rocks during the day and become active at night. During lobster season, adventurous divers can harvest their own with a proper fishing license.

Clawed and spiny lobsters are available on almost every coast and are shipped both alive and frozen to inland locations. Different seasons affect the flavor and texture of the shellfish.

When it comes to shopping for lobster, there are a few things to keep in mind:

HARD VS. SOFT SHELLED LOBSTER

Generally speaking, soft shelled lobsters have meat that's noticeably sweet, while hard shelled have heartier meat. This is important to keep in mind as you decide how to cook the lobster, be it grilled, baked, sautéed or boiled. Personally, I prefer the flavorful meat of hard-shelled lobster.

SOFT SHELLED LOBSTER

• When a lobster sheds its old shell, a soft shell develops. As it grows its new shell, the lobster pulls in water in order to grow into its paper-thin shell, which will harden eventually. Thus, when harvested during soft-shell season, the lobster will contain less meat and more water. Due to the extra water that accumulates in the shell, the meat is saltier but sweeter.

• They may have less meat than their hard shell friends, but soft shell lobster are much easier to crack, making things easier at the dinner table.

HARD SHELLED LOBSTER

• At the end of a hard-shell cycle, the lobster is at its most robust, since it has been filling out its shell. This is when there is the most meat in a lobster, and it is also the best-tasting time of a lobster's life.

• Since lobsters contain the highest amount of meat possible during the hard-shell season, they will increase in price, as you are paying for more, better-tasting meat.

Age – Large lobsters may look great when plated, but they tend to be a bit tough when cooked. In general, the older the lobster, the tougher the meat. Look for lobsters that are under 2 pounds. You may have heard the term "chicken lobster"—these are young lobsters that weigh under 1 pound.

Freshness – Spiny lobster tails are often flash-frozen and shipped to your grocery store. If they are thawed properly (in the refrigerator or under cold running water) and eaten immediately, they should have good flavor and texture.

Buying in-season – Lobsters are easier to transport when their shells are hard. You'll get a better selection and better quality if you educate yourself about the molting season in your area. Like other seasonal foods, the selection is finest when the food is abundant.

LOBSTER TYPES

CLAWED LOBSTER

Clawed lobster is what most people think of when picturing a lobster. These lobsters have five sets of walking legs and three sets of claws. The first set of claws is much larger than the following two sets. Clawed lobsters are important for the seafood industry, because they have become the expected type of lobster.

REEF LOBSTER

Reef lobsters also have claws but are considered to be separate from clawed lobsters. Reef lobsters only have the set of claws on the first set of appendages and not on the subsequent pairs.

SPINY LOBSTER

Spiny lobster, also known as rock lobster, do not have claws and are distinguishable because of the oversized, thick antennae that give them the "spiny" appearance. This variety is known for its firm and sweet tail meat. They range in size and are often less expensive and more readily available than Maine lobster.

SLIPPER LOBSTER

Slipper lobsters also have enlarged antennae and lack front claws. They are flatter than the other lobsters and look like their faces have been smashed. Slipper lobsters often bury themselves in the mud during the day instead of hiding in holes like the other lobster types. Because of this, they tend not to be as desirable for food.

FURRY LOBSTER

Furry lobsters have large antennae, though not as large as the spiny lobsters. Furry lobsters are named as such because of the protrusions on their body that make them appear to be covered in hair. Furry lobsters are small and manage to avoid most lobster traps.

SQUAT LOBSTER

Squat lobsters are not really a lobster at all. They resemble clawed lobster but are more closely related to crabs and hermit crabs. Squat lobsters live in crevices, though they have been known to use their claws to dig in the sand for food.

Storing Lobster

It's best to buy live lobsters on the day you plan to cook them. Once removed from their salted tanks, which is how they are typically stored, they have a limited lifespan—two days is usually the max. Once the lobster has expired, the meat will start to turn mushy and inedible.

1. Keep them moist but not wet and store them in the coldest part of your refrigerator. Moisture and temperature are among the most important factors. Like other shellfish, tap water or any non-salted water will kill the lobster.

2. Check for leg movement. Live crabs and lobsters should show some leg movement. They spoil rapidly after death, so only live crabs and lobsters should be selected and prepared.

3. Curled tail. When working with live lobster, one of the best ways to tell if it is healthy is to check its tail. Healthy lobsters will curl their tail tightly when held.

WHAT TO EAT AND WHAT TO LEAVE?

The University of Maine Lobster Institute is an excellent source of information for all things concerning clawed lobster. I've answered common questions here with help from this institution.

WHAT'S THE WHITE STUFF ON THE LOBSTER ONCE IT'S COOKED?

Coagulated blood. It's harmless and edible but does not present well. Use a warm cloth to wipe off the lobster prior to serving.

CAN I EAT THE GREEN PART OF THE LOBSTER?

Yes, you can. This is called the tomalley and is essentially the part of the shellfish that functions as the liver, pancreas and intestines. Some people enjoy this part and find it delicious, while others avoid it altogether.

IS THE RED STUFF FOUND ALONG THE TAIL SAFE TO EAT?

The red substance found along the tail of the lobster is actually lobster roe or eggs and is considered a delicacy in some parts of the world.

Steamed Maine Lobster

Steaming lobster is a gentle cooking technique that yields slightly more tender meat than grilling or oven roasting. It also preserves a little more flavor than boiling and is a faster cooking process. If you have a tendency to overcook shellfish, steaming is the way to go. See my Posh Pointers on types of lobster on page 203.

If you are squeamish about cooking live lobster, place the shellfish in the freezer for 15-20 minutes. This will put the crustacean to sleep and sedate it, making it less likely to wiggle in the pot.

You will need a steaming rack and a pot large enough to steam a couple of lobsters at a time. The whole process will take about 40 minutes. A 2-pound lobster will yield about 8 ounces of meat. During the cooking process, the lobster will turn from blue-green to a beautiful red color that is often associated with Maine lobster.

For a perfect-looking lobster, rub it down with a warm damp tea towel once it is cooked and cooled. The white stuff is hemolymph, or coagulated blood from the lobster, according to the University of Maine Lobster Institute. It's harmless and flavorless, but like albumin on salmon, it can be off-putting for presentation purposes.

INGREDIENTS

{ Makes 5 lobsters }

- **5 medium-sized live Maine lobsters**, about 2 pounds each

- **Fresh seawater or salted water**

- **2 bay leaves**

SERVING SUGGESTIONS: LEMON WEDGES, MELTED BUTTER

DIRECTIONS

SPECIAL EQUIPMENT: STOCKPOT WITH STEAMER BASKET

1. In a stockpot with a steamer rack, pour in 3 inches of seawater or salted water, using more as needed. Set the steaming rack inside the pot and bring the pot to a rolling boil over high heat. Add the lobsters two or three at a time, taking care not to overcrowd the pot.

2. Check the water level throughout the process to make sure lobsters are sufficiently covered. Add more water as needed. Cook until done.

3. Serve immediately or allow lobsters to cool before removing them from their shells.

HERE IS A QUICK TIMING GUIDE:	
1-pound lobster	10 minutes
1½-pound lobster	14 minutes
2-pound lobster	18 minutes
3-pound lobster	25 minutes

*See lobster stock recipe on page 492 to make use of lobster shells.

Maine-Style Lobster Roll

This is the ultimate New England summer dish. Ask any local Mainer and they will tell you that the perfect lobster roll is made from a hot dog bun split down the middle, toasted, and filled with lobster that has been lightly dressed in mayonnaise and perhaps a few aromatics. Traditionally served cold or at room temperature, this simple approach really allows the lobster to shine through.

My version represents a new wave, which slightly deviates from the classic recipe and reveals my aversion to mayonnaise. I opt for creamy, tangy Greek yogurt instead—I promise, you won't miss the mayo!

New England has another treasured version of the lobster roll hailing from Connecticut, which can be found on page 110.

I like clawed lobster for this dish. You can cook your own lobster for this recipe (see page 107) or purchase it prepared from your local market. If you purchase it from a store, be sure to taste the lobster before adding salt to the dish, as some stores add salt during the cooking process.

INGREDIENTS

{ Makes 5–6 sandwiches }

- **2 pounds cooked, chilled clawed lobster meat**, cut into chunks

- **1 cup strained Greek yogurt**

- **1 tablespoon Dijon mustard**

- **1 tablespoon chopped fresh tarragon**

- **Sea salt and freshly ground black pepper to taste**

- **6 brioche buns or hot dog buns**, split down the middle

- **5–6 leaves Bibb lettuce**

- **Fresh lemon juice for finishing**, optional

DIRECTIONS

1. Preheat oven to 350°F.

2. In a large mixing bowl, combine the lobster meat, Greek yogurt, Dijon mustard, tarragon, and sea salt and pepper to taste. Stir to combine thoroughly. Taste for seasoning and adjust as needed.

3. Warm the brioche buns in the oven for 1–2 minutes.

4. Place the Bibb lettuce on the bottom of each brioche bun, then spoon in the lobster mix. Give each sandwich a spritz of lemon juice if desired. Serve immediately.

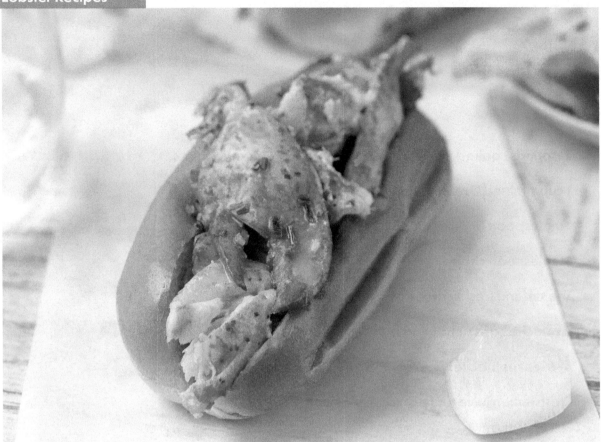

Connecticut–Style Lobster Roll

According to New England Today, the Connecticut-style lobster roll was invented by Perry's Restaurant in Milford, CT around 1929. Considered a toasted buttered lobster roll, the description is true to form. With lobster tossed in butter and served warm, the Connecticut-style lobster roll is tasty and unpretentious.

Maine or American lobster is used for this dish instead of Caribbean or spiny lobster (see page 104). You can cook your own shellfish for this recipe (see page 105), or purchase it prepared from your local market. I prefer claw meat for this dish, but feel free to use meat from your favorite section. If you purchase lobster from a market, be sure to taste it before adding salt to the dish, as some stores add salt during the cooking process.

INGREDIENTS

Makes 5–6 sandwiches

- **1 stick unsalted butter**

- **2 pounds cooked, chilled clawed lobster meat,** cut into chunks

- **Sea salt and freshly ground black pepper**

- **6 brioche buns or hot dog buns**

- **3 tablespoons chopped chives**

DIRECTIONS

1. Preheat oven to 350°F.

2. In a medium-sized saucepan, melt the butter over low heat. When the butter is melted, add the lobster meat and stir to coat in the butter. Taste and add salt and pepper as needed.

3. Meanwhile, warm the brioche buns in the oven for 1–2 minutes.

4. To serve, add equal portions of the lobster meat to the buns and garnish with chopped chives. Serve immediately.

Ecuadorian Lobster Tacos

WITH KOHLRABI SLAW

Famed for the Galápagos Islands, Ecuador is also known for its tranquil beaches, warm waters and Afro Ecuadorian gastronomy scene in which lobster plays a big role.

Spiny lobster swim in the warm waters that also play host to shrimp, squid and octopus. Their sweet flavor and firm texture work great with kohlrabi slaw, an unlikely pairing.

This kohlrabi slaw recipe is fresh and flavorful. If you are new to this root vegetable, it is a crisp and crunchy relative of cabbage that tastes like a cross between a broccoli stem and a radish. The green apple complements the kohlrabi's somewhat bitter flavor by adding a sweet note to the slaw (see page 400).

If spiny lobster proves challenging to find, swap it out for large white shrimp. See page 151 for tips on selecting shrimp. I recommend using mini street taco size tortilla shells for this recipe; they will present beautifully this way. If you are feeling creative, you can use a variety of taco shells, corn or flour tortillas, jicama shells (see page 420) or lettuce leaves.

INGREDIENTS

Makes 5–6 sandwiches

- **1 pound uncooked lobster meat,** cut into bite-sized pieces

- **2 tablespoons avocado oil,** separated

- **1 small lime,** juice and zest

- **¼ cup chopped fresh cilantro,** 1 tablespoon reserved for garnish

- **1 small serrano pepper,** minced

- **Sea salt and freshly ground black pepper to taste**

- **1 cup kohlrabi slaw** (see page 400)

- **12–15 tortillas of your choice** (see page 160 for tips on heating corn and flour tortillas)

DIRECTIONS

Marinate the lobster:
In a medium-sized bowl, combine the uncooked lobster, 1 tablespoon of the avocado oil, lime juice and zest, cilantro, serrano pepper and sea salt and pepper to taste. Mix thoroughly to coat the lobster with the seasoning and allow it to marinate while you prepare the kohlrabi salad and dressing (see page 400).

Cook the lobster:
In a large skillet, heat the remaining tablespoon of avocado oil over medium-high heat. Strain any residual moisture from the lobster bowl, then add the lobster to the skillet. Sauté for 3 minutes then turn off the heat, taking care not to overcook. Set aside.

Serve the tacos:
To serve the tacos, add a scoop of the lobster to your tortilla of choice and top with the kohlrabi slaw and fresh cilantro as desired. Repeat with the remaining tortillas and serve immediately.

Honduran Lobster Quesadillas

Honduras, a republic located in Central America, is the second-largest producer of Caribbean spiny lobster after Nicaragua. It is encapsulated by the Caribbean Sea on one side and the Pacific Ocean on the other. The cuisine in this part of the world is a mix of cultures—Indigenous, African, European and Asian. Coconut typically dominates this region's cuisine, but seafood is equally popular.

Quesadillas are a decadent, easy-living kind of meal. They are universally adored and can be made in about 10 minutes. This is one of my husband's favorite treats.

Aside from the lobster, I usually have most of the ingredients in this recipe readily available. This makes it easy to put together a quick and satisfying meal with whatever protein I have in my refrigerator or pantry. Alternatives to lobster are black beans, crab, crawfish, smoked salmon, canned salmon, shrimp, swordfish or sautéed mushrooms.

112

INGREDIENTS

2 cups uncooked spiny lobster
meat, cut into bite-sized pieces

2 teaspoons ground cumin

2 teaspoons chili powder

1 teaspoon garlic powder

1 medium lime, juice and zest

2 tablespoons avocado oil,
separated, plus more as needed

Sea salt and freshly ground black
pepper to taste

1 medium Spanish onion, thinly
sliced

5 10-inch or 12-inch flour tortillas

¾ cup shredded Mexican
cheese blend

2 cups spinach, stems removed

¼ cup chopped fresh cilantro
leaves

SERVING SUGGESTIONS:

*MANGO SALSA
(SEE PAGE 566),
SHREDDED LETTUCE, SALSA,
AVOCADO CREMA
(SEE PAGE 546)*

DIRECTIONS

Marinate the lobster:
In a medium-sized bowl, combine the lobster meat, cumin, chili powder, garlic powder, lime juice and zest, 1 tablespoon of avocado oil, and sea salt and black pepper to taste. Mix thoroughly, cover, and set aside to marinate.

Cook the lobster:
Meanwhile, heat the remaining tablespoon of avocado oil in a large skillet over medium-high heat. Add the onion and sauté until soft and fragrant. Add the marinated lobster and sauté for about 2 minutes, taking care not to overcook. Remove the lobster from the heat and set aside to cool.

Prepare the quesadillas:
Lightly coat the bottom of a large skillet with avocado oil and heat over medium-high heat. Add one flour tortilla and cook for a few seconds on one side, then flip and cook for another few seconds on the other side to heat through.

Next, add a generous sprinkling of the Mexican cheese blend, about 2 tablespoons, to one side of the tortilla along with a scoop of the lobster mix and a few spinach leaves. Fold the tortilla over to close and cook until golden brown, then flip over and brown on the other side—about 1 minute each. Repeat with the remaining tortillas, cheese, spinach and lobster mix.

To serve, slice quesadillas into thirds and place on a plate. Garnish with fresh cilantro and add optional toppings as desired. Repeat with the remaining quesadillas.

Oyster Recipes

- Emerald Coast Oysters on the Half Shell

- Chesapeake Bay Fried Oysters

- Long Island Oven-Roasted Oysters

- Sea Island Oyster Gravy Over Shrimp & Rice

- Galveston Bay Barbecued Oysters

- Lowcountry Oyster Gravy over Fried Green Tomatoes

Oyster Overview

Oysters are a magnificent shellfish that you either love or avoid altogether. To be totally transparent, I'm an oyster hound—in other words I will empty my pockets and drive an inordinate amount of miles to acquire and imbibe oysters any way possible. I prefer them au naturel, but I have no shame in frying up a batch, wrapping them in French bread and enjoying them as a New Orleans-style 'po boy or served on a plate doused with a little hot sauce and lemon juice.

Oysters are related to a host of ocean life including octopuses and clams. Legend has it that oysters are safe to eat only in months ending with the letter "R." Thank goodness this is only a rumor, which came about at a time when refrigeration controls were practically nonexistent. These days, oysters are always in season thanks to modern cultivation. Hallelujah!

There are a handful of oyster species harvested in North America. Their primary differences are based on location, the water they filter, and harvesting method. These combined factors are known as meroir, the ocean's version of terroir—the characteristic tastes and flavors imparted by the growth habitat of wine and other crops.

Most of the oysters you'll find in your market will be cultivated, or farmed. Just like wine and some cheese varieties, oysters are named for the region in which they are grown.

ATLANTIC OYSTERS

Native to the Atlantic Ocean and Gulf coast, eastern oysters are also known as American cupped oysters, North American East Coast Oysters, American oysters and Atlantic oysters. They tend to be strongshelled and strong-flavored, with a salty, briny, metallic finish. They hold up well to heat and are great on the barbecue.

EUROPEAN FLAT OR BELON OYSTERS

Native to Europe, this variety is related to the Olympia oyster but is much larger in size with a metallic, robust flavor. A true Belon oyster is harvested from the Belon River in Brittany, France, but thanks to early attempts at cultivation in North America, they can be found wild around the cold waters of Maine. These are best enjoyed on the half shell but are also great in stews.

OLYMPIA OYSTERS

The only oyster native to the West Coast, Olympia Oysters are found only in Puget Sound in the state of Washington. Slightly larger than a quarter, they only reach about 1½ inches in diameter. They are delicate and, unfortunately, practically extinct at this moment in time. Efforts are being made to bring Olympias, or Olys, back after being wiped out from overharvesting. According to the Washington Department of Fish and Wildlife, there are a number of restoration efforts underway. Like crawfish and salmon, Olys were an important part of Native American cuisine. This treasured oyster is briny with a sweet metallic finish.

PACIFIC OYSTERS

Originally transplanted from Japan, Pacific oysters begin life as male then function as a female after one year. Contrary to their name, they are not native to the West Coast, but rather to Asia Pacific. They are sweeter and less briny than Atlantic oysters. With a beautifully fluted shell, Pacific Oysters make for a delicious display on the half shell. Pacifics are small, sweet and have a crisp saltiness. I enjoy westerns raw or with very little dressing. Regional examples of these oysters include Fanny Bay, Hog Island and Kumiai.

KUMAMOTO OYSTERS

Named after their birthplace, Kumamotos were imported to North America from Kumamoto, Japan and are one of the most popular oysters on the market. They are now cultivated in Baja California, Washington, and other areas. They grow much slower than other varieties, and are small, deep-cupped oysters with a gorgeous briny flavor that is very approachable. They are eaten raw by novices and pros alike.

ASK THE EXPERT

If it's not clear where your oysters are from, ask your fishmonger or the fish market staff to see the shellfish tag.

This is a tag that is attached to each bag of shellfish, oysters, clams and mussels to identify and track shellfish as they move through the market. **These tags identify the harvest location and date** in order to provide a detailed point of reference as required by the United States Federal Government. Shellfish sellers are required to keep the tag on for 90 days after delivery date.

Live oysters are considered fresh and in their most delicious state when they have ample liquor (the liquid inside the shell) and maintain their aroma and flavor from harvest—they should smell briny and fresh. Like most shellfish, they should be tightly closed or should close when you tap them. Unless you buy them in bulk, your fishmonger should do this for you.

Like most shellfish, oysters do not come with a "best by" date; from a food safety standpoint, they can theoretically be safe to eat for months if stored properly. These bivalves have historically been stored in pits and underground cellars to be kept cool and preserved through winter—a technique called "pitting" or "wintering." I don't recommend this approach unless you are guided by an experienced hand.

My preference is to use live oysters within 1–3 days of purchase for two basic reasons: one, limited space and two, food safety.

Refrigerator space is prime real estate in my home! Regardless of the variety, live oysters are bulky and take up room in the refrigerator. Since I typically like to buy a few dozen, this limits the number of other goodies that I can store.

My 3-day rule came about when I realized that the daily ins & outs of accessing my fridge brings down the temperature, making food safety a concern. When properly handled and stored, live oysters fare well and remain fresh between 34 and 43 degrees. The back of the fridge usually works well; just make sure to cover your oysters with a damp cloth and stash them in an open container. Keep in mind that other sources may offer up a timeline between 5 and 7 days after harvest, but this is under ideal handling situations and if you know the harvest date. When I hear about people getting sick from eating raw shellfish it is rarely the shellfish that is to blame. Mishandling is one of the main causes of oyster-related foodborne illness.

Shucking your own

I love ordering oysters when dining out and when visiting oyster farms, but it's just as easy to prepare them at home!

In addition to fish markets and grocery stores, you can also take live oysters to go from your favorite seafood restaurant or order them online straight from the source. Some companies will curate a selection for you, which gives you a chance to enjoy varieties from all over the country.

THERE ARE A FEW WAYS TO OPEN—OR SHUCK—AN OYSTER, AND A FEW TOOLS YOU SHOULD HAVE ON HAND.

1. Generally, an oyster will have a flat side and a round side. With the flat side up, hold the oyster very steady on a table with the palm of your hand. You can wear a protective glove or use a tea towel to protect your hand.

2. Where the oyster comes to a point (at its anterior edge), you will find the hinge where the two half shells are connected. The first step in shucking an oyster is to break the hinge.

3. Take an oyster knife and carefully force the tip of the knife into the hinge. It may take a little practice to find the right angle for each individual oyster, so just be patient (try to aim the knife at the table and not at your hand).

4. Once you have the tip of the knife inside the hinge, you will have to pry the two half shells apart. This may take twisting or turning the knife—find the angle that gives you the most leverage.

5. Once the hinge has been broken, drag the knife along the underside of the flat side, aiming for the adductor muscle, which is found on the right side of the oyster when the hinge is facing you. This muscle must be severed in order to remove the flat shell from the rest of the oyster.

6. Once you have removed the flat side, carefully sever the adductor muscle from the round side of the shell. Make sure to reserve as much nectar (liquid) in the half shell as possible during the shucking process.

Emerald Coast Oysters

ON THE HALF SHELL

France is home to a handful of oyster producing regions, including Normandy, Vandée, Marennes Oléron, Arcachon and the Mediterranean Sea, but Brittany is one of the most celebrated. A peninsula located in the glimmering blue-green waters of the Emerald Coast, Brittany is home to hu tres plates or flat Belon oysters, an iconic oyster that is one of the most popular in Europe.

Oysters have been a part of French gastronomy for centuries and are a treasured part of the traditional Christmas Eve and New Year's Eve meals known as le réveillon, a meal composed of luxurious and decadent food that extends well into the evening.

Served on the half shell with a classic French mignonette sauce, these oysters are simply delightful.

INGREDIENTS

{ Makes 2 dozen oysters }

- **½ cup white or red wine vinegar**

- **1 tablespoon coarsely ground black pepper**

- **½ cup minced shallot**

- **Sea salt to taste**

- **2 dozen whole live oysters,** open on the half shell (see page 121

- **1 tablespoon minced fresh thyme or tarragon leaves**

SERVING SUGGESTIONS: LEMON WEDGES, TABASCO SAUCE, RUSTIC BREAD, SALTINE CRACKERS

DIRECTIONS

1. In a small bowl, combine the vinegar, ground pepper and shallot and mix thoroughly. Taste for seasoning and add salt as needed. Set aside.

2. Place the oysters on a plate or platter and artfully add a few fresh thyme leaves to each shell. Serve immediately with the mignonette sauce on the side, as well as lemon wedges, Tabasco sauce, bread and saltine crackers if desired.

Chesapeake Bay Fried Oysters

Some people dream of starting a tomato garden; I fantasize about having an oyster farm in my backyard! I simply can't get enough of these briny bivalves.

I had a chance to enjoy a curated selection of local seafood during my last trip to the state of Maryland, which is beloved for its blue crab, with oysters coming in at a close second.

There are dozens of oyster cultivators dotted along the waters of the Chesapeake Bay, an estuary where freshwater mixes with the Atlantic Ocean. Oysters from these waters have a golden hue and a distinct merroir, with a sweet and slightly briny flavor that most describe as well balanced.

These fried oysters can be stuffed into a 'po boy, served atop a salad, or eaten moments after leaving the frying pan with a squeeze of lemon and Tabasco. What makes this recipe distinct to the Chesapeake Bay region is the use of crushed cracker crumbs. I prefer to use jarred oysters for this recipe—save the fresh-shucked oysters for roasting or enjoying on the half shell.

INGREDIENTS

{ Serves 2 }

- **2 8-ounce jars oysters, drained, or 8 large oysters,** shucked

- **Rosemary sea salt to taste (see page 502)**

- **½ teaspoon cayenne pepper**

- **1 teaspoon dried thyme**

- **1 teaspoon white pepper**

- **1 cup all-purpose flour**

- **2 sleeves saltine crackers, crushed into crumbs, about 2 cups (alternately, you can use bread crumbs)**

- **1½ cups canola oil,** for frying

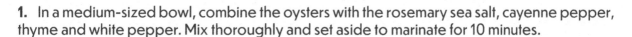

SERVING SUGGESTIONS: PEPPER SAUCE, FRESH LEMON WEDGES, SPRINKLE OF OLD BAY SEASONING

DIRECTIONS

1. In a medium-sized bowl, combine the oysters with the rosemary sea salt, cayenne pepper, thyme and white pepper. Mix thoroughly and set aside to marinate for 10 minutes.

2. In a large brown paper bag, carefully pour in the all-purpose flour and cracker crumbs (or bread crumbs, if using). Add the oysters to the bag a few at a time and shake gently to coat, holding the bottom of the bag for extra security. Remove the oysters and place them on a plate or clean surface to rest for 3–5 minutes; this will help form a thin crust. Proceed with the remaining oysters.

3. Meanwhile, in a Dutch oven or a heavy-bottomed skillet, heat the oil to 375°F.

4. Fry the oysters in batches until golden brown, then drain on a bed of paper towels or a cooling rack. Serve immediately with your favorite toppings and seasonings.

Long Island Oven-Roasted

Long Island is a densely populated island in southeastern New York State. It is separated from the mainland by the Long Island Sound and bound on both sides by the Atlantic Ocean. The island is home to a string of seaside communities and a popular summer destination known as the Hamptons.

Long Island is a seafood hotspot with clams, lobster, blue fish and oysters among the most popular choices. The Long Island Sound is home to Blue Points, which are big, strong-shelled and meaty oysters.

Large eastern oysters are a good choice for this recipe because their size holds up well to cooking. Check with your fishmonger for other options and review page 121 for more on oyster varieties. I can eat this entire serving by myself! So, buy more if you are as much of an oyster aficionado as me.

INGREDIENTS

{ Makes 2 dozen oysters }

- **½ cup panko breadcrumbs**

- **2 tablespoons ghee**

- **1 tablespoon chopped fresh mixed herbs** (such as thyme, tarragon and basil)

- **1 tablespoon grated Parmesan cheese**

- **1 teaspoon rosemary sea salt (see page 552)**, more or less as needed

- **2 dozen fresh oysters on the half shell**, see page 121 for tips on shucking oysters

DIRECTIONS

1. Preheat oven broiler to 500°F.

2. In a small bowl, combine the panko breadcrumbs with the ghee, fresh herb blend and Parmesan cheese. Taste for seasoning and add rosemary sea salt as needed.

3. On a baking sheet, place a thick layer of rock salt, plain dry rice or dry beans to help nestle the oysters while cooking. Place the oysters on the sheet, taking care not to spill the liquor (i.e. the oyster's natural luscious juice). Top each oyster with the breadcrumb mixture.

4. Place the pan in the broiler and cook for 3–4 minutes. Use a pair of tongs and transfer oysters to plates or a platter. Serve immediately.

Sea Island Oyster Gravy

OVER SHRIMP & RICE

The Sea Islands are a chain of more than 100 sandy islands on the Atlantic Ocean sprinkled throughout South Carolina, Georgia and Florida. Originally inhabited by Native Americans, this subtropical region grew cotton, indigo, sugar, rice and later crab, shrimp and oysters prior to the Civil War.

Each of the Sea Islands has its own personality. Some are developed world-class resorts with luxurious amenities, like Hilton Head, while others are desolate with wildlife as the only inhabitants. Dwelling among the state's rich riverbanks, creeks and salt marshes, wild oysters were once harvested in South Carolina en masse and enjoyed by people of all persuasions, since they were cheap and plentiful. These days, like in other parts of the world, oysters are now mostly cultivated.

If you are new to seafood gravy, just know that it is a thing, and it is out of this world! The ingredients for this oyster gravy are simple and accessible, and the result is absolutely scrumptious.

I use this recipe in a variety of ways: poured over grilled toast and scrambled eggs for brunch; as a flavorful base for pescatarian poutine; and served over pan-fried shrimp and rice. Freshly shucked medium-sized oysters or high-quality jarred oysters work well for this recipe. I recommend using large white shrimp (see page 152) for their firm texture and beautiful presentation.

INGREDIENTS

{ Serves 6 }

OYSTER GRAVY:

- ¼ cup all-purpose flour

- ¼ cup vegetable oil

- 3 stalks celery, finely diced

- 1 small white onion, finely diced

- 2 large scallions, chopped, 2 tablespoons reserved for garnish

- 2 sprigs fresh thyme, leaves only

- 2 teaspoons garlic powder

- 1 cup water

- 1 cup half-and-half

- 10–12 large oysters, chopped

- Sea salt and freshly ground black pepper to taste

PAN-FRIED SHRIMP:

- 1½ cups cornmeal

- 1 cup all-purpose flour

- 24 large shrimp, peeled and deveined (leave tails on for presentation if desired)

- Sea salt and freshly ground black pepper to taste

- 2 teaspoons garlic powder

- 1 tablespoon cayenne pepper

- Vegetable oil, for frying

- Steamed Carolina Gold rice or steamed white rice

SERVING SUGGESTIONS: LEMON WEDGES, TABASCO SAUCE

DIRECTIONS

Make the gravy:

In a medium saucepan, whisk the flour and oil together over medium heat to make a light roux. Stir constantly to avoid burning. Cook until the mixture is the color of peanut butter. Add the celery, white onion and scallions, and cook for 6–8 minutes or until the vegetables have softened. Add the thyme and garlic powder and mix thoroughly.

Cook for 2 minutes, stirring to combine. Turn the heat to low and pour in the water followed by the half-and-half. Use a small whisk to remove any lumps. The roux should be smooth and slightly thick. Add a little more water if needed to thin it out. Add a pinch of salt and freshly ground black pepper.

Add the chopped oysters and gently fold them into the roux, taking care not to break them up too much. Cook for another 1½ minutes and taste for seasoning, adjusting as needed. Set aside while you make the shrimp.

Prepare the shrimp:

Place the cornmeal and flour in a medium-sized paper bag and set aside.

Season the shrimp with salt, black pepper, garlic powder and cayenne pepper. Place the shrimp in the bag containing the cornmeal and flour. While holding the top of the bag closed, give the bag a shake to coat the shrimp. Wait a few seconds and shake again. Remove the shrimp and set aside on a clean surface while the oil heats.

In a large skillet, add ½ inch of vegetable oil and heat over medium-high heat. Shake off any excess cornmeal and flour and add the shrimp to the skillet. Be careful not to overcrowd the pan. Cook the shrimp for 2 minutes on each side and drain on paper towels. Cook in batches as needed.

Serve:

To serve, divide cooked rice evenly among 6 individual plates along with equal portions of the pan-fried shrimp. Pour 2 tablespoons of the oyster gravy over the top of each plate (use more as desired). Garnish with lemon slices and scallions and serve with Tabasco sauce on the side if desired.

Using Natural Lump Charcoal

You'll find several recipes throughout this book that encourage you to get outside and use your grill just like they do in most warm coastal communities, where the weather is nice nearly all year long.

Natural lump charcoal is my preference for grilling. It imparts an unmistakably delicious flavor and consistent heat when cooking. This variety of fuel is an ideal way to infuse an authentic vibe into the fish since most of the world uses wood or natural lump charcoal to cook outside.

Lump charcoal is made by slowly burning pure wood until all of the natural elements like sap and moisture are burned out of the wood. It's known to burn hotter and ignite faster than briquettes and is created from wood varieties that impart a mild flavor, like oak and cherry. The pieces look like petrified wood. It is slightly more expensive than briquettes but well worth it, in my opinion!

Charcoal briquettes are made by slowly burning down sawdust and wood in the same way lump charcoal is made, but with additives added during the process. They burn longer than natural lump charcoal and have a mild chemical smell. When cooking foods for a long time, briquettes come in handy.

In parts of the Caribbean, pimento wood is used primarily to barbecue the infamous jerked foods, and in Hawaii, guava wood is used to add subtle sweet aroma to food. Classic barbecue from the American south often relies on apple, cherry, oak and other fruit and nut tree charcoal for authentic regional flavor.

Galveston Bay Barbecued Oysters

Lots of people forget that the state of Texas, with its sweltering heat and steak-loving cowboy culture, has a large coastline, miles of beaches, and a big love for seafood.

As with other states that run along the Gulf of Mexico, Texas waters are home to shrimp, stone crab and eastern oysters. Galveston Bay is situated on the upper coast of Texas and is the region's primary oyster growing location. It is the largest estuary in Texas and as such, produces oysters with various merroir. For example, the bivalves grown on the eastern side of the reef are saltier than those grown in the western part, which tend to be larger and sweeter.

Oysters grilled over natural lump charcoal take on a gorgeous, smoky flavor. They cook fast and hot on the grill, so you'll need to be on standby with a pair of tongs to get them on and off the grill quickly—2 minutes max!

Check out page 121 for tips on opening fresh oysters if you are new to the process, and page 122 to learn about the primary difference between western and eastern oysters.

INGREDIENTS

{ Makes 5 dozen oysters }

- **5 tablespoons ghee, at room temperature**

- **4 cloves garlic, minced**

- **4 tablespoons chopped fresh parsley**

- **5 dozen medium-sized western oysters, scrubbed clean and opened on the half shell**

SERVING SUGGESTIONS: LEMON WEDGES, TABASCO SAUCE, RUSTIC BREAD, SALTINE CRACKERS

DIRECTIONS

1. Prepare the grill on medium-high heat.

2. Mix the ghee, garlic and parsley together to make a compound ghee.

3. Place the oysters on a baking sheet or platter, taking care not to spill the liquor. Using a small spoon, add a dollop of the compound ghee to each one.

4. Using a long pair of tongs, place the oysters, open face up, on the grill. Cook for 1–2 minutes, or until the ghee is melted and the oysters begin to sizzle and cook. When done, remove the oysters from the grill using the tongs.

5. Transfer oysters to a serving platter and serve immediately with saltine crackers, Tabasco sauce and lemon wedges if desired.

Lowcountry Oyster Gravy

OVER FRIED GREEN TOMATOES

The Lowcountry is a geographic region of the United States that is historically and culturally significant. It encompasses coastal Georgia and South Carolina, including the Sea Islands. Lowcountry cuisine is heavily influenced by the Gullah people, who are members of the first group of enslaved Africans brought to the region to work the land.

Lowcountry people were locavores before it became cool! The cuisine relies on seasonal ingredients that are grown and harvested locally, and seafood like crab, shrimp and oysters play a big role.

Fried green tomatoes are an iconic summer dish from the southern region of the United States, of which the Lowcountry is a part. Green tomatoes are not a specific type of tomato (although some heirloom varieties like green zebras remain green all season long); they are essentially unripe tomatoes that are mildly tart, crunchy and full of flavor. This dish when combined with oyster gravy will give you a taste of Lowcountry flavors.

INGREDIENTS

OYSTER GRAVY:

- **¼ cup all-purpose flour**
- **¼ cup avocado oil**, separated
- **3 stalks celery**, finely diced
- **1 small white onion**, finely diced
- **2 scallions**, chopped
- **2 sprigs fresh thyme**, leaves only
- **2 teaspoons garlic powder**
- **1 cup whitefish fumet** (see page 490)
- **1 cup half-and-half**
- **Sea salt and freshly ground pepper to taste**
- **12–15 medium-sized oysters**, shucked

FRIED GREEN TOMATOES:

- **4 large firm green tomatoes,** thickly sliced (about ¼ inch)
- **2 large eggs**
- **2 cups all-purpose flour**
- **1 tablespoon cornmeal**
- **Sea salt and freshly ground black pepper,** as needed
- **1 cup vegetable oil,** more as needed
- **Fresh thyme leaves,** for garnish

DIRECTIONS

Make the gravy:

In a medium-sized heavy-bottom pan or Dutch oven, whisk the flour and oil together over medium heat to make a light roux. Stir constantly to avoid burning. Cook until the mixture is the color of peanut butter, about 8 minutes.

Add the celery, white onion and scallions and cook for 4–6 minutes or until the vegetables have softened. Add the thyme and garlic powder and mix thoroughly. Cook for 2 minutes, stirring to combine. Turn the heat to low and pour in the seafood stock followed by the half-and-half. Whisk constantly to remove any lumps. The roux should be smooth and slightly thick. Add a little more seafood stock or water if needed to thin it out. Add a pinch of salt and freshly ground black pepper.

Gently pour in the oysters and their liquid and gently fold them into the roux, taking care not to break them up too much. Cook for another 1½ minutes and taste for seasoning, adjusting as needed. Cover the pan with a lid and set aside.

Prepare the tomatoes:

Lightly salt the sliced tomatoes on both sides and set aside. Allow the tomatoes to sit for 5 minutes—this will help draw out excess moisture. When the time is up, blot the tomatoes with paper towels to remove the excess liquid.

Serve:

To serve, divide cooked rice evenly among 6 individual plates along with equal portions of the pan-fried shrimp. Pour 2 tablespoons of the oyster gravy over the top of each plate (use more as desired). Garnish with lemon slices and scallions and serve with Tabasco sauce on the side if desired.

Crack the eggs into a shallow bowl and whisk to combine; set aside. In another shallow bowl, combine the flour and cornmeal; set aside.

Next, dip each tomato slice in the egg, coating both sides, then place in the flour mixture to coat on both sides. Set aside on a clean surface and sprinkle with sea salt and pepper as desired. Repeat with the remaining tomatoes.

Pan-fry the tomatoes:

Meanwhile, add the vegetable oil to a large cast iron skillet and heat to medium-high, about 350°F. Use a thermometer to test or add a cube of bread to the pan; when it turns golden brown, the oil is ready. Working in batches, add a few of the tomatoes, making sure not to overcrowd the pan. Cook on one side until lightly golden brown, about 2 minutes, then use a pair of tongs to flip over to the other side and cook for another 2 minutes or so. Remove the tomatoes from the pan and drain on a bed of paper towels.

If necessary, reheat the gravy over a low simmer. To serve, divide the tomatoes among individual plates and pour equal portions of the oyster gravy over the top. Garnish with fresh thyme leaves and enjoy immediately.

Scallop Recipes

- Icelandic Sea Scallops with Basil Lemon Butter

- Oahu Bay Scallop Salad with Citrus, Kiwi & Macadamia Nuts

- Mediterranean Sea Scallops in Tomato-Saffron Sauce with Crispy Potatoes

- Barcelona Lemon Scallops with Judión Beans & Fresh Tomatoes

Diving into Scallops

~~~~~~~~

Scallops are the beauty queens of the shellfish world. With their fancy fan-shaped shells, this bivalve is related to clams, mussels and oysters.

Although the entire contents of the scallop are edible, like oysters, the version of the shellfish that we experience most often is the adductor muscle. This is the meaty, white portion of the scallop that holds the two shells together. Scallops have a particularly large adductor muscle, which can grow as heavy as 2 ounces in larger varieties.

Out of all the shellfish, scallops can be the most challenging to prepare, yet they're oh, so rewarding! One reason that scallops can be intimidating is that they can easily be overcooked, plus there are so many purchasing options. Terms like diver, wet, dry, bay and blushing can cause confusion and make any consumer feel bewildered. This section of the book is designed to help you gain a better understanding of scallops and how to cook them.

Years ago, when I first began experimenting with scallops, I tried to recreate the beautiful plates of shellfish pasta that I enjoyed while living in Santa Barbara, California. Without much knowledge or familiarity with the mollusk, I continually overcooked them until it finally clicked that less was more. I soon learned that a quick toss in a hot pan of ghee, olive oil or a simple pan sauce was all it took to cook scallops to perfection. They are at their best when seared perfectly outside with a luscious soft interior— served with just a squeeze of lemon.

The U.S. FDA requires that the moisture content in scallops be less than 80%—this is due to the fact that some scallops are treated with sodium tripolyphosphate (STP), which helps preserve shelf life and plump the scallops upward of 30%. This is the reason treated scallops turn watery and ooze when cooking. Scallops with more than 84% water cannot be sold. Fish fillets and shrimp are also often treated with STP.

Some varieties of wild scallops have blue eyes! This is a fun fact I learned from a Washington Post article. The scallop's front edge has a row of 50 (or more—up to 100!) tiny eyeballs, which help the shellfish sense light. What's more, most scallops are hermaphrodites, possessing both female and male sex organs.

THERE ARE A HANDFUL OF COMMON SCALLOP VARIETIES AVAILABLE ON THE MARKET.

DRY SCALLOPS   Untreated scallops.

DIVER SCALLOPS   A rare catch with a high price tag, these large, dry scallops are hand-harvested by professional fishers who are licensed SCUBA divers.

DAYBOAT SCALLOPS   These prized scallops are harvested by a small fleet of fishers and brought back within 12–24 hours of the fleet's departure.

BAY SCALLOPS   These petite scallops live in shallow waters like bays, estuaries and harbors. They are typically the size of a thumbnail and cook up very quickly.

BLUSHING OR PINK SCALLOPS   These demure-sounding scallops are female scallops that are harvested during spawning. According to Seafood Source, pink scallops are the rarest commercially available seafood worldwide.

QUEEN SCALLOPS   With a royal-sounding moniker, these medium-sized scallops are found in places like the Mediterranean Sea, Norway, the Canary Islands, Cape Verde Islands and the Azores.

SINGING   These are small pink and spiny scallops found in Northwestern waters. They don't make a sound as their name implies; rather, they open and close their shells quickly when disturbed. You will find these live at the market, like oysters and mussels, and they require very little preparation or cooking. Washington State is the mecca for singing scallops.

WET SCALLOPS   Treated with sodium tripolyphosphate (STP), wet scallops tend to be bright white, versus the natural ivory, off-white color of dry scallops, and are often sitting in a milky whitecolored liquid. Wet scallops are controversial because the STP adds water weight to the shellfish, costing consumers more for less.

Overall, when shopping for scallops, look for off-white or ivory-colored shellfish and avoid those sitting in liquid.

Icelandic Sea Scallops

WITH BASIL LEMON BUTTER SAUCE

Iceland is a Nordic island located in the North Atlantic. The capital city of Reykjavík has a dramatic landscape with massive glaciers, volcanoes and hot springs. The country is surrounded by pristine water and offers a gastronomy scene with plenty of fresh-caught seafood.

Recognized for their beautiful, fluted shells, Icelandic sea scallops range in color from opaque white to soft pink. They are slow-growing and typically live on the seafloor in sand, gravel, shell fragments and stones. Their flavor is sweet and their texture firm.

Plentiful in the waters around Newfoundland, Greenland, Norway and Iceland, Icelandic scallops can be swapped out for any dry sea scallop—see page 141 for info on types of scallops.

INGREDIENTS

{ Serves 2 }

- **10 large dry sea scallops**

- **½ teaspoon rosemary sea salt** (see page 552), more or less to taste

- **½ teaspoon white pepper**, more or less to taste

- **1/3 cup all-purpose flour**, as needed

- **2 tablespoons ghee**

- **1 shallot**, minced

- **1 medium lemon**, juice and zest

- **1 tablespoon basil lemon butter** (see page 536), at room temperature

- **1/3 cup olive oil**

- **1½ cups baby spinach**

- **¼ cup water**, as needed

- **½ teaspoon red pepper flake**

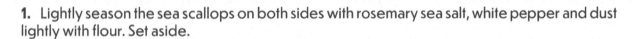

DIRECTIONS

1. Lightly season the sea scallops on both sides with rosemary sea salt, white pepper and dust lightly with flour. Set aside.

2. In a large nonstick or cast iron skillet, heat 1 tablespoon of the ghee over high heat. When the ghee is hot, add the scallops, making sure each one touches the bottom of the pan. Be careful not to overcrowd the pan or the scallops will steam instead of sear. Cook for 1½ minutes on one side, then turn and cook on the other side for 1 minute. Remove from the pan and set aside.

3. Add the remaining tablespoon of ghee, shallot, lemon juice, basil butter, olive oil, spinach and red pepper flake to a food processor and blend until smooth, add in the water as needed. Add the mix to the skillet and cook until slightly reduced and heated through, about 2 minutes.

4. To serve, place equal portions of the sauce to plates along with the sea scallops and serve immediately.

Oahu Bay Scallop Salad

WITH CITRUS, KIWI & MACADAMIA NUTS

Macadamia nuts are sometimes referred to as Queensland nuts, bush nuts or Hawaii nuts. Although famously grown in the Oahu region of Hawaii, they are not native to the island; in fact, they originated on the eastern shore of Australia and are also produced in South Africa.

Once removed from their shells and roasted, macadamia nuts make the perfect snack or addition to recipes with their crunchy texture and luxurious flavor. Salads are a nice way to combine ingredients for maximum flavor, with each element enhancing the other. This bright, fresh dish can be assembled in a flash if you prep the ingredients in advance. Bay scallops are ideal in salads since they are the perfect fork size—no chopping or dicing required.

I call for macadamia nut oil in this salad because the nuttiness of the oil complements the citrus juices used in the dressing. Specialty oils like almond, hazelnut, macadamia nut, pumpkin, pistachio and roasted walnut are considered finishing oils—you don't cook with these. If you can't find macadamia nut oil, any of these delicious oils will do the trick. After trying this recipe as written, make it your own by swapping out the bay scallops for different types of seafood and adding avocado, jicama and chickpeas.

INGREDIENTS

DRESSING

- **2 limes**, juice only

- **1 cup orange juice**

- **1 teaspoon honey**

- **¼ cup macadamia nut oil**

- **1 teaspoon toasted sesame seeds**

- **½ teaspoon sea salt**

SALAD

- **4 cups butter lettuce**, chopped

- **1 small jicama**, peeled and julienned

- **1 small red onion**, thinly sliced

- **2 scallions**, thinly sliced

- **3 green kiwis**, peeled and sliced

- **1 can mandarin oranges**, drained

BAY SCALLOPS

- **1 tablespoon butter**

- **2 pounds bay scallops**

- **Freshly ground black pepper to taste**

- **½ cup toasted macadamia nuts**

DIRECTIONS

Make the dressing:

In a medium-sized bowl, whisk together the lime juice, orange juice, honey, macadamia nut oil, toasted sesame seeds and sea salt. Taste for seasoning and adjust as needed. Set aside.

Prepare the salad:
In a large shallow bowl, artfully arrange the butter lettuce, jicama, red onion, scallions, kiwi and mandarin oranges. Cover with a lid or plastic wrap and set aside while you cook the bay scallops.

Cook the scallops:

In a large non-stick or cast iron skillet, heat 1 tablespoon of butter over high heat. When hot, add the scallops, making sure each one touches the bottom of the pan. Be careful not to overcrowd the pan or the scallops will steam instead of sear. Cook for 30 seconds, then shake the pan to ensure that even heat is applied to the scallops.

When scallops are ready, drizzle the salad with the citrus dressing and use tongs or salad forks to toss and combine. Add the scallops and the juice from the pan and garnish with toasted macadamia nuts. Serve immediately.

Mediterranean Sea Scallops in Tomato-Saffron Sauce

WITH CRISPY POTATOES

I'm attributing this recipe to the Mediterranean because the ingredients are used all over the region. The saffron-tomato cream sauce is fantastic with delicate sea scallops and also works well with shrimp, salmon, squid and clams.

Saffron is a sophisticated fragrant spice derived from the flower of the Crocus sativus flower. Its fiery bold color is what gives classic dishes like paella their unique color. The flavor is earthy and mild, yet distinct—you'll know it when you taste it! It is one of the most expensive ingredients due to its rate of production, but it's worth the splurge.

INGREDIENTS

- ¼ teaspoon saffron threads

- ½ cup hot water

- 16 large sea scallops

- Sea salt and freshly ground black pepper to taste

- 2 tablespoons ghee

- 1 tablespoon olive oil

- 1 medium shallot, minced
  ½ cup white wine

- 2 tablespoon tomato paste

- ½ teaspoon red pepper flake

- 2 tablespoons heavy cream or half-and-half

- Crispy St. Petersburg Potatoes (see page 396)
  ½ bunch fresh parsley, chopped, for garnish

DIRECTIONS

1. In a small bowl, stir the saffron and hot water together. Let the bowl rest for 20 minutes, allowing the saffron to bloom. Set aside.

2. Place the sea scallops on a clean surface and season with sea salt and freshly ground black pepper to taste. Set aside while the skillet heats.

3. In a large skillet, heat the ghee over high heat. Add the sea scallops, taking care not to overcrowd the pan—you may need to do this in two phases so that the shellfish sears and does not steam. Cook the scallops for 3 minutes on one side, then flip over and cook for 2 minutes. Remove the scallops and place them on a clean plate.

4. In the same skillet, add the olive oil and shallot and cook for 1 minute. Shake the pan occasionally to move the shallot around. Reduce heat to a simmer and add the wine and tomato paste, using a large spoon to mix the ingredients. Cook for 2 minutes and add the red pepper flake, a dash of sea salt, and freshly ground black pepper. Taste for seasoning and adjust as needed.

5. Stir in the heavy cream or half-and-half and add the cooked scallops to the pan. Simmer for about 1 minute, or long enough to reheat the shellfish.

6. Place the crispy potatoes on a platter and pour the scallop mixture over the top. Garnish with fresh parsley and serve immediately.

Barcelona Lemon Scallops

WITH JUDIÓN BEANS & FRESH TOMATOES

On a recent visit to Barcelona, Spain, I got overzealous while shopping at a fresh seafood market and bought more ingredients than I intended, namely large sea scallops. With only two days left in the city before heading out to our beachfront rental in Castelldefels, my husband and I had some work to do—cooking and eating!

Using the ingredients that I purchased at the market along with those provided by my generous loft owners, I created this dish. It's a nice and easy recipe to have in your back pocket when you are on the road because you only need a few fresh ingredients. You can have supper on the table in about 20 minutes. I used a jar of cooked Spanish Judión beans—a large, white butter bean cultivated in Northern Spain. These beans cook up plump, tender and silky.

Spanish sofrito is a combination of garlic, onion, bell pepper, olive oil and spices. Matiz is the brand I use in this recipe, but feel free to shop around! You can also change things up as desired and swap out the scallops for shrimp, squid, mussels or chunks of whitefish.

INGREDIENTS

- **3 tablespoons Spanish olive oil**, separated

- **1 dozen large dry sea scallops**

- **1 tablespoon butter**

- **½ cup Spanish sofrito sauce**

- **4 fresh tomatoes**, chopped

- **1 tablespoon Spanish paprika**

- **1 small lemon**, juice and 1 teaspoon zest

- **1 20-ounce jar cooked Judión beans** (such as El Navarrico brand), rinsed

- **Sea salt and freshly ground black pepper to taste**

- **1 bunch fresh spinach**

- **Rustic bread**, optional

DIRECTIONS

1. In a large skillet, heat 1 tablespoon of the Spanish olive oil over high heat. When the oil is hot, add the sea scallops and sear on one side for 2 minutes until brown, then turn over and cook for 1 minute. Remove from the pan, place on a clean plate, and set aside.

2. In the same pan, lower the heat to medium-high and add the butter, the remaining two tablespoons of Spanish olive oil, the sofrito and tomatoes. Cook for 3–4 minutes, stirring occasionally, then add the paprika, lemon juice and zest, and the Judión beans, and stir to combine. Taste for seasoning and add salt and pepper as needed. Cook for an additional 2 minutes to heat the beans through.

3. Next, add the cooked sea scallops and spinach to the pan and heat long enough for the spinach to wilt, about 1 minute. Remove the pan from the heat. Divide the Judión bean mixture among 4 individual plates and top with equal portions of the sea scallops and a slice of rustic bread if desired. Serve immediately.

Shrimp Recipes

- Isle of Capri Lemon Garlic Scampi Pasta

- Gullah Island Shrimp Perloo

- Trinidad & Tobago Curried Shrimp

- Lowcountry Shrimp, Tomatoes & Okra over Carolina Gold Rice

- Florida Gold Coast Rock Shrimp Tacos with Mango Salsa

- Baja Shrimp Tacos with Avocado Crema

The Skinny on Shrimp

Shrimp is one of the most popular types of seafood varieties on the planet next to cod and salmon, and the varieties you'll find available largely depend on your geographical location. For example, the shrimp that I find fresh in California (spot prawns) are very different from what are available in the gorgeous seafood markets of Mexico, Louisiana and Spain.

Thanks to modern freezing techniques, however, shrimp or prawns from various parts of the world are available year-round.

The difference between shrimp and prawns is slight and the terms are often used interchangeably. Americans tend to use "shrimp" to define all types of these lovely crustaceans, while the rest of the world uses "shrimp" and "prawns" interchangeably, with "prawn" often suggesting a large-sized shrimp. According to the U.S. National Oceanographic and Atmospheric Administration (NOAA), prawns have an extra pair of claws on their front legs, a slightly different body shape than shrimp, and are found in freshwater. Shrimp, on the other hand, live in both fresh and saltwater.

Remember to look for shrimp that are sustainably farmed and responsibly caught. Look for designations like the Marine Stewardship Council and the Monterey Bay Aquarium Seafood Watch program.

TYPES OF SHRIMP

In general, you'll find six types of shrimp on the market. This list will look different depending on where you live, but you're likely to find an assortment of the following:

1. **BROWN SHRIMP** – Found along the Atlantic coast from Florida to the Yucatan, brown shrimp have an earthy, robust flavor. They can reach up to 7 inches in length and tend to be firm in texture and smaller in size than other types of shrimp.

2. **PINK SHRIMP** – Sweet and mild in flavor, "pink shrimp" is a blanket term to describe a variety of species. They are found along the cool waters of the Atlantic and Pacific Northwest and are one of the most popular varieties. Often called "salad shrimp" due to their small size, pink shrimp are available both frozen and canned.

3. **WHITE SHRIMP** – The term "white shrimp" covers many species and describes the translucent gray-green shrimp that are on the sweeter side and among the largest shrimp you will find. White shrimp are found along the east coast of the United States and Mexico and are prized for their tender texture and mild flavor. They take on flavor well and are one of my top choices for gumbo, sautés and the grill.

4. **ROCK SHRIMP** – With their rigid, hard-as-a-rock outer shells, rock shrimp live up to their name! They are often compared to lobster due to the firm texture and sweet flavor of their meat and are sometimes referred to as a "little shrimp with a big lobster taste." Their tough shells require special equipment to break through and remove. They are deep water relatives to the pink and white shrimp found in the Southeastern U.S. Particularly popular in Florida, rock shrimp are found along the coasts of western Atlantic and the Gulf of Mexico.

5. **ROYAL RED SHRIMP** – Popular around the Gulf Coast of the U.S., royal red shrimp are large in size with briny flavor and rich buttery meat that is often compared to sea scallops. They live at extreme depths and are only fished commercially in a few locations.

6. **SPOT PRAWNS** – Sometimes called Santa Barbara spot prawns, these elegant-looking prawns look like a small lobster and have a buttery texture and sweet, juicy flavor. They are typically served head-on and some people prefer to eat the shell. They are also sometimes eaten raw.

7. **STIGER PRAWNS** – Named so for their striped likeness to their jungle-dwelling namesake, tiger prawns are one of the most popular types of farmed shrimp, ubiquitous in steak houses and upscale restaurants. Native to the Indo-West Pacific Ocean, tiger prawns can grow up to 13 inches in size, according to Seafood Source. Tiger prawns are known for their firm texture and buttery flavor.

SIZE MATTERS

In the U.S., shrimp is sold by size and the standard quantitative of count per pound. The "U" designation you'll often see associated with shrimp stands for "under," meaning less than the count per pound. For example, a U/10 designation means that the shrimp are large enough that fewer than 10 make up a pound. The lower the number, the bigger the shrimp!

Here are the typical unit numbers you'll find at the market:

SHRIMP SIZE	COUNT PER POUND U = UNIT	IDEAL USAGE
Extra Colossal	U/10	Shrimp & grits, scampi, skewers, kabobs
Super Colossal	U/12	Shrimp & grits, scampi, skewers, kabobs
Colossal	U/15	Shrimp & grits, scampi, skewers, kabobs
Extra Jumbo	16/20	Grilling, scampi, pan-frying, seafood boils
Jumbo	21/25	Grilling, ceviche, scampi, gumbo, pan-frying, tacos, seafood boils, spring rolls
Extra Large	26/30	Gumbo, ceviche, chowder, soup, gravy, stir-frying, quesadillas, spring rolls
Large	31/40	Chowder, soup, shrimp salad, tacos, quesadillas
Medium	41/50	Chowder, soup, shrimp salad, tacos, stuffing
Small	51/60	Shrimp salad, tacos, mixed shrimp cocktail, stuffing
Tiny	61/70	Shrimp salad, mixed shrimp cocktail

Isle of Capri Lemon Garlic Scampi Pasta

The Island of Capri, located in Italy's Bay of Naples, is known for its rugged beauty, gorgeous hotels and upscale shopping. The gastronomy of the island is heavily focused on vegetables, olive oil and fresh seafood. Scampi are popular shellfish throughout the country.

Scampi, also known as langoustine, are tiny lobsters found throughout the Mediterranean and other parts of the world, including Scotland, Ireland and Norway. They are often referred to as Dublin Bay Prawns or Norway Lobster, and though they possess an orange-pink shell similar in appearance to some shrimp, they differ in their lobster-like body shape and size of their front pincers.

INGREDIENTS

{ Serves 4 }

- **½ pound linguine or fettuccine noodles**

- **¼ cup garlic thyme butter**
  (see page 542)

- **3 tablespoons olive oil**, separated

- **1 large lemon**, juice and zest

- **2 teaspoons red pepper flake**

- **1 pound scampi or large white shrimp**,
  peeled and deveined

- **1 cup baby spinach**, stems removed

- **Sea salt and freshly ground black
  pepper to taste**

- **1/3 cup chopped fresh parsley**

- **Grated parmesan or other Italian
  cheese**, optional

DIRECTIONS

1. Cook pasta per package instructions. Drain, then place in a food storage bag with 1 tablespoon of olive oil and secure shut. Set aside.

2. In a large skillet, add the garlic thyme butter, 2 tablespoons of olive oil, the lemon juice and zest, and the red pepper flake. Add the scampi and cook for 3 minutes. Add the spinach and pasta to the pan and toss with tongs to combine. Add sea salt and black pepper to taste, then remove from the heat. Garnish with fresh parsley and cheese if desired, and serve family-style or on 4 individual plates.

Trinidad & Tobago Curried Shrimp

Trinidad and Tobago, affectionately known as T&T, is a dual island Caribbean nation located near Venezuela. The local gastronomy is influenced by myriad cultural flavors, from West Africa to South Asia, China and Portugal. The region is famous for its Soca music and its carnival that takes place in February or March known by music enthusiasts as "The Mother of All West Indian Carnivals." This recipe is a nice way to add a little West Indian-inspired island flavor to an everyday seafood meal and a great way to make use of the spices in your pantry.

This is an easy recipe that you can have on the table in about 20 minutes. If preferred, feel free to use your favorite bottled salt-free curry powder blend instead. You'll need about 3 tablespoons.

INGREDIENTS

- **3 tablespoons avocado oil**

- **1 small thumb fresh ginger,** grated

- **1 medium onion,** minced

- **2 cloves garlic,** minced

- **2 teaspoons ground allspice**

- **1 tablespoon ground cumin**

- **1 tablespoon ground coriander**

- **1 tablespoon ground turmeric**

- **2 teaspoons red pepper flake**

- **1 cup canned crushed tomatoes**

- **1 small habañero pepper**

- **3 sprigs fresh thyme**

- **1 cup vegetable broth**

- **1 14-ounce can coconut milk**

- **Smoked paprika sea salt**
  (see page 548)

- **Freshly ground black pepper to taste**

- **1½ pounds large or extra-large raw shrimp,** peeled and deveined, tails on for presentation

- **¼ cup chopped fresh cilantro leaves**

- **2 large scallions,** green part only, sliced

- **½ teaspoon soy sauce**

SERVING SUGGESTIONS: COCONUT RICE (SEE PAGE 418), PARATHA OR NAAN

DIRECTIONS

1. In a large Dutch oven or heavy-bottomed pot, heat the avocado oil over medium-high. Add the ginger, onion and garlic and cook until fragrant. Toss in the allspice, cumin, coriander, turmeric and red pepper flake or 3 tablespoons bottled curry powder if using. Cook for 3 minutes until fragrant.

2. Add the crushed tomatoes, habañero pepper, fresh thyme, vegetable broth and coconut milk. Reduce the heat to simmer and cook for 10 minutes. Taste for seasoning and add smoked paprika sea salt and freshly ground black pepper as needed.

3. Stir in the shrimp and fresh cilantro, cover, and cook for 4 minutes. Turn off the heat and allow the pot to rest for 2 minutes. Stir in the scallions and soy sauce. Serve with coconut rice, paratha or naan.

Lowcountry Shrimp, Tomatoes & Okra

OVER CAROLINA GOLD RICE

Book-ended by the Atlantic Ocean and the sea islands, the American South region known as the Lowcountry is named for the 80-mile stretch of low-elevation land stretching from Georgia's Savannah River to Pawleys Island of South Carolina.

The Lowcountry is a fascinating part of the world complete with saltwater marshes, 100-year-old live oaks draped in Spanish moss, stately former plantations and a gastronomy scene heavily influenced by the Gullah people. This community originated from enslaved Africans who were brought to this region for their deep knowledge of rice growing. They were responsible for the discovery of Carolina "Gold" rice, according to Yale University's Gilder Lehrman Center for the Study of Slavery, Resistance and Abolition.

Carolina Gold is a variety of rice that was widely cultivated in South Carolina, North Carolina and parts of Georgia in the 1700s; it was so popular that the region was once referred to as the Rice Coast. This variety of rice is historically important and is now a highly sought-after heirloom grain that can be found in markets, specialty stores and online. The rice is starchy, a bit sticky and has a sweet, nutty flavor and aroma with subtle floral and green tea notes.

INGREDIENTS

{ Serves 4 }

- **2 cups Carolina Gold rice,** soaked for 1 hour and drained

- **3 cups water**

- **Pinch salt**

- **1 tablespoon avocado oil**

- **1 tablespoon butter**

- **1 medium Spanish onion,** chopped

- **2 cloves garlic,** minced

- **2 teaspoons cayenne pepper**

- **1 small chili pepper,** minced

- **1 cup crushed tomatoes,** diced

- **4 fresh tomatoes,** diced

- **3 sprigs thyme, leaves only**

- **2 large scallions,** sliced

- **1½ pounds fresh okra,** chopped

- **2 pounds Gulf shrimp,** peeled and deveined

- **Sea salt and freshly ground black pepper to taste**

- **2 tablespoons water,** plus more as needed

- **¼ cup fresh parsley,** chopped

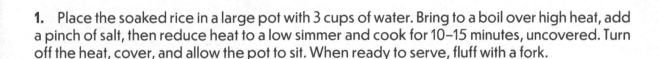

SERVING SUGGESTIONS: COCONUT RICE (SEE PAGE 416), PARATHA OR NAAN

DIRECTIONS

1. Place the soaked rice in a large pot with 3 cups of water. Bring to a boil over high heat, add a pinch of salt, then reduce heat to a low simmer and cook for 10–15 minutes, uncovered. Turn off the heat, cover, and allow the pot to sit. When ready to serve, fluff with a fork.

2. Meanwhile, in a large cast iron skillet, add the avocado oil, butter, onion, garlic, cayenne pepper and chili pepper. Cook until the onion is fragrant and soft, about 5 minutes.

3. Add the crushed tomatoes, fresh tomatoes, thyme and scallions and cook for 3 minutes. Add the okra and shrimp and continue to cook for 4 minutes. Taste and add sea salt and freshly ground pepper as needed. Add water if the dish is too stiff. Turn off the heat, cover, and allow the pot to sit for a few minutes. Serve over steamed Carolina Gold rice and garnish with fresh parsley

Heating Tortillas

You will find recipes throughout this book that feature approachable dishes from seaside regions of Mexico and Central America, including seafood tacos, enchiladas, wraps, quesadillas and more. With this in mind, I thought it wise to give you some tips on handling tortillas, specifically Mexican and Central American style tortillas, which are types of flatbread, not the Spanish dish made from potatoes.

My time spent in Mexico helped solidify my love for tortillas and Mexican flatbreads of all types. I also have the benefit of having grown up in California and having access to arguably some of the best Latin food on the planet. Tortillas are a central component of a meal similar to baguettes in France and cornbread in the American South.

I prefer to buy my tortillas from boutique markets called tortillerias, or tortilla bakeries. Central America and Mexico are hubs for these stores that produce masa for tamales, tortillas, tostada shells, crispy tortilla chips and sopes (a thick tortilla with pinched sides) on a daily basis. Some markets run full-scale restaurants, provide catering services, and sell their wares in other markets.

The most common types of tortillas are corn and flour:

— **Corn tortillas** are common throughout Mexico and Central America and are made from white, yellow and blue corn (maize). This type of tortilla has a slightly nutty corn flavor with a firm texture. I prefer corn tortillas for tacos, enchiladas, tostadas and tortilla chips.

— **Flour tortillas** are sometimes referred to as Sonoran or Northern Mexican style tortillas and are made from flour rather than corn, as the name implies. Flour tortillas are pliable, soft, chewy and dotted with golden brown blisters from the cooking process on the griddle. Quesadillas, burritos, and wraps are good uses for this style of tortilla.

Tortilla sizes vary from small street-sized versions that fit in the palm of your hand, about 5 inches, to taco size, roughly 8 inches, and burrito size, which range from 10 to 16 inches. Unless I have a party on the horizon, I typically buy my tortillas in packages of 12, half of which end up in my refrigerator for the next use, typically for wraps, burritos, tacos, quesadillas and tortilla chips. Refrigerating tortillas changes their texture, but it's nothing a little heat won't fix!

TORTILLA HEATING TIPS

One thing to note is that corn tortillas last in the refrigerator for about 4–6 weeks, while the flour variety lasts about 2–3 weeks. Warming tortillas brings them back to life so that they become soft and pliable. **Here are a few options for getting yours nice and toasty:**

• **Oven-Warming** – Wrap a stack of five or fewer tortillas in a packet of aluminum foil and place in a preheated 350°F oven for 10–15 minutes or until heated through. You can do multiple packets of five tortillas each all at the same time.

• **Microwave** – Put five or fewer tortillas on a microwavable plate and cover them with a damp paper towel. Microwave in 30-second bursts until they are warmed through. Repeat in batches of five tortillas until all tortillas are warm.

• **Stove Top** – Place tortillas in a dry (no oil) stainless-steel skillet over medium heat and cook for about 10–15 seconds, flipping intermittently. Keep warm under a tea towel.

• **Gas Range** – This is admittedly a more adventurous style of heating tortillas (read: be extra careful)! I've been doing it forever and it is my preferred method of warming both corn and flour tortillas. I like to char the tortillas directly over the flames of my gas range for a few seconds using tongs, flipping intermittently until warm and toasted.

Florida Gold Coast Rock Shrimp Tacos

WITH MANGO SALSA

The Gold Coast of Florida encompasses the cities of Miami, Fort Lauderdale and West Palm Beach. This region is sandwiched between the Atlantic Ocean and the Everglades and is one of the state's most popular areas with its gorgeous beaches and tons of tourist attractions.

This is a vacation-worthy, Florida-inspired meal crafted with succulent rock shrimp, which are native to the region and have a lobster-like flavor and appearance. Their rock-hard shells explain their name—these tough shells are removed with specialized equipment. Outside of local Gold Coast markets where rock shrimp thrive, you will likely find them shelled, deveined and frozen. They are small and a pound yields about 20–25 shrimp.

Cilantro and lime is a classic flavor combination that is a sure-fire crowd-pleaser. The marinade also serves as a sauce, enveloping the shrimp in flavor.

INGREDIENTS

- **1 pound rock shrimp**, peeled and deveined (defrosted if frozen, see page 152)

- **1 cup chopped fresh cilantro**

- **2 teaspoons ground cumin**

- **2 cloves garlic**, peeled

- **1 small jalapeño pepper**, halved

- **1 teaspoon white pepper**

- **4 key limes**, juice of all 4 and zest of 1

- **¼ cup avocado oil**

- **10 corn tortillas** (see page 160 for tips on warming tortillas)

- **1 tablespoon water**, as needed

- **Sea salt to taste**

- **Mango salsa** (see page 566)

SUGGESTED TOPPINGS:

SHREDDED CABBAGE, SALSA, GUACAMOLE, SOUR CREAM, PICKLED JALAPEÑOS AND SHAVED RED ONION

DIRECTIONS

{ Makes 10 tacos }

1.   Place the shrimp in a large bowl or resealable food storage bag and set aside.

2.   **Make the cilantro-lime marinade:**

Add the cilantro, cumin, garlic, jalapeño pepper, white pepper and lime juice and zest to a blender or food processor. Turn the machine to medium and slowly drizzle in the avocado oil. The marinade will begin to come together. Add a tablespoon of water if the mixture gets too thick.

3.   Pour the marinade over the shrimp and stir with a large spoon to combine. You can also use your hands but be sure to use gloves since the jalapeño can sting. Cover the shrimp and place in the refrigerator for 15 minutes to marinate.

4.   Meanwhile, heat your tortillas and keep them warm (see page 160) while you prepare the shrimp.

5.   **Prepare the shrimp:**

Heat a large skillet over medium-high heat. With a slotted spoon, remove the shrimp from the bowl or bag. Shake off any excess marinade and add the shrimp to the skillet. Cook for 4 minutes. Cover the skillet with a lid and set aside.

6.   **Assemble the tacos:**

Divide equal portions of the cooked shrimp among the corn tortillas and add your favorite toppings. Top with mango salsa and serve immediately.

Baja Shrimp Tacos

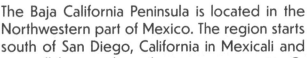

WITH AVOCADO CREMA

The Baja California Peninsula is located in the Northwestern part of Mexico. The region starts south of San Diego, California in Mexicali and goes all the way down the gorgeous coast to Cabo San Lucas. Baja, as it is commonly known, is surrounded on the west by the Pacific Ocean and on the east by the Gulf of Mexico. The area is an incredibly popular tourist location with world-class gastronomy including fresh seafood and a remarkable seafood taco scene!

Traditional Baja-style tacos are battered, fried and served with classic Mexican toppings like avocado crema, fresh salsa, simple cabbage slaw and a squeeze of lime. The batter often includes beer instead of water, which adds a nice depth of flavor. If you can find them, I encourage you to use large wild Mexican shrimp for their authentic flavor. I do not recommend using Argentine red shrimp for these tacos since their texture is too delicate. See page 152 for a shrimp use chart.

Avocados are a standard Mexican fruit and one of my all-time favorite ingredients. As one of the world's largest producers of the crop, Mexico prepares this fruit in all kinds of ways. Combined with Mexican crema, a tangy, creamy white sauce similar to sour cream, avocados make for a decadent sauce—see page 546 for my recipe!

INGREDIENTS

{ Makes 8-10 tacos }

- **1 cup all-purpose flour**

- **1 teaspoon baking powder**

- **1 cup beer** (or sparkling water if desired)

- **1½ pounds medium-sized shrimp,** peeled, deveined and tails removed

- **8–10 corn or flour tortillas** (see page 160 for tips on warming tortillas)

- **2 cups vegetable oil,** for frying

- **Sea salt and freshly ground black pepper to taste**

- **Avocado crema** (see page 546)

SUGGESTED TOPPINGS: FRESH LIME, SALSA, AVOCADO, SHREDDED CABBAGE, COTIJA CHEESE

DIRECTIONS

Prepare the batter:
In a medium-sized bowl, combine the flour, baking powder and beer or sparkling water. Whisk thoroughly and allow the batter to rest for 10–15 minutes.

Meanwhile, in a large skillet, heat 1 cup of vegetable oil to 375°F. Set up a draining rack or a bed of paper towels to drain the shrimp.

Prepare the shrimp:
Using a fork or kitchen tweezers, dredge each shrimp in the batter and place it in the hot oil. Cook until golden brown on both sides. Repeat for all of the shrimp in batches. When the shrimp are cooked, drain them on the rack or paper towels.

Assemble the tacos:
Place equal portions of shrimp in each tortilla shell and add toppings of choice: fresh lime, salsa, avocado slices, shredded cabbage and cotija cheese. Top with avocado crema and serve immediately.

Squid Recipes

- Central Coast Fried Calamari

- Santorini Calamari Greek Wrap

- Central Golden State Calamari Steak Salad

- Santa Barbara Squid with Spinach and Fettuccine

- Bangkok Fried Squid with Steamed Rice

Becoming Squid Savvy

Squid, often called by its Italian name, calamari, is a versatile shellfish that typically gets typecast as golden fried morsels served with a side of lemon or cocktail sauce. Although fried calamari is a delightful dish (see recipe on page 170), there is so much more to this abundant cephalopod.

California market squid and jumbo squid harvested in Mexico's Gulf of California are my favorite types and what I am most familiar with, being based on the West Coast. These are among the most sustainable varieties. When in doubt, check out the Monterey Bay Aquarium's Seafood Watch website or the smartphone app to get the latest information on sustainable sources of seafood.

The flavor and texture of squid can be described in myriad ways—chewy, dense, firm and sweet are what I typically experience. This is what makes it so special and a popular delicacy around the globe.

The important thing to know when cooking squid is that you either need to cook it fast and hot, about 3–4 minutes, or low and slow, 30–45 minutes. Anything in between will result in the squid turning out very tough and rubbery.

Unless you are buying it fresh off the fishing boat or catching it yourself, most of the squid on the market will be frozen or previously frozen. If you are buying it frozen, it will likely come in a 3- or 5-pound block. You can defrost the squid overnight in the refrigerator or under cool running water.

Frozen whole squid is relatively inexpensive. This is mostly due to the fact that it's a do-it-yourself type of seafood, meaning it requires cleaning. You can purchase cleaned raw squid in various forms—tubes and tentacles, rings, pineapple cut or in steak form—but it will practically double the price.

There are a few different ways to clean squid depending on how the squid will be cooked (fried, stewed, steamed or stuffed).

Squid steaks, which you'll find recipes for throughout this book, are typically ½-inch thick cuts of squid harvested from the center or mantles of large Peruvian Humboldt or Grande Calamari varieties. The steaks are typically tenderized prior to shipping using a needle machine, which gives them a characteristic punctured look.

CLEANING SQUID

- The process of cleaning squid is simple, though some would say time-consuming. The edible portion of squid after cleaning is roughly two-thirds of the total weight.

- Look for translucent gray squid mottled with black spots. In older squid, the black spots will begin to break down and turn pink. The pinker the squid, the flatter the flavor. As with most seafood, if the squid smells fishy, pass it up.

- The first step is to cut off the tentacles, which are edible. Slice right below the eyes, as close to the eyes as possible—this helps keep the tentacles neatly together. Rinse and reserve for use. Next, squeeze out the beak—a tiny hard piece of cartilage located at the base of the tentacles where they connect to the head. Discard the beak and clean the inside.

- Gently hold the body of the squid and pull out the intestines and inner cartilage, which resembles a pen quill. Throw these away unless you plan to harvest the squid ink, which is edible, but something I leave to my fishmonger to manage. You'll be left with the hollow squid body, or tube, which you should rinse and leave whole for stuffing or for cutting into strips or rings. The skin is also edible, and removing it is optional. Removing it will result in the squid cooking up white in color.

Central Coast Fried Calamari

The Central Coast of California comprises an area that includes the cities between Ventura and Monterey Bay. In this beautiful part of the world, you will find a moderate climate, rocky shorelines, ideal surfing conditions and incredible ingredients ranging from strawberries to artichokes and seafood.

My mom is the ultimate connoisseur of calamari. During warm summer days, she and my dad head down Pismo Beach for a lunch of fried squid and a couple of libations! Tubes and tentacles can be found in most restaurants, and my version uses calamari steaks, which offer a denser, meatier texture.

INGREDIENTS

 Serves 5-6

- **3 pounds calamari steaks**, cut into
- **¼-inch strips**
- **3 cups all-purpose flour**, more as needed
- **Sea salt and freshly ground black pepper to taste**
- **1 cup vegetable oil**, for frying
- **2 tablespoons fresh parsley**, chopped

SERVING SUGGESTIONS: LEMON WEDGES, MARINARA SAUCE

DIRECTIONS

1. Rinse the calamari, leaving a little moisture on the fish—this will help form a crust. In a large brown paper bag, add the flour, salt and pepper. Toss in the calamari steaks and shake the bag, holding the top closed and the bottom for security.

2. Remove the steaks from the bag, place on a clean surface, and allow them to rest for 5–6 minutes—this will help the flour form a crust.

3. Meanwhile, heat your frying oil to 375°F. Shallow-fry the calamari steaks until light golden brown. Drain on paper towels, garnish with fresh parsley, and serve with lemon wedges or marinara sauce.

Santorini Calamari Greek Wrap

As part of Greece's Cyclades islands, Santorini is located in the Aegean Sea. It is one of the most recognizable Greek Islands, with its white and red sands and active volcanoes. Given that the area is surrounded by water, it's not surprising that seafood plays a key role in the region's gastronomy.

Octopus and squid are two seafood varieties that are highly revered in Greece and in my coastal Southern California community, where we have dozens of Greek restaurants. This is a simple, satisfying dish that I revisit time and again.

INGREDIENTS

{ Serves 5-6 }

- **4 Greek pitas or soft pita breads**

- **4 tablespoons tahini**

- **4 servings fried calamari** (see page 170)

- **1 cup thinly sliced Romaine lettuce**

SERVING OPTIONS: FETA CHEESE, SLICED KALAMATA OLIVES, SLICED TOMATOES, CHOPPED CUCUMBER, GREEK YOGURT

DIRECTIONS

1.   Heat a large skillet or grill pan over medium-high heat. When the skillet is hot, warm each pita until lightly toasted.

2.   To make the sandwich, spread one tablespoon of tahini on each pita, then add equal portions of the calamari and top with the Romaine lettuce and Mediterranean salad. Add feta cheese, Kalamata olives and Greek yogurt if desired.

Golden State Calamari Steak Salad

California is also known as the Golden State for its long association with the 1848 Gold Rush period. With nearly 900 miles of coastline, my home state shares a border with Canada to the north and Mexico to the south, and boasts a gastronomy scene that is heavily influenced by fresh produce, wine, cheese and seafood.

Combining fresh salad greens and juicy Central California peaches with crispy calamari makes for a flavorful 'Best Coast' salad that is delicious served warm or at room temperature.

INGREDIENTS

- **¼ cup fresh orange juice**

- **¼ cup olive oil**

- **1 tablespoon balsamic vinegar**

- **1 small Fresno chili**, minced

- **1 tablespoon honey**

- **4 cups mixed salad greens** (Romaine, kale, iceberg, butter and red leaf lettuce)

- **3 large ripe peaches**, sliced

- **1 purple scallion**, green and purple parts, sliced

- **1 large tomato**, diced

- **3 tablespoon sliced almonds**, toasted

- **3 pounds fried calamari steaks** (see page 170)

DIRECTIONS

1.   To make the salad dressing, combine the orange juice, olive oil, balsamic vinegar, Fresno chili and honey in a medium bowl. Whisk to combine and set aside.

2.   To make the salad, artfully arrange the mixed greens, sliced peaches, purple scallion, tomato and toasted almonds in a large bowl. Pour the dressing over the top and toss to combine. Divide the salad among 4 bowls and top with the fried calamari. Serve immediately.

Santa Barbara Squid

WITH SPINACH AND FETTUCCINE

Located on California's Central Coast, nestled between the Santa Ynez mountains and the Pacific Ocean, Santa Barbara is a popular destination known as the "American Riviera."

I had the pleasure of attending the University of California, Santa Barbara (UCSB) for my undergrad education. It was on the campus of UCSB that I met my husband and closest friends while gaining an appreciation for elegant, beautifully plated seafood dishes thanks to the gorgeous restaurants that dotted State Street. This squid and fettuccine recipe is one of my favorites and cooks up quickly, making it a good weeknight meal.

Be sure to cook the squid hot and fast to achieve the best texture.

INGREDIENTS

{ Serves 4 }

- **1 pound fettuccine noodles**
- **2 tablespoons olive oil,** separated
- **2 tablespoons unsalted butter**
- **1 medium shallot,** minced
- **2 cloves garlic,** minced
- **2 teaspoons red pepper flake**
- **3 pounds squid tubes and tentacles, cleaned, tubes cut into ½-inch rings**

- **2 Roma tomatoes,** diced
- **1 large lemon,** juice and zest
- **1 cup fresh baby spinach or kale**
- **Sea salt and freshly ground black pepper to taste**
- **2 tablespoons chopped fresh parsley,** for garnish
- **Grated Romano cheese,** optional

DIRECTIONS

1. Cook the fettuccine al dente according to package directions. Drain and place the pasta in a large bowl or plastic bag and toss with 1 tablespoon of olive oil to keep the noodles from sticking. Cover and refrigerate until ready to use.

2. In a medium-sized skillet, heat the butter and the remaining tablespoon of olive oil over medium-high heat. Add the shallot, garlic and red pepper flake and sauté until fragrant.

3. Turn the heat to high and toss in the squid, tomatoes, lemon juice and zest and sauté for 4 minutes until the squid turns pink. Add sea salt and freshly ground black pepper to taste.

4. Add the cooked pasta to the skillet. Toss to coat in the sauce, add the spinach or kale, and simmer for 2 minutes. To serve, place the squid and pasta in a large bowl and serve family-style, or divide equally among 4 bowls. Garnish with fresh parsley and grated Romano cheese if desired. Serve immediately.

Bangkok Fried Squid

~~~~~

WITH STEAMED RICE

Bangkok is the capital city of Thailand known for its vibrant nightlife, ornate shrines and incredible food scene. Gastronomy tours are a popular activity for visitors, and the region's fresh vegetables, everpresent rice, and fresh seafood are highlighted with restaurant tasting visits and cooking lesson.

Squid is a local favorite and an affordable seafood that is enjoyed throughout Asia. This dish is inspired by Thai street food and cooks up quick and flavorful—the ultimate fast food!

The scallions are an important component of this dish, offering a bright and earthy, yet mellow onion flavor that makes them mild enough to be eaten raw. Combined with the shrimp paste, these flavors make for a truly authentic Thai dish.

Shrimp paste is called for in this dish, which can be found in most Asian markets or purchased online. This fermented shellfish paste is a centuries-old ingredient that provides a salty, pungent flavor. It can be purchased dry and firm or as a sauce.

This is a simple dish that cooks up fast over high heat. If you don't have a wok, a large skillet will work, just be mindful of overflow.

INGREDIENTS

{ Serves 4 }

- **3 tablespoons vegetable oil**, for frying

- **3 cloves garlic**, minced

- **1 teaspoon shrimp paste**

- **2 pounds squid tubes and tentacles**, cleaned

- **1 tablespoon oyster sauce**

- **1 teaspoon red pepper flake**

- **4 scallions, green part only**, bias sliced

- **Kombu rice** (see page 414)

DIRECTIONS

1.   Heat a wok over medium-high heat. When hot, add the oil and fry the garlic and shrimp paste until the garlic is fragrant.

2.   Add the squid, oyster sauce and red pepper flake and cook for 3–4 minutes. Toss in the scallions and cook for another minute. Remove from heat and serve immediately with kombu rice.

Black and Green-Lipped Mussel Recipes

- Southeast Asian Coconut-Lime Black Mussels

- New Zealand Green-Lipped Mussels with Garlic & Herbs

- Prince Edward Island (PEI) Mussels in Gingered Carrot Broth

- Knokke-Heist Beach Moules Frites

- North Beach Garlic Mussels with Marinara and Mozzarella

- Amalfi Coast Lemon and Garlic Grilled Mussels

Muscling up on Mussels

Growing up with a family of piscators, I grew up eating all kinds of seafood. The one thing that did not show up on the dinner table, however, was mussels. Although abundant, these bivalves never made it to my mom's shopping list. Things have changed these days, and blue mussels appear on my menu about once a month. They are delicious, affordable and versatile.

Out of all the shellfish around, mussels are often overlooked in some parts of the world. I think it's because they are misunderstood. They are bold-looking—often mottled with white spots and sometimes decorated with scratchy beards. For centuries, mussels have been an ethnic food enjoyed in places like Belgium, France, Portugal, Spain and Italy. Think of Belgium's classic Moules-Frites or mussels with fries (see recipe on page 188).

Mussels are bivalve mollusks belonging to the marine family Mytilidae. There are other families that live in freshwater but only mussels harvested from seawater are edible. The most common variety of edible mussels are blue mussels, also called black mussels. They are recognized by their smooth outer shell and pearlescent inner shell. The other commercially available variety is green-lipped mussels, which are strikingly hued and exotic-looking.

According to the Encyclopedia of Fish Cookery, wild mussels begin their lives as tiny free-swimming spats that eventually find a home in large colonies on rocks, gravel and seawalls. They will adhere to any willing surface by secreting byssus, silken anchor threads composed of protein that hardens on contact with seawater. Legend has it that these threads were collected and used to make gloves in ancient Greece. They were kept in buckets of seawater to keep them durable and lasted long enough to be passed down through generations.

Modern-day mussels are cultivated on large sea farms. Black mussels thrive in cool water and are produced in many parts of the world. Their tender meat is a bit tangy with a hint of smokiness. Green-lipped mussels are large, sweet and succulent and are at their best when prepared simply. Green lips are exclusively produced in New Zealand and exported so you will likely find these frozen on the half shell or unshelled. Don't be alarmed if you find the meat of the mussels in two colors—the orange is female and creamy white is male. Both blue and green mussels are harvested in similar ways, either via longline suspension systems or from the seafloor. These days, the longline suspension method is the most common.

You can harvest your own wild mussels in some unique places. They can be collected using a rake or from a boat using a dredge. You'll need a permit in some locations and there are some daily limits; in Maine for example, there is a two-bushel limit.

Because they are filter feeders, mussels, like clams and oysters, are vulnerable to bacterial pollution. This is the reason the water from which your shellfish is harvested makes all the difference. Commercially harvested shellfish is safe; it's when you harvest your own that you must be cautious.

Southeast Asian Coconut–Lime Black Mussels

The vast area known as Southeast Asia, a tropical region nestled between the Indian and Pacific oceans, is made up of 11 countries with diverse religions, languages and history all influenced by Chinese, Indian and Western cultures. Due to its year-round warm weather and unforgettable beauty, it is one of the world's most popular tourist destinations with coastal destinations such as Ha Long Bay, Vietnam; Bali, Indonesia; and Phuket, Thailand ranking among the top.

Although the gastronomy of each state is unique, most cultures share a cuisine that is infused with limes, coconut milk, chili, garlic and ginger. Catfish, tilapia, milkfish, crab, squid, shrimp and mussels are local favorites and are delicious when bathed in these flavorful ingredients.

This simple tropical black mussel dish cooks up quickly and works equally well with clams.

INGREDIENTS

- **1 cup canned coconut milk**
- **1 cup white fish fumet** (see page 490)
- **2 tablespoons water**
- **½ cup chopped fresh cilantro**
- **1 large kaffir lime,** juice and zest
- **1 teaspoon lemongrass powder or 1 stalk fresh lemongrass,** sliced
- **1 teaspoon garlic powder**

- **2 cloves garlic,** minced
- **1 teaspoon freshly ground black pepper**
- **½ teaspoon salt**
- **1 Thai chili**
- **2 tablespoons vegetable oil**
- **5 pounds live mussels**

SERVING OPTIONS: RICE NOODLES (VERMICELLI), JASMINE RICE, KOMBU RICE (SEE PAGE 414)

DIRECTIONS

1. To make the coconut lime sauce, combine the coconut milk, white fish fumet, water, cilantro, kaffir lime juice and zest, lemongrass powder or stalk, garlic powder, garlic cloves, black pepper, salt and Thai chili in a food processor or blender. Blend until smooth and refrigerate for 2 hours.

2. To make the mussels, heat a large stockpot on high heat and add the vegetable oil. Add the prepared coconut lime sauce and cook for 3–4 minutes. Once the sauce becomes fragrant, add the mussels and stir to coat them in the sauce. Cover with a tight lid and simmer for 6–8 minutes or until the mussels begin to open. Turn off the heat to give the mussels time to absorb the sauce.

3. To serve, place the mussels and the coconut lime sauce in a large bowl and serve family-style, or divide among 4–6 bowls. Serve with rice noodles, jasmine rice or kombu rice if desired.

New Zealand Green-Lipped Mussels

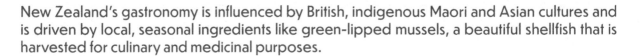

Made up of two main landmasses, North Island and South Island, the country of New Zealand is situated in the South Pacific and boasts more than 9,000 miles of coastline. With its dramatic topography—a mix of jagged mountains, volcanic zones and scenic beaches—the country is a dream location for surfers, divers, hikers and wine connoisseurs alike.

New Zealand's gastronomy is influenced by British, indigenous Maori and Asian cultures and is driven by local, seasonal ingredients like green-lipped mussels, a beautiful shellfish that is harvested for culinary and medicinal purposes.

Green lips are large and succulent mussels that are at their best when prepared simply. Outside of New Zealand, you will likely find these frozen on the half shell or unshelled. Don't be alarmed if you find the meat of the mussels in two colors—the orange is female and the creamy white is male.

Beyond being delicious, the high level of omega-3 fatty acids in New Zealand green-lipped mussels is cause for celebration for arthritis sufferers. The extract has been discovered to have anti-inflammatory properties, which help relieve the pain and discomfort associated with osteoarthritis and rheumatoid arthritis.

INGREDIENTS

- **4 tablespoons garlic thyme butter** (see page 542)

- **2 cloves garlic**, minced

- **3 shallots**, minced

- **1 cup dry white wine**, such as chardonnay, dry riesling or pinot grigio

- **2 tablespoons chopped fresh parsley**

- **2 teaspoons red pepper flake**

- **1 large lemon**

- **¼ cup heavy cream or half-and-half**

- **Rustic bread**, optional

DIRECTIONS

1. To make the coconut lime sauce, combine the coconut milk, white fish fumet, water, cilantro, kaffir lime juice and zest, lemongrass powder or stalk, garlic powder, garlic cloves, black pepper, salt and Thai chili in a food processor or blender. Blend until smooth and refrigerate for 2 hours.

2. To make the mussels, heat a large stockpot on high heat and add the vegetable oil. Add the prepared coconut lime sauce and cook for 3–4 minutes. Once the sauce becomes fragrant, add the mussels and stir to coat them in the sauce. Cover with a tight lid and simmer for 6–8 minutes or until the mussels begin to open. Turn off the heat to give the mussels time to absorb the sauce.

3. To serve, place the mussels and the coconut lime sauce in a large bowl and serve family-style, or divide among 4–6 bowls. Serve with rice noodles, jasmine rice or kombu rice if desired.

Prince Edward Island (PEI) Mussels

IN GINGERED CARROT BROTH

Prince Edward Island is one of Canada's smallest Provinces, yet its seafood offerings span North America. The mussels cultivated in the cold, pristine waters surrounding PEI are briny, meaty and nutritious and are known for their world-class quality. Mussels cultured in this part of the world are grown in mesh stockings that are suspended from long lines.

The mild taste of mussels combined with warm and spicy gingered carrot broth makes for an easy exotic meal. As with most shellfish recipes, this one cooks up quickly. I like this as an entrée or a starter.

INGREDIENTS

{ Makes 2 generous servings }

- **2 tablespoons ghee** (clarified butter)

- **3 pounds live mussels**, sorted and debearded

- **2 cloves garlic**, minced

- **1 cup fresh carrot juice**

- **½ cup water**

- **2 tablespoons minced fresh ginger**

- **¼ cup chopped fresh cilantro**

- **1 lime**, juice and zest

SERVING OPTIONS: GRILLED GARLIC BREAD, BAGUETTE ROUNDS

DIRECTIONS

1.   In a large pot, melt the ghee over medium heat and sauté the garlic for 1 minute—stir regularly to ensure it doesn't burn. Add the carrot juice, water and ginger, and bring to a boil until the liquid reduces by half.

2.   Next add the cilantro, lime juice and zest, and the mussels. Cover the pot with a lid and turn heat to high to steam until the mussels open. Shake the pot occasionally to encourage the mussels to open—this should take about 8–10 minutes.

3.   Remove the pot from the heat and let sit for 3–5 minutes, allowing the flavors to blend.

4.   To serve, divide equal portions of the mussels and broth among 2 bowls, or place the mussels and broth in a large serving bowl to serve family-style. Discard any unopened mussels and serve warm with grilled bread or baguette rounds if desired.

Knokke-Heist Beach Moules Frites

~~~~~

MUSSELS WITH FRIES

A 90-minute drive from the capital of Brussels, the sophisticated beach city of Knokke-Heist, Belgium, has five lovely beaches with a gorgeous nature preserve. Once visitors tire of the ocean waves, the local art galleries, golf courses or the casino, they head to the local restaurants and bars for a cold beverage and a bite to eat. Those in the know seek out moules-frites or mussels with fries.

A simple combination of European-style fried potatoes paired with steamed mussels in a sauce of white wine, butter and aromatics, Moules Frites is the national dish of Belgium. Popular along the coast and in Brussels, this dish can be found in high-end restaurants and street carts alike throughout the country. Legend has it that mussels gained favor centuries ago with Belgians as a substitute for fish, especially during winter months.

INGREDIENTS

- **1 pound russet potatoes,** skin on

- **4 cups vegetable oil for frying,** more as needed

- **5 tablespoons unsalted butter**

- **2 shallots,** minced

- **4 cloves garlic,** minced

- **3 cups dry white wine**

- **1 bunch fresh flat-leaf parsley,** chopped (¼ cup), with 1 tablespoon reserved for garnish

- **5 pounds blue mussels,** cleaned

- **Finishing salt such as fleur de sel,** optional

DIRECTIONS

Partially cook the frites:

Slice the potatoes into chunky sticks—use a mandoline for simplicity and to make uniform cuts. Place the cut potatoes in an ice bath to keep them from oxidizing (browning).

In a large Dutch oven, heat 4 cups of vegetable oil to 320°F or 330°F.

Remove the cut potatoes from the ice water and dry them on paper towels or tea towels until completely dry. Set aside.

When the oil reaches the correct temperature, add the potatoes and cook for 3 minutes, then remove with a slotted spoon or spider strainer and place on paper towels or a draining rack. Continue in batches until all of the potatoes are partially cooked. Set aside to cool.

Make the mussels:

In a large heavy-bottomed pot, add the butter, shallots and garlic and sauté until fragrant, about 2 minutes. Pour in the wine and parsley and bring to a boil. Add the mussels and stir to combine. Cover and steam for about 5 minutes, lifting the lid halfway through to stir. Remove from the heat and set aside.

Finish the frites:
Turn the heat up on the Dutch oven to 375°F, then add the partially cooked potatoes and fry until crispy and golden brown. Drain on paper towels. Garnish with finishing salt if desired. To serve, gently ladle mussels and broth into serving bowls, garnish with parsley, and serve with a side of frites.

North Beach Garlic Mussels

WITH MARINARA AND MOZZARELLA

North Beach is a San Francisco neighborhood steeped in Italian history and is considered to be the city's Little Italy. The district is filled with cafes, delicatessens and restaurants that serve traditional favorites and some creative dishes like these mussels with marinara and mozzarella.

This recipe is a good introduction to mussels for anyone new to shellfish. Marinara sauce and mozzarella are nice easy flavors to ease into, especially for pizza lovers.

I call for New Zealand green-lipped mussels in this dish because they are large and impressive, but large-sized black mussels will work just as well. In a pinch, use what you have access to and double the recipe to make up for size.

INGREDIENTS

Makes 2
dozen mussels

- **1 cup rock salt or kosher salt,** plus more as needed

- **24 large green-lipped mussels on the half shell**

- **2 tablespoons olive oil**

- **2 teaspoons garlic powder**

- **1 teaspoon dried mixed herbs**

- **1 cup prepared marinara sauce**

- **1 cup shredded mozzarella cheese**

- **Pecorino Romano cheese**, grated, for garnish

- **Rosemary sea salt** (see page 552) or fleur de sel, for finishing

DIRECTIONS

1. Preheat oven to 475°F.

2. Lay a piece of parchment paper on a baking sheet and cover with a thin layer of rock salt or kosher salt. Place mussels on the baking sheet, nesting each one in the salt to help secure them during the cooking process. Set aside.

3. In a small bowl, combine the olive oil, garlic powder and herbs. Spoon equal portions of the garlic mixture onto each mussel, followed by the marinara sauce. Sprinkle with the mozzarella cheese, then place the baking sheet in the oven for 4–5 minutes or until the cheese is golden brown and melted.

4. Remove the pan from the oven and add a pinch of the Pecorino Romano cheese and a little rosemary sea salt to each mussel as desired. Serve immediately on individual plates, or place mussels on a large platter and serve family-style.

Amalfi Coast Lemon and Garlic Grilled Mussels

The Amalfi coast is located on Italy's northern coast along the Gulf of Salerno. This region of the world is known for its breathtaking cliff-edge terraces that serve as gardens filled with lemon trees. The large fresh citrus fruit called Cedro citrons is used in classic Italian beverages (limoncello), desserts and seafood recipes.

These simple lemon and garlic mussels are made even more delicious by cooking over natural lump charcoal, which adds smoky flavor. You can also put these in the oven at 450° if you prefer.

INGREDIENTS

{ Serves 4 }

- **24 black mussels, sorted and debearded**

- **2 tablespoons salted butter**

- **2 tablespoons olive oil**

- **3 cloves garlic,** minced

- **1 tablespoon chopped fresh parsley**

- **2 tablespoons fresh thyme leaves**

- **4 large lemons,** cut into thick rounds

- **Grilled bread, optional**

DIRECTIONS

1. Preheat a natural lump charcoal grill to medium-high heat.

2. In a small saucepan, add the butter, olive oil, garlic, parsley and thyme. Cook over low heat until the butter melts, then remove from the heat. Set aside.

3. Place the mussels in a pot or Dutch oven large enough to hold them and cover with the lid. Place the pot on the grill along with the lemon slices and close the grill lid. Cook for 5–6 minutes until the mussels open and use tongs to turn the lemons halfway through. Using protective hand mitts, remove the pot from the grill, and remove the grilled lemon slices with tongs, placing them on a clean plate. Set aside.

4. Remove the lid from the mussel pot and use tongs to remove any mussels that are not open (discard these). Pour the garlic olive oil sauce over the mussels and toss in the grilled lemon. Stir gently to combine. To serve, divide equal portions of the mussels, grilled lemon and sauce among individual bowls, or pour the mussels and sauce into a large bowl and serve family-style. Serve with grilled bread if desired.

WHITE FISH RECIPES

A Word on White Fish

~~~~~~~~~~~~~~

White fish (or whitefish) is a general term for many saltwater and freshwater fish species with fins and white flesh that are demersal, or that live and feed on the bottom of seas and lakes. They are generally mild in flavor and are low in fat, with some exceptions. I have outlined some of the most popular and sustainable white fish varieties in the list below.

Atlantic cod is one of the most popular fish in the world—so much so that fisheries have had trouble keeping up with demand. This species can grow up to 6 feet long and can weigh in at more than 200 pounds.

According to the organization Oceana, cod has been fished for thousands of years and once drove the coastal economies of North America. This is the same fish that was salted, dried and cooked up as an important food source during the early days of colonization of the Caribbean, and that was the original fish in the U.K.'s classic fish & chips (though pollock is now often substituted). The stocks for Atlantic cod vary, so be sure to look for fish that comes from a sustainable fishery, likely to come from a cultivated source. There are entire books dedicated to the history of cod and cod fisheries—For Cod and Country is a good one.

Wild Pacific cod also goes by the names Alaskan cod and true cod. They are caught off the waters of Alaska and are one of the most abundant sources of white fish in North America. The flavor profile is mild, firm and flaky.

Black cod is not cod at all, but a colloquial term that refers to sablefish, a deep-sea fish that inhabits the North Pacific Ocean. Its small scales feel like fur when touched, thus the name sablefish. The fish has a supple and buttery smooth flavor and is one of the most oil-rich of all white fish, which gives it its unique flavor. Black cod can be found in California, the Bering Sea and all the way to Japan.

Flatfish is a catch-all term that describes a group of more than 700 fish including flounder, halibut, sole and turbot that belong to the ray-finned order of fish. These fish spend most of their time on the bottom of the ocean in search of food. They begin life round, then eventually flatten out as they mature, and one eye migrates to either the left or right while the mouth twists to one side.

Alaskan pollock, also known as walleye pollock, is a wild fish harvested in the cold waters of Alaska. According to Seafood Source, the wild pollock fishery in Alaska is one of the largest in the world. The variety of pollock harvested in Alaska differs from that found on the Atlantic coast.

Pollock is a mild-flavored white fish similar to cod in texture; they are the thinner, less robust cousin to cod. The best part is that this lean white fish is budget-friendly. A pound of pollock costs about $3–4 per pound.

Wild Alaskan pollock can be found in a variety of forms, including fresh, frozen and in some of the world's most popular breaded fast-food fish sandwiches as well as fish sticks and surimi—fish products designed to imitate crab, lobster, scallops and shrimp.

FUN FACT Did you know that McDonald's Fillet-o-Fish® sandwich is made from sustainably harvested Alaskan pollock? I'm not promoting the consumption of fast food, but just thought you'd like to know.

Sea bass, unlike striped bass and white bass, lives in the ocean. "Sea bass" is a fairly generic term used to describe a variety of species. The flavor of each type of fish varies, but for the most part they all have lean white flesh with large flakes and delicate flavor.

Patagonian toothfish has a unique story. Ever heard of this fish? You may know it by its stage name—*Chilean sea bass.*

Most of the fish labeled "Chilean sea bass" do not come from Chile, but from the Arctic region. According to an article in Priceonomics magazine, it's not even a bass but a type of cod. This previously ignored fish underwent a marketing makeover in the mid -1970s and soon became the darling of the seafood world next to lobster.

Other fish that have undergone name changes are the slimehead, known by its more fortunate stage name orange roughy, and the goosefish, which currently goes by monkfish.

Other white fish varieties to look out for:
Barramundi, bass, haddock, sablefish, tilapia

Catfish, Cod, Halibut, Sea Bass, Tilapia and More

- South Asian Catfish with Green Chutney & Saffron Rice
- Southern Blackened Catfish with Steamed Collards
- Mississippi Fried Catfish
- Lowcountry Pan-Fried Catfish with Stewed Tomatoes & Okra
- Hawaiian Opakapaka with Vanilla Cream Sauce & Macadamia Nuts
- South African Hake with Quinoa and Pumpkin
- Australian Barramundi with Kiwi-Mango Salsa
- Brittany Lotte (Monkfish) en Papillote
- Seoul Barbecued Fish Collars
- Crispy Baja Fish Tacos with Avocado Crema

- Wild Alaskan Pollock Burger

- Aleutian Islands Fish & Chips

- Alaskan Halibut Steaks with Tomatillo Sauce

- Caribbean Char-Grilled Halibut

- Israeli Falafel-Crusted Turbot with Tabbouleh Salad

- Tokyo Miso-Ginger Glazed Sablefish

- Puerto Rican-Inspired Sofrito Cod

- Boracay Tilapia in Coconut Milk with Coconut Rice

- Pinoy Banana-Wrapped Whole Tilapia

- Balinese Island Tilapia with Nasi Kuning (Yellow Rice)

- Tulum Beach Cilantro-Lime Tilapia Burritos

South Asian Catfish

WITH GREEN CHUTNEY & SAFFRON RICE

The region known as South Asia is one of the most populous on earth! Boundaries are soft in this area, which includes Afghanistan, Bangladesh, Bhutan, India, Maldives, Nepal, Pakistan and Sri Lanka. In this part of the world, cooking traditions embrace chili, ghee, herbs, legumes, spices, rice and yogurt—think spicy seafood curries, steamed basmati rice and rich coconut stews.

INGREDIENTS

- **4 4-ounce catfish fillets**

- **Sea salt and freshly ground black pepper to taste**

- **1 bunch fresh cilantro**

- **1 tablespoon toasted cumin seeds**

- **1 small serrano pepper**, minced

- **1 1-inch piece fresh ginger**

- **4 cloves garlic**, halved

- **1 large lemon**, juice only

- **2 teaspoons paprika sea salt** (see page 548)

- **½ teaspoon honey**

- **½ cup olive oil**

- **2 tablespoons water as needed Saffron rice** (see page 412)

DIRECTIONS

1. Preheat oven to 375°F.

2. Place the fish on a clean platter and season with a little sea salt and freshly ground black pepper. Set aside.

3. In a food processor, combine the cilantro, toasted cumin seeds, serrano pepper, ginger, garlic, lemon juice, paprika sea salt, honey and olive oil and blend to create a paste. Add one tablespoon of water if needed to help smooth the mixture out. Reserve 2 tablespoons of the chutney for serving; set aside.

4. Place the fish and green sauce in a resealable food storage bag and let marinate for 10 minutes. Place the marinated fish on a baking sheet or a cast iron skillet and place in the oven. Cook for 8–10 minutes. Divide the fish fillets among 4 plates and add a scoop of saffron rice. Top fish fillets with a spoonful of the reserved chutney and serve immediately.

Southern Blackened Catfish

~~~~~~~~~~~

WITH STEAMED COLLARDS

Catfish are an important part of the culinary fabric of the American South. Officially known as channel catfish or channel cats, these lean and meaty whiskered fish are caught wild in the lakes and rivers around the region and are cultivated in places like Alabama, Arkansas and the Mississippi Delta. They are shipped to both domestic and international markets.

The inedible skin of catfish has the slick, rubbery texture of a neoprene wetsuit and is sold in a handful of ways—whole, filleted, and in nugget and steak form. Channel catfish have a mild, clean flavor that is well-suited for herbs and spices, like blackening seasoning.

You will need to be comfortable with getting your cast iron skillet really hot. The trick to a good sear is using a temperature higher than what is typically used for sautéing and pan-frying—about 400–450°F. As an alternative to the stovetop, you can drizzle the seasoned fish with oil and bake in the oven at 400–450°F.

INGREDIENTS

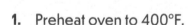

{ Serves 2 }

- **2 3-ounce U.S.-harvested catfish fillets**

- **2 tablespoons blackening seasoning** (see page 530)

- **1 teaspoon paprika sea salt** (see page 548)

- **3 tablespoons avocado oil**

- **Steamed collard greens** (see page 372)

SERVING SUGGESTIONS: LEMON WEDGES, STEAMED RICE, HOT WATER CORNBREAD

DIRECTIONS

1. Preheat oven to 400°F.

2. On a clean dry surface, sprinkle the blackening seasoning on both sides of the fish along with the paprika sea salt. With clean hands, rub the spices into the fish and set aside to marinate for 15 minutes.

3. In a cast iron or ovenproof skillet, heat the avocado oil over high heat. Add the fish and sear on one side for about 4 minutes. Using a spatula, flip the fish and cook for 2 minutes, then immediately place the skillet in the oven for 5 minutes until cooked through. Freshwater fish should be cooked thoroughly, but definitely not overcooked, lest it turns dry and overly firm.

4. To serve, divide the fish among 2 plates and serve with steamed collards and other optional sides as desired.

Mississippi Fried Catfish

The Southern American state of Mississippi is the nerve center for catfish cultivation. In fact, the U.S. is the home to the largest catfish aquaculture industry in the world, according to the site Mississippi History Now. Channel catfish are the variety farmed in this region and are typically harvested at a weight of 1–3 pounds.

Fried fish in general is incredibly tasty, but catfish hits the mark for me because of its meaty texture and mild flavor that cook up so moist. One non-traditional element I bring to this recipe is brining. I like to brine catfish in a quick salt water bath to help impart flavor, which results in a delicious fried fish that doesn't need tons of hot sauce or other condiments.

I grew up enjoying wild catfish in its many forms—fillets, whole, and cut into fingers once my grandpa chose how he'd serve up supper. My grandmother—a stellar angler in her own right—taught me to use a large brown paper bag to coat my fish with flour and cornmeal. Practical and effective. To honor the tradition, I've included this as the tried-and-true method in this recipe. A plastic bag will work in a pinch.

INGREDIENTS

BRINE

- 4 tablespoons sea salt

- 3 cups hot water

- 5 cups ice

FRIED CATFISH:

- 4 4-ounce catfish fillets

- 2 eggs

- 1 cup milk or buttermilk

- 2 cups all-purpose flour

- ½ cup cornmeal

- 1 tablespoon cayenne pepper

- 1 tablespoon garlic powder

- 2 teaspoons freshly ground black pepper

- 1 teaspoon sea salt

- 3–4 cups vegetable oil, for frying, more as needed

- 4 servings Southern green beans and red potatoes (see page 392)

- Hot sauce, optional

DIRECTIONS

Serves 4

1. In a large container, whisk the sea salt and hot water together until the salt has dissolved. Add the ice to cool the mixture. Place the fish in the cooled brine and set aside to marinate for 2 hours.

2. When the fish is ready, beat the eggs and milk (or buttermilk) together in a large bowl and set aside. Next, add the flour, cornmeal, cayenne pepper, garlic powder, black pepper and sea salt to a large brown paper bag; set aside.

3. Rinse each piece of catfish and pat dry, then place on a clean surface.

4. Rinse each piece of catfish and pat dry, then place on a clean surface.

5. Dredge one piece of catfish in the egg mixture, then place it in the bag of seasoned flour. Shake the bag gently to coat the fish, then place the fish on a clean surface or plate. Repeat with the remaining catfish pieces. Allow the fish to rest for a few minutes to allow a crust to form.

6. Add the fish, two pieces at a time, to the hot oil and cook on one side until golden brown, about 5 minutes. Flip over and cook on the other side for 3–4 minutes. Remove and drain on a bed of paper towels. Repeat with the remaining fish.

7. To serve, divide the catfish pieces among 4 plates along with a portion of the green beans and red potatoes and hot sauce if desired. Serve immediately.

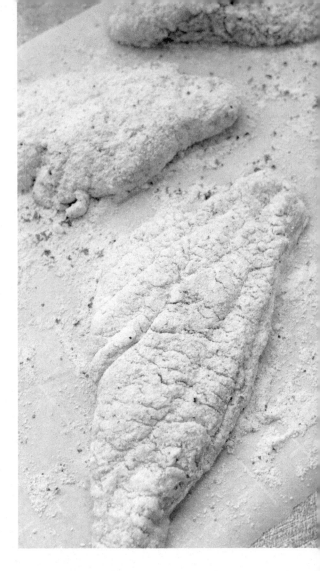

Lowcountry Pan-Fried Catfish

WITH STEWED TOMATOES & OKRA

The Southern American style of cuisine referred to as Lowcountry cooking is defined by ingredients that are grown and harvested in the coastal area between Georgia and South Carolina. It's the original farm-to-table style of dining!

Crab, catfish, shrimp and oysters are some of my favorite Lowcountry ingredients, along with okra, tomatoes and rice. This dish is a culmination of the regional cuisine and comes together pretty quickly. Pan-frying creates fish that is tender and succulent inside, with a slightly crispy exterior.

INGREDIENTS

PAN-FRIED CATFISH

- **4 catfish fillets or steaks**
- **Sea salt and freshly ground black pepper to taste**
- **1 tablespoon cayenne pepper**
- **1 tablespoon smoked paprika**
- **1 teaspoon ground thyme**
- **1 cup all-purpose flour**
- **¼ cup vegetable oil**

STEWED TOMATOES & OKRA

- **1 large white onion,** sliced
- **1 clove garlic,** minced
- **1 cup crushed tomatoes,** including the juice
- **3 sprigs fresh thyme**
- **Sea salt and freshly ground black pepper to taste**
- **1 pound fresh okra,** sliced

SERVING SUGGESTIONS: CAROLINA GOLD RICE, JASMINE RICE

DIRECTIONS

1. Place the catfish on a clean plate and season on both sides with sea salt and freshly ground black pepper to taste, cayenne pepper, smoked paprika and ground thyme. Rub the spices into the fish with clean hands and set aside. Add the flour to a paper bag, then add the fish and gently shake the bag to evenly coat the fish. Remove the fish from the bag, shake off any excess flour, and set aside.

2. In a large cast iron skillet, heat the vegetable oil over medium-high heat. When the oil is hot, add the fish and cook for 3 minutes on both sides. Place on a bed of paper towels to absorb any excess oil.

3. In the same pan, add the onion and garlic and cook for 3 minutes. Add the tomatoes, thyme sprigs, and a pinch of sea salt and freshly ground black pepper. Stir and cook for 3–4 minutes. Add the okra and stir to combine. Cook for 3–4 minutes. Taste for seasoning and adjust as needed.

4. Divide the catfish fillets among 4 plates and top with the tomato & okra mixture along with a scoop of rice if desired. Serve immediately.

Hawaiian Opakapaka

**WITH VANILLA CREAM SAUCE
& MACADAMIA NUTS**

Hawaiian pink snapper, or opakapaka, is a lean, pink-colored fish similar to sea bass with a delicate sweet flavor. Opakapaka is typically found between the tropical archipelagos of Hawaii and Tahiti.

This fish is a part of the Hawaii "Deep 7"—a special group of fish that are important and highly valued in the Pacific. The group includes ehu (ruby snapper), kalekale (Von Siebold's snapper), onaga (long tail red snapper), gindai (oblique-banded snapper), lehi (silver mouth snapper), hapu`upu`u (Hawaiian grouper) and opakapaka (pink snapper), which are bottom fish that are heavily monitored in the area by local and federal agencies.

This fish is a part of the Hawaii "Deep 7"—a special group of fish that are important and highly valued in the Pacific. The group includes ehu (ruby snapper), kalekale (Von Siebold's snapper), onaga (long tail red snapper), gindai (oblique-banded snapper), lehi (silver mouth snapper), hapu`upu`u (Hawaiian grouper) and opakapaka (pink snapper), which are bottom fish that are heavily monitored in the area by local and federal agencies.

Combined with the mild, rich flavor of vanilla and the crunch of toasted macadamia nuts, this opakapaka makes a simple and elegant meal. A whole vanilla bean is called for in this recipe. Pure vanilla extract can work in a pinch but will not impart the same flavor.

Halibut, wahoo, sea scallops and other firm white fish are great alternatives if you want to mix things up.

INGREDIENTS

{ Serves 4 }

- **4 4-ounce opakapaka fillets**
- **Sea salt and freshly ground black pepper to taste**
- **2 tablespoons olive oil**, separated
- **1 shallot**, minced

- **¼ cup dry vermouth**
- **½ cup vegetable stock**
- **1 whole vanilla bean**, split and scraped
- **1 cup heavy cream**
- **½ cup toasted macadamia nuts**, crushed

SERVING SUGGESTIONS: KOMBU RICE (SEE PAGE 414), CAULIFLOWER PARSNIP PURÉE (SEE PAGE 424)

DIRECTIONS

1. Preheat oven to 375°F.

2. Lightly season the fish with sea salt and black pepper on both sides. In an ovenproof skillet, heat one tablespoon of olive oil over medium-high heat. Cook the fish on one side for 2 minutes, then place the pan in the oven while you make the sauce.

3. In a small saucepan, heat the remaining tablespoon of olive oil over medium heat, then add the shallot and sauté until soft. Add the vermouth, vegetable stock and vanilla bean. Whisk in the cream and taste for seasoning. Add salt and freshly ground black pepper to taste. Cook for 3–4 minutes until the sauce is reduced.

4. Remove the fish from the oven and divide evenly among 4 plates. Top with one or two tablespoons of the vanilla sauce and toasted macadamia nuts. Serve immediately with kombu rice or parsnip purée if desired.

South African Hake

WITH QUINOA AND PUMPKIN

South Africa occupies the entire southern region of the African continent and boasts more than 1,700 miles of rugged coastline. Straddled by the Atlantic and Indian Oceans, the nation is known for its diverse cultures and religions, massive great white sharks and legendary seafood scene. Coastal cities and towns along the water love their braaivleis or barbecues!

Hake is a popular white fish harvested in the waters surrounding South Africa. It is a lean white fish that is similar to cod and pollock. I found this dish on a recipe card a few years ago and made it my own with a few tweaks here and there.

Pumpkin is a favorite ingredient in South African cuisine and the surrounding region. Pumpkin fritters are popular, as is roasted pumpkin. This large orange slightly sweet squash works great with fish when prepared in a savory manner. If you can't find hake, firm white fish like cod, pollock and sea bass are good alternatives for this dish.

INGREDIENTS

- **2 cups pumpkin,** peeled and diced

- **2 tablespoons olive oil,** plus more as needed

- **½ teaspoon paprika**

- **½ teaspoon cayenne pepper**

- **Sea salt and freshly ground black pepper to taste**

- **4 4-ounce boneless,** skin-on hake fillets, at least 1 inch thick

- **1 cup cooked quinoa,** any color

- **1 cup feta cheese**

- **½ cup chopped fresh parsley**

- **½ cup chopped fresh cilantro**

- **2 tablespoons lemon juice**

DIRECTIONS

1. Preheat oven to 375°F.

2. In a medium-sized bowl, toss the pumpkin in 1 tablespoon of olive oil along with the paprika, cayenne pepper and a pinch of salt and pepper. Place the pumpkin in a baking dish and roast for 35–40 minutes, turning once until tender and slightly golden brown. Remove from the oven and set aside to cool.

3. Season the fish with sea salt and freshly ground black pepper to taste and a drizzle of olive oil. Place in an ovenproof dish, skin side up, and bake for 10–12 minutes or until opaque. Remove from the oven and set aside.

4. In a medium-sized bowl, combine the cooked pumpkin, cooked quinoa and feta cheese with the parsley, cilantro, lemon juice and the remaining tablespoon of olive oil. Mix to combine, taste for seasoning and adjust with salt and pepper as needed.

5. To serve, divide the quinoa and pumpkin mixture among 4 plates and top with a fillet of roasted hake. Serve immediately.

Australian Barramundi

WITH KIWI-MANGO SALSA

Barramundi is a type of sea bass that inhabits the waters that span from Australia all the way up to Southeast Asia, where it is known as Asian sea bass. According to The Better Fish, a site dedicated to Barramundi, the fish are born in the ocean and develop in freshwater—the opposite of salmon. Along with black cod, Barramundi are high in omega-3 fatty acids and have a sweet mild flavor and firm texture.

Barramundi are born male and turn female when they turn 3 or 4 years old. Once caught wild, Barramundi are now responsibly cultivated in Australia and the Indo-Pacific region. Native Aboriginals named the fish, which loosely translates into "large-scaled silver fish." On a romantic note, these fish spawn on the full moon and their iridescent skin can be seen shimmering from afar during their "love dance."

INGREDIENTS

{ Serves 4 }

BARRAMUNDI

- **1 tablespoon paprika**
- **½ teaspoon sea salt**
- **1 teaspoon black pepper**
- **1 tablespoon lime juice**
- **1 1-inch piece fresh ginger, grated**
- **1 tablespoon avocado oil**
- **4 4-ounce barramundi fillets, skin on**

KIWI-MANGO SALSA

- **4 large green kiwis, peeled and diced**
- **¼ cup chopped red onion**
- **2 large firm, ripe red mangoes, peeled and diced into ¼-inch pieces**
- **¼ cup chopped fresh cilantro leaves**
- **Sea salt, as needed**

DIRECTIONS

1. Preheat oven to 375°F.

2. In a small bowl, combine the paprika, sea salt, black pepper, lime juice, ginger and avocado oil. Add the barramundi to a plate and use a pastry brush to coat the fish in the seasoning mix. Set aside.

3. For the salsa, combine the kiwi, red onion, mango, cilantro leaves and a pinch of sea salt. Stir and taste for seasoning. Add more salt as needed. Cover and refrigerate until ready to use.

4. Add the fish to a cast iron skillet or a baking sheet lined with parchment paper and place in the oven. Cook for 7–8 minutes, then remove and set aside.

5. To serve, divide the fish among 4 individual plates and top with the kiwi-mango salsa.

Brittany Lotte (Monkfish)

EN PAPILLOTE

Lying in the Northwest corner of France, Brittany is a distinctive and culturally significant region with spectacular coastlines and medieval towns and is one of the country's major suppliers of seafood.

Often referred to as "goose fish" and "sea devil" in the region, monkfish is one of the ugliest fish around; so much so that it is typically sold with its head removed. Looks aside, monkfish is outstanding—with plump and tender tail meat that is like a cross between lobster and mild white fish.

Fish en papillote, or fish cooked in parchment paper, is a French technique that works well for most types of seafood. It's one of my favorite ways to cook frozen fish when I'm short on time or on the road and need a quick meal. Wrapping the fish in parchment paper allows the fish to gently steam in its own juices, keeping it moist and succulent. Feel free to swap out the monkfish for your favorite whitefish, salmon or shellfish.

INGREDIENTS

{ Serves 2 }

- **1 lemon**, sliced into 6 rounds

- **2 6-ounce pieces of monkfish or other white fish such as black cod or halibut**

- **Sea salt and freshly ground black pepper to taste**

- **1 large ripe tomato**, diced

- **1 tablespoon chopped fresh tarragon**

- **2 teaspoons olive oil**

- **1 tablespoons basil butter**, separated

- **1 tablespoon capers in brine**, drained

- **Optional: Zucchini slices, fresh spinach, fresh swiss chard**

SERVING SUGGESTIONS: SAFFRON RICE (SEE PAGE 412)

DIRECTIONS

1. Preheat oven to 400°F.

2. Cut two large rectangles of parchment paper that are double the size of the fish. Place 3 lemon rounds on each piece of parchment and place the piece of fish directly on top. Season with salt and pepper and add equal portions of the tomatoes, tarragon, olive oil, capers and optional ingredients as desired.

3. Fold the parchment paper around the fish tightly. Start on one side and fold, pleating the edges together and seal. Be sure to press as you fold to seal the packets well, otherwise the steam will escape. Arrange the packets on a baking sheet and bake until the fish is cooked through, about 12 minutes. Remove from the oven and allow to rest for 2 minutes, use a kitchen knife or scissors to cut the parchment paper open and add a piece of butter and serve immediately with saffron rice if desired.

Seoul Barbecued Fish Collars

Seoul is the capital of South Korea. The city is known for its BBQ, kimchi and seafood. The emblematic Noryangjin Fish Market is a chaotic and bustling place where everything from fresh abalone to live octopus and unusual cuts of fish, like these fish collars, are for sale.

The fish collar is a particular cut of fish that lies between the neck and the body; it is an unsung and underrated cut, as it offers some of the most rich, succulent meat on the fish. Some fishmongers offer this cut on a regular basis or only on special occasions—I advise finding a quality fishmonger and calling ahead! Halibut, yellowtail and salmon are my favorites. This recipe works great on the grill or in the broiler.

INGREDIENTS

{ Serves 4 }

- **1 large lime**, juice only

- **1 small orange**, juice only

- **1 large scallion**, sliced

- **¼ cup soy sauce**

- **¼ cup yuzu sauce**

- **2 tablespoon dark sesame oil**

- **1 tablespoon sea salt**

- **4 large fish collars**

SERVING SUGGESTIONS: KOMBU RICE (SEE PAGE 414), SAUTÉED BOK CHOY

DIRECTIONS

1. Preheat a natural lump charcoal grill over medium-high heat.

2. To make the marinade, whisk together the lime juice, orange juice, scallion, soy sauce, yuzu sauce, dark sesame oil and sea salt in a medium-sized bowl. Set aside.

3. Lightly season the fish with sea salt on both sides. Place the fish and the marinade in a resealable plastic food storage bag and close. Gently shake to coat the fish and allow it to rest for 10 minutes.

4. Place the collars in a fish grate and secure shut. Place the grate on the grill and cook for 3–4 minutes on each side. Remove from heat and allow to rest for 1 minute, then serve immediately with kombu rice and sautéed bok choy as desired.

Crispy Baja Fish Tacos

WITH AVOCADO CREMA

Mexico has seemingly endless miles of coastline that include the Gulf of California and the Pacific Ocean. In Baja California, an important part of coastal Northern Mexican gastronomy, seafood is king. The peninsula is also famous for its excellent wine, world-class diving and beautiful natural habitat.

Beach cities dotted along the Baja coast are known for their simple seafood dishes like ceviche, guacamole and fish tacos. You will find versions of these crispy fish tacos in restaurants and seafood shacks alike. Most firm white fish will work for this recipe—think cod, haddock, pollock or snapper.

The avocado crema is an optional addition to these tacos, but I highly recommend it! Avocados are a classic Mexican fruit and one of my all-time favorites. If you are new to crema, it is akin to crème fraîche or sour cream and has a thick, creamy texture. In a pinch you can swap it out for sour cream. Shrimp is also a popular choice for these tacos—see page 164 for the recipe.

INGREDIENTS

{ Serves 4 }

- **1 cup all-purpose flour**

- **1 teaspoon baking powder**

- **1 cup beer or plain seltzer water**

- **4 cups vegetable oil**, for frying

- **2 pounds boneless, skinless white fish,** cut into 2-inch long pieces (wild Alaskan pollock, cod, haddock, halibut and sea bass are good options)

- **Sea salt and freshly ground black pepper to taste**

- **8–10 corn or flour tortillas** (see page 160 for tips on warming tortillas)

- **Avocado crema** (see page 544)

SUGGESTED TOPPINGS: FRESH LIME WEDGES, MANGO SALSA (SEE PAGE 566), SHREDDED CABBAGE, AVOCADO SLICES, COTIJA CHEESE, SOUR CREAM

DIRECTIONS

1. In a medium-sized bowl, whisk together the flour, baking powder and beer or seltzer water. Set aside and allow the batter to rest for 10–15 minutes.

2. Meanwhile, in a large skillet, heat 1 cup of oil to 375°F. Set up a draining rack or a bed of paper towels to drain the fish.

3. Using a fork or kitchen tweezers, dredge each piece of fish in the batter and add it to the hot oil. Cook until golden brown on both sides. Repeat in batches for all of the fish. Drain the fried fish pieces on the draining rack or paper towels.

4. When the fish is done, it's time to build the tacos. Place equal portions of fish in each tortilla shell and top with the avocado crema and your favorite toppings. Serve immediately.

Wild Alaskan Pollock Burger

Alaska Pollock is considered Alaska's most abundant fish. A cousin of codfish, pollock is harvested from the icy and pristine waters of the North Pacific and the Bering Sea, the same waters where king crab and other delicacies are usurped. The fish has a mild taste and flaky white flesh.

Wild pollock burgers are a 'Best Coast' dish that has become increasingly more popular as major food brands have jumped in with both feet to create commercial versions, which are typically found in the frozen section. While store bought varieties are tasty and come in handy for large parties, I find it rewarding to make my own whenever possible.

This recipe calls for the pollock to undergo a quick spin in a food processor, which will change the texture slightly and give the burger a nice mouthfeel. The goal is to reach a smooth consistency reminiscent of your favorite burger.

Burger buns make all the difference, and brioche is my bun of choice. The flavor and texture are exquisite and they upscale almost any burger patty. If brioche is not possible, use the best tasting bun possible.

Hake, halibut and salmon are good options for this burger.

INGREDIENTS

{ Makes 4 burgers }

- **2 pounds wild Alaskan pollock fillets,** cut into pieces

- **2 scallions,** chopped

- **1 teaspoon water,** more as needed

- **1 tablespoon onion powder**

- **1 tablespoon garlic powder**

- **1 tablespoon dried savory**

- **½ bunch cilantro,** leaves only

- **1 small lemon,** juice and ½ teaspoon zest

- **½ cup dried breadcrumbs or Panko breadcrumbs** (if needed)

- **3 tablespoons olive oil or your favorite vegetable oil,** separated

- **½ teaspoon sea salt,** plus more as needed

- **Freshly ground black pepper to taste**

- **4 brioche burger buns or your favorite type of burger bun**

DIRECTIONS

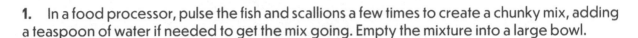

1. In a food processor, pulse the fish and scallions a few times to create a chunky mix, adding a teaspoon of water if needed to get the mix going. Empty the mixture into a large bowl.

2. Add the onion powder, garlic powder, dried savory, cilantro, lemon juice, lemon zest, 1 tablespoon of olive oil, ½ teaspoon sea salt and several cracks of black pepper. The mix should be firm and hold its shape, if the mix it too loose, which can happen if using frozen fish, add the breadcrumbs, stir to combine and refrigerate for 20–30 minutes.

3. Once the fish mixture has rested, heat a little olive oil in a skillet over medium-high heat. When the pan is hot, scoop out a little of the pollock burger mix, form a small patty, and add it to the skillet—this is your test burger. Cook on both sides for 20–30 seconds, then taste for seasoning. Adjust as needed.

4. Rinse each piece of catfish and pat dry, then place on a clean surface.

5. Make the burgers by equally dividing the pollock mixture into four sections and use your hands to form patties about 1 inch thick. Place the patties on a plate and set aside.

6. Heat a stovetop grill pan to high heat. Brush the brioche buns or other buns of choice with a little olive oil and add them to the pan, toast them lightly, then remove and set aside.

7. Next, add the pollock burgers to the grill pan and cook on each side for 3–4 minutes. Be careful not to overcook. When done, remove the fish patties from the pan and place on a clean plate.

8. To make the burgers, dress the buns with desired toppings and a cooked pollock patty. Serve immediately.

SUGGESTED TOPPINGS:
SLICED RED ONION, ICEBERG LETTUCE, MUSTARD, SLICED PICKLES, PINEAPPLE RING, AVOCADO OR OTHER FAVORITE BURGER TOPPINGS

OPTIONS:
ADD A DOLLOP OF HARISSA, CHIMICHURRI OR CURRY POWDER TO THE BURGER MIX FOR ADDED FLAVOR AND TEXTURE

Aleutian Islands Fish & Chips

The Aleutian Islands, located in the Bering Sea, are home to one of the busiest fishing ports in North America. It's a remote region and ecotourism destination, filled with water activities like thermal hot springs, hiking, site-seeing and of course, fishing.

The waters in this area are teeming with life and are known for some of the most abundant seafood around, including Dungeness crab, snow crab, red king crab, Pacific cod, black cod, halibut and pollock, among other seafood.

Pollock, a cousin of cod, the old-time treasured fish & chips favorite, is wonderful when baked, stewed or roasted, and it really shines when it's battered, fried and combined with potatoes, or "chips," in this case. This fish & chips recipe uses a classic beer batter for a flavorful take on a beloved comfort food.

INGREDIENTS

{ Serves 4 }

CHIPS

- **1 pound russet potatoes,** skin on

- **4 cups vegetable oil for frying,** more as needed

FISH

- **2 pounds boneless,** skinless white fish cut into ¼-inch pieces (pollock, cod and halibut are good options)

- **Sea salt and freshly ground black pepper to taste**

- **1 cup all-purpose flour**

- **1 teaspoon sea salt**

- **1 teaspoon baking powder**

- **1 tablespoon garlic powder**

- **1 cup beer or plain seltzer water**

- **4 cups vegetable oil,** for frying

DIRECTIONS

1. Preheat oven to 375°F.

2. Slice the potatoes into thin sticks—use a mandoline for simplicity and to make uniform cuts. Place the cut potatoes in an ice bath to keep them from oxidizing (browning).

3. In a large Dutch oven, heat 4 cups of vegetable oil to 320°F or 330°F.

4. Remove the cut potatoes from the ice water and dry them on paper towels or tea towels until completely dry. Set aside. Meanwhile, set up a bed of paper towels or a draining rack for the cooked potatoes.

5. When the oil reaches the correct temperature, add the sliced potatoes and cook for 3 minutes, then remove with a slotted spoon or spider strainer and place on paper towels or a draining rack. Continue in batches until all of the potatoes are partially cooked. Set aside to cool and turn the heat on the stove to low.

6. Place the fish on a clean surface and sprinkle a bit of sea salt and freshly cracked black pepper on each side. Set aside.

7. To finish the chips, turn the heat up on the Dutch oven to 375°F, then add the partially cooked potatoes and fry until crispy and golden brown. Drain fried potatoes on paper towels, then place on a baking sheet and place in the oven to keep warm.

8. To prepare the fish, combine the flour, sea salt, baking powder, garlic powder, sea salt and beer in a large bowl. Whisk to combine. Allow the batter to rest for 5 minutes; this will give the baking powder time to activate. Meanwhile, set up a bed of paper towels or a draining rack for draining the cooked fish.

9. Lightly dust the pollock pieces in flour, then dredge in the beer batter and add to the hot oil. Cook for 3–4 minutes or until golden brown. Use a slotted spoon or spider strainer to remove the fish from the oil and drain on paper towels or draining rack. Repeat the process until all the fish is cooked.

10. Remove the chips from the oven.

11. To serve, divide the fish among 4 individual plates along with equal portions of chips. Enjoy immediately.

Caribbean Char-Grilled Halibut

This recipe is perfect for those of us who like things on the hot and spicy side! This char-grilled Caribbean halibut recipe calls for Scotch bonnet or habañero pepper—a classic ingredient in Caribbean fare. Halibut are not native to the Caribbean, but I enjoy the flavors of this meaty fish combined with island flavors and cooking techniques.

Using natural lump charcoal is highly recommended and practically a must for this dish. It provides an authentic smoky island flavor that cannot be replicated by liquid smoke or standard charcoal briquettes. Lump charcoal can be found at most grocery stores, ethnic markets or online. See page 131 for info on charcoal.

One thing to note is that I like to use a fish grate when I barbeque fish. It's a safety precaution that ensures that my fish won't stick to the grill and makes for easy turning. I highly recommend purchasing one for fuss-free grilling.

Halibut is a versatile fish that is very lean. It's important that you keep an eye on the grill when cooking to prevent the fish from becoming overly dry and tough.

INGREDIENTS

2 Scotch bonnet or habañero peppers

3 green cardamom pods, seeds only

1 medium white onion, quartered

4 scallions, sliced

2 cloves garlic, peeled

1 3-inch piece fresh ginger, peeled and halved

3 sprigs fresh thyme, leaves only

1 tablespoon ground allspice

½ teaspoon cinnamon teaspoon or a pinch of nutmeg

Sea salt to taste

1 tablespoon freshly ground black pepper

2 large limes, juice and zest

2 tablespoons avocado oil, divided

1 tablespoon water, more as needed

5 4-ounce halibut steaks

DIRECTIONS

1. Start by splitting the Scotch bonnet or habañero peppers in half and removing the white ribs and seeds. You may want to use gloves for this, as the natural oils from the peppers can remain on your hands and nails and can cause a little discomfort.

2. To make the marinade, add the peppers to a food processor, along with the cardamom, onion, scallions, garlic, ginger, thyme leaves, allspice, cinnamon, nutmeg, sea salt, black pepper, lime juice and zest, 1 tablespoon avocado oil and 1 tablespoon water. Blend until smooth. The result should be a slightly chunky paste. Set aside.

3. Place the fish on a shallow plate and spread the marinade on both sides using a spoon or rubber spatula. Cover the fish with plastic wrap and refrigerate for 20 minutes, allowing the flavors of the spice blend to permeate the fish.

4. Meanwhile, heat the coals on your barbecue to medium-high.

5. When the fish is ready, use a spoon or other kitchen utensil to scrape off any excess marinade from the fish and place the steaks in the fish grates.

6. Using a pastry brush, spread a light layer of the remaining avocado oil to both sides of the fish to help prevent it from sticking to the fish grate and the grill. Close the fish grate.

7. When the coals are hot, place the fish on the grill and cook over indirect heat for 6–8 minutes on each side. Remove the fish from the grill and allow the fish to rest for 1–2 minutes before gently removing from the fish grate. Serve immediately with plantains, coconut rice and salad as desired.

Israeli Falafel- Crusted Turbot

WITH TABBOULEH SALAD

Falafel is a Middle Eastern patty made from chickpeas and fava beans (some cooks solely use chickpeas) combined with herbs and spices and fried golden brown. It is served all day long in some places like Egypt, Israel and Sudan and can be eaten hot or cold.

My first experience with falafel was in the '90s in Paris, France at an Israeli restaurant where the artist Lenny Kravitz visited, which was mentioned in a local article. I'm a big Kravitz fan, so of course I dragged my then-boyfriend (current husband) to the spot. The restaurant was packed with customers and for good reason—the falafel was awesome!

Turbot is a large, sandy-colored fish that is highly prized throughout Europe. It's one of the most consumed flatfish in the region and is a relative of other flatfish like halibut and sole. Mostly harvested in the Atlantic Ocean and Mediterranean, Turbot is now cultivated in Galicia, Spain.

Salmon, tilapia and hake are good options, but this recipe works particularly well with turbot, a flatfish that needs some structural support in the pan.

INGREDIENTS

{ Serves 4 }

- **2 cups chickpea and fava bean flour mix**
- **2 tablespoon dried parsley**
- **2 tablespoon dried cilantro**
- **1 tablespoon ground cumin**
- **1 tablespoon ground coriander**
- **2 teaspoons garlic powder**

- **2 teaspoon onion powder**
- **1 teaspoon cayenne pepper**
- **1 teaspoon kosher salt**
- **1 teaspoon freshly ground black pepper**
- **1½ pounds (4 large) turbot fillets**
- **1 cup grapeseed oil**

SERVING SUGGESTIONS: *GREEK YOGURT, TAHINI SAUCE, PITA BREAD, TABBOULEH SALAD*

DIRECTIONS

1. In a large bowl, combine the chickpea and fava bean flour with the parsley, cilantro, cumin, coriander, garlic, onion, cayenne pepper, kosher salt and black pepper. Mix thoroughly, then empty the mixture into a sturdy paper bag. Set aside.

2. Rinse the turbot fillets under cool water and gently shake to remove excess moisture. While the fillets are relatively wet, place them in the bag with the falafel mix—the wetness of the fish will allow the dry mix to adhere to the flounder without having to use an egg wash.

3. Hold the top of the bag to keep it closed and gently shake until the fish is evenly coated. Remove fish from the bag and set it on a clean dry surface—this will help form a crust. Set aside.

4. To cook the fish, heat the grapeseed oil in a large skillet over medium-high heat. Add the fish one piece at a time. Cook on one side until golden brown, about 1½ minutes, then flip over and cook until golden brown on the other side.

5. Remove from heat and allow the fish to drain on a rack. Divide fillets among 4 plates and serve immediately with tabbouleh salad, minty yogurt sauce, tahini sauce and pita bread as desired.

Tokyo Miso-Ginger Glazed Sablefish

Black cod, also known as sablefish and butterfish, is a favorite fish on the tables of Japanese kitchens and restaurants alike. The fish is high in omega-3 fatty acids, which lends a moist flavorful flavor and melt-in-your-mouth texture. Although sablefish can be found in the waters surrounding Japan, most of the fish is imported from North America.

This miso-ginger recipe is a popular one, and most cooks have their own twist on this classic dish. For example, I use honey instead of sugar and yellow miso paste instead of white miso because I like the flavor. Mirin is a white Japanese cooking wine that adds sweetness and a nice tangy flavor. It adds interest and variety to other dishes like ramen bowls.

Yuzu is a sour and tart citrus fruit that is widely found in China, Korea and Japan. It's the size of a tangerine and is mostly used for its juice and zest. Is important to this dish, so try to find it. A good substitute is lemon juice.

INGREDIENTS

{ Serves 2 }

- **1 pound black cod fillets**, cut into two pieces

- **2 tablespoon mirin**

- **3 tablespoon yuzu juice or lemon juice**

- **3 tablespoons yellow miso paste**

- **1 tablespoons honey**

- **1 1-inch piece fresh ginger**, grated

- **2 teaspoons avocado oil**

SERVING SUGGESTIONS: KOMBU RICE (SEE PAGE 414), SOBA NOODLES

DIRECTIONS

1. Preheat oven to 450°F.

2. Place the fish on a large shallow plate and lightly season with salt and black pepper. Set aside and allow to rest while you prepare the marinade.

3. Add the mirin, yuzu, miso paste, honey and grated ginger to a bowl and whisk in the avocado oil. Place the fish in a plastic bag and pour in the marinade. Gently massage the bag to evenly distribute the marinade and refrigerate for 10 minutes.

4. Drain the marinade from the bag and blot the fish with a paper towel to remove excess moisture.

5. In an ovenproof dish, add the fish and place in the oven, about 4 inches from the heat. Cook for about 4–5 minutes or until cooked through. Remove from the oven and allow to rest for 1 minute. Serve with kombu rice or soba noodles as desired.

Puerto Rican -Inspired Sofrito Cod

The flavors of Puerto Rico are mild and savory, unlike other Caribbean nations that like to keep things hot and spicy! Sofrito is the base of most traditional dishes in the region and is easy to put together by combining onion, pepper, garlic, tomato, cilantro. Like most sauces, the ingredients vary by household.

Salt cod is traditionally used in the recipe, but I discovered that the unsalted version makes for a tasty meal. I use frozen Alaskan cod pieces, but any white fish will do; mahi-mahi, shark, swordfish, tilapia, rockfish or black grouper are good options.

Cuban Moros y Cristianos is a good pairing (see page 370), as are Belizean red beans & coconut rice see page 580 for the recipe.

INGREDIENTS

- **1 pound cod**, cut into chunks

- **Sea salt and freshly ground black pepper to taste**

- **1 cup all-purpose flour**

- **2 tablespoons avocado oil**

- **2 tablespoons annatto seed**

- **4 medium onions**, finely chopped

- **2 cloves garlic**, minced

- **2 green bell peppers**, chopped

- **1 habañero pepper**, finely chopped

- **3 large tomatoes**, chopped (about 2 cups)

- **1 small bunch fresh cilantro**, chopped, a few tablespoons reserved for garnish

- **¼ cup water**, as needed

- **1 large lime**, sliced, for garnish

DIRECTIONS

1. Place the cod on a shallow plate and season with sea salt and black pepper to taste. Coat the fish in all purpose flour and allow to rest for 1–2 minutes.

2. In a large skillet, head one tablespoon of the avocado oil over medium-high heat. Add the fish to the pan and fry until light brown on all sides. Remove from the skillet and place on a clean plate. Set aside and prepare the sofrito.

3. Rinse and dry the large skillet and add the remaining tablespoon of oil and the annatto seeds. Cook for 1–2 minutes or until the annatto is fragrant and has released its golden red color. Use a spoon to remove the seeds and discard.

4. Add the onion, garlic, bell pepper, habañero pepper, tomatoes and cilantro to the pan and sauté for 3 minutes. Add a little water if needed to make a sauce. When the vegetables are soft and fragrant, add the cooked cod and cook for 3–4 minutes until heated through—take care not to break up the cod too much.

5. Garnish with lime slices and cilantro and serve immediately over steamed rice or as desired.

Boracay Tilapia in Coconut Milk

WITH COCONUT RICE

Located in Southeast Asia, the Republic of the Philippines is made up of more than 7,000 islands. The cooking style of the country is a mashup of Chinese, Malay and Spanish gastronomy.

The island of Boracay is one of the most popular tourist destinations in the region. Known for its beaches and resorts, Boracay also has an exciting food scene that is a combination of classic street eats, international fare and local favorites, like this tilapia in coconut milk dish.

Along with milkfish, tilapia is one of the most popular freshwater fish in the Philippines. Both posh and practical, this is a dish you'll find on the menu of an upscale restaurant and on dinner tables of local residents.

INGREDIENTS

- **4 large tilapia fillets**, skinless, cut into large pieces

- **Sea salt and freshly ground black pepper to taste**

- **2 tablespoons ghee**

- **1 medium onion**, diced

- **2 cloves garlic**, minced

- **1 tablespoon ground ginger**

- **1 teaspoon ground turmeric**

- **2 green chiles**, halved, seeds optional

- **1 small head fresh cauliflower** (about 2 cups), cut into bite-sized pieces

- **2 large tomatoes**, diced, or 1 cup drained canned tomatoes

- **1 cup water**

- **1½ cups coconut milk** (1 14-ounce can)

- **1 bunch fresh cilantro**, chopped, a few leaves reserved for garnish

- **4 heads bok choy**, halved

DIRECTIONS

1. Place the tilapia on a clean surface and season with sea salt and freshly ground black pepper. Set aside.

2. In a large skillet or Dutch oven, heat the ghee over medium-high heat. When the ghee is melted, add the onion and garlic and cook until soft and fragrant, about 2 minutes. Add the ginger, turmeric, green chiles, cauliflower and tomatoes and cook for 2 minutes, stirring intermittently—this will give the cauliflower time to brown and absorb the flavor and color of the turmeric.

3. Stir in the water, coconut milk and cilantro and bring the pot to a low boil for 5 minutes. Taste the sauce for seasoning and adjust as needed with sea salt and freshly ground black pepper. Add the fish to the pot along with the bok choy and cover with the lid slightly ajar. Reduce the heat to low and cook for 5 minutes. Turn off the heat and allow the pot to rest for 2–3 minutes, giving the fish and bok choy time to finish cooking.

4. To serve, place scoops of coconut rice in 4 bowls along with equal portions of the tilapia and sauce. Garnish with lime slices and serve immediately.

SERVING SUGGESTIONS:
COCONUT RICE (SEE PAGE 418), LIME WEDGES

Pinoy Banana-Wrapped Whole Tilapia

In general, the word 'Pinoy' refers to anything related to Filipino people and culture. Tilapia, also known as St. Peter Fish, is a popular choice in the region and is available year-round thanks to the advent of fish farming or aquaculture. These fish are prepared fried, grilled, curried, and as in this recipe, wrapped in banana leaf.

Banana leaf imparts an earthy flavor to the fish that is impossible to replicate. It's important to know that banana leaf is inedible and is only used as a cooking vessel.

A traditional Filipino style of eating is called kamayan, which means "by hand" in Tagalog. Portions of food, along with a healthy dose of rice, are placed on a banana leaf and scooped up by hand to enjoy. This way of dining is optional, and I present it here in case you want to mix it up with a little island flair at the dinner table.

INGREDIENTS

{ Serves 2-4 }

- **2 whole tilapia**, dressed

- **2 large limes**

- **Sea salt and freshly ground black pepper to taste**

- **2 large banana leaves**, large enough to wrap around the fish

- **1 bunch fresh cilantro**

- **1 thumb fresh ginger**, grated

SERVING SUGGESTIONS: COCONUT RICE (SEE PAGE 418), CANE VINEGAR

DIRECTIONS

SPECIAL EQUIPMENT: COOKING TWINE

1. Preheat oven to 400°F.

2. Place the tilapia on a clean surface. Use a knife to make three cuts on both sides of the fish. Squeeze the lime over both sides of the fish and sprinkle with sea salt and freshly ground black pepper to taste. Set aside for 10 minutes.

3. Place one piece of banana leaf on a clean surface and add one fish. Stuff the fish with half of the cilantro and half of the fresh ginger. Fold the fish in the banana leaf using the cooking twine as needed. Repeat with the other fish.

4. Place each banana leaf package on a baking sheet. Place in the oven and cook for 15–20 minutes. Remove from the oven and allow to rest for 3–5 minutes.

5. To serve, cut open the banana leaf package and serve with a scoop of coconut rice. Drizzle with cane vinegar as desired and serve immediately.

Balinese Island Tilapia

WITH NASI KUNING (YELLOW RICE)

Affectionately known as The Island of the Gods, Bali is nestled in the Indonesian archipelago between Java and Lombok. The island is surrounded by the Indian Ocean and the Java Sea and boasts a rich and diverse culture.

As the country's most popular tourist destination, visitors fall in love with Bali for its beautiful white sand beaches, steamy jungles, centuries-old architecture and iconic terraced rice paddies that create an elaborate, lush landscape. Rice is an important cultural and culinary ingredient.

Nasi kuning, or yellow rice, is a dish that is gilded with turmeric for color, and flavored with ginger, garlic and lemongrass. Stacked high on a plate, it looks like a pile of gold and is often served at parties and ceremonies as a symbol of good luck and prosperity. Paired with fish, another Balinese staple, this dish will bring the flavors of the island to your kitchen.

INGREDIENTS

TILAPIA

- **4 tilapia fillets,** cut into large pieces

- **Sea salt and freshly ground black pepper to taste**

- **1 thumb ginger,** grated

- **2 red chilis,** chopped

- **2 tablespoons kecap manis** (sweet soy sauce)

YELLOW RICE

- **Avocado oil,** as needed

- **1 medium Spanish onion,** minced

- **2 cups medium-grain rice**

- **1 cup coconut milk**

- **2 cups vegetable broth**

- **½ teaspoon ground turmeric**

- **1 stem lemongrass,** halved

- **1 bay leaf**

- **3 whole cloves**

- **1 small cinnamon stick**

- **4 green cardamom pods,** seeds only

DIRECTIONS

{ Serves 4 }

1. Place the tilapia fillets, sea salt and freshly ground black pepper, ginger, red chilis and kecap manis in a large resealable food storage bag. Seal the bag and massage to coat the fish. Place the bag in the refrigerator for 15 minutes.

2. To make the yellow rice, heat 1 tablespoon of avocado oil in a large saucepan over medium heat. Add the onion and cook until soft and fragrant. Add the rice and cook for 2 minutes, coating the grains in the oil. Stir in the coconut milk, vegetable broth, turmeric, lemongrass, bay leaf, cloves, cinnamon stick and cardamom seeds. Bring to a boil for 2 minutes, then reduce heat to a simmer. Cook for 15 minutes with the lid slightly ajar. When the time is up, fully cover with the lid and let the pot sit for 10 minutes, allowing the rice to finish steaming. Set aside.

3. Remove the tilapia from the refrigerator and drain the excess liquid from the bag. In a medium-sized skillet, add enough avocado oil to coat the bottom. Add the tilapia and cook until brown on both sides, about 3 minutes each. for 2–3 minutes, giving the fish and bok choy time to finish cooking.

4. To serve, divide yellow rice among 4 plates and top with the cooked tilapia. Enjoy immediately.

Tulum Beach Cilantro-Lime Tilapia Burritos

Surrounded by natural beauty and deep-rooted history, the Caribbean town of Tulum is nestled along the coastline of the Yucatán Peninsula. Its 11 municipalities make up the area known as Quinta Roo, Mexico.

Culturally important to Central America, Tulum is sought after for its Mayan archaeological sites, stunning beaches and inviting gastronomy scene. Burritos, tacos and seafood, no doubt, are popular menu options on restaurant and resort menus. This cilantro-lime tilapia burrito is a dish to look for while visiting and are an easy meal to whip up at home. Fill the flour tortillas with your favorite suggested toppings.

INGREDIENTS

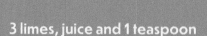

- 3 limes, juice and 1 teaspoon of zest

- 1 bunch fresh cilantro

- 2 cloves garlic, halved

- ½ cup minced white onion

- 1 serrano pepper

- 1 teaspoon ground cumin

- 1 teaspoon dried Mexican oregano

- 1 tablespoon water, more as needed

- 2 tablespoons avocado oil, separated

- Sea salt and freshly ground black pepper, as needed

- 1½ pounds tilapia fillets, cut into bite-sized pieces

- 4 large flour tortillas

DIRECTIONS

1. In the bowl of a food processor, add the lime juice and zest, cilantro, garlic, onion, serrano pepper, cumin, Mexican oregano, water, 1 tablespoon avocado oil and a generous pinch of sea salt and freshly ground black pepper. Pulse to make a smooth marinade. Add water in half-teaspoon increments as needed to smooth out the mixture. Set aside.

2. Place the tilapia pieces in a large plastic food storage bag and pour in the cilantro-lime marinade. Place in the refrigerator for 15 minutes.

3. Remove the tilapia from the refrigerator and drain the excess marinade from the bag. Set aside.

4. In a large skillet, heat the remaining tablespoon of avocado oil over medium-high heat. When the pan is hot, add the marinated fish. Cook for 6–8 minutes or until the fish is firm and opaque, turning occasionally with tongs or a spatula. Turn off the heat and cover with a lid; set aside.

5. Warm the tortillas (see page 160) and assemble by adding equal portions of cilantro-lime tilapia to the center along with your favorite optional toppings and fold the sides and ends to make a wrap. For added texture, add the wrapped burritos to a hot lightly oiled pan and toast on sides before serving.

FILLING SUGGESTIONS:
MOROS Y CRISTIANOS (SEE PAGE 370), SPANISH SAFFRON RICE (SEE PAGE 410), SHREDDED CHEESE, MANGO AVOCADO SALSA (SEE PAGE 564), BLACK BEANS, AVOCADO CREMA (SEE PAGE 546 SHREDDED CABBAGE

Mahi Mahi, Opah, Swordfish, Tuna, Yellowtail, Wahoo & Other Large Game Fish Recipes

- Polynesian Honey-Lime Mahi-Mahi with Avocado Salsa

- Mediterranean Spicy Chermoula Mahi-Mahi with Vegetable Couscous

- Spanish Mahi-Mahi with Espinacas con Garbanzos (Chickpeas & Spinach)

- Yucatán Mahi-Mahi Tacos with Habañero Sour Cream

- Key West Grilled Lime-Mustard Swordfish with Avocado Salad

- Maltese Spinach & Artichoke Stuffed Swordfish

- Cuban Swordfish Brochettes with Moros y Cristianos (Black Beans & Rice)

- Costa Rican Pink Guava Basted Swordfish Casado

- La Jolla Yellowtail with Grape & Walnut Salad

- Sri Lankan Curried Tuna & Dhal (Red Lentils)

- Sicilian Spaghetti al Tonno (Tuna) with Eggplant

Polynesian Honey-Lime Mahi-Mahi

WITH AVOCADO SALSA

Polynesia is a region of Oceania that encompasses more than 1,000 tropical islands, including Fiji, Hawaii, New Zealand, Samoa and Tonga. The name alone evokes dreamy images of clear blue water, fruity umbrella-clad cocktails and poi-infused luaus, but the archipelago is also a culturally rich region with traditional languages, iconic art, and a gastronomy scene that boasts fresh, delicious ingredients.

Along with seafood, fruit is a common addition to recipes throughout Polynesia, along with the occasional dash of honey. Tuna, swordfish and mahi-mahi are cultural favorites and the honey that you are likely to find is from macadamia blossom, ōhia lehua blossom and wilelaiki blossom, according to Big Island Bee Company.

Mahi-mahi, also known as dolphinfish or dorado, is a beautiful and meaty catch with a mild, yet distinct flavor. They are a predatory fish that feed on squid, crustaceans and smaller fish, and can grow up to 40 pounds. Because of their lean, low-in-fat flesh, mahi-mahi can be easily overcooked, resulting in a tough, dry texture. In this recipe, adding a little honey to the marinade helps keep it moist, as does keeping a watchful eye on the cooking time.

INGREDIENTS

{ Serves 4 }

- **4 3-ounce mahi-mahi fillets,** skinned with bloodline removed

- **1 large lime,** juice and zest

- **1 tablespoon honey**

- **2 cloves garlic,** crushed

- **1 tablespoon ground cumin**

- **2 teaspoons cayenne pepper**

- **2 tablespoons avocado oil,** divided

- **Sea salt and freshly ground black pepper to taste**

- **2 cups avocado salsa** (see page 548)

DIRECTIONS

1. In a medium-sized bowl, combine the lime zest and juice, honey, garlic, cumin, cayenne pepper, 1 tablespoon avocado oil, and sea salt and black pepper to taste. Whisk thoroughly and set aside.

2. Place the fish in a resealable food storage bag large enough to hold all four pieces and pour in the marinade. Close the bag and shake gently to allow the marinade to fully coat the fish. Place the bag in the refrigerator for 5 minutes.

3. When the mahi-mahi has finished marinating, remove from the bag using your hands or a pair of tongs, then place on a clean plate. Blot the fish with a paper towel to remove any excess moisture; set aside. In a large cast iron skillet, heat the remaining tablespoon of avocado oil over medium-high heat. Add the fish and cook for 3–4 minutes on each side until lightly browned. Remove the mahi-mahi from the pan and place on a clean plate. Allow the fish to rest for 1–2 minutes—do not keep it in the pan or the residual heat will continue to cook the fish.

4. To serve, divide fillets among 4 plates and top with avocado salsa.

Mediterranean Spicy Chermoula Mahi-Mahi

~~~~~~~~~~~

WITH VEGETABLE COUSCOUS

The light and refreshing flavors of the Mediterranean shine through in this bright garlicky green sauce commonly used for fresh fish and vegetables in North Africa. It's called chermoula and it is simple to prepare. Combined with mahi-mahi or other firm white fish like swordfish or tuna, it makes for a mouthwatering meal.

In this region, which includes the countries of Algeria, Egypt, Libya, Morocco and Tunisia, most dishes are served with couscous, an iconic ingredient that is as important to North African cuisine as rice is to Asian cuisine. It can be served plain as a side dish but is best when dressed up with other ingredients like chickpeas, vegetables, preserved lemons, spices and herbs, as seen in my recipe for Tunisian vegetable couscous found on page 408.

INGREDIENTS

- **4 4-ounce mahi-mahi fillets,** bloodline removed

- **Sea salt and freshly ground black pepper to taste**

- **1 bunch fresh cilantro**

- **1 tablespoon toasted cumin seeds**

- **1 small serrano pepper,** minced

- **1 1-inch piece fresh ginger**

- **4 cloves garlic,** halved

- **1 large lemon,** juice only

- **½ preserved lemon,** cut into chunks

- **2 teaspoons paprika sea salt** (see page 548)

- **½ teaspoon honey**

- **½ cup olive oil**

- **2 tablespoons water,** or as needed

- **Tunisian vegetable couscous** (see page 420)

DIRECTIONS

{ Serves 4 }

1. Preheat oven to 375°F.

2. Place the mahi-mahi on a clean platter and season with a little sea salt and freshly ground black pepper. Set aside.

3. In a food processor, combine the cilantro, toasted cumin seeds, serrano pepper, fresh ginger, garlic, lemon juice, preserved lemon, paprika sea salt, honey and olive oil. Blend to create a smooth paste and add one tablespoon of water if needed to smooth the mixture. Reserve 1 or 2 tablespoons of the chermoula sauce for serving.

4. Place the fish and chermoula sauce in a resealable food storage bag and marinate for 10 minutes. Once it has marinated, place the fish on a baking sheet or in a cast iron skillet and place in the oven. Bake for 8–10 minutes.

5. Remove from the oven and allow the fish to rest for 1–2 minutes before serving. Divide the fillets among 4 individual plates and spread a little extra chermoula sauce on top. Add a scoop of Tunisian vegetable couscous and serve immediately.

Spanish Mahi-Mahi with *Espinacas con Garbanzos*

CHICKPEAS & SPINACH

This recipe is my pescatarian play on a popular dish from Seville called espinacas con garbanzos, or spinach with garbanzos. It's typically served as a tapas offering in Spanish bars, especially when the weather cools down.

Chickpeas are popular throughout the Mediterranean. During my time spent in Spain, I often found them tucked into stews, swimming side-by-side with roasted tomatoes and slow-roasted with fish. For this saucy dish, mahi-mahi is a nice meaty choice. Cod, swordfish, tuna and large shrimp are good alternatives.

You can make your own garbanzos using my recipe on page 378 or use a canned or jarred variety.

INGREDIENTS

1 medium lemon, juice only
1 teaspoon honey

3 tablespoons Spanish olive oil, separated

Sea salt and freshly ground black pepper to taste

1½ pounds mahi-mahi, skinned, bloodline removed, cut into ¼-inch pieces

1 medium Spanish onion, thinly sliced

4 cloves garlic, minced

1 small bell pepper, thinly sliced

1 15-ounce can crushed tomatoes (with juice)

1 tablespoon water, more as needed

2 teaspoons smoked Spanish paprika

2 Padrón peppers (Anaheim or shishito peppers are good substitutes), minced

1½ cups cooked garbanzo beans (chickpeas)

2 cups raw baby spinach

DIRECTIONS

{ Serves 4 }

1. In a small bowl, combine the lemon juice, honey, 1 tablespoon of olive oil and salt and pepper. Whisk together to make a simple marinade. Place the fish pieces in a resealable food storage bag and pour in the marinade. Seal the bag and shake to coat the fish in the marinade on all sides. Place the bag in the refrigerator for 10 minutes. When the fish has marinated, open the bag slightly and fully drain the marinade. Set aside.

2. In a medium-sized skillet, heat the remaining olive oil over medium-high heat. Add the onion, garlic and bell pepper and cook for 2 minutes until soft and fragrant. Stir in the crushed tomatoes along with the water, paprika, Padrón peppers and garbanzo beans. Cook for 4–5 minutes, stirring occasionally. Taste for seasoning and add sea salt and freshly ground black pepper as needed.

3. Remove the mahi-mahi from the bag and place the fish in the skillet; use a spoon to cover the fish in the sauce. Place a lid on the pot and cook for 2 minutes, then toss in the spinach and cook, covered, for 2–3 minutes or until the spinach has wilted.

4. Remove the pot from the heat and allow it to rest with the lid on for 2–3 minutes; this will allow the fish to finish cooking through and absorb the flavors. To serve, divide equal portions of the espinacas con garbanzos among 4 bowls and enjoy immediately.

Yucatán Mahi-Mahi Tacos

WITH HABAÑERO CREMA

Habañero peppers are an important ingredient in cuisine of the communities along the Yucatán Peninsula, an area of Mexico that separates the Gulf of Mexico and the Caribbean Sea. Parts of the Yucatán also encompass the Central American countries of Belize and Guatemala.

A few years ago, I visited the region for a two-week vacation and fully enjoyed exploring the beaches, the culture, and of course, the food scene. I certainly had my fair share of fish tacos, which are generally prepared with grilled fish, instead of the crispy, battered version that is popular in Baja California, Mexico (see page 164).

Mahi-mahi is a lean, meaty fish that works great for tacos. The texture of the fish, paired with the corn tortillas and spicy toppings, makes for a delicious experience.

INGREDIENTS

- **1 cup Mexican crema**

- **1 medium lime**, juice and zest

- **Sea salt and freshly ground black pepper to taste**

- **1 large habañero pepper**, seeded and minced

- **1 pound mahi-mahi fillets**, skinned, diced

- **¼ cup chopped fresh cilantro**

- **¼ cup thinly sliced white onion**

- **1 teaspoon granulated garlic or garlic powder**

- **2 tablespoons ground cumin**

- **2 tablespoons avocado oil**

- **12 corn tortillas** (see page 160 for tips on warming)

DIRECTIONS

1. In a food processor, blend the crema, 1 teaspoon lime juice, a pinch of sea salt and black pepper, and habañero pepper together. Pour the mixture into a bowl, cover, and refrigerate until ready to use.

2. In a plastic food storage bag, combine the mahi-mahi, lime zest, remaining lime juice, cilantro, onion, garlic, sea salt and black pepper to taste, cumin and avocado oil. Place in the refrigerator and let marinate for 30 minutes.

3. Once the fish has marinated, remove from the refrigerator, drain any excess liquid from the bag, and set aside.

4. In a grill pan, heat the avocado oil over high heat. When the oil is hot, toss in the mahi-mahi along with the contents of the bag and sauté for 4 minutes, turning the fish intermittently. Turn off the heat, cover, and set aside.

5. Warm the tortillas (see page 160) and assemble the tacos. Divide equal portions of the fish among tortillas and add a dollop of the habañero crema and your favorite toppings. Serve immediately.

Key West Grilled Lime- Mustard Swordfish

WITH AVOCADO SALAD

The Florida Keys are a unique set of tropical islands located on the southern tip of Florida. They are a popular destination for snorkeling, SCUBA diving and big-game fishing. Swordfish is an impressive prize and can be caught in local waters year-round.

Swordfish is a single species that makes up its own family and is found throughout the tropical and warm temperate oceans of the world. Swordfish is a large predatory species that migrates widely in search of food. Ninety percent of the time, the swordfish you'll find in the market will be sold in steak form and require very little trimming aside from removing the bloodline.

Key limes, also known as West Indian or Mexican limes, are used in this dish for their authentic regional flavor—Florida is famous for its Key lime pies. This variety of lime is grown all over the world and has more seeds than common Persian limes; their flavor is also much more tart. They are picked when green and turn yellow when ripe.

As with other char-grilled recipes throughout this book, I use a fish grate to protect the fish and to keep my cooking stress free. I highly recommend it.

INGREDIENTS

{ Serves 4 }

- **4 4-ounce swordfish fillets**, bloodline removed

- **Rosemary sea salt** (see page 552) and freshly ground black pepper to taste

- **4 key limes**, juice and zest

- **3 sprigs fresh thyme**, leaves only

- **4 tablespoons Dijon mustard**

- **1 tablespoon olive oil**

- **1 clove garlic**, minced

- **Avocado salad** (see page 544)

SERVING SUGGESTIONS: SAFFRON RICE (SEE PAGE 412)

DIRECTIONS

1. Preheat a natural lump charcoal grill to medium-high.

2. Lightly season both sides of the swordfish with rosemary sea salt and black pepper to taste; set aside.

3. In a small bowl, combine the key lime juice and zest, fresh thyme, Dijon mustard, olive oil and garlic. In a large food storage bag or shallow baking dish, cover the swordfish with the marinade, making sure that both sides of the fish are well coated. Place the fish in the refrigerator to marinate for 10 minutes.

4. Once the fish has marinated, remove it from the bag and place it on a clean surface. Blot the fish to remove any excess marinade then place in a fish grate and secure the grate closed. Place the grate on a preheated grill and cook for 4–5 minutes on each side.

5. When the fish is finished cooking, remove it from the grill and allow it to rest for a minute or two. Serve with avocado salad on the side and saffron rice if desired.

Maltese Spinach & Artichoke Stuffed Swordfish

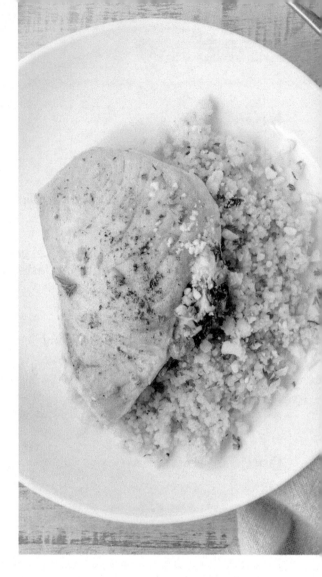

The Republic of Malta is an archipelago that sits between Sicily and North Africa. It's made up of three islands known as Gozo, Comino and Malta, the latter of which is the largest of the three islands and serves as the republic's cultural and administrative hub.

Malta, as the set of islands is often referred to, has a gastronomy scene colored by its proximity to Europe and Africa as well as the various cultures that have inhabited the islands. Tomatoes, olives and cheese are commonly used ingredients, and this recipe for stuffed swordfish is an excellent way to enjoy the flavors of the island.

Stuffing fish is a simple and delicious preparation—you simply make a small pocket in the fish and add flavorful ingredients. When I first began stuffing fish, particularly swordfish, salmon and catfish, I had a tendency to over-stuff, resulting in the filling oozing all over the pan. Since those early days, I have learned to be more modest in my approach and have achieved beautiful results. I encourage you to do the same.

A couple of things to keep in mind when making this recipe: When you cut the pockets in your fish, make sure you cut right in the center so that both sides of the fish are even. Also, once the fish is cooking on the stove, you can use the back of a spoon to force the stuffing back into the fish.

INGREDIENTS

- **Olive oil**, as needed

- **2 cloves garlic**, minced

- **1 pound baby spinach**, chopped

- **1 8-ounce jar roasted artichokes**, chopped

- **3 sun-dried tomatoes in oil**, minced

- **1 large lemon**, juice and zest

- **¼ cup crumbled feta cheese**

- **4 4-ounce swordfish steaks**, about 1 inch thick, with bloodline removed

- **Sea salt and freshly ground black pepper to taste**

SERVING SUGGESTIONS:
SAFFRON RICE (SEE PAGE 412)

DIRECTIONS { Serves 4 }

1. Preheat oven to 375°F.

2. In a large skillet, heat 1 tablespoon of olive oil over medium heat. Add the garlic and cook for 1 minute. Add the spinach and cook until it wilts. Place mixture in a bowl and set aside to cool.

3. Once the spinach is cool, add roasted artichokes, sun-dried tomatoes, lemon juice and zest, and feta cheese to the bowl and mix to combine. Taste for seasoning and adjust with sea salt and freshly ground black pepper as needed. Set aside.

4. Place the swordfish steaks on a clean surface. with a small paring knife, cut a 1½–2-inch slit in the side of each steak. Season steaks with a pinch of sea salt and freshly ground black pepper on both sides. With a spoon, stuff each swordfish steak with about 1 tablespoon of the spinach stuffing, pushing the mixture as far in as possible without tearing the flesh. Set aside.

5. In a large cast iron skillet, heat 1 tablespoon of olive oil over medium-high heat. Once hot, add the swordfish, flat side down, and cook for 3 minutes—you may have to do this in two batches, depending on the size of your skillet. If this is the case, line a baking sheet with parchment paper and set the fish steaks on top once the 3-minute cooking time is done.

6. With a large spatula, turn the fish over and cook for 2 minutes. Add a little more olive oil to the pan if it seems dry. Once all the fish is done, place the steaks on a lined baking sheet and bake in the oven for 5 minutes to finish cooking through.

7. Allow the fish to rest briefly before serving with saffron rice or your favorite side dish.

Cuban Swordfish Brochettes

~~~~~~~~~~

WITH FRESH CILANTRO SOFRITO

Surrounded by the Caribbean Sea, the Gulf of Mexico, and the Atlantic Ocean, the island nation of Cuba contains more than 3,500 miles of stunning tropical coastline. It is the largest island in the Caribbean, followed by Hispaniola, which is made up of two independent nations—the Dominican Republic and the Republic of Haiti.

The gastronomy of the island is heavily influenced by the flavors of Africa, North America, Spain and indigenous people. The cuisine of the region is flavorful, but not spicy as often assumed.

Cubans love their pork and beef, but seafood plays a big role in the local fare. Black beans and rice, otherwise known as Moros y Cristianos, is a staple food in the country that can be made up to one day in advance— see the recipe on page 370.

INGREDIENTS

{ Serves 4 }

- **½ bunch fresh cilantro**

- **2 cloves garlic**

- **1 large lime**, juice and zest

- **2 tablespoons ground cumin**

- **2 tablespoons olive oil**

- **½ teaspoon sea salt**

- **1 tablespoon water**

- **2 pounds swordfish steaks**, bloodline removed, cut into 1-inch pieces

- **2 medium bell peppers (any color)**, seeded and cut into 1-inch pieces

- **8-10 fresh pineapple chunks**

- **1 large onion**, cut into 1-inch pieces

SERVING SUGGESTIONS: CUBAN MOROS Y CRISTIANOS (SEE PAGE 370), TOSTONES (SEE PAGE 404), AVOCADO SALAD (SEE PAGE 544)

DIRECTIONS

SPECIAL EQUIPMENT: METAL SKEWERS

1. In a food processor, combine the cilantro, garlic, lime juice and zest, cumin, olive oil and sea salt. Pulse until smooth. Add a little water if needed. Set aside.

2. Place the fish in a large resealable food storage bag and add the marinade, making sure all the fish pieces are thoroughly coated. Close the bag and refrigerate for 20 minutes.

3. Meanwhile, heat a natural lump charcoal grill to medium-high heat.

4. Once the grill is hot and the fish has marinated, remove the fish from the refrigerator. Artfully add a piece of fish to a skewer, followed by a piece of bell pepper, onion and pineapple. Repeat with the remaining fish and vegetables. Place the skewers on the grill and cook on one side for 3 minutes, then rotate skewers and close the lid. Cook for another 2 minutes, being careful not to overcook. Remove the skewers from the grill and place on a clean platter.

5. Serve the skewers with a scoop of Moros y Cristianos, a side of tostones and a serving of avocado salad as desired.

Costa Rican Pink Guava -Basted Swordfish Casado

Located in Central America, Costa Rica is a fascinating country that boasts a coastline of more than 800 miles along the Caribbean Sea and the Pacific Ocean. Roughly one quarter of the country is protected jungle territory and known as one of the most biodiverse places on the planet.

Costa Rica's climate fosters a diverse mix of tropical produce, including guava, a large tropical berry that can be found throughout the Caribbean, Central America, Mexico and South America. It has beautiful pink flesh and a sweet flavor and floral essence. Some describe guava as tasting like a cross between a strawberry and pear. There are six different varieties of guava, which are classified by the color of their flesh.

I use guava paste for this recipe—a dense purée of guava fruit and sugar that comes in a spongy block. The habañero pepper gives the guava sauce a little kick that delightfully contrasts with the sweetness of the guava.

A Casado is a typical Costa Rican plate of food that includes beans, rice, plantains, tortillas, salad and a protein of choice. It is traditionally the largest meal of the day. The word Casado means "married man" in Spanish and the dish is thought to have been created when local restaurant customers asked to be treated as casados in hopes of getting a home-cooked meal.

INGREDIENTS

- 2 tablespoons minced white onion

- 1 clove garlic, minced

- 1 tablespoon avocado oil, plus more as needed

- ½ cup water

- 3 ounces or a 2-inch piece of solid Guava paste, diced

- 2 tablespoons ketchup

- 2 large lime, juice and 1 teaspoon zest

- 1 large orange, juice only

- 1 small habañero pepper, halved

- Sea salt and freshly ground black pepper to taste

- 4 4-ounce swordfish steaks, bloodline removed

- 1 tablespoon avocado oil or your favorite vegetable oil

- 4–8 warmed corn tortillas (see page 160), for serving

DIRECTIONS

1.   Preheat a lump charcoal grill to medium-high.

2.   In a medium-sized saucepan, sauté the onion and garlic in a little avocado oil over medium heat; cook until softened. Reduce the heat to low and add the water and pieces of guava paste. Stir occasionally with a rubber spatula, breaking up the guava pieces until the paste dissolves. Add the ketchup, lime juice and zest, orange juice and habañero pepper and stir to combine. When the mixture is smooth, taste for seasoning and add sea salt and black pepper as needed. Set aside and allow the mixture to cool.

3.   Place the swordfish on a clean surface and season with sea salt and freshly ground black pepper, then rub each side with avocado oil. Using a pastry brush, add a light layer of the cooled guava sauce on both sides of the fish. Place the swordfish in fish grates and secure; or if adding directly to the hot barbecue grill, use a little avocado oil to wipe down the grill grates. Place the fish on the grill and cook on each side for 4–6 minutes, until the outside browns and the inside remains slightly pink.

4.   Once done, remove the fish from the grill and allow it to rest for a couple of minutes—the residual heat will cook the fish through.

5.   To serve, place the fish pieces on individual plates and add your Casado ingredients of choice. Serve immediately with the warmed tortillas.

SERVING SUGGESTIONS:
BRAZILIAN FEIJOADA (SEE PAGE 376), STEAMED RICE, TOSTONES (SEE PAGE 404) OR MUDROS PLANTAINS (SEE PAGE 406), AVOCADO SALAD (SEE PAGE 544)

La Jolla Yellowtail

WITH APPLE & WALNUT SALAD

La Jolla is a seaside city in San Diego County with a gorgeous, rugged Pacific coastline. Along with its beauty and world-class zoo, the city is also known for its fishing excursions that offer plenty of opportunities to catch large game fish like mahi-mahi, swordfish and yellowtail.

With its sweet mild flavor, yellowtail works great alongside these California-inspired ingredients. This dish is a great occasion to break out your favorite specialty oil for the salad.

Specialty oils are high-end culinary oils used for finishing dishes or as part of a dressing. I often receive them as gifts around the holidays, and I love it—my friends and family know me well! Though they can sometimes be a splurge budget-wise, I always find them to be worth it. Natural almond, macadamia, pumpkin and walnut seed oil are delicious finishing oils, as are infused oils like lemon or garlic.

Crisp, mildly sweet apples like Fuji and Gala are my top choices for this dish, Granny Smith is another favorite.

INGREDIENTS

VINAIGRETTE DRESSING:

½ cup orange juice

1 tablespoon honey

¼ cup champagne vinegar

2 shallots, minced

3 sprigs fresh mint, chopped

1 tablespoon Dijon mustard

¼ cup avocado oil or your favorite specialty oil

Sea salt and freshly ground black pepper to taste

YELLOWTAIL:

4 4-ounce yellowtail fillets, skin and bloodline removed

2 tablespoon lemon juice

1 tablespoon avocado oil (for drizzling fish)

Pinch sea salt and freshly ground black pepper

WALNUT SALAD:

2 large Fuji or Gala apples, sliced

¼ cup crumbled feta cheese

½ cup toasted walnuts

6 cups salad greens: a mix of Bibb, Romaine and radicchio

Sea salt and black pepper to taste

DIRECTIONS

{ Serves 4 }

1. To make the vinaigrette, whisk together the orange juice, honey, champagne vinegar, shallots, mint and Dijon mustard in a mixing bowl. Gradually add the avocado oil or specialty oil in a steady stream while whisking to emulsify, then season with salt and pepper. Taste for seasoning and adjust as needed; set aside.

2. To make the vinaigrette, whisk together the orange juice, honey, champagne vinegar, shallots, mint and Dijon mustard in a mixing bowl. Gradually add the avocado oil or specialty oil in a steady stream while whisking to emulsify, then season with salt and pepper. Taste for seasoning and adjust as needed; set aside.

3. Meanwhile, in a large mixing bowl, combine the apples, feta cheese, walnuts, salad greens and sea salt and black pepper to taste. Mix thoroughly, cover, and refrigerate.

4. To cook the fish, heat a grill pan to medium-high heat. Drain any residual marinade from the dish. Blot any excess moisture off the yellowtail with a paper towel, then place in the hot pan. Cook for 3 minutes on each side, taking care not to overcook. Remove fish from heat and allow it to rest for about 1 minute.

5. To serve, drizzle the salad with the vinaigrette and toss to combine. Divide salad evenly among 4 plates and top with a piece of fish. Serve immediately.

Sri Lankan Curried Tuna & Dhal (Red Lentils)

Perched just outside of India is the tropical South Asian island of Sri Lanka, a country famous for its curries and rice. In fact, the national dish is rice and curry. When visiting you will no doubt be exposed to spicy, saucy dishes of every persuasion with a dash of coconut milk. One of my favorite meals from this region is tuna curry.

Sri Lankan seafood curries are chunky and generous, with lots of gorgeous sauce—the perfect bed for a bowl of fluffy basmati rice. Tuna is often used in fragrant and savory dishes in places like Colombo, the capital city that has its own world-renowned curry blend which is used here. Yellowfin and bigeye are the most common of the nine tuna varieties found in the Bay of Bengal. Mahi-mahi and yellowtail are good substitutes for tuna.

INGREDIENTS

{ Serves 4 }

- **2 tablespoons avocado oil**

- **1 tablespoon ghee**

- **1 large white onion**, chopped

- **2 cloves garlic**, minced

- **1 large carrot**, chopped

- **1 tablespoon Colombo curry spice blend** (see page 538)

- **2 cups water**

- **2 teaspoons ground dried shrimp**

- **1 bunch (1 cup) fresh cilantro**, large stems removed, chopped

- **1 cup red lentils**, rinsed

- **1 teaspoon white pepper**

- **2 pounds tuna fillets** (or other firm white fish) cut into 2-inch chunks

- **1 cup coconut milk**

- **Sea salt to taste**

- **1 large lime**, sliced into 4 pieces, for serving

SERVING SUGGESTIONS: SAFFRON RICE (SEE PAGE 412) AND NAAN, CHAPATI OR PITA BREAD

DIRECTIONS

1. In a large Dutch oven or soup pot, heat the avocado oil and ghee and over medium-high heat. Add the onion, garlic, carrot and Colombo curry spice blend. Cook until the vegetables are soft and fragrant, but not brown, about 3 minutes.

2. Next, add the water along with the ground shrimp, half of the fresh cilantro, lentils and white pepper. Bring to a boil, then reduce the heat to simmer and cover for 5 minutes.

3. Add the fish and coconut milk; cover and cook for another 5 minutes.

4. Taste for seasoning and add salt as needed. Cover and let the pot sit for a few minutes before serving. Serve with lime wedges and garnish with remaining fresh cilantro. Serve family-style in a large serving dish or divide among 4 individual bowls. Serve immediately with steamed rice and naan, chapati or pita bread as desired.

Sicilian Spaghetti al Tonno (*Tuna*)

WITH EGGPLANT

The gastronomy of the Italian island of Sicily is a culmination of the various cultures that have influenced the region including France, Greece, North Africa and Spain.

Bluefin tuna is the most common variety of tuna found in the waters of Italy, which once had a thriving commercial market. This recipe calls for high-quality canned or jarred tuna in oil, which is excellent for this dish. Though it is botanically considered a fruit due to its seeds, eggplant is culinarily treated as a vegetable. The eggplants in Sicily are legendarily large and are purple with white stripes—earning them the name "graffiti" eggplant.

Salting the eggplant will trigger a process called osmosis, which draws water out of the plant. This will help prevent the fruit from getting waterlogged while in the sauce and will reduce the amount of oil it absorbs. It also helps condense the flavor of the vegetable, so don't skip this step!

INGREDIENTS

1 large purple Italian or Sicilian eggplant, peeled and sliced into rounds

Sea salt, as needed

Freshly ground black pepper, as needed

1 pound dried spaghetti noodles

3 tablespoons olive oil, plus more as needed

2 cloves garlic, minced

1 large shallot, minced

2 sprigs fresh oregano, leaves only, or 1 teaspoon dried oregano

1 cup crushed tomatoes

2 teaspoons capers in brine, drained

2 teaspoons red pepper flake

2 anchovy fillets

8 ounces Italian tuna in oil, drained and the oil reserved

8-10 pitted green olives

½ bunch fresh Italian parsley, chopped for garnish

DIRECTIONS

1. Place the eggplant slices on a clean surface and lightly salt both sides. Set aside for 15 minutes, allowing the excess moisture to draw out from the plant. When the time is up, rinse the eggplant and use paper towels to pat dry, gently squeezing as needed. Add a few cracks of black pepper and set aside.

2. Cook the pasta per package instructions. Drain and place in a resealable food storage bag along with a splash of olive oil. Set aside.

3. In a large non-stick pan, heat 1 teaspoon of olive oil over medium-high heat. Add the eggplant in batches and cook on one side for 2–3 minutes until lightly brown and supple. Add more oil to the pan as needed. Use tongs to turn the eggplant slices over and cook for another 2–3 minutes. Place on a clean plate and set aside.

4. In the same pan used to cook the eggplant, heat a tablespoon of olive oil over medium-high heat. Add the reserved tuna oil, garlic, shallot and oregano. Cook until fragrant, about 1 minute. Add the crushed tomatoes, capers, red pepper flake and the anchovies and stir to combine. Reduce heat to a simmer and cook for 5 minutes.

5. When the eggplant is cool to the touch, chop into bite-sized pieces and add it to the pan along with the tuna and olives. Stir to combine. Taste for seasoning and adjust as needed. Cook for 3–4 minutes or until the tuna is heated through.

6. Add the cooked pasta to the pan and use a pair of tongs and toss to combine in the sauce. To serve, place equal portions of the spaghetti on 4 or 6 plates. Garnish with fresh parsley and serve immediately.

Kadavu Island Wahoo Fish Tacos

The Republic of Fiji is a group of volcanic islands in the South Pacific Ocean made up of roughly 1,200 miles of coastline and more than 330 islands. The sublimely beautiful island of Kadavu (pronounced kahn-da-voo) is the fourth largest Island in the archipelago. This rugged and remote island is a SCUBA diver's paradise with crystal-clear water and the Great Astrolabe Reef to explore. It's also an angler's paradise.

Sportfishing is big in this area. So important in fact, that local restaurants on Kadavu often offer a catch-and-eat service where guests are invited to bring their catch of the day in for preparation and dining. Wahoo is a popular choice.

Also known as ono (meaning "delicious" or "good to eat" in Hawaiian), wahoo is a large, highly prized game fish. It has an elongated body and looks a little like tuna. Wahoo are found in tropical and subtropical waters of the Atlantic, Indian and Pacific Oceans, including the Caribbean and Mediterranean seas. They also go by the name "Pacific kingfish" in some territories. They are closely related to king mackerel and have lean flesh that cooks up similar to swordfish.

INGREDIENTS

{ Serves 4 }

- **1 large orange**, juice and zest

- **1 large lime**, juice only

- **1 cup coconut milk**

- **1 thumb ginger**, grated

- **1 small Fijian bongo chili or habañero pepper**, halved

- **½ teaspoon sea salt**

- **1 pound wahoo**, skin and bloodline removed, cut into large chunks

- **8 corn tortillas**

  2 cups mango salsa (see page 564)

- **1 cup shredded green cabbage**

SERVING SUGGESTIONS: COCONUT RICE (SEE PAGE 418), AVOCADO SALAD (SEE PAGE 544)

DIRECTIONS

1. Preheat a natural lump charcoal grill to medium-high.

2. In a medium-sized bowl, whisk together the orange juice and zest, lime juice, coconut milk, ginger, bongo chili or habañero pepper, and sea salt. Pour the marinade into a large resealable food storage bag. Add the fish, seal the bag, and refrigerate for 15 minutes.

3. Once the fish has marinated, remove the bag from the refrigerator and drain the liquid. Place the fish pieces on a clean surface and add them to metal or wooden skewers. Place the fish skewers on a well oiled preheated grill and cook for 3–4 minutes, turning occasionally. When done, remove from the heat and set aside.

4. Meanwhile, warm the tortillas (see page 160) and set aside.

5. To make the tacos, add equal portions of the grilled wahoo to each tortilla. Top with mango salsa and shredded cabbage. Serve immediately with coconut rice or avocado salad as desired.

Shark
& Skate
Recipes

Taking a Bite out of Shark

Cue the eerie music. I know what you may be thinking, but despite its status as an ocean villain, the average shark is more likely to end up on your plate than the other way around.

Much like cilantro or mayonnaise, shark is something that you either have an affinity for or avoid altogether. I happen to love the flavor and texture of this slightly gamey fish.

Seafood has been a long-standing food source around the world for centuries, and shark has played a major role in places like Asia, where it's considered to have medicinal properties, and in Iceland, where the national dish is shark that is dried, fermented and made into a pungent dish called Hákarl.

Not all sharks are edible. Blacktip, mako and thresher are the most highly prized species of edible shark and the best tasting. These are smaller sharks—we're not talking Jaws here. At market size, these sharks are about 125 pounds and 12–14 feet in length. The flesh of these sharks is moist and slightly sweet, with a full-bodied, meaty taste.

U.S shark fisheries are among the most sustainable and lead the industry with best practices. For decades, fishers from the U.S have worked under some of the most robust standards established. According to the National Oceanographic and Atmospheric Administration (NOAA), the idea that all sharks are endangered is false, although in some countries overfishing remains an issue. When shopping for shark, look for varieties from the U.S. or those with the MSC label.

Maracas Bay Bake & Shark Sandwich

Can you hear the soca music playing in the background? The twin islands of Trinidad and Tobago, or "T&T" for short, are known for their biodiverse environments, tropical rainforests and pulsating music scenes.

One of the region's most popular beaches is Maracas Bay, located on the north side of Trinidad and arguably one of the finest beaches in the area. The classic street food called bake & shark can be found at the dozens of food stalls strewn along the beach, where hundreds of these fried fish sandwiches are served daily. One of the most celebrated of these food stalls is Richard's Bake & Shark, a favorite of both tourists and locals.

The "bake" is a humble fried bread and the "shark" is a boneless shark fillet marinated in a spice blend and deep fried. They combine to make a simple sandwich served with lots of toppings and condiments. Shark is sometimes substituted with tilapia, skate or another firm white fish.

Every household on the island has their own recipe for the shark marinade, and some cooks even choose to marinate the fish overnight. My recipe is designed for minimal time in the kitchen with maximum flavor. One thing to note is that the shark is traditionally fried for this dish, but it works great grilled over natural lump charcoal.

The bake recipe below is adapted from a popular Caribbean website called Simply Caribbean. For an authentic experience (and if you are feeling extra ambitious), you can make your own fry bread, but I have found that good-quality brioche or telera rolls make good alternatives.

INGREDIENTS

PAN-FRIED SHRIMP:

- **4 4-ounce shark fillets**, skin and bloodline removed, sliced into ½ inch or ¾ inch fillets

- **1 large lime**, juice and zest

- **2 cloves garlic**, peeled

- **1 cup cilantro**, leaves only

- **2 tablespoons fresh thyme**, leaves only

- **½ habañero pepper** (optional)

- **1 small white onion**, peeled and halved

- **2 scallions**, green and white parts, sliced

- **2 tablespoons water**, more as needed

- **1½ cups all-purpose flour**

- **Sea salt and freshly ground black pepper to taste**

- **2 cups vegetable oil**, plus more as needed for frying

BAKE:

- **2 cups all-purpose flour**

- **2 teaspoons baking powder**

- **1 teaspoon sea salt**

- **½ cup butter**, room temperature

- **1 teaspoon sugar**

- **¾ cup warm water**, more as needed

- **2 cups vegetable oil for frying**, more as needed

DIRECTIONS

Make the Bake:

In a large bowl, sift together the flour, baking powder and salt. Add the butter and sugar and mix with a fork or pastry cutter. Make a well in the center of the flour and slowly add the water, using your hand to stir, and add more water as needed until a soft smooth dough comes together.

Add the dough to a clean surface that has been dusted with a bit of flour and gently knead. Place the dough in a clean bowl, cover with a damp tea towel, and let rest for 25 minutes.

Divide the dough into 6–8 pieces and roll into balls. Flatten into discs using a rolling pin—take care not to flatten too much or the bread will turn out stiff. Set aside.

Heat the oil over medium-high heat and fry the dough until brown on both sides. The bread will puff up but flatten while cooling. Remove and set aside.

Make the Shark:

Place the fish on a plate and squeeze the lime juice over both sides. Set aside.

In a food processor add the garlic, cilantro, thyme, habañero pepper, onion, scallions, lime zest and water and pulse to combine into a thick paste. Add the paste to a plastic bag along with the fish. Gently massage the marinade into the fish to ensure the shark is well coated. Refrigerate for 20 minutes or overnight.

After the fish has marinated, remove it from the bag and dredge it thoroughly in the flour. Set aside. In a large skillet, heat the oil over medium-high heat and cook the shark for 2–3 minutes on each side. Drain the fish on a rack or bed of paper towels.

To assemble the sandwiches, slice each bake in half lengthwise, add a piece of shark, and layer on the toppings as desired. Serve immediately.

SUGGESTED TOPPINGS:
MANGO CHUTNEY, THINLY SLICED RED ONION, AVOCADO, LETTUCE, CUCUMBER, TOMATO, PINEAPPLE SLICES, TAMARIND SAUCE, PEPPER SAUCE, COLESLAW, PINEAPPLE CHOW (SEE PAGE 540), CUBAN PLÁTANOS MADUROS (SEE PAGE 406)

Channel Islands Wild Shark

IN TOMATO SAUCE

Made up of five islands along the Santa Barbara Channel, Channel Islands National Park is a region often referred to as the "Galápagos of North America." The islands are home to more than 2,000 plant and animal species, including Pacific thresher sharks.

Thresher is among the most sustainable of all sharks and is particularly popular with big game anglers around Catalina Island, one of the five landmasses that make up the Channel Islands.

The flesh of thresher sharks is moist and slightly pink with a firm texture. The flavor is mild and slightly gamey—in a good way. If you have a hard time finding shark, you can substitute it with swordfish, mahi mahi or yellowtail.

INGREDIENTS

{ Serves 2-4 }

- **2 tablespoons avocado oil**

- **2 cloves garlic**, minced

- **1 cup (about ½ large) Spanish onion,** sliced

- **1 cup canned crushed tomatoes**

- **½ cup water**

- **2 tablespoons fresh thyme**, leaves only

- **2 tablespoons toasted pine nuts,** roughly chopped

- **2 teaspoons red pepper flake**, crushed

- **1 large lime**, juice and zest

- **Smoked paprika sea salt to taste**

- **Freshly ground black pepper to taste**

- **2 pounds boneless thresher or mako shark fillets**, skinned and cut into 1-inch cubes

- **1 bunch fresh cilantro**, leaves only

SERVING SUGGESTIONS: COOKED PASTA, STEAMED RICE, TUNISIAN VEGETABLE COUSCOUS (SEE PAGE 420), CRUSTY FRENCH BREAD

DIRECTIONS

1. In a large cast iron skillet or Dutch oven, heat the avocado oil over medium-high heat. Add the garlic and onion and sauté until soft and fragrant. Pour in the crushed tomatoes, water, thyme leaves, toasted pine nuts, red pepper flake, lime juice and zest, and smoked paprika sea salt and black pepper to taste. Stir to combine and cook for 8–10 minutes over low heat.

2. Add the cubed shark and stir, coating the fish in the tomato sauce. Cover and cook for 6–8 minutes over medium heat. Taste the sauce for seasoning and adjust as needed.

3. Turn off the heat and allow the fish to rest for a couple of minutes before serving. Garnish with fresh cilantro. Serve immediately with pasta, steamed rice, Tunisian vegetable couscous or French bread.

Isla Mujeres Shark Tacos

WITH AVOCADO CREMA

Isla Mujeres is an unforgettable island where life seems to slow down immediately upon arrival. The turquoise blue water, balmy weather and island vibe are intoxicating. This "Island of Women" is considered a part of the Mexican Caribbean and is a short boat ride from Cancun that boasts lots of water sports, fishing expeditions, SCUBA diving and good food.

During my first visit to the island, my boyfriend (now husband) and I rented a motorbike and set off for a tour of the area. As we rolled along the rocky coast-lined highway, the wind at our backs, we stopped to enjoy tacos and cerveza at the various food huts along the way. This shark taco recipe is my version of the one that I enjoyed on the trip.

INGREDIENTS

Makes 10-12 Tacos

- **2 pounds shark**, skinned and bloodline removed, cut into strips or chunks

- **3 tablespoons avocado oil**, separated 1 lime, juice and zest

- **½ bunch fresh cilantro or ¼ cup**, leaves only

- **2 cloves fresh garlic**, minced, or 1 teaspoon garlic powder

- **1 serrano pepper**, seeded (optional) and minced

- **Sea salt**, to taste

- **Avocado crema** (see page 556)

- **12 corn tortillas**, warmed (see page 158)

SERVING SUGGESTIONS: LIME WEDGES, SLICED RED ONION, MANGO SALSA (SEE PAGE 548), PICKLED CARROTS, COTIJA CHEESE, SHREDDED CABBAGE

DIRECTIONS

1. Add the shark to a resealable food storage bag along with 1 tablespoon of the avocado oil, lime juice and zest, cilantro, garlic, serrano pepper and a pinch of salt. Gently shake the bag to combine and marinate for 20 minutes.

2. Heat a grill pan or skillet over medium-high heat.

3. Drain any excess moisture from the shark marinade then add the fish to the hot pan and cook for 2–3 minutes on each side, taking care not to overcook.

4. To serve, add equal portions of the shark to the tortillas, add desired toppings, and serve immediately.

Rolling with Skate

Skate is a bottom-dwelling fish that is a member of the ray family and a close relative of sharks. The edible portions of the fish are its large pectoral muscles that resemble wings since skates are shaped like a kite. This shape allows them to lay flat and disappear into the sand on the bottom of the ocean floor.

Served up at fancy restaurants the world over from Beijing to Paris, skate wings can be quite expensive, yet most markets sell them at an attractive price, making home cooking not only economical, but adventurous. The muscle structure of the wing makes for a beautiful, exotic-looking presentation with its flesh situated long narrow strips.

Skates can grow very large, but those caught commercially are usually between 1½ and 2 feet wide. Each wing has a thin layer of meat on either side with a layer of cartilage in between. The skin is inedible so wings are typically sold skinless, although you can find them whole skin-on in some places. Tender with mild gamey flavor, skate cooks up fast.

When shopping, look for fish that are reddish in color with shiny, moist looking flesh. You can buy skate as whole wings, filleted or as cheeks and most often frozen. If buying fresh, store them in the coldest part of your refrigerator and use immediately. Skate is highly perishable and needs to be used within the first or second day of purchasing. As with sharks, the circulation system of skate makes it important to ice the fish immediately after capture to prevent the development of ammonia—skate and shark excrete waste through their skin. If you happen to smell a hint of ammonia on your skate wings, there is no need to worry, it will disappear during the cooking process. If the scent is overwhelming, however, it is ill advised to cook them, as doing so may result in funky tasting fish.

Thaw frozen skate in the refrigerator overnight or sealed in plastic in a bath of cool water. In a pinch, fillets can be cooked from frozen en papillote style, wrapped in parchment paper and baked in the oven.

My favorite ways to enjoy skate are cooked with capers and tomatoes or served as fish & chips—recipes you'll find in the following section.

La Rochelle Skate Wings

WITH LEMON & CAPERS

La Rochelle is a coastal town located in Southwestern France that is filled with bustling markets, interesting architecture, and the faint scent of an ocean breeze! The gastronomy scene is exciting with streets filled with bars, restaurants and bistros. The city also has a gorgeous open air market, Marché du Centre Ville, where you will find fishmongers selling all types of seafood, including skate wings tucked in among the prawns, monkfish, seabass and oysters.

Skate is a favorite fish in France and the UK. This recipe uses classic ingredients to create a simple, flavorful meal.

INGREDIENTS

{ Serves 4 }

- **4 skate wing fillets**

- **Sea salt and freshly ground black pepper to taste**

- **1 cup all-purpose flour for dusting**

- **3 tablespoons olive oil**, more as needed

- **1 tablespoon ghee** (clarified butter)

- **1 tablespoon fresh lemon juice**

- **1 teaspoon dried thyme**

- **2 tablespoons capers in brine**, drained

SERVING SUGGESTIONS: CAULIFLOWER PARSNIP PURÉE (SEE PAGE 424)

DIRECTIONS

1. Preheat the oven to 375°F.

2. Sprinkle both sides of the skate wings with a pinch of sea salt and black pepper and allow to rest for 5-10 minutes.

3. In a large bowl or paper bag, dredge the skate wings in the flour and shake off any excess; set aside.

4. Heat a large ovenproof skillet over medium heat and add the olive oil and the ghee. When the oil is hot, add the skate wings and cook for about 2 minutes on one side until lightly golden brown. Flip over, cook for 1 minute, then add the lemon juice, capers and thyme. Turn down the heat and shake the pan gently to combine the ingredients, then place the skillet in the oven. Cook for 4 minutes until the skate wings are cooked through.

5. To serve, place the wings on individual plates along with the pan sauce and a scoop of cauliflower parsnip purée.

Buenos Aires Chimichurri Skate Wings

Located on the southern half of South America, Argentina is a country with more than 3,000 miles of coastline. The region loves its asado or barbecue, and steak is king, but the country also has a place in its heart for seafood.

Salmon and shrimp are likely what you'll find on the menus of most restaurants in the region, but if you go the extra mile, you'll find seafood options that range from octopus to squid and if you're lucky— skate wings! Chimichurri is a simple gorgeous green sauce that is used as a condiment, marinade or sauce. Combined with barbecued skate wings, it's a great way to enjoy the flavors of Argentina.

Depending on the size of your skate wings, you can add them to a fish grate to make things easy when flipping and removing the fish from the grill. Otherwise, make sure you add a little oil to the barbecue grates to keep the fish from sticking.

INGREDIENTS

{ Serves 4 }

- **4 large skate wings**, skin removed

- **Sea salt and freshly ground black pepper**

- **1 teaspoon olive oil**

- **1 cup chimichurri sauce** (see page 556), divided

- **Lemon wedges**, for serving

DIRECTIONS

1. Place the skate wings on a clean surface and add a pinch of sea salt and freshly ground black pepper. Set aside for 5 minutes.

2. Place the fish in a large plastic bag along with the olive oil and ½ cup of chimichurri sauce. Seal the bag and use your hands to massage the marinade into the fish to equally distribute. Place the bag in the refrigerator for 15–20 minutes.

3. Meanwhile, using natural lump charcoal, heat the barbecue over moderately high heat.

4. When the coals are ready, remove the bag of fish from the refrigerator. Open the bag, shake off any excess marinade from each skate wing and place them in a fish grate or directly on an oiled grill. Cook for 3 minutes on one side, then flip over and cook for another 3 minutes with the lid closed.

5. Remove the fish from the heat and allow it to rest for 3–4 minutes. To serve, place the fish on individual plates along with a dollop of the remaining chimichurri sauce and lemon wedges.

Shetland Islands Skate Cheeks & Chips

Skate is a popular variety of fish that is prized throughout the United Kingdom. Places like the Shetland Islands have embraced it as part of its "fish & chips" or "chipper" culture and serve up skate as often as haddock, cod and squid rings. Cheeks are a part of the fish located in the jaws and right below the eyes. They are succulent morsels that work great grilled or baked and, in this case, lightly battered and served up with chips.

The Shetland archipelago is brimming with gorgeous local produce and fresh seafood, boasting some of the most productive waters in the world. Wild and cultivated fish are harvested in this region and some of the UK's plumpest and juiciest mussels are grown here.

The chips in this recipe are made in a traditional European style, meaning they require a two-step frying process for authentic texture. Experienced cooks can have two fryers going at the same time to ensure that the skate cheeks and fries are both crispy when serving; if you choose this path, note that you will need to double the amount of oil.

The cheeks of halibut, monkfish or turbot are good substitutes for skate.

INGREDIENTS

{ Serves 4 }

CHIPS

- 1 pound russet potatoes, scrubbed clean and peeled if desired
- 1½ quarts vegetable oil for frying, more as needed

SKATE CHEEKS:

- 1½ pounds skate cheeks or 20 cheeks
- Sea salt and freshly ground black pepper to taste
- 1 cup all-purpose flour, plus more as needed
- ¼ cup rice flour or cornstarch
- 2 teaspoons baking powder
- 1 teaspoon sea salt
- 1 teaspoon paprika
- 1 teaspoon garlic powder
- 1 12-ounce bottle of cold Guinness or your favorite dark beer

DIRECTIONS

1. Preheat oven to 200°F or turn on the warming oven tray.

2. For the chips, slice potatoes into thick sticks—I highly recommend using a mandoline for simplicity and to achieve uniform cuts. Place the cut potatoes in an ice bath to keep them from oxidizing (browning).

3. Remove the cut potatoes from the ice water and dry them on paper towels or tea towels until completely dry. Set aside.

4. In a large Dutch oven, add 1 quart of vegetable oil and heat to 320°F or 330°F.

5. When the oil is ready, add the cut potatoes in batches and cook for 3 minutes. Use a slotted spoon or spider strainer to remove and drain on a paper towel-lined baking sheet. Continue in batches until all of the potatoes are partially cooked. Set aside to cool.

6. To finish cooking the chips, bring the oil up to 375°F, then add the partially cooked potatoes and fry until crispy golden brown. Drain on paper towels. Place drained potatoes on a baking sheet and place in the oven or warming tray to keep warm while you prepare the skate.

7. Place the skate wings on a clean surface and add a dash of sea salt and freshly cracked black pepper to each side and dust with a bit of flour on both sides. Set aside.

8. In a large bowl, add the flour, rice flour, baking powder, sea salt, paprika, garlic powder and beer. Whisk to combine. Allow the batter to rest for 5 minutes; this will give the baking powder time to activate.

9. With the same oil used to cook the chips, turn the temperature to 375°, and add more oil if needed.

10. Lightly dust the skate wings in flour to help the batter adhere, then dredge in the beer batter and add to the hot oil. Cook for 3–4 minutes, turning once, until golden brown. Use a slotted spoon or spider strainer to remove the fish from the oil and drain on paper towels. Repeat the process until all of the skate wings are cooked.

11. To serve, place the fish on individual plates along with equal portions of chips. Serve with malt vinegar, tartar sauce, lemon wedges and ketchup as desired.

SUGGESTED TOPPINGS:
MANGO CHUTNEY, THINLY SLICED RED ONION, AVOCADO, LETTUCE, CUCUMBER, TOMATO, PINEAPPLE SLICES, TAMARIND SAUCE, PEPPER SAUCE, COLESLAW, PINEAPPLE CHOW (SEE PAGE 540), CUBAN PLÁTANOS MADUROS (SEE PAGE 406)

Côte d'Azur Skate Wings Au Poivre

France has a coastline that spans 2,000 miles. One of the most popular communities is the Côte d'Azur or the French Riviera, the glamourous southeastern portion of the country's Mediterranean coastline known for luxury beach resorts and seafood.

Au poivre translates into "with peppercorns" or "with pepper." It's typically used for steak, but it works equally as well with skate wings. This is a classic French bistro recipe, so it shouldn't be surprising that the dish includes wine and cognac. The amounts of alcohol called for are not significant enough to cause intoxication.

The sauce is also excellent on swordfish and pan-fried turbot.

INGREDIENTS

SKATE:

- **4 skate wings fillets or whole wings,** skin removed

- **2 tablespoons olive oil,** more as needed

- **1 tablespoon ghee** (clarified butter)

- **1 cup all-purpose flour**

- **Sea salt and freshly ground black pepper as needed**

PEPPER SAUCE

- **1 tablespoon black peppercorns**

- **2 tablespoons brandy or cognac**

- **1 shallot,** peeled and minced

- **½ cup vegetable broth**

- **½ cup dry white wine**

- **2 tablespoons unsalted butter**

- **Juice of 1 lemon**

- **1 teaspoon lemon zest**

- **¼ cup cream or half-and-half**

- **1 tablespoon corn starch slurry** (corn starch mixed with equal part water), if needed

DIRECTIONS {#} { Serves 4 }

1. Preheat the oven to 200°F or turn on the warming oven tray.

2. To toast the peppercorns, place them in a heavy-bottomed skillet and heat over medium until fragrant, taking care not to burn. Place them in a mortar and crush coarsely with a pestle. Set aside.

3. Season the skate wings with a pinch of sea salt and freshly ground black pepper and dredge in flour; set aside.

4. In a heavy-bottomed skillet, add the olive oil and butter and heat over medium-high heat. Add the skate wings and cook on both sides until golden brown. Remove the fish and place in an ovenproof dish, then place in the oven or warming tray to keep warm. Reserve the pan to make the sauce.

5. Place the pan over high heat and deglaze with the brandy or cognac. Use a wooden spoon to scrape the bottom to release any brown bits and cook for 2 minutes, giving the alcohol time to burn off.

6. Reduce the heat to medium, add the shallot and cook until fragrant, then pour in the vegetable broth and white wine and cook for 2–3 minutes. Add the lemon juice, lemon zest and peppercorns. Stir to combine, then add the half-and-half. Continue to stir, taste for seasoning, and adjust as needed. If the sauce is too thin gradually stir in the corn starch slurry. Cook for 1–2 minutes, then turn off the heat.

7. Remove the skate wings from the oven. Place each piece on individual plates and pour the pepper sauce over the top. Serve immediately.

Salt
Cod

~~~~~~~~~~~

 Mount Pelée Marinades Accras de Morue (Salt Cod Fritters)

Brazilian Codfish & Potato Balls

287

Savoring Salt Cod

Salt cod is an ingredient you'll find throughout the Mediterranean in places like France, Italy, Portugal and Spain. It's also very popular in the Caribbean, which some sources date back to the 15th century. It also goes by the names of saltfish and bacalao.

Salt has served as a food preservative for centuries and gradually became less popular with the advent of refrigeration; however, salt cod has been one of the last holdouts. I suspect that it's because the flavor and texture are hard to replicate any other way. The salt-based dehydration process changes the nature of the fish, which becomes interesting and complex over time.

When buying salt cod, look for the thick center-cut pieces. Tail pieces will be a bit stringy. To make it edible, the salt has to be removed either by soaking overnight or via the "quick boil" method.

TRADITIONAL PREPARATION METHOD

Remove the salt cod from its packaging and rinse under cold water to remove the top layer of salt. Place the cod in a bowl large enough to accommodate its size and add enough cold water to cover the fish. Place the bowl in the refrigerator and soak overnight, changing out the water every 4 to 6 hours to remove the salt.

When ready, drain and rinse the fish well. Remove any bones or skin. Place the fish in a saucepan and cover with cold water. Bring the fish to a boil, then reduce the heat to medium. Cover the pan and simmer for 10 minutes, then drain and rinse the fish under cold water. Set aside until ready to use.

QUICK-BOIL METHOD

Rinse the fish under cold running water for 10–15 minutes. Place the fish in a pan and cover with water, bring to a low simmer, then boil for 3 minutes. Drain the fish, rinse under cold water, then add more water to the pot and repeat 3–4 times. When the fish has cooled, feel for bones and remove.

Mount Pelée Marinades Accras de Morue (Salt Cod Fritters)

WITH AVOCADO CREMA

This recipe hails from Martinique, a French Caribbean island that is the third largest landmass in the Lesser Antilles. One of my favorite college professors was from this island and my fascination for the place has never waned.

The largest town on the island, Fort-de-France is a fun place to visit the island's breathtaking beauty, exciting water sports and delightful Creole cuisine. Mount Pelée is the volcano that dominates the island and brings a sense of mystique to the area. Inspired by the variations of this snack found throughout the Caribbean, these marinades (mah-ree-nods), or salt cod fritters also known as accras de morue, are a delicious start to any island-inspired meal. Unlike other regions of the world that make fritters, this version uses baking powder.

When you think of Caribbean food you likely think of fresh fish roasting over a barbecue, which is often the case. Salt cod, however, is the exception.

INGREDIENTS

- **1½ pounds dried salt cod**, prepared (see page 291)

- **¼ cup chopped scallions**, green part only

- **1 bunch fresh cilantro**, roughly chopped

- **2 cloves garlic**

- **1 small Spanish onion**, finely chopped

- **1 small habañero or Scotch bonnet pepper**, seeded

- **2 sprigs or 1 teaspoon fresh thyme**, leaves only

- **1 cup all-purpose flour**, sifted

- **1 teaspoon baking powder**

- **3½ cups cold water**

- **1½ gallons vegetable oil**, for frying

SERVING SUGGESTIONS: SLICED LIMES, PEPPER SAUCE

DIRECTIONS

1. Flake the prepared salt cod and set aside.

2. In a food processor, combine the scallions, cilantro, garlic, onion, habañero pepper and thyme, pulsing until well combined. Add a bit of water if needed. The mix should be a bit chunky and not smooth. Pour the aromatic mixture into a small bowl and set aside.

3. In a large bowl, combine the flour, baking powder and water, whisking to make a batter. Fold in the aromatic pepper mixture and the salt cod flakes and let stand for 5–6 minutes. The batter is ready when it is thick enough to coat the back of a spoon.

4. Meanwhile, heat the cooking oil to 375°F and set up a bed of paper towels to drain the fritters.

5. When the oil is ready, use a 1-ounce scoop or spoon and drop one fitter into the fryer—this is your test fritter, which is very important. Cook for 2–3 minutes; note that the batter will drop to the bottom then float. Use a pair of chopsticks or a slotted spoon to turn the fritter to ensure it cooks on all sides. When the fritter turns golden brown, use a slotted spoon to remove the fritter, then place on a bed of paper towels. Taste for flavor and doneness. Make adjustments as needed and continue with the remaining batter. Serve immediately with sliced lime as desired.

Brazilian Codfish & Potato Balls

Popular in places like Brazil, Spain, Portugal and New England, this version of salt cod fritters uses potatoes to create a savory, creamy snack. Proper cooking results in light and crispy fish balls with a moist interior. I attribute this recipe to Brazil because it's where I first experienced these fritters; however, the origin of the dish is Portuguese.

Keep the mix light and the cod balls small for crispy, creamy bites.

These require a bit of preparation ahead of time in order to rehydrate the salt cod. See page 291 for tips on how to do this.

INGREDIENTS

{ Serves 4 }

- 3 large russet potatoes, peeled and diced small
- 2 tablespoons ghee or avocado oil
- ½ cup minced Spanish onion
- 3 cloves garlic, minced
- 1½ pounds salt cod, prepared (see page 291)
- 3 tablespoons chopped fresh parsley
- 1 tablespoon paprika
- 1 tablespoon lemon juice
- 2 teaspoons white pepper
- Sea salt to taste
- 2 eggs, yolks and whites separated
- 2 tablespoons all-purpose flour, separated
- 2 cups breadcrumbs
- 1½ quarts vegetable oil, for frying

SERVING SUGGESTIONS: LIME WEDGES AND PEPPER SAUCE

DIRECTIONS

1.   Place the potatoes in a pot and cover with water. Bring to a boil over high heat and cook for 20–25 minutes or until tender. Set aside.

2.   Meanwhile, in a medium saucepan, melt the ghee and sauté the onion and garlic until fragrant and soft. Set aside to cool.

3.   In a food processor, pulse the cod until shredded or use your hands to break up the fish.

4.   In a large bowl, mash the potatoes using a potato masher. Add the cod, the onion and garlic mixture, and the parsley, paprika, lemon juice and white pepper. Mix thoroughly, taste for seasoning, and add salt and additional white pepper as needed. Add the egg yolks and 1 tablespoon of the flour and stir to combine.

5.   In a clean bowl, whip the egg whites into stiff peaks using a hand mixer with a clean whisk attachment (alternately, you can use a stand mixer for this). Gently fold the egg whites into the cod and potato mixture. The mixture should be firm enough to form a ball—if not, stir in the second tablespoon of all purpose flour.

6.   Place the breadcrumbs on a clean surface. Use a 1- or 1½-ounce scoop to measure out portions of the cod mixture, then roll the balls in the breadcrumbs to coat and place them on a baking sheet. Repeat with the rest of the mixture and place the cod balls in the refrigerator for 20 minutes to chill (this will help them stay together during the cooking process).

7.   Meanwhile, in a large Dutch oven, heavy-bottomed pot or deep fryer, heat the oil to 375°F. Set up a cooling rack or a bed of paper towels to drain the finished cod and potato balls.

7.   When the oil is ready, carefully drop the cod balls, a few at a time, into the oil; be careful not to crowd the pan. Cook for 2–3 minutes until golden brown. Use a slotted spoon or spider strainer to remove them and place on the cooling rack or paper towels. Serve immediately with lime wedges or pepper sauce as desired.

Arctic Char, Salmon, Trout & Other Oily Fish Recipes

Know Your Salmon, Arctic Char and Trout

Salmon is a perennial favorite for seafood lovers and casual fish consumers alike. It has consistently been one of the most consumed seafood products worldwide, often coming in second to shrimp as the most globally consumed seafood, according to the Global Aquaculture Alliance. Even people who don't consider themselves fish fanatics often enjoy it—who can turn away a fresh piece of wild-caught sockeye or king salmon with a squeeze of fresh lemon?

In addition to serving as a delicious source of protein for millions, salmon is a culturally important fish and an invaluable economic resource for many communities around the globe, especially for some Native American tribes, who have built spiritual and cultural traditions around this fascinating fish. For Native Nations of the Pacific Northwest, who call themselves Salmon People, salmon is revered and celebrated as one of the First Foods, along with berries, wild game and pure water. The annual salmon harvest represents a rite of passage from one generation to the next.

You'll find two varieties of salmon at the market: **Atlantic and Pacific.**

Atlantic Salmon

Atlantic salmon is native to the North Atlantic Ocean and rivers. Unlike its Pacific counterparts, Atlantic salmon can spawn more than once. Due to its ample fat content, it is great for smoking and candying. All of the Atlantic salmon sold commercially is cultivated or farmed-raised in places like Canada, Chile and Norway. Commercial fishing for wild Atlantic salmon is prohibited in the U.S. because wild population levels in the eastern U.S. are extremely low.

Cultivated Atlantic salmon is primarily sold fresh or frozen, available as dressed fish (with viscera, scales, fins and head removed), or in fillet or steak form.

According to the Food and Agriculture Organization of the United Nations, Atlantic salmon cultivation spans back to the early 19th century in the U.K., where freshwater was stocked with parr (baby salmon) to boost wild fish yield for anglers. Norway took the lead on sea cage cultivation in the 1960s, which started a trend in Scotland, Ireland, Farro Island and later in Canada, the U.S. and Chile. A small level of cultivation also occurs in France, Spain and New Zealand. With this in mind, don't be surprised to find salmon recipes in this book from the unlikeliest of places, like Brazil.

Pacific Salmon

Of the seven species of Pacific salmon, six are native to North America—Chinook (king), coho (silver), sockeye, chum, pink and steelhead. Copper River salmon, the variety that heroically navigates Alaska's 300-mile Copper River to spawn, is not its own species, but can be either coho, king or sockeye varieties. The seventh Pacific salmon, known as masu or cherry salmon, is found only in the western Pacific mostly off the coasts of Japan, Korea and Russia, and will not be covered in this book.

They are not called "kings" for nothing! Chinook, or king salmon, are the largest of the Pacific species and are named for the indigenous Chinookan peoples of the Pacific Northwest. Chinook salmon, celebrated for both their large size and succulent flavor and texture, are commercially harvested in Alaska, Washington and Oregon, and in smaller amounts in California. In North America, Chinook range from Monterey Bay to Alaska, and in other parts of the world like Asia, king salmon inhabit the waters of Siberia all the way south to Hokkaido, Japan.

King salmon account for about 20 percent of the total salmon fished in the Pacific and are one of the most commercially valuable fish in the world. Often weighing more than 30 pounds, Chinook are dubbed "king" both for their large size and reputation as one of the world's most prized salmon varieties.

Coho salmon are one of the most beautifully colored salmon of all. Their ruby-red flesh is worthy of its own lipstick color, nail polish shade, or wall cover hue! Coho are also known as silver salmon because of their dark metallic backs and silver sides and are also sometimes referred to as "medium red," which is a canning term. Coho are the second largest of the Pacific salmon species and can grow up to 25 pounds in size—roughly the Washington State record, as of 2001. Coho can live in both fresh and saltwater and are found throughout the North Pacific Ocean from Alaska to California, all the way to Japan and Russia. Though many places are home to coho—even the landlocked Great Lakes of the U.S.—the majority of the coho harvest comes from Alaska.

Coho salmon have a 3-year life cycle. After spending a little over a year feeding in the ocean, they return to their home stream or river to spawn, according to NOAA Fisheries.

Sockeye salmon are also famous for their vividly colored, neon-like deep orange flesh. With its unmistakably rich, intense flavor and firm texture, sockeye is often considered one of the best-tasting Pacific salmon—there are certainly plenty of sockeye devotees. Weighing in between 5 and 15 pounds, sockeye are among the smallest of the Pacific salmon species and have a lifespan of 3 to 7 years. All commercially available sockeye salmon is caught by U.S. fishers, mainly in Alaskan waters.

Chum salmon are the most widely distributed of all Pacific salmon, according to the Alaska Department of Fish and Game, and are one of the largest next to Chinook, weighing up to

35 pounds. Chum falls closely behind pink salmon as one of the most harvested species, and though it often gets billed as a less desirable salmon variety, it is actually quite delicious. Chum, also known as calico, chub, dog and keta salmon, have their special place in the world as a prized source of dried, smoked and canned fish that is often exported to Asia and Europe. I use chum to make salmon burgers and salmon jerky, and it is always a great choice.

Pink salmon are the smallest of the Pacific salmon, averaging between 3 and 5 pounds, according to the Alaska Department of Fish and Game. Pinks have the shortest life cycle—they mature and complete the circle of life within a two-year time span. What they lack in size, they make up for in abundance—they are the most plentiful of all salmon species and have been harvested and canned since the 1800s. Almost all of the pink salmon harvested in the U.S. comes from Alaskan fisheries, with lesser amounts coming from the states of Washington and Oregon. If you have ever purchased tinned salmon, it's very likely pink salmon, unless otherwise specified.

Pink salmon is one of the main ingredients in my salmon sausage recipe because of its mild flavor, light color, and its ability to take on flavor remarkably well.

Steelhead salmon, often referred to as steelhead trout, salmon trout, rainbow trout, ironhead and steelie, is included in this section because it has been long argued that rainbow trout, especially steelhead, have anatomical and behavioral traits that closely match those of Pacific salmon. They differ from other salmon in that they return to spawn multiple times. With a lifespan of up to four years, steelhead is a prized game fish that can weigh up to 20 pounds. Steelhead has a mild, nutty flavor with tender flesh, making it a deliciously versatile fish.

Rainbow trout and **steelhead** are the same species, but trout live in freshwater only, whereas steelhead are anadromous, meaning they dwell in both fresh and saltwater, like all other salmon species. Rainbow trout is a delicate fish with mild, pleasant flavor. They are one of the top game fish in North America and can usually reach up to 8 pounds. Most of the rainbow trout you'll find in the market will be cultivated and found whole, butterflied or filleted.

Arctic char is a freshwater fish also known as char, sea trout or alpine trout. They are distinguished from their salmon cousins (salmonid) by their light spots and lack of teeth on the bottom portion of their mouth. They are a close relative of the brook trout and have an average weight of 2 to 8 pounds. Char has the characteristics of salmon, trout and steelhead with a meaty texture and mild, delicate buttery flavor.

The range of the Arctic char spans across the polar regions of the world, with the species' largest populations dwelling in the cold waters of Alaska, Iceland, Newfoundland and Russia, where they were an important food source for Native inhabitants. The fish support a variety of sport and commercial fisheries in Canada and Europe, according to the Alaska Department of Fish and Game. A highly sustainable fish, char can be found both wild and cultivated.

In Canada, Arctic char has been harvested since the 1960s, but Inuit and Native populations have been enjoying this fish for centuries and continue to do so, according to the organization Ocean Wise. Char is an important subsistence and cultural food for many indigenous peoples.

FUN FACT Arctic char was served to the Queen of England during her visit to Canada and was the fish option at the U.S. White House dinner during the Clinton Administration in the 1990s.

Once you have selected your salmon fillet, be it the Atlantic or Pacific variety, you will likely need to remove the pin bones that are buried deep in the fish's flesh. If you have selected steaks for a whole fish you can skip this step.

Some salmon producers use machines to remove the pin bones from the fish, but it's always a good idea to check.

Pin bones are thin, needle-like floating bones found along the center of the salmon. Essentially calcified nerve endings that are unattached to the main skeleton, these little bones work to send signals to other salmon and help them sense when another salmon is swimming nearby. They are fairly easy to remove with a pair of kitchen tweezers or a clean pair of needle nose pliers. You don't have to remove pin bones, but doing so will make eating more enjoyable. Here is a simple technique:

- **Run your fingertips along the flesh side of the fillet until you feel the pin bones.**

- **Take a large bowl and turn it upside down. Take care not to tear the flesh and gently lay the fish over the convex of the bowl, which will expose the bones. You can also lay the fish flat and use your fingers to search out the bones.**

- **Using tweezers or pliers, grasp the top of each bone and pull it straight out and away from you. Pulling too far upward or backward will tear the flesh.**

- **Continue until all of the bones have been removed.**

This technique also works on Arctic char and trout. You can leave the pin bones in the fish, but they can be distracting and a bit dangerous if swallowed.

Reducing Albumin

The white stuff that appears on some kinds of fish is not fat. It's a simple protein called albumin that is most evident in salmon and some white fish like halibut. Regardless of how your fish is prepared— broiled, baked or barbecued, this harmless, curd-like substance can appear at any time.

According to the University of Alaska's Seafood Science department, albumin lives in fish in liquid form and appears when the muscle fibers in fish are heated and contract, pushing out the white-colored protein.

Some cooks believe that albumin only appears when fish is cooked fast and hot, but my experience proves that it is unpredictable and appears randomly. Every fish is unique, so the amount of albumin released in each fish varies.

Although perfectly safe to eat, albumin can be viewed as unsightly for some cooks.

There are two good options to help with presenting a fish covered in albumin. You can use a moist paper towel to blot away the protein, followed up by a little detail work using the pointed end of a chopstick to clean things up. Alternately, you can simply use a beautiful, full garnish.

A more proactive approach is to quickly brine your fish prior to cooking. A quick soak in a blend of salt and water—1 tablespoon per cup of water—will help dissolve the muscle fibers of your fish and will help minimize the appearance of albumin.

Another option is to salt the fish and let it sit for 20–30 minutes. It will begin to sweat and release the protein. It's easier than brining, and it's convenient in a pinch.

Emerald City Slow-Roasted Salmon Steaks

Seattle, Washington is also known as the Emerald City—not because Dorothy, Toto and the Wizard of Oz live there, but rather due to the city being surrounded by stunning greenery all year long thanks to the region's unique weather conditions and constant rainfall.

My friends who live in the area harvest salmon on a regular basis, often stashing several pounds in the freezer, and are always looking for new ways to experience this fish. An interesting way to enjoy salmon is by slow-roasting it. Cooking salmon low and slow results in a luscious, almost creamy texture.

This recipe calls for salmon steaks, a cross-section of the whole drawn (gutted) fish that contains bones. Cooking fish on the bone adds rich flavor and a good serving of collagen, a protein that has multiple health benefits.

INGREDIENTS

{ Makes 2 pounds salmon steaks }

- 2 pounds salmon steaks
- Sea salt and black pepper

DIRECTIONS

1. Preheat oven to 250°F.

2. Season the salmon with sea salt and black pepper. Place the fish in a large cast iron skillet or on a baking sheet and bake for 25 minutes.

3. Remove the fish from the oven and serve as desired—I suggest serving with cauliflower parsnip purée (see page 424), sautéed Broccolini (see page 422).

Central Coast Char-Grilled Salmon Brochettes

WITH SPICY APRICOT SAUCE

Savory salmon combined with sweet and tart apricot is a wonderful flavor combination with roots in Central California. This recipe shines at parties and outdoor cookouts. It's mouthwatering and easy to make, since the spicy apricot sauce can be prepared well in advance and the salmon brochettes can be assembled up to a day ahead.

Using jarred barbeque sauce and apricot jam cuts down on prep time, and the spicy red pepper flake adds a nice kick of flavor. Feel free to add veggies like onion and bell pepper if you'd like.

I use both wooden skewers and metal skewers for this depending on the occasion—wooden for outdoor parties for easy clean-up, and metal for home fêtes, where I can easily stick them in the dishwasher. A fish grate also comes in handy here; I use one to ensure stress-free cooking.

INGREDIENTS

{ Serves 5 }

- **¼ cup water**

- **1 cup of your favorite barbeque sauce**

- **½ cup apricot jam**

- **1 small clove garlic**, minced

- **2 tablespoons red pepper flake**

- **2 teaspoons dried ginger**

- **3 sprigs fresh thyme**, leaves only

- **1 small lemon**, juice and zest

- **Sea salt and freshly ground black pepper**

- **2 pounds Atlantic salmon**, cut into 20 1-inch chunks

- **Optional: Onion, bell pepper, lemon**

SERVING SUGGESTIONS: SAFFRON RICE (SEE PAGE 412)

DIRECTIONS

1. To make the sauce, combine the water, barbeque sauce, apricot jam, garlic, red pepper flake, dried ginger, thyme, 1 tablespoon of lemon juice and 1 teaspoon of lemon zest in a small saucepan. Whisk thoroughly and simmer over low heat for 3 minutes. The sauce should be thick and coat the back of a spoon. Turn off the stove and allow sauce to cool. Taste for seasoning and adjust with salt and pepper as needed. Set aside

2. Meanwhile, heat the coals on your barbecue to medium-high.

3. To prepare the brochettes, add four salmon pieces to each skewer, then place on a clean, flat surface. Using a pastry brush, coat the fish with the spicy sauce on all sides. Allow the fish to rest for 5 minutes, providing enough time for the sauce to adhere to the fish, then add the brochettes to a fish grate and secure shut. Set aside.

4. When the coals are ready, add the fish to the grill and cook for 4 minutes on one side with the grill open, then turn and cook on the other side with the grill closed for 2 minutes. Serve immediately with saffron rice if desired.

Santa Cruz
Turtle Bean & Salmon Chili

Known for its vintage beach boardwalk, as well as its world-class university and laid-back vibe, Santa Cruz, California has a stellar seafood scene with a reputation for being a great place to catch King salmon. The waters around Santa Cruz are some of the most bait-rich in the world, playing host to some of salmon's favorite treats—anchovy, herring, sardine and squid.

Black beans, or turtle beans, named so for their shiny black coating, are one of my favorites to use for chili. I discovered a vegetarian version of this recipe during my college years when it was called "hippie chili," a nod to the 1960s vegetarian movement in the U.S., when legumes as part of a healthy lifestyle were becoming all the rage.

The creamy texture of black beans combined with the richness of wild salmon makes for a luscious and hearty meal. Black beans made from scratch take a bit of time, unless you have a pressure cooker. Prepared using either method, they are delicious. If you are new to cooking dry beans, check out page 368 for instructions.

INGREDIENTS

- 2 tablespoons ghee

- 1 bell pepper, chopped

- 1 large carrot, diced

- 2 stalks celery, diced

- 1 medium onion, chopped

- 2 cloves garlic, minced

- 1 tablespoon each: coriander, cumin, chili powder and cayenne pepper

- 1 pound (2 cups) dried black beans, sorted and soaked overnight

- 4 cups water, more as needed

- 3 cups salmon bone broth (see page 484) or store-bought prepared seafood stock

- 1 bay leaf

- Smoked paprika sea salt (see page 548) to taste

- Freshly ground black pepper to taste

- 2 tablespoons avocado or vegetable oil

- ½ pound wild salmon, such as sockeye, coho or Chinook, cut into chunks

- ¼ cup chopped fresh cilantro

DIRECTIONS { Serves 6-8 }

1. In a large Dutch oven or heavy-bottomed pot, heat the ghee over medium heat. Toss in the bell pepper, carrot, celery, onion, garlic, coriander, cumin, chili powder and cayenne pepper, and stir for 2 minutes until fragrant.

2. Add the soaked beans, water, salmon or seafood stock, and bay leaf to the pot. Cover and bring to a boil for 10 minutes, then cover with the lid slightly ajar and simmer for 60 minutes.

3. After one hour, add the smoked paprika sea salt and black pepper to taste. Check the beans for doneness and flavor. Adjust the seasoning as needed and check the liquid level. Add more water if needed—the water should be about 1 inch above the beans. Reduce the heat to a simmer and cook for an additional 45 minutes.

4. Taste the beans again for doneness—they should be flavorful, tender and slightly creamy. Turn off the heat and let the pot sit for 20 minutes before serving, allowing time for the flavors to meld. If the beans are not done, cook in additional 10-minute intervals until your ideal level of doneness is reached. Set aside.

5. Season the salmon with paprika sea salt to taste. In a medium nonstick skillet, heat the avocado or vegetable oil and sauté the salmon for 4–6 minutes, or until cooked through. To serve, ladle a hearty scoop of chili into individual bowls and add equal portions of the salmon to each serving. Garnish with fresh cilantro, top with your favorite toppings, and serve.

SERVING SUGGESTIONS:
SLICED SCALLION, CHOPPED ONION, JALAPEÑO, SOUR CREAM, DICED TOMATO AND SHREDDED CHEESE

Pacific Coast Blackened Salmon Pasta

WITH HABAÑERO CREMA

Like the rest of my nieces and nephews, my niece Sarah (who is also my Goddaughter) has big love for salmon. During our long weekends spent together during the summer, I typically pack a lunch and we head to the beach for an afternoon. I prepare some of her favorite things—lavender lemonade, fresh fruit and this blackened salmon pasta dish.

Salmon is one of the most popular seafood varieties around and is often an easy sell with kids. I created this dish years ago when I began to study southern American cuisine and got heavily into blending my own spices. I attribute this dish both to Louisiana's own Chef Paul Prudhomme, who introduced the world to blackened seafood in the 1980s, and to the abundance of salmon available to me on the West Coast.

Most pasta varieties will work for this recipe, but my preference is for long, thin pastas like fettuccine or thick spaghetti. Penne and cavatappi are also good options. Make this your own by tossing in veggies like grilled zucchini or spinach

INGREDIENTS

{ Serves 4 }

- **1 pound dry fettuccine or thick spaghetti**
- **3 tablespoons olive oil**, separated
- **2 cloves garlic**, minced
- **1/3 cup chopped Spanish onion**
- **3 fresh Roma tomatoes**, diced
- **1½ cups flaked cooked blackened salmon**
- **½ fresh lemon**, juice and zest
- **Rosemary sea salt** (see page 552) to taste

- **Freshly ground black pepper to taste**
- **2 tablespoons half-and-half**
- **1 cup pasta sauce**
- **1 teaspoon red pepper flake**
- **¼ cup chopped fresh parsley**
- **Grated Parmesan or Pecorino Romano cheese**, optional
- **Optional: Grilled zucchini or fresh spinach**

DIRECTIONS

1. Cook the pasta per package instructions. Drain, rinse, then add the cooked pasta to a plastic resealable food storage bag with 1 tablespoon of olive oil—this will keep the noodles moist. Refrigerate the noodles while you prepare the salmon.

2. In a large non-stick skillet, heat the remaining 2 tablespoons of olive oil over medium-high heat. Add the garlic and onion and sauté until fragrant but not brown—about 1 minute. Add the tomatoes, salmon, and the lemon juice and zest, and toss. Add rosemary sea salt and black pepper to taste.

3. Add the cooled cooked noodles to the pan along with the half-and-half and red pepper flake and optional veggies as desired. Toss to coat the pasta in the sauce and serve immediately—this recipe is great served family-style or individually. Garnish with fresh parsley and grated cheese as desired.

Wenatchee Valley Apple and Salmon Quesadilla

Washington state is renowned for its apples and is affectionately called the "Apple Capital of the World." There are five apple-growing regions in the state—Okanogan, Lake Chelan, Columbia Basin, Yakima Valley and Wenatchee Valley, one of my favorites.

Wenatchee is loaded with eye-catching waterfront orchards that produce crisp, delicious apples that find their way into lunch bags, pies and cider. My husband and I discovered this area during our road trip from Lake Washington through the Cascade Mountain Range on our way to Winthrop for a week of snowshoeing and fat biking. We enjoyed stopping at roadside stands to buy apples that were sold by growers along the way.

Chinook salmon are common in the waters surrounding Wenatchee, namely the Columbia River. Salmon combined with apples and cheese makes for a delightful combination—ever heard of apple pie with a slice of cheddar? According to food historian Charles Perry, it is an English tradition that dates back to the 17th century, and it's easy to see (and taste) why it's stood the test of time!

If you are new to quesadillas, they are essentially flour tortillas stuffed with a mixture of cheese and other ingredients, then grilled until toasted. They can be sweet or savory, and this version is a bit of both.

INGREDIENTS

{ Makes 4 quesadillas }

- ¼ cup avocado oil

- 4 8-inch flour tortillas

- 1 cup shredded Mexican cheese blend (Monterey Jack, mild cheddar, asadero & queso quesadilla)

- 1 cup cooked black beans

- 1 cup cooked Chinook salmon or another variety

- 1 large Granny Smith apple, thinly sliced ¼ cup Cotija cheese

SERVING SUGGESTIONS: AVOCADO SLICES, GUACAMOLE, CHOPPED CILANTRO, DICED TOMATO, SALSA

DIRECTIONS

1. Heat a little avocado oil in a large grill pan over medium heat. Place a tortilla in the skillet and cook for 10–15 seconds on both sides.

2. This is the part where you'll need to use your instincts and preferences. With the tortilla lying flat, add enough of the Mexican cheese blend to cover one half of the tortilla (about 2 tablespoons), along with a portion of black beans and a few tablespoons of the salmon. Add two slices of apple and 1 tablespoon of the Cotija cheese and fold the tortilla over to make a half-moon shape.

3. Add the quesadilla to the hot pan and cook for 2–3 minutes on each side, allowing time for the cheese to melt and the tortilla to brown. When the cheese has melted and the outside of the tortilla is crispy, remove from the heat. Cover with a tea towel or place in the warmer tray of your oven to keep warm. Repeat with the remaining tortillas and ingredients.

4. When ready, serve with your choice of toppings.

Montenegro Baked Pastrva (Trout) in Filo Pastry

Montenegro is a small Balkan country with a lot to offer with its array of natural and manmade wonders. It has always been a land of mystery and intrigue with its medieval villages, spectacular mountains, breathtaking landscapes and picturesque beaches along the Adriatic coast. The gastronomy of the region is influenced by the surrounding nations of Hungary, Turkey, Serbia and other Central European nations.

Fishers often refer to Montenegro as the "Fishing Paradise of the Balkans," and angling is one of the most popular summer activities. Share a fishing boat with a local and you'll likely imbibe a shot of rakia, a favorite national alcohol drink (similar to brandy).

According to the Trout Restoration Group website, the first mention of Montenegrin trout was in 1858. This is a beautifully presented dish that is surprisingly simple to make. It will work with any type of trout or salmon.

INGREDIENTS

{ Serves 4 }

- **1 tablespoon ghee**

- **1 large onion**, finely diced

- **2 cups flaked baked or poached trout**, skin and bones removed

- **1 cup ricotta cheese**

- **1 small lemon**, zest only

- **1 small bunch fresh basil** (about 4 tablespoons)

- **2 large eggs**

- **½ pound filo dough sheets**, thawed if frozen

- **5–6 tablespoons butter**, melted

- **Salt and freshly ground black pepper to taste**

DIRECTIONS

1. Preheat oven to 375°F.

2. In a large sauté pan or nonstick skillet, melt the ghee and sauté the onion until soft, taking care not to brown. Transfer to a medium-sized bowl and let cool slightly. Add the cooked trout, ricotta cheese, lemon zest and basil. Season to taste and stir in the eggs.

3. Unroll the filo dough and pull off one sheet. Lay it crosswise on the table and cover the remaining filo dough with a moist tea towel or paper towel to prevent it from drying out. Using a pastry brush, brush the sheet lightly with melted butter and top with another filo sheet. Brush again with butter and add a third sheet. Brush the top with butter and spread enough of the salmon mixture to cover, making sure to go to the edge.

4. Rolling parallel (one side of the square to the other) or diagonal (from one corner of the dough to another), gently roll the dough and filling until the filling is covered, then fold in the ends. Roll the rest of the way, forming a neat log. Gently transfer, seam side down, onto a lightly buttered baking sheet. Repeat with three more sheets of filo dough and the remaining filling (you should have two wrapped fish pastries). Brush the tops and sides with a little more butter and bake for 20–30 minutes, or until golden brown.

5. Allow to cool for 5–10 minutes before cutting and serving.

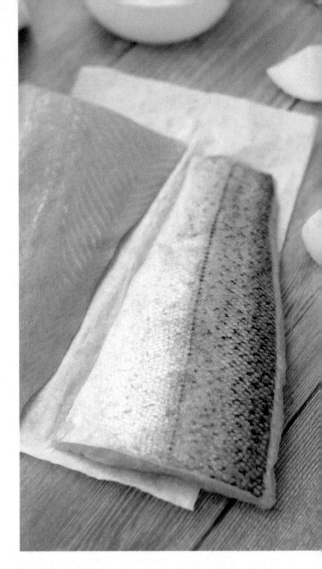

Cambridge Bay Arctic Char

WITH CREAMY DILL SAUCE

The area of Canada known as Cambridge Bay is a hamlet located on the southeast coast of Victoria Island, a quick and beautiful ferry ride from Vancouver. The water surrounding the regions is part of the Arctic Ocean, the smallest and shallowest of the world's five oceans. If the stars are aligned and the season is right, you can spot dolphins, orcas and other whales along the passage.

One Christmas holiday, my husband and I traveled to the island. We enjoyed traditional English high tea with Canadian flair midday and Arctic char for supper. Arctic char is an emblem of the local culture and an important part of the diet. According to the Vancouver Aquarium's Ocean Wise program, Arctic char has been commercially harvested around Victoria Island since the 1960s; however, Inuit communities have harvested it for centuries.

This recipe is my version of a simple, satisfying supper we relished on our trip.

INGREDIENTS

{ Serves 4 }

- **4 4-ounce Arctic char fillets**, skin-on

- **½ teaspoon sea salt**

- **1 cup sour cream**

- **1 small shallot**, peeled and minced

- **1 clove garlic**, minced, or 1 teaspoon garlic powder

- **1 lemon**, juice and zest

- **½ bunch or 3 tablespoons fresh dill**, fronds only

- **Freshly ground black pepper to taste**

- **2 tablespoons avocado oil or ghee**

SERVING SUGGESTIONS: SAUTÉED BROCCOLINI (SEE PAGE 422), SAFFRON RICE (SEE PAGE 412)

DIRECTIONS

1. Preheat oven to 400°F.

2. Place the Arctic char on a clean surface and sprinkle with sea salt. Allow the fish to rest for 10–15 minutes; this will help prevent an overabundance of albumin (see page 301).

3. Meanwhile, make the dill sauce. In a medium-sized bowl, combine the sour cream, shallot, garlic, lemon juice and zest, dill, and a pinch of freshly ground black pepper. Mix thoroughly and taste for seasoning, adjusting as needed. Set aside and prepare the fish.

4. In a cast iron or ovenproof skillet, heat the avocado oil or ghee over high heat. When the oil is hot (about 10–15 seconds), add the fish to the pan, skin side down, and cook for 2–3 minutes. Gently flip the fish over with a large spatula, taking care not to damage the fish. Place the skillet in the oven and cook for 3 minutes.

5. After 3 minutes, remove fish from the oven and set aside. To serve, divide the fish among individual plates and top with the dill sauce, a scoop of saffron rice (see page 412), and Broccolini (see page 422) as desired.

Nunavut Maple Dijon Arctic Char

WITH CAULIFLOWER PARSNIP PURÉE

On one of my last trips to Canada, I ended up buying a new suitcase just for all of the maple syrup products I purchased and brought back to the states! I had it all—maple sugar, taffy, and of course grade A maple syrup.

It was during this trip that I learned about the Nunavut territory, a region located in the very northern part of Canada. Sparsely populated and isolated, Nunavut is known for indigenous Inuit artwork and Arctic char.

A favorite fish served on dinner tables and restaurants alike in this area, Arctic char is an important part of the gastronomy for commercial fishers and Inuit communities. The cold waters around Victoria and the Arctic Ocean make for high-quality fish with a high-fat content—a good thing!

This simple recipe uses maple syrup and tangy Dijon mustard to enhance the mild flavor of delicate Arctic char without being overpowering.

Cauliflower parsnip purée is the perfect partner; it is delicious and helps balance out the sweetness of the maple syrup. Traditional mashed potatoes or roasted sweet potatoes will also work in a pinch.

INGREDIENTS

{ Serves 4 }

- **½ cup real maple syrup**

- **3 tablespoons Dijon mustard**

- **1 large lemon,** juice only

- **2 sprigs fresh thyme,** leaves only

- **1 tablespoon rosemary sea salt**
  (see page 552)

- **2 tablespoon olive oil**

- **½ teaspoon sea salt**

- **4 4-ounce Arctic char fillets,** skin on

- **Sea salt**

- **Cauliflower parsnip purée**
  (see page 424)

DIRECTIONS

1. Preheat oven to 375°F.

2. In a medium-sized bowl, whisk together the maple syrup, Dijon mustard, lemon juice, fresh thyme leaves, rosemary sea salt, olive oil and sea salt. Combine thoroughly and set aside.

3. Place the fish on a clean surface and sprinkle each piece with a pinch of salt to help reduce the appearance of albumin (see page 301). Set aside for 10–15 minutes.

4. When ready, place the Arctic char on a baking sheet lined with parchment paper and blot the fish with paper towels to remove any moisture. Using a pastry brush, spread the marinade on the fish. Take care to coat evenly, but don't overdo it. Place the fish in the oven and cook for 12 minutes, then remove from the oven and allow it to rest for a minute or two. Add a scoop of the cauliflower parsnip purée to four individual plates and top with the fish. Garnish with fresh rosemary and a slice of lemon. Serve immediately.

California Poached Steelhead

WITH JERUSALEM ARTICHOKE PURÉE

Steelhead trout can be found along the coast of Southern California all the way to the frigid waters of Alaska. They present like salmon but cook up like trout. In fact, some authorities report that steelhead are coastal rainbow trout. Sometimes caught in the wild, this fish is mostly cultivated and is considered a responsible choice.

I will be the first to tell you that poaching fish is not my go-to cooking technique; I prefer the texture of grilled, seared and roasted fish. However, a trip to a local market in Portland, Oregon changed my mind after a long day of filming my show "Appetite for Adventure!" I discovered an incredibly tasty salad featuring poached steelhead that was lightly sauced with mustard.

If you are new to poaching, it is a simple cooking technique that imparts lots of flavor while the fish simmers in water or flavored liquid until done.

Jerusalem artichokes, also known as sunchokes, have nothing to do with Jerusalem or artichokes. These tubers are a big knobby root vegetable that happens to taste a lot like artichokes or water chestnuts.

Some sources believe that the word "Jerusalem" is a distortion of the Italian name for the plant name, girasole. As for the artichoke, it's rumored that an early explorer described the plant as tasting like artichokes when it was introduced to Europe in the 1600s.

Native to the Americas, sunchokes have been a staple food for Native Americans for centuries. They are thin-skinned and delicious roasted and puréed, which is how I use them in this recipe. Choose sunchokes that are firm, heavy and devoid of black spots.

INGREDIENTS

POACHED STEELHEAD TROUT

1 small fennel bulb, sliced

1 tablespoon black peppercorns

1 small orange, sliced

2 cloves garlic, peeled and halved

1 tablespoon rosemary sea salt (see page 552)

4 4-ounce steelhead trout fillets

JERUSALEM ARTICHOKE PURÉE

1 pound Jerusalem artichokes, scrubbed and diced

1 teaspoon sea salt

2 cloves garlic, peeled

½ pound russet potatoes, peeled and diced

2 tablespoons unsalted butter

1 small lemon, juice and zest

Freshly ground black pepper to taste

DIRECTIONS

 { Serves 4 }

1.   In a large high-rimmed pan, add 2 cups of water along with the fennel, black peppercorns, sliced orange, garlic and rosemary sea salt. Bring the pot to a simmer for 10–15 minutes, allowing the flavors of the ingredients to release.

2.   Meanwhile, add the Jerusalem artichokes, sea salt and garlic to a pot and cover with water. Bring to a boil and cook until fork tender, about 6 minutes. Using a slotted spoon, remove the sunchokes and add them to the bowl of a food processor. Reserve the water in the pot—you will use it to cook the fish.

3.   Add the potatoes to the pot of water that the sunchokes were cooked in and boil for 10–12 minutes or until fork tender. With a slotted spoon, add the potatoes to the food processor containing the sunchokes. Reserve the liquid for poaching the fish and set aside. Blend until smooth and pour into a large bowl. Stir in the butter, lemon juice, lemon zest and freshly ground black pepper to taste. Mix to combine and taste for seasoning, adjusting as needed. Cover and set aside.

4.   Place the fish flesh side down in the pot with the reserved sunchoke/potato liquid and simmer on low for 4 minutes—be careful not to boil. The liquid should cover the fish; if not, add a little water. Once the time is up, remove the fish from the liquid and set aside on a clean plate.

5.   To serve, add a scoop of the Jerusalem artichoke purée to individual plates and top with a poached steelhead fillet. Serve immediately.

Napa Chardonnay & Mustard Steelhead Trout

This is a simple, wine country inspired dish that's great for dinner parties or holiday celebrations. I like to serve this tangy steelhead trout with a light green salad and mashed potatoes to give the sauce a nice place to land.

Steelhead is a silver-colored fish with bright orange flesh. It is similar to salmon in a number of ways but is more like a close cousin of the tomatillo. The flavor profile is a cross between salmon and trout. Arctic char and rainbow trout are good substitutes for the steelhead in a pinch.

This recipe calls for white pepper, which is hotter than black pepper and has a milder flavor. Fun fact: white and black pepper are berries that come from the same plant; the difference is in how they are processed.

You can prepare the fish for this recipe as individual servings or use a large whole fillet, which is great served family-style.

INGREDIENTS

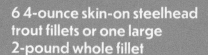

6 4-ounce skin-on steelhead trout fillets or one large 2-pound whole fillet

2 teaspoons rosemary sea salt (see page 552), plus more as needed

1 teaspoon white pepper, plus more as needed

2 tablespoons olive oil

1 tablespoon water

4 tablespoons Dijon mustard

5 sprigs fresh thyme, leaves only, 1 teaspoon reserved for garnish

½ cup chardonnay

2 cloves garlic, minced

¼ cup half-and-half

Lemon wedges, for serving

DIRECTIONS

{ Serves 6 }

1. Preheat oven to 375°F.

2. Place the fish on a clean dry surface and season the flesh side with rosemary sea salt and white pepper. Set aside.

3. Meanwhile, heat 1 tablespoon of olive oil in a large ovenproof skillet over high heat. When the oil is hot, add the fish and sear, flesh side down, for 2 minutes. Use a spatula to turn the fish over and cook for an additional 30 seconds—just enough time to lightly crisp the skin side. Turn off the heat and place the fish in the oven for 5 minutes to finish cooking.

4. As the fish cooks, make the sauce: In a small saucepan, whisk together the remaining tablespoon of olive oil, water, Dijon mustard, thyme, wine and garlic and heat over low heat. Stir and simmer for 4 minutes until slightly reduced. Taste for seasoning and adjust with rosemary sea salt and white pepper as needed. Stir in the half-and-half and simmer for another 2 minutes; cover and turn off the heat.

5. When the fish is ready, use an oven mitt to remove the skillet from the oven. Allow the fish to rest for 1–2 minutes before removing it from the pan.

6. If serving individual fillets, divide fillets among 6 individual plates and spoon a tablespoon of the mustard chardonnay sauce over top. Use more or less of the sauce as desired. Garnish with fresh thyme leaves and a lemon wedge on the side and serve immediately.

7. If using a large whole filet, add the fish to a large serving platter and pour the sauce over top. Garnish with fresh thyme leaves and a small plate of lemons on the side. Serve immediately.

Italian Spicy Mackerel Spaghetti

A member of the tuna family, mackerel is a delectable, yet underrated fish that deserves more attention! A firm, high-fat fleshed fish, it's known for bold, savory flavor. Tinned mackerel is popular throughout the Mediterranean in places like Italy, where it's referred to as sgombro (Atlantic mackerel) and enjoyed in sandwiches, salads and right out of the can.

In most cases you will find tinned fish boneless and skinless, but if you prefer, you can buy it intact. It will be labeled accordingly.

This spicy recipe calls for whole wheat pasta, which I think adds another flavor dimension with its nutty, earthy characteristics. The briny capers help cut through the richness of the fish and the arugula adds a bright note. Tinned sardines in olive oil will work equally as well for this dish.

INGREDIENTS

{ Serves 4 }

- **6 ounces tinned mackerel in olive oil**

- **3 Roma tomatoes,** diced

- **2 tablespoons capers in brine,** drained

- **1 pound whole wheat spaghetti**

- **3 tablespoons olive oil**

- **½ cup tomato sauce**

- **2 tablespoons fresh lemon juice**

- **1 tablespoon chopped fresh thyme**

- **Rosemary sea salt (see page 552) to taste**

- **1 teaspoon freshly ground black pepper**

- **1 teaspoon red pepper flake**

- **1 cup wild arugula or spinach,** rinsed and chopped

- **4-5 kalamata olives,** pitted and chopped (or left whole if desired)

- **¼ cup freshly grated parmesan cheese**

DIRECTIONS

1. Place the mackerel and its oil in a large bowl. Flake the mackerel, add the diced tomatoes and capers, and set aside.

2. Cook the pasta to al dente according to package directions, drain, and place in the bowl with the mackerel; the warmth from the pasta will help the flavors blend. Add the olive oil, lemon juice, thyme, rosemary sea salt, freshly ground black pepper, red pepper flake, tomato sauce and arugula or spinach and kalamata olives. Toss and taste. Adjust seasoning as required. Finally, toss in the freshly grated parmesan cheese. Serve immediately.

Boston Baked Bluefish

On the East Coast of the United States, bluefish is a very big deal. There are festivals dedicated to this meaty, oily fish that is found along the Atlantic coastline in places like Boston in the U.S., as well as Africa, Australia and the Mediterranean.

Bluefish are a popular recreational fish that have moist flesh with a slightly coarse texture. The flavor is full and rich, similar to mackerel.

INGREDIENTS

{ Serves 4 }

- 4 4-ounce bluefish fillets, skin on

- Sea salt and freshly ground black pepper to taste

- 2 tablespoons avocado oil, separated

- 2 cloves garlic, minced

- 1 shallot, minced

- 1 tablespoon capers in brine, drained

- 3 large fresh tomatoes, diced, or 1 generous cup canned tomatoes

- 1 tablespoon balsamic vinegar

- Fresh parsley, for garnish

SERVING SUGGESTIONS: CRUSTY BREAD, COOKED PASTA OR SAFFRON RICE (SEE PAGE 412)

DIRECTIONS

1. Preheat oven to 400°F.

2. For crispy-skinned fish, place the bluefish skin side up on a bed of paper towels and allow to rest in the refrigerator for 60–90 minutes. This will allow the skin to dry out and firm up during the cooking process.

3. Once the fish is ready, lightly sprinkle the flesh side with sea salt and freshly ground black pepper. Set aside.

4. In a medium-sized skillet, heat 1 tablespoon of avocado oil over medium-high heat. When the oil is hot, add the garlic and shallot and cook until fragrant, stirring occasionally. Add the capers, tomatoes and balsamic vinegar and cook for 1–2 minutes, then turn the heat to low. Cook until the tomatoes break down, about 3–4 minutes, stirring intermittently. Remove from the heat and set aside.

5. In a large cast iron skillet or an ovenproof pan, heat the remaining avocado oil over high heat. When the oil is hot, about 20–30 seconds, place the fish in the skillet, skin side down. The pan will sizzle and pop, which is a good sign. Cook for 2 minutes, then pour the tomato mixture on top and place the pan in the oven. Cook for 10 minutes, then remove from the oven using heat-proof oven gloves.

6. Garnish with parsley and serve immediately with crusty bread, pasta or rice as desired.

Whole Fish

✳ Colombian Whole Fried Fish with Plantains

✳ Mediterranean Chargrilled Whole Branzino

✳ Belizean Whole Grilled Fish with Coconut Rice & Red Beans

✳ West Indies Grilled Snapper with Pineapple Chow

✳ Korean Salty Mackerel with Forbidden Rice

Colombian Whole Fried Fish with Plantains

The culinary traditions of Colombia are a mix of African, Indigenous and Spanish cultures. This South American country has both a Caribbean and Pacific coastline that spans more than 1,990 miles.

My first time experiencing Colombian food was actually in Barcelona, Spain. I was staying in a small flat in an area near the University District where the sidewalks were dotted with tapas bars in addition to dozens of Latin and Caribbean restaurants. After sampling a few places, I found my favorite spot and ate there several days in a row, enjoying pan-fried fish, plantains and black beans with an avocado salad.

This popular dish, called mojarra frita, is quintessential Colombian coastal fare and is one of the region's most popular dishes.

INGREDIENTS

{ Serves 4 }

- **4 whole drawn tilapia**

- **2 large cloves garlic**, sliced

- **2 large limes**, juice only

- **Sea salt and freshly ground black pepper**, as needed

- **1½ cups vegetable oil**

- **½ cup all-purpose flour**

- **Mudros plantains (see page 406) or patacones (see page 404)**

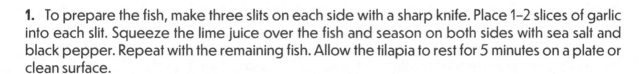

SERVING SUGGESTIONS: BRAZILIAN FEIJÃO (SEE PAGE 376), COCONUT RICE (SEE PAGE 418) OR AVOCADO SALAD (SEE PAGE 544)

DIRECTIONS

1. To prepare the fish, make three slits on each side with a sharp knife. Place 1–2 slices of garlic into each slit. Squeeze the lime juice over the fish and season on both sides with sea salt and black pepper. Repeat with the remaining fish. Allow the tilapia to rest for 5 minutes on a plate or clean surface.

2. Meanwhile, in a large, deep skillet, heat the vegetable oil to 350°F. Use a thermometer to check the temperature or add a small cube of bread to the skillet—when it turns golden brown, the oil is ready.

3. To cook the fish, lightly dredge both sides with the flour, shaking off any excess. Add the fish to the hot oil, using tongs to protect your fingers. Fry the fish for about 3–4 minutes per side, or until golden brown. You may have to do this in batches.

4. Use tongs to remove the fish from the oil and place it on a rack or a bed of paper towels to drain. Serve immediately with pan-fried plantains or patacones and Brazilian feijão, coconut rice, or avocado salad.

Mediterranean Chargrilled Whole Branzino

The 21 countries surrounding the Mediterranean Sea can be divided into three culinary regions: Eastern Mediterranean, Southern Mediterranean and North African. With a moderate climate, the area boasts more than 28,000 miles of coastline.

As a midpoint between Africa, Asia and Europe, the region was once an ancient trading hub where ingredients like spices and other goods were exchanged. These same ingredients are now reflected in the gastronomy of the region. Vegetables, grains, olive oil and legumes make up the base of most meals, with seafood making a frequent appearance.

Branzino, also known as branzini, loupe de mer or European sea bass, is popular in the area and is one of my favorite fish to prepare whole. It is native to the Mediterranean Sea but can be found as far as West Africa and Norway.

If you are new to cooking whole fish, this recipe is a good place to start. The flavor of branzino is mild yet distinct, the flesh firm, and the bones easy to work around with their high amounts of cartilage. This means that when the fish gets hot, instead of drying out, the cartilage melts and creates a moist and tender flesh.

INGREDIENTS

{ Serves 2 }

- **1 tablespoon garlic powder**

- **2 tablespoons dried oregano**

- **2 tablespoons ground coriander**

- **2 tablespoons ground cumin**

- **2 tablespoons dried thyme**

- **2 whole lemons,** juice and zest of 1, the other quartered

- **¼ cup Spanish olive oil**

- **2 2-pound whole branzino,** drawn

- **1 bunch fresh rosemary,** or enough to stuff two fish

- **Sea salt and freshly ground black pepper to taste**

SERVING SUGGESTIONS: SAFFRON RICE (SEE PAGE 412) OR SAUTÉED BROCCOLINI (SEE PAGE 422),

DIRECTIONS

1. Preheat a lump charcoal grill to medium-high heat.

2. In a small bowl, combine the herbs, spices, the juice and zest of ½ lemon, and enough olive oil to create a paste, about 2 tablespoons. Mix thoroughly and set aside.

3. Using a sharp knife, score the fish three times on each side. Stuff the cavity with fresh rosemary and place the fish on a clean surface. Repeat with the remaining fish.

4. Season with a little sea salt and black pepper, then slather one side of the fish with the herb and spice paste and place it in a fish grate, marinated side down. Add additional paste to the other side of the fish and secure the grate closed. Repeat with the other fish.

5. When the barbecue coals are ready, add the fish to the grill. Cook for 6 minutes on one side, closing the grill halfway through, then turn and cook for another 5–6 minutes on the other side with the grill closed.

6. Remove the fish from the grill and allow it to rest for 1–2 minutes before removing from the fish grate. Place on a serving platter and serve immediately with saffron rice or sautéed Broccolini.

Belizean Whole Grilled Fish

WITH COCONUT RICE & RED BEANS

On the northeastern coast of Central America, you will find Belize, a gem of a country that is as culturally rich as it is beautiful. Dotted with fun-loving cays and culturally significant coastal villages, this region features a vibrant, infectious assortment of music, dance and food reflective of African, Creole, European, Garifuna and Mayan influences.

This whole grilled fish dish is similar to one I enjoyed while dining beachside in Hopkins Village, a small Garifuna village located in the Stann Creek district. The Garifuna people are made up of native Caribbean tribes who mingled with shipwrecked enslaved Africans hundreds of years ago. This encounter resulted in the creation of a new culture with its own language, storytelling and food traditions.

Rice & beans are a staple dish and served with almost every meal in Belize—I even had a bowl for breakfast one morning with fry jacks—a traditional fry bread eaten for breakfast or as a snack.

I experienced rice & red beans a few ways during my travels in Belize. Some cooks left the pot of beans whole, others kept things slightly on the mashed and soupy side, and on occasion the beans and rice were combined. All versions were tasty. My preference is to cook the rice and beans separately, as this allows guests to choose their portion size of each. Preparing them separately also gives you more options for using up any extras—for example, the beans are great with tortillas and scrambled eggs for a hearty breakfast.

INGREDIENTS

RICE AND BEANS:

- **3 tablespoons coconut oil,** separated

- **1 medium bell pepper (any color),** chopped

- **1 medium white onion,** chopped

- **2 cloves garlic,** minced

- **1 large carrot,** chopped

- **2 stalks celery,** chopped

- **1 cup dry red kidney beans, soaked overnight, or 2 cups cooked kidney beans, rinsed**

- **4 cups water,** more as needed

- **2 bay leaves**

- **2 sprigs fresh thyme,** leaves only

- **Sea salt and freshly ground black pepper to taste**

- **1 cup long-grain white rice,** rinsed

- **1 cup plain coconut water**

- **1½ cups unsweetened coconut milk or 1 13.5-ounce can**

- **1 scallion,** sliced

- **1 small whole habañero pepper**

GRILLED FISH:

- **2 large whole snapper or other white fish, dressed**

- **2 large limes, halved**

- **Sea salt and freshly ground black pepper to taste**

DIRECTIONS

Prepare the beans:

In a large Dutch oven or heavy-bottomed pot, add 2 tablespoons of the coconut oil along with the bell pepper, white onion, garlic, carrot and celery and sauté for 3 minutes until fragrant. Add the beans, water, bay leaf and thyme and bring to a boil for 10 minutes. Reduce heat to a simmer and cook covered with the lid slightly ajar for 90 minutes. Check the water level on occasion—the beans should always be covered in water. When the time is up, check the beans for doneness—they should be tender yet firm.

Cook for an additional 30 minutes or until the desired level of tenderness is achieved. Set aside. In a large wide pot over medium-high heat, melt 1 tablespoon of coconut oil with the rice. Stir the pot to lightly toast and coat the rice in the oil, about 4 minutes. Add the coconut water, coconut milk, scallion and habañero pepper. Stir to combine and cover with the lid slightly ajar. Cook for 15 minutes then fully place the lid on the pot, turn off the heat and let stand for 10–15 minutes—this is important because it allows the rice to steam and absorb the flavors of the coconut milk. Set aside while the fish is cooking.

Cook the fish:

Preheat a lump charcoal grill over medium-high heat.

Place the fish on a clean surface and use a knife to make three slits on both sides. Squeeze the lime juice over the fish and allow it to rest for 5 minutes. Add a pinch of sea salt and black pepper. Place the fish in a fish grate and add it to the grill. Cook on one side for 5 minutes, then flip the fish over, close the lid, and cook for another 5 minutes. Remove the fish from the heat and the fish grate.

To serve family-style, place the fish on a platter and serve with a bow.

SERVING SUGGESTIONS: : MUDROS PLANTAINS (SEE PAGE 406), MANGO SALSA (SEE PAGE 566), AVOCADO SALAD (SEE PAGE 544), MARIE SHARP'S PEPPER SAUCE OR OTHER HABAÑERO HOT SAUCE

West Indies Grilled Snapper

WITH PINEAPPLE CHOW

The area known as the West Indies is made up of more than 7,000 islands comprising the Bahamas, Greater Antilles and the Lesser Antilles. The vibrant and lively flavors of this archipelago are no doubt some of my favorites.

In this part of the world, African, Asian, European, Indian and native cultures combine to create distinctly rich and flavorful Caribbean dishes. Hot peppers, plantains, coconut, peas & rice, roti and roasted fish make up an important part of the gastronomy.

This whole grilled snapper topped with pineapple chow reminds me of the bustling market in Marigot, the capital city of picturesque Saint Martin, where my husband and I spent time having lunch and shopping for souvenirs during our honeymoon. The food vendors cooked roasted vegetables and fish over natural lump coals, which gave the food a wonderful smoky flavor. See page 131 for more on natural charcoal.

INGREDIENTS

{ Serves 2 }

- **2 limes, juice only**

- **2 large snapper, or other firm meaty fish like drum or sea bass**

- **2 cups finely chopped fresh pineapple**

- **1 large scallion,** sliced

- **1 small habañero pepper, minced**

- **2 sprigs fresh thyme**

- **2 cloves garlic,** minced

- **Sea salt and freshly ground black pepper to taste**

SERVING SUGGESTIONS: TOSTONES (SEE PAGE 404), PILAU RICE (PAGE 410), MOROS Y CRISTIANOS (SEE PAGE 370) OR A BIG GREEN SALAD

DIRECTIONS

1. Preheat a lump charcoal grill over medium-high heat.

2. Squeeze the juice of one lime over the fish and allow it to rest for 10 minutes. Meanwhile, make the pineapple chow.

3. In a medium bowl, combine the chopped pineapple with the scallion, habañero pepper, the remaining lime juice and the garlic, sea salt and black pepper.

4. Stuff each fish with one sprig of thyme, add the fish to a fish grate and place it on the grill. Cook for 6–8 minutes, then remove from the heat and set aside for 1–2 minutes. Place the fish on a serving platter, top with the pineapple chow, and serve.

Korean Salty Mackerel

WITH FORBIDDEN RICE

Surrounded by water on three sides, South Korea is located on the southern half of the Korean peninsula. The country's cosmopolitan capital of Seoul is balanced by its lush, green countryside, ancient temples and traditional dance ceremonies, which are some of the most elegant and impressive in the world.

With 1,400 miles of coastline, South Korea has an enviable food scene made up of unpretentious soups and stews, complex noodle and vegetable dishes, and flavorful seafood. Local favorites include crab, scallops, tuna, octopus and mackerel. This grilled salty mackerel recipe is simply seasoned and grilled, a favorite style of cooking in Korea.

Mackerel is an oily fish, like salmon and sardines. Its firm meaty flesh has a distinct pleasantly fishy flavor due to its high oil content. This recipe comes from an old technique of preserving fish with salt. I use a metal fish grate to make the grilling process easier.

INGREDIENTS

{ Serves 4 }

- **2 cups black rice**, rinsed

- **1 bay leaf**

- **3 teaspoons sea salt**, separated

- **3½ cups water**, more as needed

- **1 lemon**, juice only

- **1 tablespoon fresh grated ginger**

- **4 8-ounce whole mackerel**, dressed and butterflied

DIRECTIONS

1. Add the rice to a bowl with enough water to cover. Allow the rice to soak for 5 minutes, then rinse. Add the rice to a pot along with the bay leaf, 1 teaspoon sea salt and the water. Bring to a boil for 8–10 minutes, then cover with the lid slightly ajar and cook for 30 minutes. When the time is up, fully cover with the lid, turn off the heat and allow the rice to finish steaming for 10 minutes. Set aside.

2. Meanwhile, preheat a lump charcoal grill to medium-high.

3. Combine the lemon juice and ginger in a small bowl. Set aside.

4. Make three slashes across the skin side of the mackerel. Season each side of the fish with ½ teaspoon of sea salt. Set aside and allow to marinate for 20 minutes.

5. When the time is up, add the fish to a fish grate. Place the fish on the grill and cook for 3 minutes on each side. Remove and allow the fish to rest for 2 minutes. Drizzle with the lemon and ginger sauce. Serve with cooked black rice.

Relishing Raw Seafood

I have a real passion for raw seafood dishes. Whether it be ceviche, crudo or poke, send it my way! And I'm not alone—raw fish has been eaten by people all over the world for centuries, and for good reason. The flavor and texture of quality uncooked fish is complex and delicious. Consider the delicacies of the Inuit from Northern Alaska, who at one point in time subsisted on a diet of raw walrus meat and seal oil.

Growing up, all of the fish that I enjoyed was cooked—mostly barbecued, grilled or fried. I didn't develop a taste for raw fish until my 20s. It started on my honeymoon when my husband and I took a boat from St. Martin to St. Barts and enjoyed an amazing raw yellowfin tuna dish that had me ordering seconds. A couple of weeks after arriving home, I started experimenting with raw seafood recipes and now enjoy raw fish a few times a month.

If you are new to raw fish, once you try it you will wonder why you took so long to come around. One of the first things I learned during my kitchen experiments and research is that raw seafood dishes should only be made from saltwater fish. This is a rule without exception and is centered around the matter of parasites, which exist in most animals and produce, according to the U.S. FDA. They are natural and unavoidable.

Heat and very cold temperatures kill these parasites, which is why any fish that you plan to use raw should be placed in the freezer before preparing. In fact, it is illegal to serve sushi or raw fish in the U.S. if it has not been previously frozen—tuna is one of the only exceptions.

It is advisable to freeze fish for 24-48 hours before serving raw. The good news is that this process does not dramatically alter the fish in any way.

One thing to keep in your back pocket when buying fish for raw dishes: Terms like "organic" and "sushi grade" are often tossed around to imply some level of freshness, but in the U.S., there are no regulations around the use of these terms, and they don't have any real value when it comes to selecting seafood. It's worth noting that most fish served as sushi or sashimi in Japan—the Mecca for raw fish dishes—is frozen before serving.

The good news is that you will likely never get a parasite from eating raw fish, but it would be irresponsible for me not to mention the possible risks associated with it, especially if you are pregnant or have a compromised immune system (see page 39).

HERE IS A STRAIGHTFORWARD OVERVIEW OF POPULAR RAW SEAFOOD DISHES.

JAPANESE STYLES – maki, nigiri, sashimi, temaki and uramaki. All are typically served with ingredients like soy, pickled ginger, wasabi (Japanese horseradish) and ponzu.

- Maki is rice and filling tightly wrapped in seaweed; otherwise known as sushi rolls.

- Nigiri is fish (or another topping like Spam) served atop rice.

- Sashimi is raw seafood made from saltwater fish not served with rice. The fish used for sashimi is prepared using a method that paralyzes and kills the fish quickly, which maintains the quality of the flesh. The process minimizes buildup of lactic acid, which can result in sour, mushy meat.

- Temaki are similar to maki and are often referred to as hand rolls.

- Uramaki are similar to maki but with the rice on the outside of the seaweed and filling.

PESCE CRUDO – Pesce crudo means "raw fish" in Italian and Spanish. It is similar to sashimi and is served with a dash of lime juice, sea salt and olive oil. Crudo implies a particular shape and size of the fish, which is thinly sliced, delicate and quite refreshing. Pesce crudo can be made from white or oily fish. Some cooks add specialty toppings for variety.

CEVICHE – Fresh and tangy with bold flavors, ceviche is a staple in Central and South America. While sashimi is enjoyed relatively unadorned, ceviche likes to get dressed up—it's cured in citrus juices and topped with chilies, cilantro, mango, onion, tomato, avocado and more.

I enjoy ceviche often, and my favorite fish for this preparation include sea bass, snapper, halibut, lionfish, scallops and shrimp. I avoid oily fish like salmon and mackerel. In the Philippines, you'll find a similar dish known as kinilaw, and in Fiji there is a version called kokoda, which is enriched with coconut milk to balance out the acid.

Maki rolls have been a fun way to introduce the kiddos in my family to raw dishes. They now look forward to our sushi parties and have been able to further develop their palates.

HERE IS A STRAIGHTFORWARD OVERVIEW OF POPULAR RAW SEAFOOD DISHES.

TARTARE – A traditional French dish with its roots in finely chopped raw beef, tartare has been extended to include fish. Tartare is most commonly seen on menus as tuna tartare, where the fish is diced, then dressed in flavorful seasonings like salt, olive oil, lime juice, pepper and more. It is usually served on a bed of avocado or spooned onto crackers or toast.

GRAVLAX – Gravlax is a Nordic delicacy made from unsmoked salmon that is cured in sugar, salt, and importantly dill. The herby flavors of the fish are great as an appetizer. Gravlax is easier to make at home than most people think.

POKE – Prominent on the island of Hawaii, poke is made from cubed raw fish dressed in soy sauce and toasted sesame oil and prepared with other ingredients such as onion, avocado, aioli and mango. It is sometimes served with rice.

CARPACCIO – Similar to pesce crudo, carpaccio is a dish made from sliced meat pounded thin and served raw. Fish carpaccio is served with simple ingredients like olive oil, lemon juice and good-quality vinegar.

If you are interested in getting into raw seafood, one of the best ways I know of is to explore maki rolls, which are made up of seafood wrapped in rice and a nori (seaweed) wrapper along with vegetables like avocado and cucumber. Popular varieties are the classic California roll, spicy tuna, tempura shrimp and surimi—a seafood product made from Alaskan pollock flavored with lobster, crab and shrimp, which is very popular in parts of Asia.

Raw Seafood Recipes

- Wild Alaskan Halibut Ceviche with Mango
- Big Island Ahi Tuna Poke
- Spicy Island Ahi Tuna Poke
- Japanese Hamachi
- Tahitian Poisson Cru
- Hokkaido Opah Tataki
- Peruvian Shrimp Ceviche
- Scottish Salmon Tartare with Cucumber Chips
- Chilean Crudo (Sea Bass)
- New Zealand Crudo Hapuka (Sea Bass)
- Venetian Tonno (Tuna) Carpaccio

Wild Alaskan Halibut Ceviche

WITH MANGO

Halibut are a quirky, funny-looking flatfish that swim sideways with one side facing down. According to the Alaska Department of Fish and Game, female halibut grow faster and larger than males, and small fish are referred to as chickens. This variety of fish can be found in the Bering Sea, along the California coast and near Hokkaido, Japan.

Throughout their lifecycle, halibut nosh on plankton in their early days, then slowly graduate to eating small shrimp-like organisms and small fish. As halibut grow, clams, crab, herring, sablefish and octopus become primary sources of sustenance. Their diet influences their flavor, which is meaty and mild tasting.

Halibut works great for oven roasting, fish & chips, and served "raw" as in this ceviche recipe. See page 340 for tips on preparing raw fish.

INGREDIENTS

{ Serves 2-3 }

- **½ pound Pacific halibut**, boneless and skinless, diced

- **6 large limes**

- **1 tablespoon freshly grated ginger**

- **1 teaspoon minced fresh habañero pepper**

- **½ cup diced red onion**

- **1 tablespoon olive oil**

- **2 medium mangoes**, peeled and diced

- **Sea salt and white pepper to taste**

DIRECTIONS

1. In a medium-sized bowl, combine the diced fish with the zest from 1 lime, juice from 4 of the limes, and the ginger. Cover the bowl with plastic wrap and refrigerate for 4 hours

2. When the fish is ready, drain the liquid. Add the juice of another lime and marinate in the refrigerator for an additional 30 minutes. When the time is up, drain the bowl and add the habañero pepper, red onion, olive oil, mango, sea salt and white pepper to taste, and the juice of the remaining lime. Combine thoroughly and serve immediately.

Big Island Ahi Tuna Poke

A more traditional version of Hawaiian poke (pronounced poh-kay), this ahi tuna version has become a family favorite, requested by my sister Leslie on most occasions. This is my go-to recipe. The Big Island is named as such because it is the largest of the islands in the Hawaiian archipelago.

Fishing for tuna and other large gamefish is a popular sport in the area. I like to keep this dish pretty simple, as do most Hawaiian locals—just the fish and a few simple ingredients. If so inclined, you can take a contemporary approach and serve this poke "bowl" style by adding your favorite ingredients like chopped cucumber, avocado slices, steamed rice and mango.

The recommended "cooking" time for this recipe is 10 minutes or up to 1 hour; however, some people enjoy this dish after it has spent 8 hours in the fridge. Be sure to check out my Posh Pointers on page 340 for safety tips on preparing raw seafood.

INGREDIENTS

{ Serves 4 }

- **1 8-ounce ahi tuna fillet, skin and bloodline removed,** cut into ½-inch cubes

- **½ small sweet Hawaiian onion,** thinly sliced (about 1 cup)

- **1 small thumb fresh ginger,** grated (about 1 tablespoon)

- **4 large limes,** juice only

- **1 tablespoon lime zest**

- **2 teaspoons red pepper flake**

- **¼ cup tamari (dark soy sauce)**

- **1 pinch ground white pepper**

- **1 teaspoon sea salt**

- **2 large scallions,** green part only, thinly sliced

- **2 tablespoons toasted sesame seed oil**

- **2 tablespoons soy sauce**

- **2 tablespoons white and black sesame seeds,** for garnish

SERVING SUGGESTIONS: STEAMED COCONUT RICE (SEE PAGE 418), JICAMA TOSTADA SHELLS (SEE PAGE 421).

DIRECTIONS

1. In a medium-sized bowl, combine the tuna, onion, ginger, lime juice and zest, red pepper flake, tamari, white pepper and sea salt.

2. Cover the bowl with plastic wrap and refrigerate for 15 minutes or up to 1 hour. Keep in mind that the longer you leave the fish to marinate, the more "cooked" it will be from the lime juice.

3. Remove the tuna from the refrigerator 15–20 minutes before plating and toss with 2 tablespoons of scallions, toasted sesame seed oil and soy sauce.

4. To serve, divide equal portions of poke among 6 small plates or small serving bowls. Artfully garnish with the remaining scallions and toasted sesame seeds as desired. Serve immediately.

Spicy Island Ahi Tuna Poke

Ahi tuna also goes by two other names: bigeye and yellowfin. It has a rich flavor and great texture and is outstanding when eaten raw. The addition of sambal oelek, an Indonesian chili paste, turns my Hawaiian inspired ahi tuna poke recipe into a fiery and flavorful treat.

The recommended "cooking" time for this recipe is 15 minutes or up to 1 hour; however, some people enjoy this dish after 8 hours in the fridge, when the fish becomes firm and changes hue. Be sure to check out my Posh Pointers on page 340 for safety tips on preparing raw seafood.

INGREDIENTS

{ Serves 4 }

- **2 pounds ahi tuna**, skin and bloodline removed, cut into ½-inch chunks

- **½ small sweet Hawaiian onion**, thinly sliced

- **1 small thumb fresh ginger**, grated (about 1 tablespoon)

- **4 large limes**, juice and 1 tablespoon of zest

- **¼ cup soy sauce**

- **Sea salt to taste**

- **3 tablespoons sambal oelek**, plus more if desired

- **2 tablespoon toasted sesame seed oil**

- **2 large scallions**, green part only, thinly sliced

- **2 tablespoons white and black sesame seeds**, for garnish

DIRECTIONS

1. In a medium-sized bowl, combine the tuna with the onion, ginger, lime zest and juice, soy sauce and sea salt to taste. Fold the ingredients together.

2. Cover the bowl with plastic wrap and refrigerate for 15 minutes or up to 1 hour. Keep in mind that the longer you leave the fish to marinate, the more "cooked" it will be from the lime juice.

3. Remove the tuna from the refrigerator 15–20 minutes before plating and toss with the sambal oelek and toasted sesame seed oil.

4. To serve, divide equal portions of poke among 4 small plates or small serving bowls. Artfully garnish with scallions and sesame seeds. Serve immediately.

Japanese Hamachi

Hamachi are a part of the amberjack family, a genus of fish found in Atlantic and Pacific waters. Yellowtail are a part of this group, and in Japanese terminology, yellowtail is referred to as hamachi when it reaches between 6–10 pounds.

Yellowtail has firm pink flesh with a rich, buttery flavor, and is excellent served raw. I had a chance to catch my own in San Diego, California while I was taping an episode of my show, "Appetite for Adventure!" The captain and team helped me catch 30 fish in total.

This is hardly a recipe; it's more like an assembly of Asian-inspired ingredients that work great with raw fish. Be sure to read the section on preparing raw fish (page 340). You'll need small bowls or containers to serve this dish.

INGREDIENTS

{ Serves 4-5 }

- **2 pounds fresh hamachi**, skin and bloodline removed, thinly sliced

- **2 tablespoons soy sauce**

- **2 tablespoons yuzu sauce**

- **2 tablespoons toasted sesame seed oil**

- **2 teaspoons toasted sesame seeds**

- **1 large lime**, cut into 6 pieces

DIRECTIONS

1. Artfully arrange the fish on a chilled platter and serve alongside the soy sauce, yuzu sauce, toasted sesame seed oil, chives, toasted sesame seeds and lime. Enjoy by dipping the fish in the various condiments.

Tahitian Poisson Cru

Located in the Pacific Ocean, Tahiti is the largest island in French Polynesia and is known as "Queen of the Pacific." Most of the island's residents reside near the shore, leaving the inland part of the island feeling almost untouched. Barracuda, bonito, mahi-mahi, yellowfin tuna and wahoo are common species found in the waters surrounding the island.

The gastronomy of Tahiti is a combination of French and Polynesian cultures, making for an interesting mix. Poisson cru means "raw fish" in French, and in Polynesian it's called ia ota (pronounced ee-ah-ottah). You can find this dish on most menus throughout the South Pacific, although it goes by different names depending on the island. The Cook Islands, Fiji, Samoa, Tonga and others call the same dish by a different name.

INGREDIENTS

{ Serves 4 }

- **2 pounds meaty fish (such as tuna, sea bass, snapper, halibut, mahi-mahi or wahoo),** skinned and deboned, chopped into bite-sized pieces (see page 340 for preparing raw fish)

- **4 large limes,** juice only

- **2 large lemons,** juice only

- **1 small red onion,** shaved or very thinly sliced

- **1 large red chili,** minced

- **3 ripe tomatoes,** seeded and diced

- **3 scallions,** green part only, sliced

- **½ teaspoon sea salt**

- **Freshly ground black pepper to taste**

- **2 cups coconut milk**

- **Lime wedges,** for serving

SERVING SUGGESTIONS: JICAMA TOSTADA SHELLS (SEE PAGE 420), COCONUT RICE (SEE PAGE 418)

DIRECTIONS

1. In a resealable food storage bag, combine the fish with the juice of two of the limes and the two lemons. Seal the bag closed and refrigerate for 15 minutes.

2. Once the fish has marinated, drain the liquid from the bag. Place the fish in a large bowl and add the juice from the remaining limes, as well as the red onion, red chili, tomatoes, scallions, sea salt, black pepper to taste and the coconut milk. Mix gently to combine. Taste for seasoning and adjust as needed. Garnish with lime wedges and serve immediately as desired.

Hokkaido Opah Tataki

One of Japan's northernmost islands, Hokkaido is known for its hot springs, ski areas and mouthwatering seafood dishes. Boiled crab, sea urchin, squid and raw fish are some of the most beloved.

Tataki is a Japanese word that has two meanings derived from the verb tataku. The first is "hammer" or "to pound," while the second refers to a style of cooking fish and meat that involves searing the outside while leaving the inside moist and rare. The secret to tataki is a very hot pan. The Japanese Times reports that the tataki technique was invented by a samurai in the 17th century. Skipjack and ahi tuna are commonly used for tataki, but salmon and opah are becoming more popular. Opah, also known as sunfish or moonfish for its large round body, can be found in tropical waters. The flesh is sweet and tender, similar to tuna. Try to get your hands on a thick loin of opah; it will cook evenly and present well. Otherwise, a thick meaty portion of fish will work, but you'll need to do a little extra work to make sure all sides are seared—a pair of tongs will come in handy.

Karashi, or Japanese mustard, is hot and spicy and typically used as a condiment. Not only does it add flavor to this dish; it also helps the sesame seeds stick to the fish.

INGREDIENTS

{ Serves 4-6 }

TATAKI DIPPING SAUCE:

- **¼ cup soy sauce**

- **1 tablespoon toasted sesame oil**

- **1 large scallion**, green part only, sliced

- **2 tablespoons yuzu sauce**

- **1 tablespoon grated fresh ginger**

- **1 large lime juice**

- **1 cup shaved red onion**, for garnish

OPAH:

- **1½ pounds fresh opah loin**

- **2 tablespoons karashi (Japanese mustard)**

- **½ cup toasted sesame seeds (a mix of black and white)**

- **1 teaspoon kosher salt**

- **Avocado oil or favorite vegetable oil**, as needed

SERVING SUGGESTIONS: KOMBU RICE (SEE PAGE 414)

DIRECTIONS

1. Place the opah on a clean surface. With a pastry brush, spread the Japanese mustard on all sides—this will add flavor and help the sesame seeds stick. On a separate plate or in a large shallow bowl, combine the sesame seeds and kosher salt. Using tongs, coat the fish in the sesame seed and salt mixture, applying pressure as needed (use clean, dry hands to help as needed). Wrap the fish in plastic wrap and chill for 20 minutes.

2. Meanwhile, make the tataki sauce. In a small bowl, whisk together the soy sauce, toasted sesame seed oil, scallion, yuzu sauce, grated ginger and lime juice. Taste for flavor and adjust as needed. Set aside.

3. Lightly coat the bottom of a large cast iron skillet with vegetable oil and heat over medium-high heat. When the skillet is hot, cook the fish on each side for 40–45 seconds. When done, place the fish on a plate and refrigerate.

4. Once it is cooled, slice the fish against the grain with a sharp knife and place the slices on a clean platter. Garnish with shaved red onion and serve with the dipping sauce and kombu rice if desired.

Peruvian Shrimp Ceviche

The city of Lima, Peru is famous for its seafood, and ceviche is a dish that is widely enjoyed throughout the region. Seafood ceviche is an important part of Peruvian gastronomy. Peruvian ceviche is not hot and spicy like Mexican ceviche; it is simple, fresh and flavorful. My version uses poached shrimp dressed in traditional ceviche ingredients. White fish, squid, scallops and octopus are also delicious options.

Unlike tuna or salmon, shrimp must be poached prior to making ceviche. Because it uses heat, this recipe is technically a cross between a shrimp cocktail and a ceviche. I'm calling it a ceviche because of the way it is dressed and how it hearkens back to flavors I enjoyed in Peru.

This is one of those dishes that I like to serve family-style. Slicing the shrimp in half lengthwise makes for a beautiful presentation and gives the appearance of a more abundant bowl.

INGREDIENTS

{ Serves 6 }

- **4 cups water**

- **2 tablespoons sea salt**, plus more as needed

- **1 tablespoon whole black peppercorns**

- **1 large lemon**, halved

- **3 pounds white shrimp**, peeled, deveined and halved

- **4 large fresh tomatoes**, chopped

- **1 large red onion**, thinly sliced

- **2 medium jalapeño peppers**, minced

- **1 bunch (1 cup) fresh cilantro**, leaves only

- **1 tablespoon avocado oil**

- **2 large limes**, juice only

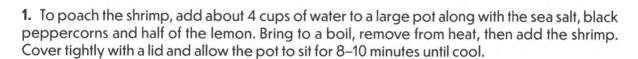

SERVING SUGGESTIONS: TORTILLA CHIPS, JICAMA TOSTADA SHELLS (SEE PAGE 420), TOSTONES (SEE PAGE 404), OR LETTUCE CUPS

DIRECTIONS

1. To poach the shrimp, add about 4 cups of water to a large pot along with the sea salt, black peppercorns and half of the lemon. Bring to a boil, remove from heat, then add the shrimp. Cover tightly with a lid and allow the pot to sit for 8–10 minutes until cool.

2. Drain the pot and add the shrimp to a large bowl along with the tomatoes, red onion, jalapeño pepper, cilantro, avocado oil and lime juice. Mix to combine.

3. Taste for seasoning and add salt and the juice of the remaining lemon half as needed. Cover and refrigerate for at least 1 hour or overnight if needed. Serve family-style with tortilla chips, jicama tostada shells, tostones or lettuce cups.

Scottish Salmon Tartare

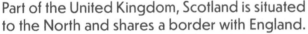

WITH CUCUMBER

Part of the United Kingdom, Scotland is situated to the North and shares a border with England.
Rich with Celtic, Norse, and Scottish heritage, the county is home to dazzling landscapes, crumbling castles and more than 800 small islands including the Shetland Isles and Orkney Isles.

The county is surrounded by different bodies of water that range in topography from wild coastlines to pristine beaches. The sparkling clean waters of Scotland boast some of the world's best seafood, including oysters, langoustines and salmon. Scottish salmon was the first cultivated salmon to be given the coveted Label Rouge designation by the French government. The fish was originally produced as a niche market but quickly grew to be one of Europe's most sought-after fish, according to the Scottish Salmon Producers Organization.

This beautiful and sophisticated Scottish salmon tartare dish is a nod to its French association while also celebrating the fine flavor of the fish. The cucumber "chips" are a result of using a mandoline to achieve even slices.

Check out my Posh Pointers on page 340 for safety tips on preparing raw seafood.

INGREDIENTS

{ Serves 6 }

- **1 large English cucumber**, chopped fine

- **1½ pounds center-cut Scottish salmon or Atlantic salmon**, skin and pin bones removed

- **1 medium shallot**, minced

- **1 tablespoon chopped flat-leaf parsley**

- **1 medium lemon**, juice and zest

- **2 tablespoons minced fresh chives**

- **1 tablespoon olive oil**

- **½ teaspoon sea salt**

- **½ teaspoon freshly ground black pepper**

DIRECTIONS

1. Use a mandoline or a sharp knife to slice the cucumber into round "chips" or thin slices—use your judgement and cut them to your preference. Add to a platter, cover with plastic wrap, and set aside.

2. Using a sharp knife, cut the salmon into ½- to ¼-inch cubes.

3. In a medium-sized bowl, gently fold together the salmon, shallot, parsley, lemon juice and zest, and 1 tablespoon of chives. Add the olive oil, sea salt and black pepper, and gently fold into the mixture. Cover the bowl with plastic wrap and refrigerate for 30 minutes or up to 8 hours. Keep in mind that the longer you leave the fish to marinate, the more "cooked" it will be from the lemon juice.

4. Remove the salmon tartare from the refrigerator 15 minutes before serving. Add equal portions to 6 plates and top with the chopped cucumber. Serve immediately.

Chilean Crudo (Sea Bass)

The laid-back country of Chile has a long coastline surrounded by Argentina, Bolivia, Paraguay and Peru. The exotic country is known for its association with Chilean sea bass, a highly prized white fish that adorns the menus of high-end restaurants and sells for top dollar in seafood markets.

Also known as Patagonian toothfish, Chilean sea bass underwent a name change decades ago in the 1970s to help make it more marketable. These highly prized fish subsist on a diet of squid, crustaceans and other fish and can grow as large as 200 pounds. They are deep-sea dwellers that swim alongside sperm whales and elephant seals and are often their prey, according to the organization Oceana.

Before starting this dish, be sure to check out my Posh Pointers on page 340 for safety tips on preparing raw seafood.

INGREDIENTS

{ Serves 4 }

- **1½ pounds fresh boneless,** skinless Chilean sea bass, sliced into ¼-inch pieces

- **2 large limes,** juice only

- **1 small chili pepper,** minced

- **2 tablespoons chopped fresh cilantro leaves,** with a few leaves reserved for garnish

- **1 small white onion,** thinly sliced

- **2 large radishes,** thinly sliced on a mandoline

- **2 tablespoons olive oil**

- **Sea salt and freshly ground black pepper to taste**

DIRECTIONS

SPECIAL EQUIPMENT: CHILLED PLATE OR SERVING DISH

1. To assemble the crudo, place the fish slices on a chilled plate, overlapping the pieces in a decorative pattern. Squeeze the lime juice over the top, making sure to cover every piece of fish. Wrap the plate in plastic wrap and refrigerate for 20 minutes.

2. To make the dressing, combine the chili pepper, cilantro, onion, radish, olive oil and a pinch of sea salt and freshly ground black pepper in a small bowl. Taste for seasoning and adjust as needed. Set aside.

3. When the fish is ready, remove the plate from the refrigerator. Pour the dressing over the fish and serve immediately.

New Zealand Crudo Hapuka (Sea Bass)

As a Pacific Island country, New Zealand is home to spectacular caves, glaciers, sandy beaches and tons of glorious seafood! Hāpuku, also referenced as hāpuku or whapuku, is a popular catch in New Zealand and ranges from sweet, mild and delicate to juicy and flaky depending on the age and size of the fish. Like its misnomered friend Chilean sea bass, hāpuku, though sometimes referred to as New Zealand sea bass, is in fact, not a sea bass at all but a species known as groper.

This raw hapuka dish is delightful and easy to make. My preference for macadamia nut oil is based on the way the nutty flavor of the oil complements the sweetness of the fish and the toasted macadamia nuts called for in the recipe.

If hāpuku is challenging to find, swap it out for ahi tuna, opah, wahoo, dry sea scallops or salmon. Before starting this dish, be sure to check out my Posh Pointers on page 340 for safety tips on preparing raw seafood.

INGREDIENTS

{ Serves 4 }

- **3 tablespoons macadamia nut oil**

- **1 large lemon,** juice only

- **2 tablespoons chopped fresh cilantro leaves,** with a few leaves reserved for garnish

- **2 large cloves garlic,** minced

- **Sea salt and freshly ground black pepper to taste**

- **2 pounds boneless,** skinless hapuka, sliced into ¼-inch slices

- **2 large limes,** juice only

- **¼ cup toasted macadamia nuts,** crushed

DIRECTIONS

SPECIAL EQUIPMENT: CHILLED PLATES OR A SERVING DISH

1. To make the dressing, whisk together the macadamia nut oil, lemon juice, cilantro, garlic, and sea salt and black pepper in a small bowl. Taste for seasoning and adjust as needed. Set aside.

2. To assemble the crudo, place the fish slices on a chilled plate, overlapping the pieces in a decorative manner. Squeeze the lime juice over the top, making sure to cover every piece of fish. Wrap the plate in plastic wrap and refrigerate for 20 minutes.

3. When the fish is ready, pour the dressing over the fish, using only enough to lightly coat the fish. Decoratively sprinkle the macadamia nuts over the top along with the reserved cilantro. Serve immediately.

Venetian Tonno (Tuna) Carpaccio

Thinly sliced pieces of tuna combined with a drizzle of lemon juice and olive oil are all it takes to escape to Northern Italy, a city without roads, only canals lined with Renaissance palaces and Byzantine mosaics. Carpaccio is a classic Italian dish created in the 1950s by Giuseppe Cipirano, a Venetian barkeep. It is traditionally served as a starter but also works well as an entrée when served with a salad and fresh bread.

Big eye tuna, also known as ahi, are large, fast-growing tuna that can grow as large as 5 feet in length. They get their name from their strong body and large eyes. This succulent fish is at the top of the food chain and enjoys a diet of crustaceans, fish (including other tunas) and squid.

The key to making a good seafood carpaccio is slicing the fish wafer-thin, about the thickness of a coin. Make sure to chill your plate for best results. There are many versions of carpaccio; some are made with blood orange, lime or topped with arugula.

Alternative fish: Halibut, lionfish, octopus, sea scallops, sea bass and salmon.

INGREDIENTS

{ Serves 4 }

- **2 pounds big eye tuna**, skinned and bloodline removed

- **5 tablespoons lemon juice**

- **1 small lemon**, quartered, for serving

- **6 tablespoon Italian olive oil**, separated

- **Sea salt and freshly ground black pepper to taste**

- **4 fresh basil leaves**, julienned

- **Optional: capers in brine**

DIRECTIONS

SPECIAL EQUIPMENT: 4 SMALL PLATES, CHILLED

1. Going against the grain, carefully slice the fish in coin-thin pieces. Add the fish to each plate, being careful not to overlap the pieces. Set aside.

2. In a small bowl, blend the lemon juice with the olive oil and a pinch of salt and pepper. Spoon equal portions of the mix over the fish. Cover with plastic wrap and refrigerate for 30 minutes.

3. To serve, discard the plastic wrap and drizzle a little olive oil over each plate and garnish with fresh basil and capers as desired.

Side Dishes and Legumes

- Cuban Moros y Cristianos

- California Steamed Collard Greens

- Mediterranean Gigantes (Gigantic) Beans

- Brazilian Feijão (Black Bean Stew)

- Global Chickpeas

- Belizean Red Beans & Coconut Rice

- Louisiana Red Beans & Rice

- Goan Cauliflower, Coconut & Lentil Soup

- Middle Eastern Red Lentil Lemon Soup

- Cuban Accaras (Black-Eyed Pea Fritters)

- Southern Green Beans and Red Potatoes

- Native American Crawfish Cornbread

- Crispy St. Petersburg Potatoes

- Uruguayan Buñuelos de Algas (Seaweed Fritters)

- German Kohlrabi Slaw

- Albanian Tomato and Cucumber Salad

- Caribbean Tostones (Fried Green Plantains)

- Cuban Plátanos Maduros (Sweet Plantains)

- Tunisian Vegetable Couscous

- Tanzanian Pilau Rice with Spices

- Spanish Saffron Rice

- Global Coconut Rice

- Asian Kombu Rice

- Japanese Sushi Rice with Kombu

- Jicama Tostada Shells

- Italian Sautéed Broccolini

- German Cauliflower Parsnip Purée

Cooking Dried Legumes

~~~~~~

Legumes are a big part of coastal cooking around the globe—from the classic red beans and rice from the American south, to gigante beans from the Mediterranean and black-eyed pea fritters from West Africa. They come in various colors, shapes and sizes and are universally delicious!

Legumes are essentially any form of bean, pea or seed from the Fabaceae or Leguminosae botanical family, according to the Grains and Legumes Nutrition Council. They can be found fresh, dried, canned or frozen. This section of the book includes some of my favorite bean, lentil and pea recipes. Pescatarians eat a plant-based diet that is supplemented with seafood and legumes—a wonderful addition to the lifestyle.

Rumor has it that cooking dried beans from scratch can be fussy and laborious work. Although they do require some attention if cooking on the stovetop, legumes are pretty easy to make and just need a little time and attention. If you own a pressure cooker as I do, you will find cooking dried beans an easy-peasy process.

The Bean Institute, a U.S.-based cooperative of bean growers from the Midwest, outlines a four-step method for cooking beans on the stovetop, and one that I agree with wholeheartedly.

TRADITIONAL COOKING METHOD

1. Thoroughly rinse beans in cold water and remove any rocks or debris.

2. Soak beans overnight or up to 12 hours—this will help rehydrate the beans and speed up the cooking process.

3. Rinse the beans and cook them in fresh water or broth over medium heat. Since beans expand when cooking, you may need to add more liquid as they cook. Stir on occasion.

QUICK-SOAK METHOD (WHEN YOU DON'T HAVE TIME FOR SOAKING)

1. Cover the beans generously with cold water in a large saucepan and bring to a boil.

2. Simmer for 2 minutes, then turn off the heat, cover tightly with a lid, and let them sit for 1 hour.

3. When ready to use, drain and rinse the beans.

4. Transfer them to a large soup pot along with water or a broth and cook for 60–90 minutes, or until the desired level of tenderness is reached.

In most cases I use a traditional mirepoix (celery, carrot and onion) along with a bay leaf to add flavor and texture to my pot of legumes. In the South where carrots don't grow well, celery, bell pepper and onion make up the base for legumes, soups and gravies. Once you have a foundation of flavor, you can have fun and add ingredients that interest you—tomatoes, smoked salmon belly, garlic, herbs, spices, or whatever floats your boat!

PRESSURE COOKER METHOD

1. To cook your beans with a pressure cooker, please follow the manufacturer's instructions.

2. Once the beans are cooked, I recommend letting them rest in the cooker for 30–60 minutes to give them time to absorb the flavors. The benefit of pressure cooking is that the process is fast, but it cannot fully replace the time needed for the co-mingling of flavors.

Cuban Moros y Cristianos

BLACK BEANS AND RICE

Rice and beans are staple foods throughout the Caribbean and Latin America. Moros y Cristianos is a classic Cuban dish that is served practically everywhere on the island. The name translates into Moors and Christians. The dish had a deep history in the country and refers to a point of contention in the early 8th century between Spanish Christians and African Muslims and commemorates the Reconquista, a long battle between the two groups.

There is some debate as to whether the original dish used red or black beans, but my experience has been black beans all the way. The key to this dish is reserving the color of the black beans by not over rinsing. The dark color is part of its charm.

INGREDIENTS

- **8 cups water**

- **½ pound dry black beans**, soaked overnight

- **2 tablespoons vegetable oil**

- **1 small bell pepper**, chopped

- **1 small white onion**, chopped

- **2 cloves garlic**, crushed and chopped

- **1 cup long grain white rice**

- **1 tablespoon cumin powder**

- **2 tablespoons tomato paste**

- **4½ cups vegetable broth**

- **1 tablespoon apple cider vinegar**

- **1 teaspoon dried oregano**

- **1 bay leaf**

- **1 teaspoons sea salt**

- **Freshly ground black pepper to taste**

DIRECTIONS

1. In a large Dutch oven or heavy-bottomed pot, add the water and black beans and cook covered for about 2 hours over medium-high heat. Keep an eye on the liquid level; the beans should always be covered. Set aside.

2. In a medium sauté pan over medium-high heat add the bell pepper, onion and garlic and sauté for 2 minutes, then reduce the heat to sweat the vegetables until they are soft and fragrant. Add the rice and coat in the vegetable mixture (also known as sofrito). Set aside.

3. Drain the black beans, reserving 1 cup of liquid. Add the black beans back to the pot along with the bean liquid, cumin, tomato paste, vegetable broth, apple cider vinegar, oregano, bay leaf, sea salt, black pepper and the vegetable and rice mix. Stir to combine and bring to a boil for 5 minutes, then cover and simmer for 50 minutes or until the rice absorbs the liquid. Remove from heat and allow the pot to rest for 10 minutes. Fluff and serve as desired.

California Steamed Collard Greens

I grew up eating all types of greens. My grandparents grew all sorts on their Central California farm, which often accompanied Sunday dinners. My parents currently grow many varieties including kale, mustard, turnip and collards in their large organic garden, and in true tradition, I have some growing in my own garden.

My preference is to steam my collards until just tender, versus other recipes that call for braising the vegetable for 1 hour or more to create a very tender, melt-in-your-mouth texture. Using a good-quality vegetable bouillon gives the greens a lovely umami flavor; alternatively, you can substitute vegetable broth for the water and omit the bouillon.

INGREDIENTS

- **1 tablespoon vegetable oil**

- **2 cloves garlic**, peeled and chopped

- **3 bunches or 3 cups collard greens**, rinsed, stems removed and chopped

- **1 tablespoon vegetable bouillon or vegetable base**

- **1 teaspoon crushed red pepper flake**

- **Kosher salt and freshly ground black pepper to taste**

- **1 cup water**

DIRECTIONS

1. Add the oil to a Dutch oven or a medium-sized pot along with the collard greens and garlic. Sauté on medium-high heat for 3 minutes then add the water and bouillon. Mix to combine, then reduce the heat to medium and simmer for 18 minutes or until the greens are tender. Serve immediately as desired.

Mediterra- nean Gigantes (Gigantic) Beans

Big in size and equally large in flavor, these gorgeous large white beans are common in parts of Europe and are used throughout Mediterranean in Greece, Portugal and Spain. Gigantes are similar to fava and butter beans with a meaty texture and slightly sweet flavor.

These beans are great on their own but are even more amazing with the addition of smoked salmon belly or a few anchovies. Feel free to experiment.

INGREDIENTS

{ Serves 4-6 }

- **4 tablespoons olive oil**

- **1 large white onion**, chopped

- **4 cloves garlic**, minced

- **2 stalks celery**, diced

- **2 large carrots**, diced

- **2 cups water**, more as needed

- **4 cups low-sodium vegetable broth**

- **2 tablespoons tomato paste**

- **½ pound gigante beans**, soaked overnight (12–14 hours)

- **3 sprigs fresh thyme**

- **Sea salt and freshly ground black pepper to taste**

- **1 bunch fresh parsley**, chopped, for garnish

SERVING SUGGESTIONS: TOASTED PITA, CRUSTY BREAD OR ROASTED FISH

DIRECTIONS

1. In a large Dutch oven or heavy-bottomed pot, heat the olive oil over medium-high heat. Add the onion, garlic, celery and carrot, and cook for 3–4 minutes until fragrant.

2. Add the water, vegetable broth, tomato paste, gigante beans and thyme and stir to combine. Bring to a boil and cook for 5 minutes, then cover with the lid slightly ajar and simmer for 2 hours and 30 minutes— stir occasionally and add more water if needed. The beans should always be covered in liquid.

3. When the time is up, taste the beans for flavor and add sea salt and freshly ground black pepper to taste. Check the doneness of the beans, which should be tender and creamy. Cover the pot fully and cook for another 30–60 minutes as needed. Turn off the heat and let the pot sit for 20 minutes; this will allow the flavors to meld and will help the beans become wonderfully flavorful. Garnish with fresh parsley and serve as desired.

4. Serve as a side dish with roasted fish or on its own with toasted pita or crusty bread.

Brazilian Feijão (Black Bean Stew)

Black beans in South America are practically mother's milk! They are central to the country's gastronomy and are, in fact, Brazil's national dish. Called feijão, this dish is a Portuguese-inspired black bean stew with pork and vegetables. My pescatarian version excludes the meat but has just as much flavor.

Dendê oil, also known as red palm oil, is a thick, rich and highly flavorful traditional ingredient used in the cooking styles of Bahia, a notable region of Brazil with roots steeped in West African culture. Arriving in Brazil along with millions of enslaved Africans, this reddish-orange colored oil is used to create black beans and another of my favorite South American dishes called moqueca or seafood stew.

Dendê oil is essential to this dish in order to create authentic flavor, but coconut oil makes a good substitute.

INGREDIENTS

{ Serves 6-8 }

- **2 tablespoons dendê oil**, or coconut oil

- **1 bell pepper**, chopped

- **1 large carrot**, diced

- **2 stalks celery**, diced

- **1 medium onion**, chopped

- **2 cloves garlic**, chopped

- **1 tablespoon ground coriander**

- **2 tablespoons ground cumin**

- **1 tablespoon chili powder**

- **1 pound (2 cups) dried black beans,** sorted and soaked overnight

- **3 cups vegetable stock**

- **4 cups water**, more as needed

- **1 bay leaf**

- **Smoked paprika sea salt (see page 548) and freshly ground black pepper to taste**

- **¼ cup chopped fresh cilantro**

DIRECTIONS

1. In a large Dutch oven or heavy-bottomed pot, heat the dendê or coconut oil over medium-high heat. When the oil is hot, toss in the bell pepper, carrot, celery, onion, garlic, coriander, cumin and chili powder, and cook for 2–3 minutes until soft and fragrant.

2. Add the black beans, vegetable stock, water and bay leaf and bring to a boil for 10 minutes, then cover with the lid slightly ajar and reduce the heat to a simmer. Cook for 60 minutes.

3. After one hour, stir in the smoked paprika sea salt and black pepper to taste. Check the beans for doneness and flavor, adjusting the seasoning as needed. Check the liquid level and add more water if needed—the water should be about 1 inch above the beans. Reduce the heat to a simmer, cover fully with the lid, and cook for an additional 45 minutes.

4. Taste the beans again for doneness—they should be flavorful, tender and slightly creamy. If the beans are not done, cook in additional 10-minute intervals until your ideal level of doneness is reached. When beans are finished, turn off the heat and let the pot sit for 20 minutes before serving, giving the flavors time to meld. Garnish with fresh cilantro and serve as desired.

Global Chickpeas

Chickpeas also called garbanzos, grams, pulses and Egyptian peas, are primarily consumed in India, the Mediterranean and the Middle East. They have a buttery, nutty flavor and are often used to create soups, stews, hummus and falafel (one of my favorites). However, they are having quite a moment in North America and are all the rage.

According to Harvard School of Public Health, chickpeas appeared in Turkey around 3500 BCE, and in France in 6790 BCE. Though they are grown in more than 50 countries worldwide, India currently produces the most garbanzos, which are widely available canned, dried and in flour form.

The most common type of chickpea produced is called kabuli—these are the light or off-white colored variety. The second most popular type of chickpea is a smaller and darker type called desi, which are often dried and made into flour for baking.

I've attributed this dish to the global community since the recipe is universal and can be customized to suit most palates.

INGREDIENTS

{ Makes 4 cups }

- **2 tablespoons olive oil**
- **2 cloves garlic**
- **1 large Spanish onion**, halved
- **2 large carrots**, halved
- **2 stalks celery**, chopped
- **2 cups water**
- **4 cups vegetable broth**

- **1 bay leaf**
- **2 whole sun-dried tomatoes**
- **4 whole sprigs fresh oregano**
- **1 pound dried chickpeas**, soaked overnight and rinsed
- **Sea salt freshly ground black pepper to taste**

DIRECTIONS

1. In a large Dutch oven or heavy-bottomed pot, heat the olive oil over medium-high heat. Add the garlic, Spanish onion, carrot and celery and sauté for 3 minutes until fragrant. Add the water, vegetable broth, bay leaf, sun-dried tomatoes, oregano and chickpeas and bring to a boil for 10 minutes.

2. Reduce the heat to a simmer and cook covered with the lid slightly ajar for 60 minutes, checking the water level on occasion. The beans should always be covered by 1 inch of water.

3. After 1 hour, check the chickpeas for doneness and taste for flavor. Add sea salt and freshly ground black pepper to taste. The chickpeas should be fork tender. If you prefer a more tender chickpea, cook in intervals of 15 minutes until desired texture is reached. When the chickpeas are done, turn off the heat and use as desired.

Belizean Red Beans & Coconut Rice

Rice & beans are a staple dish of this beautifully diverse part of the world! Red beans or a scoop of rice & red beans are served with almost every meal in Belize—I even had it for breakfast one morning with fry jacks, a traditional breakfast or snack food similar to a beignet or savory donut.

I enjoyed rice & red beans a few ways during my travels in Belize. Some cooks left the beans whole and others kept things slightly on the mashed and soupy side (called stewed beans), and on occasion the beans and rice were combined. All versions were tasty. My preference is to cook them together for a more traditional experience. This dish is famously served with stewed meat or fish and affectionately called a "Sunday Dinna."

If you are new to cooking rice and beans together, it is a simple process; it just takes a little practice in terms of getting your ideal rice to bean ratio right. I like the beans more than rice, which is what you'll find in this recipe. Long-grain jasmine rice is ideal for this recipe because the rice holds up well and the grains remain firm.

You can make the beans in a crockpot or a pressure cooker; my version is cooked on the stovetop top and can be made up to a day in advance. See my Posh Pointers on cooking dry beans on page 368. In a pinch, canned kidney beans dressed up a little will also work.

This is a simple dish but it requires attention and some finesse. You will be rewarded with a delicious taste of Belize!

INGREDIENTS

- **3 tablespoons coconut oil,** separated

- **1 medium bell pepper (any color),** seeded and chopped

- **1 medium white onion,** chopped

- **2 cloves garlic,** minced

- **1 large carrot,** chopped

- **2 stalks celery,** chopped

- **4 cups water,** more as needed

- **2 bay leaves**

- **2 sprigs fresh thyme,** leaves only

- **1 cup dry red kidney beans,** soaked overnight, **or 2 cups cooked kidney beans,** rinsed

- **1½ cups unsweetened coconut milk (1 14-ounce can)**

- **1 cup plain coconut water**

- **1 scallion,** sliced

- **1 small whole habañero pepper (optional)**

- **1 cup long-grain white Jasmine rice or long grain brown rice rinsed and soaked for 30 minutes**

- **Sea salt and freshly ground black pepper to taste**

- **Marie Sharp's Belizean Habañero Pepper Sauce** (any flavor), optional

DIRECTIONS

{ Serves 4 }

1. In a large Dutch oven or heavy-bottomed pot, heat 2 tablespoons of the coconut oil over medium-high heat. Add the bell pepper, white onion, garlic, carrot and celery and sauté for 3 minutes until fragrant.

2. Add the water, bay leaves and thyme and bring to a boil for 5 minutes. Drain the beans from the soaking water and add them to the pot. Stir to combine and reduce the heat to a simmer. Cook covered with the lid slightly ajar for 90 minutes. Check the water level on occasion; the beans should always be covered by 1 inch of liquid.

3. When the time is up, check the beans for doneness; they should be tender yet firm. Cook in 15-minute increments until the desired level of tenderness is achieved.

4. Pour in the coconut milk, coconut water, scallion, habañero pepper (if using), and rice and stir to combine, adding more water if needed—keep in mind that one cup of rice absorbs about 2 cups of water. Add sea salt and black pepper to taste. Cover with the lid slightly ajar and cook for 15 minutes, then fully place the lid on the pot, remove from heat and let it stand for 10–15 minutes. This is important because it allows the rice to steam and absorb the flavors of the coconut milk.

5. To serve, scoop out portions of rice and beans and serve with pepper sauce if desired.

Louisiana Red Beans & Rice

You can't go anywhere in the American South without being offered this Southern staple at restaurants or in family homes. Red beans and rice are traditionally served with pieces of sausage, salt pork or bacon. My version uses smoked salmon belly, which can be omitted if you want to make this as a vegetarian option.

Large red kidney beans are used here. They are hearty, cook up creamy and absorb tons of flavor. Named for their resemblance to a specific internal organ, red kidney beans originated in Peru and were cultivated more than 8,000 years ago, according to the folks at Camellia® Brand Beans. They were spread by migrating tribes throughout the Americas and eventually were commercially produced by Acadian farmers in Louisiana in the 1700s. Enslaved African plantation workers prepared a spicy version of red beans and rice and emigrating Haitians put their own Caribbean spin on the dish.

Traditionally, red beans and rice were commonly eaten in New Orleans on Monday for two reasons: the start of the week was typically laundry day, a labor-intensive task that allowed the cook to sort and fold while keeping an eye on the simmering pot of beans. The second reason is that the ham bone left from Sunday supper's ham could be used for flavoring the beans.

Red beans are such a celebrated part of the fabric of this region that Jazz artist Louis "Satchmo" Armstrong occasionally signed his letters "Red Beans and Ricely Yours," according to National Public Radio (NPR) in a story called "The Culinary Habits Of Louis Armstrong."

INGREDIENTS

- 2 tablespoons avocado oil

- ¼ pound smoked salmon belly, cut into chunks

- 1 bell pepper (any color), seeded and chopped

- 1 large white onion, chopped

- 2 cloves garlic, chopped

- 3 stalks celery, chopped

- 4 cups vegetable broth

- 4 cups water, separated, more as needed

- 1 bay leaf

- 1 tablespoon paprika

- 1 tablespoon cayenne

- 1 tablespoon ground cumin

- 3 whole sprigs fresh thyme

- 3 tablespoons tomato paste

- 1 pound red beans, soaked overnight, rinsed and drained

- Sea salt and freshly ground black pepper to taste

- 2 cups cooked white rice

DIRECTIONS

{ Makes 6 cups }

1. In a large Dutch oven or heavy-bottomed pot, heat the avocado oil over medium-high heat. When the oil is hot, add the smoked salmon belly, bell pepper, white onion, garlic and celery and sauté until fragrant, about 3 minutes.

2. Next, pour in the vegetable broth and water and add the bay leaf, paprika, cayenne, cumin, fresh thyme, tomato paste and red beans. Stir to combine and bring the pot to a boil for 10 minutes.

3. Reduce the heat to a simmer and cover the pot with the lid slightly ajar for 90 minutes. Check the water level on occasion—the beans should always be covered by 1 inch of water.

4. When the time is up, check the beans for doneness, they should be tender yet still hold their shape. Taste for seasoning and add sea salt and black pepper as needed. Cook for an additional 30 minutes until the desired level of tenderness is achieved. Set aside for 10–15 minutes before serving, allowing the beans to fully absorb the flavor of the liquid. Serve as desired with Native American crawfish cornbread.

SERVING SUGGESTIONS:
TOASTED PITA, CRUSTY BREAD OR ROASTED FISH

Goan Cauliflower, Coconut & Lentil Soup

Although I grew up enjoying soup—my mom's noodle soup and grilled cheese in particular—it wasn't until the mid-2000s that I truly fell in love with this classic comfort food while living in a very diverse neighborhood in Glendale, California.

I was transitioning into becoming a pescatarian and was slowly developing my arsenal of recipes. Legume-based soups slowly became a favorite thanks to the influence of my Armenian, Greek, Indian, Jewish and Mexican neighbors.

This recipe combines easily accessible ingredients to create a flavorful Indian-inspired soup. I like this potage any time of day—for breakfast, lunch or as a light supper.

Orange lentils sometimes referred to as red lentils, cook up fast since they are de-husked and split before packaging. Cauliflower, a low-carb darling, is a firm, cruciferous vegetable that also cooks up in a flash, making this soup an everyday favorite.

A couple of things to note: The first is that I have a generous spice cabinet and enjoy making my own blends. Like all cooks, I have my list of favorite spices and will toss them into the pot as desired. If your spice cabinet is limited, feel free to purchase a dry or wet curry or powder blend for this recipe; there are several wonderful versions on the market from large and small companies. A Moroccan spice blend, ras el hanout, also works for this recipe with a dash of turmeric.

Secondly, as an artform, texture plays a big role in soup making. With this in mind, I like to prepare the lentils and cauliflower separately and combine them at the end to create the ideal soup. This allows me to control the texture of both ingredients, but mostly the cauliflower since the lentils will go soft to create the base of the soup.

I have enjoyed this soup both chunky and smooth! If you like a chunky soup, you will lightly steam the cauliflower, about 5 minutes, before combining with the lentils and other ingredients. For a silky-smooth soup, you will fully steam the cauliflower before blending. If you are a fan of one-pot cooking, you can cook the lentils and the cauliflower at the same time. In such a case I'd recommend making a smooth soup.

INGREDIENTS

~~~~~~~~

- **1 head cauliflower (or two cups)**, chopped

- **3 tablespoon ghee or vegetable oil**

- **1 medium brown onion**, diced small

- **2 large stalks celery**, diced small

- **2 large carrots**, diced small

- **1 tablespoon ground coriander**

- **1 tablespoon ground cumin**

- **1 tablespoon minced garlic**

- **1 teaspoon paprika**

- **1 tablespoon ground turmeric**

- **1 tablespoon ground ginger**

- **2½ cups low-sodium vegetable broth or water**, separated

- **1 cup red lentils**, rinsed and drained

- **1 14-ounce can coconut milk**

- **Sea salt and freshly ground black pepper to taste**

- **1 teaspoon red pepper flake**, more as needed

DIRECTIONS   { Serves 4-6 }

~~~~~~~~

SPECIAL EQUIPMENT:
STICK BLENDER, FOOD PROCESSOR OR BLENDER

1. Add the cauliflower to a large pot along with ½ cup water. Cover and cook for 5–8 minutes, depending on your desired texture. Turn off the heat, drain, and place cauliflower in a container. Set aside.

2. In the same pot used to cook the cauliflower, heat the ghee or vegetable oil over medium heat, then add the onion, celery and carrot. Cook until soft and fragrant, about 3 minutes. Toss in the coriander, cumin, garlic, paprika, turmeric and ginger and cook for another minute.

3. Add the vegetable broth or water and the lentils. Stir to combine, cover and cook for 10 minutes. The lentils should be soft. Turn off the heat and add half of the cauliflower along with the coconut milk. Use an immersion blender to mix until smooth.

4. If using a food processor or countertop blender, add the contents of the pot to the container and pulse until smooth, then add back to pot. Taste for seasoning and add sea salt and freshly ground black pepper to taste, and the red pepper flake.

5. Add the remaining cauliflower to the pot and simmer for 5 minutes. The soup should be a bit chunky and the lentils should be soft and tender. Add a little more water if the soup is too thick for your liking. Serve immediately with whole wheat pita and garnish with fresh cilantro as desired.

SERVING SUGGESTIONS:
WHOLE WHEAT PITA BREAD, FRESH CILANTRO

Middle Eastern Red Lentil Lemon Soup

During the winter of 2019 I fell in love with red lentil soup. I discovered it while caring for a dear friend in Minnesota who lived adjacent to a cozy Middle Eastern restaurant called Shish. The flavors wafting out of the doors were mesmerizing and I couldn't resist. I paid the shop a visit and soon learned that red lentil lemon soup was one of their signature offerings.

I placed an order for falafel and the soup and ended up having to wait 20 minutes for my savory supper as they had sold out. I was offered a baklava and coffee to hold me over, which I happily accepted. Upon taking my first bite, I forgot about the wait and tucked in. The savory, nutty and brightly flavored soup was outstanding.

Lentils are popular in the Middle East and used for soup, falafel, hummus, fried chickpeas and more. Often substituted for meat, they are low in fat and an excellent source of soluble and insoluble fiber.

The Meyer lemon and simple aromatics make this an easy everyday kind of soup, especially since it takes less than 30 minutes to cook. Red lentils cook up quickly because they are dehusked and split before packaging.

This soup works great as a meal served with toasted pita or as a side dish to roasted fish or salmoncakes.

INGREDIENTS

- 3 tablespoons olive oil

- 1 medium brown onion, diced small

- 2 large stalks celery, diced small

- 2 large carrots, diced small

- 1 tablespoon ground coriander

- 1 tablespoon ground cumin

- 1 teaspoon paprika

- 1 tablespoon ground turmeric

- 2 cups water

- 2 cups low-sodium vegetable broth

- 1 tablespoon tomato paste

- 2 sprigs fresh thyme, leaves only

- 1 cup red lentils

- 1 teaspoon sea salt

- ½ medium or 3 tablespoons preserved lemon, skin only, diced

- ½ Meyer lemon

DIRECTIONS

1. In a heavy-bottomed pan, heat the olive oil over medium heat, then add the onion, celery and carrot. Cook until soft and fragrant, about 3 minutes. Toss in the ground coriander, cumin, paprika and turmeric and cook for another minute.

2. Add the water, vegetable broth, tomato paste and thyme. Stir to combine and cook for 10 minutes.

3. Add the red lentils, sea salt and preserved lemon and cook for an additional 10 minutes. Taste for seasoning and adjust as needed.

4. Turn off the heat and use an immersion or "stick" blender and blend for 10–15 seconds until smooth. Alternately, if using a blender or food processor, add half of the soup to the container and blend until smooth.

5. Reduce heat to a low simmer and cook for 5 minutes. The soup should be a bit chunky and the lentils soft and tender. Add a little more water if the soup is too thick. Squeeze the juice of the Meyer lemon over the soup (use a strainer to prevent seeds) and serve immediately with toasted pita if desired.

SERVING SUGGESTIONS:
TOASTED PITA BREAD, RUSTIC BREAD

Cuban Accaras

BLACK-EYED PEA FRITTERS

Cuba is a Caribbean island surrounded by more than 2,000 miles of coastline. The country has strong gastronomic ties to its indigenous peoples, the Taíno, as well as to Spain and West Africa.

I'm attributing this fritter recipe to the island nation because it's a celebrated treat throughout the country; however, the origin of accaras is West African. The difference between the accaras you'll find in say, Nigeria or Senegal, versus Cuba is in the spices.

The key to making great accaras is to soak the peas overnight, remove the skins, and add a little baking powder to the batter. This results in light and crunchy fritters. These fritters are a labor of love and require a bit of work, but it's well worth it. Make a big batch because you'll want more the next day—the texture changes slightly, but they will still be delicious after a quick warm-up in the oven.

For a more substantial meal, treat these fritters like falafel and serve them sandwich-style with toppings.

INGREDIENTS

Makes
20–25 fritters

- **2 pounds dried black-eyed peas**, soaked overnight

- **4 cloves garlic**

- **3 large scallions**, chopped

- **1 large onion**, quartered

- **½ cup water**, or as needed

- **2 teaspoons cayenne pepper**

- **2 tablespoons baking powder**

- **2 teaspoons sea salt**, plus more to taste

- **Freshly ground black pepper to taste**

- **Vegetable oil for frying**

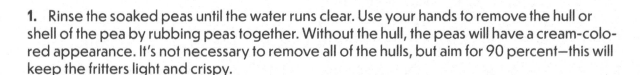

SERVING SUGGESTIONS: PEPPER SAUCE, FRESH LIME

DIRECTIONS

1. Rinse the soaked peas until the water runs clear. Use your hands to remove the hull or shell of the pea by rubbing peas together. Without the hull, the peas will have a cream-colored appearance. It's not necessary to remove all of the hulls, but aim for 90 percent—this will keep the fritters light and crispy.

2. Combine the peas, garlic, scallions and onion in a food processor. Pulse, adding a little water if needed to get the batter going. The batter should be smooth with bits of chunky peas. Pour the mixture into a large bowl and stir in the cayenne pepper, baking powder, sea salt and a few cracks of black pepper. Stir to combine and allow to sit for 10 minutes.

3. Meanwhile, heat the oil to 375°F. Use a thermometer or test the oil by adding a small cube of bread to the oil—when it turns brown, the oil is ready. While the oil is heating, set up a bed of paper towels for draining the fritters.

4. Remove the fritter from the oil using a slotted spoon or spider strainer. Taste the fritter and adjust the seasoning as needed. Proceed with the remaining batter, placing the cooked fritters on a bed of paper towels. Serve immediately with pepper sauce and fresh lime.

Southern Green Beans and Red Potatoes

Green beans sometimes referred to as string beans or haricot vert, are snap beans that can be found in shades of green and purple. They are grown on a bush or a pole and as a result are often called "bush beans" or "pole beans."

Green beans are harvested while immature and technically considered a fruit by botanists since they are pods that contain seeds. They are treated like vegetables and prepared using savory ingredients in most parts of the world.

This recipe from the American South traditionally calls for the addition of ham or ham bone. This version is vegetarian, but it benefits from a slice of smoked salmon belly if you're feeling so inclined. Served for Sunday supper, Christmas dinner, Easter lunch and other special occasions, a steaming bowl pairs well with fried catfish and roasted salmon.

I call for fresh green beans for this dish, but canned green beans will work well if they are out of season in your area. There is a saying, "Cook the can out of your beans." This means that you take canned items and mix them with fresh aromatics and seasonings or high-quality bouillon and make them your own. Like tinned seafood, canned fruits and vegetables are picked at the peak of ripeness, so they often make an excellent choice.

My maternal grandparents grew green beans on their Central California farm, among a few dozen other fruits and vegetables. During weekend and summer visits, my sisters and I were often given the task of helping my grandma with supper by "snapping" a freshly picked crop.

Red potatoes are nice for this recipe and what I grew up enjoying, but any waxy or all-purpose variety will do. Good alternatives are Yukon gold, fingerling, or even a variety of mixed baby potatoes. My cooking style results in tender potatoes and green beans, which is different from the well-done version found in some Southern homes. If you like your vegetables well-done or stewed, cook them a little longer.

INGREDIENTS

{ Serves 4 }

- **1 tablespoon avocado oil**

- **2 cloves garlic, minced**

- **1 medium onion, chopped**

- **1 pound red potatoes, quartered**

- **½ cup water**, or as needed

- **1 cup vegetable broth**

- **1½ pounds fresh green beans, trimmed and snapped in half or 2 14-ounce cans, drained**

- **2 teaspoons sea salt**, plus more to taste

- **Freshly ground black pepper to taste**

SERVING SUGGESTIONS: PEPPER SAUCE, FRESH LIME

DIRECTIONS

1. In a Dutch oven, heat the avocado oil over medium-high heat. Add the garlic and onion and cook until fragrant, about 2–3 minutes. Add the potatoes, vegetable broth and water and bring the pot to a boil for 2–3 minutes, then cover and reduce heat to medium. Cook for 5 minutes with the lid slightly ajar.

2. Add the green beans along with sea salt and freshly ground black pepper to taste. Stir to combine. Cook for 10–12 minutes covered with the lid slightly ajar, or until the potatoes are fork tender. Taste for seasoning and add salt and black pepper as needed. Remove from the heat and allow the pot to rest for 5 minutes before serving.

Native American Crawfish Cornbread

Cornbread is delicious on its own, but the addition of crawfish turns it into a real treat. An early staple of Native Americans, cornbread is a quick bread made with simple ingredients, including ground corn, which was once a major food source along with a variety of shellfish—clams, oysters, shrimp and crawfish were abundant and highly favored.

As Top Chef alum Chris Scott often says, "If you want to truly know a culture, eat their bread." Consider the baguette from France, injera from Ethiopia and the ngome from West Africa. Centuries ago, cornbread didn't taste that great; the simple mix of cooked ground corn and water cooked on an open flame was basic fare. It morphed into a more delicious and iconic southern staple through the years with the culinary influences of enslaved Africans who added ingredients to elevate the flavor. This jazzed-up version is my homage to this culturally complex dish.

INGREDIENTS

{ Serves 10–12 }

- **½ cup plus 2 teaspoons corn oil,** separated
- **1 cup finely chopped Spanish onion**
- **1 cup finely chopped bell pepper**
- **½ cup finely chopped scallions,** green part only
- **2 tablespoons chopped fresh jalapeño pepper**
- **½ teaspoon white pepper**
- **½ cup white flour,** sifted
- **1½ cups cornmeal**

- **4 teaspoons baking powder**
- **½ teaspoon baking soda**
- **1 teaspoon paprika sea salt** (see page 548)
- **3 large eggs**
- **1 cup skim milk**
- **1 cup shredded pepper jack cheese**
- **1 teaspoon herbes de Provence**
- **1 pound cooked U.S. crawfish tails,** shelled

DIRECTIONS

1. Preheat oven to 350°F.

2. In a medium-sized skillet, heat 2 teaspoons of corn oil and sauté the Spanish onion, bell pepper and scallions until the onion is transparent. Add the jalapeño and white pepper and cook for 1 minute. Set aside to cool.

3. In a large bowl, whisk together the flour, cornmeal, baking powder, baking soda, paprika sea salt, ½ cup corn oil, eggs and milk. Next fold in the onion mixture, shredded cheese, herbes de Provence and the crawfish. Pour batter into a lightly greased 9-by-13-inch pan and bake for 35 minutes or until a toothpick inserted into the center comes out clean.

4. For cornbread muffins (ideal for appetizers!), pour into a lined or oiled mini muffin tin and bake for 25 minutes. Remove from the oven and allow to rest for 5–10 minutes before serving.

Crispy St. Petersburg Potatoes

The coastline of Russia includes the Pacific Ocean to the east, the Atlantic Ocean to the north and west and the Baltic Sea, Black Sea, Caspian Sea and the Sea of Azov to the Southeast. This region has a penchant for fresh wild seafood and potato-rich side dishes.

Potatoes are a favorite food in Russia, so much so that the capital is known as the "Big Potato." The beloved tuber holds a special place in the hearts of this community and has so for centuries. Initially rejected and called the "Devil's Apples," potatoes quickly grew in acceptance and popularity, and even rivaled cabbages and beets in status, according to Mansur Mirovalev, writer for the Seattle Times. Soon the potato found multiple purposes, including vodka distilling.

These crispy St. Petersburg potatoes are based on a classic Russian comfort food called **Жареный картофель**, or home fries with garlic. It's a flavorful and simple side dish that is ideal for breakfast, brunch or supper.

INGREDIENTS

{ Serves 4 }

- **4 cups water**
- **1 pound red potatoes**
- **6 cloves garlic**, roughly chopped
- **3 tablespoons olive oil**
- **1 tablespoon paprika sea salt**
- **1 teaspoon freshly ground black pepper**
- **¼ cup fresh parsley**

DIRECTIONS

1. Preheat oven to 375°F.

2. Rinse and scrub the potatoes thoroughly. In a large pot, bring the water to a boil.

3. Meanwhile, cut the potatoes into quarters. Add them to the pot along with the garlic. Cook for 10 minutes covered with the lid slightly ajar. When the time is up, turn off the heat, fully cover the pot and let stand for 5 minutes. Drain through a fine-mesh colander, and place in a large bowl.

4. Add the olive oil, paprika sea salt and black pepper and toss to fully coat. Place the potatoes on a sheet pan lined with parchment paper and bake for 15–25 minutes until crispy. Garnish with fresh parsley and serve immediately.

Uruguayan Buñuelos de Algas (Seaweed Fritters)

Fritters are made all over the world, but few countries make them from seaweed—Uruguay is one of the few. Buñuelos de algas are a popular item along the coast and one of the first things that the locals and guidebooks will encourage you to try. Buñuelos de algas are particularly famous around the Rocha region, and most local restaurants and food stands have their own take on the recipe. The flavor is earthy with a salty, beachy vibe.

Sandwiched between Brazil and Argentina, Uruguay plays host to the world's longest carnival. This lively 40-day celebration takes place in January through February (and sometimes March) and celebrates Candomblé, an Afro-Brazilian religion that spread throughout the region between 1550 and 1888. During carnival, as the drummers beat out thunderous African rhythms called "candombe" and dancers gyrate in sequined costumes to the infectious music, morsels like these crispy seaweed fritters are being gobbled up along with a glass of clericó, a drink made of wine and fruit juice similar to sangria.

INGREDIENTS

{ Makes 12–14 fritters }

- **3 large eggs**

- **3 cups milk**

- **3 cups all-purpose flour**

- **2 teaspoons baking powder**

- **1 teaspoon paprika sea salt** (see page 548)

- **4 ounces rehydrated dulse**, kombu or lavar, minced

- **4 cups vegetable oil**, for frying

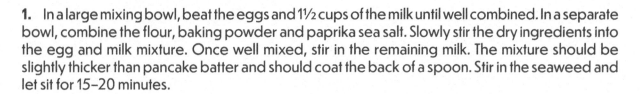

SERVING SUGGESTIONS: PEPPER SAUCE, FRESH LIME

DIRECTIONS

1. In a large mixing bowl, beat the eggs and 1½ cups of the milk until well combined. In a separate bowl, combine the flour, baking powder and paprika sea salt. Slowly stir the dry ingredients into the egg and milk mixture. Once well mixed, stir in the remaining milk. The mixture should be slightly thicker than pancake batter and should coat the back of a spoon. Stir in the seaweed and let sit for 15–20 minutes.

2. Heat the cooking oil to 375°F. Use a thermometer or test the oil by adding a small cube of bread to the oil—when it turns brown, the oil is ready. While the oil is heating, set up a bed of paper towels for draining the fritters.

3. When the oil is ready, use a 1-ounce scoop or spoon and drop one fitter into the fryer—this a test fritter, which is very important. Cook for 2–3 minutes (note that the batter will drop to the bottom then float). Use a pair of chopsticks or a slotted spoon to turn the fritter to ensure it cooks on all sides.

4. When golden brown, use a slotted spoon to remove the fritter, then place on a bed of paper towels to drain. Taste for flavor and doneness. Make adjustments as needed and continue with the remaining batter. Serve immediately with your choice of dipping sauce and sliced lime.

German Kohlrabi Slaw

The Western European country of Germany has a coastline that is divided between the Baltic Sea and the North Sea. The Baltic Sea is one of the most popular destinations for tourists. The seafood dishes found in the area include crab, mussels and trout, but what I like most about Germany's gastronomy are its vegetables.

Kohlrabi is a German turnip that is popular throughout Europe. "Kohl" means cabbage and "rabi" means turnip. There are two main varieties: white (which is actually light green) and purple. My parents grow the white variety in their organic garden in Central California and I've had a chance to play and experiment with this flavorful vegetable thanks to their generosity.

In Germany, you may find kohlrabi in a white sauce, boiled and mashed, or puréed. My slaw recipe is simple, with a light citrus dressing that goes great with grilled fish or as a topping for sandwiches.

INGREDIENTS

{ Makes 4 cups }

KOHLRABI SLAW:

- **3 large green or purple kohlrabi** (about 3 cups), peeled and cut into thin matchsticks

- **2 medium green apples,** cut into thin matchsticks

- **1 small bunch fresh cilantro,** leaves only

- **1 medium red onion,** thinly sliced

- **Kosher salt and freshly ground black pepper to taste**

CITRUS DRESSING:

- **¼ cup avocado oil**

- **¼ cup fresh orange juice**

- **2 large limes,** juice only

- **1 tablespoon honey,** room temperature

- **1 pinch kosher salt**

DIRECTIONS

1. In a large bowl, combine the kohlrabi, green apple, cilantro and red onion along with a pinch of kosher salt and freshly ground black pepper. Toss to combine and set aside.

2. To make the dressing, whisk together the avocado oil, orange juice, lime juice, honey and a pinch of kosher salt in a small bowl. Taste for seasoning and adjust as needed.

3. To make the slaw, pour the dressing over the kohlrabi mixture and toss with a pair of tongs to combine. Taste for seasoning and adjust as needed. Serve as desired.

Albanian Tomato and Cucumber Salad

Situated next to Greece along the Adriatic Sea, Albania is a small country was settled by the Illyrians about 2000 BC. It has an impressive coastline that stretches roughly 100 miles long with stunning mountain ranges and deep bays. Hiking, rock climbing, and fishing are popular outdoor activities.

Blurry cultural lines with neighboring countries have culminated into gastronomy that is truly Mediterranean. This light and easy salad is a good representation of what you'll find served at lunch and supper along with a big spread of other dishes like roasted fish.

INGREDIENTS

{ Serves 4 }

- **2 English or Persian cucumbers,** halved lengthwise and sliced

- **6 Roma tomatoes,** sliced

- **Kosher salt and freshly ground black pepper to taste**

- **1 medium white onion,** sliced

- **1 cup pitted black olives,** halved

- **¼ cup olive oil**

- **¼ cup balsamic vinegar**

- **1 cup crumbled feta cheese**

DIRECTIONS

1. In a large bowl, combine the cucumber and tomato slices with ½ teaspoon of kosher salt. Allow the vegetables to sit for 5 minutes, allowing any excess moisture to be released.

2. When the time is up, you should see a small pool of liquid at the bottom of the bowl. Use a colander to drain the bowl of the excess liquid. (There is no need to rinse the vegetables at this point since we won't be adding additional salt to the dish, unless your taste buds tell you otherwise.)

3. In the same bowl, toss in the onion, olives, olive oil, balsamic vinegar, feta cheese, and a pinch of freshly ground black pepper. Use a large spoon to combine the ingredients. Taste for seasoning and adjust as needed. Serve as desired.

Caribbean Tostones (Fried Green Plantains)

The importance of tostones to Latin-Caribbean cuisine is equivalent to the significance of rice among Asian cultures. Known by many names depending on the location; including patacones, tachinos and bananes pesées, these crispy and sometimes dense treats made from twice-fried green plantains can be eaten as a side dish or starter and are typically eaten at least once a day.

There is a special tool called a plantain masher or tostonera that makes the process go a bit faster, but a flat surface or rolling pin will work fine.

INGREDIENTS

{ Serves 6-8 }

- **5 green plantains**
- **2 cups vegetable oil**
- **Sea salt**, as needed

DIRECTIONS

1. Peel the plantains with a paring knife to remove the thick outer layer. Once peeled, slice plantains into 1-inch pieces. Set aside

2. In a large skillet, heat the oil to 375°F. Use a thermometer to check the temperature or add a small cube of bread to the skillet—when it turns golden brown, the oil is ready.

3. Place the plantain pieces, a few at a time, in the oil and cook for 30 to 60 seconds or until lightly browned. Remove with a slotted spoon and drain on a bed of paper towels. Allow to cool before flattening.

4. To keep the oil warm, turn the heat on the skillet to low.

5. When the plantains are cool enough to work with, place one piece between two sheets of parchment or wax paper. With a rolling pin or the bottom of a flat glass or plate, gently flatten the plantain into ½-inch thickness. Do this with each piece and set aside.

6. Return the cooking oil to 375°F.

7. Fry the flattened plantain pieces for 2 minutes on each side, or until golden brown. Use a slotted spoon or tongs to remove them from the oil and place them on a rack to drain. Sprinkle with sea salt as desired. Serve immediately.

Cuban Plátanos Maduros (Sweet Plantains)

Throughout the Caribbean and Africa, plantains are used at various stages of ripeness—from crispy tostones made with green plantains, to these luxuriously sweet Cuban plátanos maduros or mudros for short, made with slightly overripe plantains that are nearly black. When cooked, the flesh turns sweet and tender and caramelizes.

The best plantains to use for mudros are those with black skin. As the fruit ripens, it becomes sweeter and less starchy.

As one of the most common foods in tropical environments, plantains are ranked as one of the 10 most important staple foods in the world, according to the Plantain Council. Trees can produce year-round and the fruit is a reliable food source for many countries.

You can serve these with savory dishes or as a dessert with a little cinnamon & sugar.

INGREDIENTS

{ Serves 4 }

- **4 large overripe (black) plantains**

- **½ cup vegetable oil**, more as needed

- **Finishing salt**, such as fleur de sel

DIRECTIONS

1. Peel the plantains with a paring knife to remove the thick outer layer. Once peeled, slice them into 1-inch pieces. Set aside.

2. In a large skillet, heat the oil over high heat. Once the pan is hot, add the plantains in batches. Cook the plantain pieces for 2 minutes on each side, or until golden brown. Use a slotted spoon or tongs to remove them from the oil and place on a bed of paper towels to drain. Sprinkle with finishing salt (or cinnamon and sugar if desired) and serve.

Tunisian Vegetable Couscous

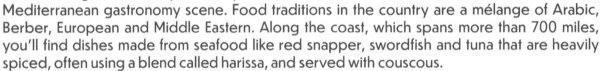

Tunisia is a North African Country that sits between Algeria and Libya and is part of the Mediterranean gastronomy scene. Food traditions in the country are a mélange of Arabic, Berber, European and Middle Eastern. Along the coast, which spans more than 700 miles, you'll find dishes made from seafood like red snapper, swordfish and tuna that are heavily spiced, often using a blend called harissa, and served with couscous.

My first experience with this dish was during college when I worked on campus at the University of California, Santa Barbara at the Multi-Cultural Center. I was hired to work an evening event for a gathering of women from North Africa—it was one-part potluck, one part book club, but I soon learned that it was mostly about the food and fellowship. As I helped set up tables and the sound system, the members brought in steaming platters of food and fragrant tagines filled with traditional homemade delicacies.

If you are new to couscous, it is a classic North African ingredient made from tiny steamed balls of semolina flour. Some think that couscous is a grain, but it is actually closer to pasta and does not require much cooking time.

INGREDIENTS

{ Serves 4-6 }

- **2 tablespoons olive oil or ghee**

- **1 carrot**, coarsely chopped

- **1 brown onion**, chopped

- **1 clove garlic**, minced

- **1 red bell pepper**, diced small

- **1 yellow bell pepper**, diced small

- **1 red onion**, sliced

- **2 zucchinis**, sliced

- **3 cardamom pods**, seeds only

- **1 teaspoon smoked paprika**

- **¼ teaspoon sea salt**

- **1 1-inch piece preserved lemon**, chopped

- **4 cups vegetable broth**

- **1 cup cooked chickpeas**, use my recipe on page 378 or used the canned version

- **1 large tomato**, coarsely chopped, or about ½ cup canned tomatoes

- **½ preserved lemon**, minced

- **2 cups dry couscous**

- **¼ cup toasted almonds**

- **¼ cup fresh cilantro leaves**

DIRECTIONS

1. In a large pot, heat the olive oil or ghee over medium-high heat. Add the carrot, onion, and garlic and cook until the onion is soft and fragrant. Add the red and yellow bell pepper, red onion, zucchini, cardamom, smoked paprika, sea salt and preserved lemon. Cook for 1 minute, stirring occasionally.

2. Add the vegetable broth, chickpeas, tomatoes and preserved lemon, and bring to a boil for 3 minutes. Reduce heat to a simmer and add the couscous. Stir to combine, turn off the heat and cover the pot. Let the pot stand for 10–15 minutes—this will give the couscous time to absorb the flavors of the dish and prevent it from becoming gummy. When the time is up, remove the lid and fluff with a fork. Garnish with toasted almonds and fresh cilantro. Serve as desired at room temperature.

Tanzanian Pilau Rice with Spices

This is a great side dish for Indian and Sri Lankan-inspired recipes; it's a classic dish that uses turmeric to give the rice a hint of golden color.

This is a dish from Tanzania with Indian roots. The primary difference between the East African version and the traditional Indian version is the amount of spice used and the addition of coconut milk. I use Basmati rice for this recipe, which can be found at most supermarkets. Soaking the rice for at least 45 minutes will allow it to cook faster, similar to lentils and beans.

INGREDIENTS

{ Serves 4-6 }

- **1 cinnamon stick, ½-inch piece**

- **6 green cardamom pods**, shelled

- **1 bay leaf**

- **4 dried clove buds**

- **¼ cup ghee**

- **1 medium onion**, chopped

- **1 clove garlic**, chopped

- **1 cup basmati rice**, rinsed and soaked for 45 minutes

- **2 cups vegetable broth**, heated

- **½ cup canned coconut milk**, heated

- **1 tablespoon ground turmeric**

DIRECTIONS

1. In a medium-sized pot, add the cinnamon stick piece, cardamom, bay leaf and clove buds. Add the ghee, onion and garlic to the pot and sauté until soft.

2. Drain the rice and add it into the pot along with the warm vegetable broth and coconut milk. Bring to a boil and stir in the turmeric. Reduce heat to a simmer, cover with a lid, and cook for 10–12 minutes or until the liquid has been absorbed. Turn off the heat and allow the rice time to steam, covered, for 10 minutes. When the time is up, fluff with a fork and serve as desired.

Spanish Saffron Rice

Saffron is an exotic aromatic herb that is harvested by hand and is one of the most expensive cultivated spices in the world. It's worth every penny in my humble opinion! The flavor is earthy and complex, and a little goes a long way. It is an indispensable ingredient in recipes like Spanish paella and French bouillabaisse.

Once used in folk medicine and Ayurvedic health systems as a sedative and expectorant, saffron was also used in various opioid preparations for pain relief in the 16–19th centuries and as a treatment for depression, according to researchers at the University of Münster's Institute of Pharmaceutical Biology and Phytochemistry.

To bring out maximum color and flavor, it's important to bloom the delicate threads in hot water prior to using.

This rice recipe is a convenient way to have flavorful paella-like rice on hand for many applications.

INGREDIENTS

{ Makes 2
cups rice }

- **2 teaspoons saffron threads**

- **2 cups water or vegetable broth,** hot

- **1 cup short-grain rice,** rinsed and soaked for 30 minutes

DIRECTIONS

1. With a mortar and pestle, crush the saffron threads and add them to the hot water or vegetable broth for about 20 minutes. Set aside.

2. Add the rice to a medium saucepan and pour in the saffron water or broth—keep the threads for a more intense flavor, otherwise strain and discard them. Bring to a boil for 5 minutes, then reduce the heat to a simmer and cover with the lid slightly ajar and cook for 15 minutes. Turn off the heat and fully cover with the lid. Allow the pot to sit for 10–15 minutes for the rice to steam and finish cooking. Serve as desired.

Asian Kombu Rice

Rice is the foundation of many Asian meals and this Japanese kombu rice recipe is a nice one to have in your tool kit. Sticky and textured with a toothsome bite, this is essentially the starter for sushi rice, but it also works on its own as a side dish.

Kombu is a type of sea kelp. If cooking with sea vegetables is new to you, know that there are many varieties—red, green and brown—that are packaged in a range of sizes from large sheets to dried slices. Classified as green algae, kombu is a favorite among Japanese cooks for the umami flavor that it brings to recipes. Seaweed adds a salty, earthy, beachy flavor that is unbeatable. Kombu is readily available online and in most Asian markets. Keep in mind that nori sheets, the seaweed wrapper used for sushi rolls, will not work for this application.

The key to making a good pot of rice is soaking the kernels prior to cooking. I did not grow up soaking rice, but once I discovered its magic, I began working it into my cooking schedule—it makes all the difference!

INGREDIENTS

{ Makes about 3 cups cooked rice }

- **1½ cups Japanese short grain rice**, rinsed and soaked for 30 minutes

- **2 cups water**

- **1 small sheet of kombu**, about a 4-inch square (dried kelp)

DIRECTIONS

1. Drain the rice from its soaking water and add it to a medium-sized saucepan along with the water. Bring the pot to a soft boil, then reduce the heat to low. Cover and simmer for 15 minutes, with the lid slightly askew, until the moisture is absorbed. Remove from the heat, cover fully with the lid, and let stand for 10–15 minutes. Fluff and serve.

Japanese Sushi Rice with Kombu

The Japanese word sushi translates into "sour taste" in English and is related to the centuries-old tradition of storing fish wrapped in fermented rice. When ready to eat, the rice was thrown out and the fish was enjoyed on its own.

Centuries later, in the new capital city of Japan, Edo (modern-day Tokyo), rice was brought back into fashion. The group of merchants responsible for the resurgence used a fermentation process that placed cooked rice seasoned with vinegar alongside a layer of fresh fish. Fast-forward to the 1920s when sushi carts popped up around the city. By the 1970s, sushi bars appeared. Los Angeles was the first city in America to embrace sushi, which is how the classic California roll was born.

When making sushi rice, there is no substitute for the short-grain variety. Its texture and stickiness are paramount to making maki (rice and filling wrapped in nori), nigiri (fish served atop rice), uramaki (rice wrapped around seaweed and filling), and temaki (hand-rolled sushi).

414

INGREDIENTS

- **1½ cups Japanese short grain rice**, rinsed and soaked for 30 minutes

- **2 cups water**

- **1 small sheet kombu (dried kelp)**

- **1/3cup rice wine vinegar**

- **3 tablespoons sugar**

- **1½ teaspoons sea salt**

DIRECTIONS

SPECIAL EQUIPMENT: SUSHI OKE (FLAT-BOTTOMED WOODEN BOWL) OR PARCHMENT-LINED BAKING SHEET, RICE PADDLE OR SPATULA, AND FAN OR PAPER PLATE

1. Drain the rice from its soaking water and add it to a medium-sized saucepan along with the water. Bring the pot to a gentle boil, then reduce the heat to low. Cover and simmer for 15 minutes with the lid slightly askew until the moisture is absorbed. Remove from the heat, cover fully with the lid, and let stand for 5 minutes.

2. In a small bowl, combine the rice wine vinegar, sugar and sea salt. Stir until the sugar and salt have dissolved. Set aside.

3. Transfer the rice to a large wooden bowl or a baking sheet lined with parchment paper and spread it out so that it cools faster. While the rice is warm, pour the sushi vinegar over the rice.

4. This is the fun part—use the paddle or spatula, slice the rice at a 45-degree angle and gently flip to mix in the sushi vinegar, intermittently use the fan or paper plate to cool down the rice mixture and continue to mix until the rice is shiny, and the vinegar has been incorporated and the mix is room temperature. Use immediately or cover with a damp towel or freeze in an airtight container for up to 1 month.

Global
Coconut
Rice

Coconut is the fruit of the palm tree with dozens of uses. According to Science Daily, coconut was originally cultivated in two specific locations: the Pacific basin and the Indian Ocean. Due to its sweet, nutty flavor, creamy rich milk, and flavorful oil, it is a wildly popular cross-cultural ingredient and valued source of nutrition.

Coconut rice is a dish that can be found in various parts of the world: Asia, Caribbean, Pacifica, South Asia and parts of Africa. I'm calling this dish "global" coconut rice as a nod to its multi-cultural heritage. I call for jasmine rice for this dish, but most varieties of long grain or medium grain rice will turn out well. Sticky coconut rice made from short grain rice is a popular recipe in Southeast Asia, but that's not what we are making here.

INGREDIENTS

{ Makes 4 cups }

- **2 cups jasmine rice**, rinsed and soaked for 30 minutes

- **1 tablespoon coconut oil**

- **1 shallot**, peeled and minced

- **1 ½-inch piece fresh ginger**, peeled and minced (or 1 teaspoon ground ginger)

- **1 clove garlic**, minced

- **2½ cups water**, more as needed

- **1 14-ounce can coconut milk**

- **1 teaspoon sea salt**

DIRECTIONS

1. Drain the soaking water from the rice and set aside.

2. In a medium-sized pot, heat the coconut oil over medium heat and add the shallot, ginger and garlic and cook until soft and fragrant. Turn up the heat and add the rice, water, coconut milk and sea salt and stir to combine. Bring to a boil for 5 minutes, then add the lid and reduce the heat to a low simmer for 15 minutes. Remove from the heat and rest the pot for 10 minutes, allowing the rice time to steam and absorb the flavors. When the time is up, use a fork to fluff and serve as desired.

Jicama Tostada Shells

I first learned to use jicama as a shell while on one of my cooking adventures in Baja, California. Ceviche was on the menu and my tour guide suggested we use jicama instead of tortilla chips. It was a crunchy, delightful and refreshing alternative.

If you are new to jicama (HEE-kah-ma), it is an edible root vegetable native to Mexico that is also sold as yam bean, Mexican turnip, or Mexican potato. All over Mexico and Central America, jicama is sold by street vendors, served raw and seasoned with lemon or lime juice and chili powder (Tajin is a favorite brand). You can find jicama year-round in the produce section of most grocery stores and Latin American markets. Look for firm, dry jicama roots with smooth skin.

Tostada shells are slightly thicker than corn tortillas. I use a mandoline to create uniform shells. The mandoline is an essential kitchen tool in my opinion and I encourage you to invest in one. You can also use a sharp knife to make these, but it is more labor intensive.

INGREDIENTS

{ Serves 4 }

- **2 medium-sized jicamas** (the size of the vegetable should fit your mandoline)

DIRECTIONS

1. Remove the skin from the jicama using a potato peeler, then use a mandoline to create ¼-inch slices using the appropriate setting. Be sure to use the guard to protect your hands.

2. When you have your first tostada shell, check it out to make sure it's to your desired thickness. Adjust as needed. Slice remaining jicama into shells.

Italian Sautéed Broccolini

Also known as baby broccoli, this deep green vegetable is a close relative to cabbage and is a hybrid of broccoli and Chinese kale. A favorite in Italian kitchens, broccolini's long, tender stems and sweet florets make for a fantastic side to rich pasta dishes as well as lighter Mediterranean-inspired fare, like chargrilled whole Branzino (see page 330).

INGREDIENTS

{ Serves 3-4 }

- **1½ pounds Broccolini,** about 3 bunches

- **2 tablespoons extra-virgin olive oil**

- **4 cloves garlic,** minced or thinly sliced

- **2 tablespoons roasted pine nuts**

- **Pinch red pepper flake,** optional

- **Sea salt and freshly ground black pepper to taste**

- **1 large lemon,** for drizzling

- **1 tablespoon water**

DIRECTIONS

1. Trim the Broccolini by cutting off the tough end of the stems. Set aside.

2. In a large skillet, heat the olive oil over medium-high heat. Add the garlic and pine nuts and cook until fragrant. Turn the heat to high and add the Broccolini, red pepper flake and season with sea salt and black pepper to taste. Sauté for 3 minutes. Add the water and cover for 2 minutes. Turn off the heat and set aside for 30 seconds before serving. Drizzle with lemon juice and serve immediately.

German Cauliflower Parsnip Purée

Parsnips are a hearty vegetable that are a favorite among German cooks. You can find them on the tables of most European households during the holiday season. They are often sold near carrots, their culinary cousins, as well as other root vegetables at the market. They are a cream-colored vegetable sometimes referred to as "white carrots," but they have quite a different flavor profile.

Parsnips have an elegantly sweet, deep, nutty and flavor. In fact, at one point in history, parsnip extract was used as a sweetener when honey was hard to come by and when sugar, a New World creation, was rare. Combined with the mild flavor of cauliflower, parsnips make for an incredibly delicious purée.

INGREDIENTS

{ Serves 4 }

- **1 pound large parsnips**, peeled and diced

- **2 cloves garlic**, minced

- **1 tablespoon sea salt**

- **1 large head cauliflower**, chopped

- **½ teaspoon rosemary sea salt (see page 552)**

- **Freshly ground black pepper to taste**

- **2 tablespoons olive oil**

- **1 small lemon**, juice and zest

DIRECTIONS

1. In a large pot, add the parsnips, garlic, sea salt and enough water to cover the parsnips. Cover, bring to a boil, then reduce heat to medium and cook until the parsnips are soft and fork- tender about 12 minutes. Remove from heat. Over a medium-sized bowl, drain the parsnips and garlic with a fine-mesh colander. Reserve the cooking water in the bowl—you will use it to cook the cauliflower. Place the parsnips and garlic in the bowl of a food processor and set aside.

2. Add the cauliflower and the reserved parsnip-garlic water to the same pot, adding more water if needed to cover the cauliflower. Cover and bring to a boil, then reduce heat to medium. Cook until the cauliflower becomes soft and fork-tender—about 10 minutes. Drain the water and add the cooked cauliflower to the food processor containing the garlic and parsnips. Blend until smooth, adding a teaspoon of water if necessary to get the mix going. Once smooth, place the mixture in a large bowl. Add the rosemary sea salt, freshly ground black pepper to taste, olive oil, and the juice and zest of the lemon. Stir to combine and adjust seasoning to taste. Serve immediately.

Appetizers and Small Bites

- English Whelks with Garlic and Basil Lemon Butter

- 'Best Coast' Salmon Cakes

- Loch Etive Scottish Smoked Trout Pâté

- Texas Gulf Shrimp Queso Fundido (Cheese Sauce)

- Scandinavian Gravlax

- Scandinavian Gruyère & Gravlax Stuffed Tomatoes

- Irish Colcannon with Smoked Trout

English Whelks

WITH GARLIC AND BASIL LEMON BUTTER

English whelks are a type of sea snail, a marine gastropod that inhabits the Atlantic Ocean. Most are spirally coiled, with really cute shells that are often found in beachside gift shops or used as musical instruments.

Once considered street food for the poor in the 19th century, whelks have made a big comeback. They are often harvested on purpose, but also end up as bycatch while fishing for lobster. Aside from whelks, conches and periwinkles are popular sea snail varieties. Snails from the sea have a dense chewy texture and briny flavor. Small ones are the best for this recipe, while larger ones should be reserved for chowders and stews. Regardless of size, whelks can be a little tough. Cooking them low and slow is my favorite way to prepare them.

Sea snails require a good scrubbing and soaking prior to cooking so keep this in mind when making this recipe.

INGREDIENTS

1 dozen fresh whelks, scrubbed and soaked for 3 hours (change water twice during soaking)

3 cups water

2 large stalks celery, roughly chopped

1 large carrot, roughly chopped

1 large onion, roughly chopped

4 cloves garlic, minced

Rosemary sea salt (see page 552), as needed

2 tablespoons basil lemon butter (see page 536)

1 large lemon, juice only

2 tablespoons olive oil

4 tablespoons fresh parsley, chopped, separated

Freshly ground black pepper to taste

Crackers or toasted garlic bread, for serving

DIRECTIONS

{ Makes 1 dozen sea snails }

1. Preheat oven to 350°F.

2. Pour out the soaking liquid from the whelks and give them a rinse. Use a small fork to gently remove each whelk from its shell, taking care not to tear the meat. Use a paring knife to cut off the tough foot, the round flat portion, and the hood, the sheath that covers a portion of the whelk. Remove the intestinal tract which is just under the skin. Repeat for the remaining shellfish. Set aside.

3. In a large pot, add the water, celery, carrot, onion, 1 teaspoon of minced garlic and ½ teaspoon of rosemary sea salt. Bring to a boil for 8 minutes, then reduce to a simmer. Add the whelks and cook covered with the lid slightly ajar for 1 hour. When the time is up, fully close the lid and allow the whelks to sit in the flavorful liquid until cool.

4. Once cooled, roughly chop the whelks into bite-sized pieces and add them to a bowl. Add the basil lemon butter, lemon juice, olive oil, 3 tablespoons of fresh parsley and the remaining garlic along with a pinch of rosemary sea salt and freshly ground black pepper. Combine thoroughly. Pour the mixture into an ovenproof pan and place in the oven. Cook for 20 minutes. To serve, add to a bowl, garnish with remaining parsley, and serve with crackers or toasted garlic bread.

'Best Coast' Salmon Cakes

These savory salmon cakes are easy to make and work great for brunch with scrambled eggs and fruit or as a satisfying starter. Salmon is king on the West Coast and available in abundance, so having fish on hand is typical depending on the season.

Aside from a couple of eggs and a little panko breadcrumb, there are no heavy binders in this recipe, making these West Coast-inspired salmon cakes tender and flaky.

You can make these up to one day in advance, and they freeze well for an easy meal down the road. I use a large fillet of cooked wild pink salmon for this recipe, though wild canned salmon works well too. For a more substantial snack, make these salmon cakes a little larger, place them in mini burger buns to create sliders, and serve with your favorite toppings.

INGREDIENTS

{ Makes 10–12
salmon cakes }

- **2 pounds cooked pink salmon (or 3 6-ounce cans of boneless, skinless salmon, drained)**

- **¼ cup chopped fresh cilantro**

- **¼ cup finely chopped red onion**

- **¼ cup panko breadcrumbs**

- **1 medium lime,** juice and zest

- **2 large eggs**

- **Sea salt and freshly ground black pepper to taste**

- **Vegetable oil for frying (preferably avocado, grapeseed or sunflower oil)**

SERVING SUGGESTIONS: LIME WEDGES, SALTED AVOCADO (SEE PAGE 560)

DIRECTIONS

1. In a large bowl, combine the salmon, cilantro, red onion, panko, lime juice, lime zest, eggs, and sea salt and freshly ground pepper as desired. Mix thoroughly and set aside.

2. Portion out the salmon mixture with a 1- or 1½-ounce scoop, forming small patties as you go. Add patties to a baking sheet lined with parchment paper and repeat until all of the salmon mix is used. Cover salmon patties with plastic wrap and refrigerate for 20 minutes—this will help them hold together when cooking.

3. Add the vegetable oil to a large skillet and heat to 375°F.

4. Remove the patties from the refrigerator and pan-fry until golden brown on both sides. Serve immediately with lime wedges, guacamole or salted avocado.

Loch Etive Scottish Smoked Trout Pâté

Loch Etive is a glacially carved sea loch and is one of Scotland's most beautiful waterways. A mix of freshwater and tidal seawater, Loch Etive is positioned in Northern Argyll on the west coast of Scotland, where it is surrounded by wild countryside and rich flora and fauna. Sea trout are native to this region, and these days, the trout coming from these waters are cultivated.

Scottish trout has brightly colored red flesh with a good healthy fat content and mild flavor often compared to salmon. Smoking your own fish can be rewarding and a delicious option, but most stores sell reliable, high-quality brands. I prefer tinned fish in oil for this dish since oil-packed fish adds a multitude of flavor.

This recipe is an adaptation of my signature smoked trout spread recipe, which is a family favorite. It works great on bagels, crackers, toast or veggies. I double and sometimes triple the recipe for my large tribe and often give it as a gift over the holidays.

INGREDIENTS

Makes about 1½ cups

- **6 ounces smoked Scottish trout packed in oil,** flaked

- **2 tablespoons crème fraîche**

- **2 teaspoons minced tarragon**

- **1 medium lemon,** juice and zest

- **4 ounces Scottish goat cheese or chèvre,** at room temperature

- **4 ounces cream cheese,** softened

- **Sea salt and freshly ground black pepper to taste**

DIRECTIONS

In a medium-sized bowl, combine the smoked trout, crème fraîche, tarragon, lemon juice and zest, chèvre, and cream cheese. Taste for seasoning and add sea salt and black pepper as needed. Chill in the refrigerator for 15 minutes prior to serving.

Texas Gulf Shrimp Queso Fundido (Cheese Sauce)

The state of Texas has more than 350 miles of coastline dotted with fun beach towns, picturesque cities and plenty of fishing opportunities. This Tex-Mex recipe featuring Gulf shrimp is a decadent melted cheese dip that conjures the flavors of Galveston Island.

Tex-Mex is a style of cooking that became popular in the United States around the 1970s. It's a distillation of Northern Mexican and Texan cuisine. The primary difference between Tex-Mex and traditional Mexican cuisine is the heavy use of ingredients like cumin, cheddar cheese and garlic. Use this queso as a dip or pour it over nachos and baked potatoes—irresistible!

INGREDIENTS

{ Makes about 4½ cups }

- **1 pound Texas Gulf shrimp**, peeled, deveined and roughly chopped

- **2 teaspoons vegetable oil**

- **2 tablespoons unsalted butter**

- **2 tablespoons all-purpose flour**

- **1 tablespoon water**

- **2 cups half-and-half**

- **4 ounces cream cheese**

- **1 large jalapeño pepper**, chopped

- **2 cups pepper jack cheese**

- **1 cup chunky salsa**

- **1 teaspoon ground cumin**

SERVING SUGGESTIONS: TORTILLA CHIPS, CHOPPED VEGETABLES

DIRECTIONS

SPECIAL EQUIPMENT: FONDUE POT

1. Preheat oven to 350°F.

2. In a sauté pan over medium-high heat, add the oil and the shrimp. Cook for 3 minutes, then remove from heat and set aside.

3. In a heavy-bottomed pan, melt the butter over medium heat and whisk in the flour to make a light roux—keep your eye on the heat and whisk constantly so that the flour doesn't burn. Next, slowly add the water and the half-and-half, whisking constantly until smooth. Add the cream cheese, jalapeño, pepper jack cheese, salsa and cumin. Continue whisking until smooth and combined.

4. Pour into an ovenproof pan and bake for 15 minutes until hot and bubbling. Consider adding sauce to a fondue pot to keep the cheese warm and melted. Serve immediately.

Scandinavian Gravlax

The countries of Denmark, Norway and Sweden comprise the stunning subregion of northern Europe known as Scandinavia. Seafood reigns supreme in this part of the world, which is famous for its pickled herring and gravlax.

Gravlax is a type of cold cured salmon, and it's a wonderful way to enjoy flavorful, succulent fish without having to cook! This dish is typically cured in a mix of salt, sugar, dill weed, Cognac and fresh spruce sprigs. It's simple enough to make at home and is definitely worth the effort!

Prior to making gravlax and finding my favorite recipe, I would buy it in large 2-pound sheets from a local market. They were often previously frozen, and the flavor was good, but the texture was always compromised—a little mushy and difficult to separate the individual slices. The funny thing is, when I make a couple gravlax at home, I freeze it with great results! Who knew?

These days, I enjoy making this dish for family holidays like Easter, Thanksgiving and Christmas.

INGREDIENTS

{ Serves 10–15 }

- **½ cup sea salt or kosher salt**

- **½ cup sugar**

- **5 juniper berries**

- **5 black peppercorns**

- **1 4-pound salmon fillet**, skin on and pin bones removed

- **8–10 sprigs fresh dill**, chopped

- **¼ cup gin**

DIRECTIONS

1. Set aside a glass or ceramic baking dish large enough to hold the salmon.

2. In a small bowl, combine the salt, sugar, juniper berries and peppercorns. Pour half of the mixture on the bottom of the baking dish. Lay 4–5 pieces of fresh dill on the bottom of the dish then add the fish skin side down. Drizzle the gin over the top of the fish, then place the remaining salt and sugar mixture on the flesh, making sure to cover the salmon evenly, then place the remaining dill on top.

3. Take a piece of plastic wrap and lay it directly on the fish, then lay a slightly smaller baking dish or another large flat object on top of the fish. Fill the top baking dish with enough dried beans or kitchen weights to weigh down the fish.

4. Place the fish in the refrigerator for up to 5 days, turning the fish over every 24 hours and placing the weighted baking dish back on top. (Drain off any liquid that accumulates at the bottom of the dish.) I prefer a 3–4-day gravlax; feel free to slice off a little sliver after day two to test your palate.

Scandinavian Gruyère & Gravlax Stuffed Tomatoes

The Scandinavian countries of Norway, Sweden and Denmark are known for their love of pickled herring and gravlax, a type of cured salmon typically cured in salt, sugar and dill weed.

Gravlax is simple enough to make at home and is a fun kitchen project; see page 436 for my recipe. It takes a few days and is definitely worth the effort! However, there are some pretty good brands on the market if you are in a pinch and don't have time to make your own. Smoked salmon is also a good alternative.

INGREDIENTS

{ Makes 20–24 stuffed cherry tomatoes or 10–12 medium-sized tomatoes }

- **20–24 fresh cherry tomatoes or 10–12 medium-sized tomatoes**
- **1 cup grated Gruyère cheese**
- **1 teaspoon garlic powder**
- **½ cup chopped gravlax or smoked salmon**
- **1 large lemon,** juice only

- **1 tablespoon olive oil**
- **½ cup breadcrumbs**
- **2 tablespoons basil lemon butter (see page 536),** melted
- **2 tablespoons chopped fresh parsley**
- **Freshly ground black pepper to taste**
- **Finishing salt (such as fleur de sel) for garnish**

DIRECTIONS

1. Preheat oven to 375°F.

2. Cut a thin top off of each tomato and discard. Place the tomatoes on a paper towel for 5 minutes to allow the excess liquid to drain.

3. In a medium bowl, combine the Gruyère cheese, garlic powder, gravlax (or smoked salmon if using), lemon juice, olive oil, breadcrumbs, basil lemon butter, 1 tablespoon of parsley, and a few pinches of freshly ground black pepper.

4. Using a melon baller or a small spoon, scoop out the seeds from each tomato and add to the bowl with the rest of the ingredients. Mix to combine, cover, and allow to rest for 5 minutes.

5. When the mixture has rested, place one tomato inside each section of a muffin tin. With a small spoon, stuff the tomatoes with the gravlax and Gruyère mixture. Bake for 25–30 minutes.

6. Remove the pan from the oven and let it rest for 1–2 minutes.

7. Garnish with finishing salt and the remaining parsley and serve.

Irish
Colcannon

WITH SMOKED TROUT

Colcannon is a classic Irish dish that combines mashed potatoes and butter with cruciferous vegetables like cabbage or kale in a simple, scrumptious dish. My pescatarian version includes savory smoked trout, which ups the deliciousness factor and celebrates the country's cuisine even more. In addition to its famous potatoes, Ireland, with its huge network of rivers and loughs (lakes), is home to gorgeous wild brown trout.

Colcannon is great any time of year, but it's especially fantastic during the holiday season when extra mashed potatoes and veggies are readily available.

INGREDIENTS

{ Serves 6 }

- **1 tablespoon ghee**

- **1½ cups finely shredded cruciferous vegetables (kale, Brussels sprouts or green cabbage)**

- **4 cups mashed potatoes**, at room temperature

- **1 teaspoon garlic powder**

- **1 tablespoon dried dill**

- **1 lemon, zest and juice**

- **¼ cup half-and-half**

- **1 teaspoon white pepper**

- **Sea salt and freshly ground black pepper to taste**

- **6 ounces smoked trout**, boneless and skinless (drain if using a tinned version)

- **2 tablespoons salted butter**, melted

DIRECTIONS

1. Preheat oven to 375°F.

2. To make the colcannon, heat the ghee in a large cast iron skillet over high heat. Add the cruciferous vegetables and sauté for 2–3 minutes until soft and fragrant. Turn off the heat and allow the vegetables to cool.

3. In a large bowl, combine the mashed potatoes, garlic powder, dill, lemon zest, a squeeze of lemon juice, half-and-half, white pepper, and sea salt and black pepper to taste.

4. Next, gently fold the smoked trout and the melted butter into the mashed potato mixture. Taste for seasoning and adjust as needed.

5. Pour the colcannon into a lightly oiled 10-inch cast iron skillet. Bake until golden brown, about 25–35 minutes. Remove from the oven and let stand for 10 minutes before serving.

Brunch, Sandwiches and Salads

- Kent Island Crab Cake Benedict

- Big Sur Dungeness Crab & Avocado Benedict

- Tillamook Bay Wild Sockeye Salmon Grilled Cheese

- 'Best Coast' Salmon Caprese Sandwich

- Monterey Bay Sardine Sandwich

- Brazilian Salmon Cobb Salad with Orange Dressing

- Thai Shrimp & Peanut Salad

- Tropical Grilled Scallop Sandwich with Sweet Plantain & Avocado Mash

- Scandinavian Seared Salmon with Lemon-Dill Cucumber Salad

- Bodega Bay Crab Cobb Salad

- Catalina Spicy Lobster Salad

- NOLA Oyster 'Po Boy

- Middle Eastern Grilled Barramundi with Tahini Sauce & Cucumber Salata

- California Avocado Salad

Kent Island Crab Cake Benedict

A popular destination, especially for visitors hailing from mainland Maryland and Washington, D.C., Kent Island is the largest of its kind in the Chesapeake Bay. It's famous for its crab cakes, which are made from local blue crab.

Blue crabs are small and have a buttery flavor, as opposed to Dungeness or Alaskan king crab, which are large and slightly sweet. Maryland-style crab cakes use saltine crackers for texture instead of panko breadcrumbs, which is my standard go-to.

Traditionally, eggs Benedict features Canadian bacon along with poached eggs and hollandaise sauce. This pescatarian version swaps out the Canadian bacon for luxurious crab cakes, while the toasted English muffin and arugula add mouthwatering texture contrast to the creamy hollandaise sauce and the tender crab cakes. It's an indulgent, restaurant-worthy brunch!

If you don't prefer a creamy egg yolk, feel free to scramble your egg instead of poaching; your kitchen, your rules! I have not always appreciated a creamy yolk, but when I tried it on smoked salmon avocado toast several years ago, I was hooked.

INGREDIENTS

{ Serves 4 }

- Hollandaise sauce (see page 532)

- 1 pound jumbo lump or backfin crab meat, picked through for shells

- 2 tablespoons minced fresh parsley, for garnish

- 10 saltine crackers, crushed

- 1 tablespoon Dijon mustard

- 1 teaspoon Worcestershire sauce

- Freshly ground black pepper to taste

- 5 large eggs

- Vegetable oil for pan-frying, as needed

- Water and ice, as needed

- 1 teaspoon white vinegar

- 2 English muffins, halved

- Fresh chives, for garnish

DIRECTIONS

Make the hollandaise with the recipe on page 532. Cover and set aside.

Make the crab cakes:
In a large bowl, combine the crab with the parsley, crushed saltine crackers, Dijon mustard, Worcestershire sauce and a few cracks of black pepper. Set aside. In a small bowl, whisk one egg, beating thoroughly with a fork. Pour the egg into the crab mixture and gently fold the ingredients together with a rubber spatula. Cover and refrigerate for 15 minutes—once cooled, the mixture will be easier to form into cakes.

When the mixture is chilled, use a 2-ounce scoop to portion out the crab mixture, then use your hands to form cakes and place them on a clean plate. Repeat until all of the crab mixture has been used. If you don't have a 2-ounce scoop, you can eyeball the portion sizes; however, I recommend using a scoop, as it will give you uniformly sized crab cakes that will cook evenly.

Next, in a large skillet, add ¼ cup of vegetable oil over medium-high heat. When the oil is hot, add the crab cakes to the pan and cook on one side for 2 minutes or until golden brown, then flip over and cook on the other side for 2 minutes or until golden brown. Store in the warming drawer of your oven or keep warm in a 200°F oven until ready to use.

Poach the eggs:
First, set up an ice bath by adding 1 cup of ice and 1 cup of water to a large bowl; set aside. In a medium-sized saucepan, add 2 cups of water and the vinegar. Bring the pot to a simmer. Crack one egg into a small bowl, then gently slide the egg into the pan of simmering water, taking care not to break up the yolk and white. Repeat with the remaining eggs. Cook for 3–4 minutes or until the whites begin to set and the yolk firms up a bit. Use a slotted spoon to gently remove the eggs from the pan and place them in the ice bath. Set aside until ready to use.

Toast the English muffins:
Turn the oven to broil, then place the halved English muffins on a baking sheet and place under the broiler to toast. (You can also use a toaster for this.) Once golden brown, remove the muffins from the oven and slather with a little butter if desired. Set aside.

Make the benedict:
Place a toasted muffin half on a plate and spread with a tablespoon of hollandaise. Add a crab cake and top with a poached egg and more hollandaise as desired. Repeat with remaining ingredients. Garnish benedicts with fresh chives and serve immediately.

Big Sur Dungeness Crab & Avocado Benedict

Located along California's Central Coast, the rugged beauty of Big Sur is arguably unmatched. Sandwiched between the Pacific Ocean and the Santa Lucia mountains, the area has an eclectic vibe that is easy to fall in love with and has something for everyone—hiking, wine tasting, surfing, shopping, waterfalls and good food.

As a child, my parents would load us all up in my dad's prized International Scout and with the music of Jimi Hendrix and Al Green alternating through the speakers, we headed north for the ocean with Big Sur, Monterey and Santa Cruz on the horizon. The view from Highway 1 approaching Big Sur was jaw-droppingly beautiful and an unforgettable memory. Even as a kid it felt like a spiritual experience. I made it a point to make sure I was awake during this part of the drive any time we made this trip.

Years later, while driving a Mustang convertible, my husband and I made the same coastal trek and stopped for breakfast along the route. The food was simple, seasonally inspired and outstanding. This recipe is reminiscent of that meal, and uses quintessential California ingredients.

The name 'Dungeness' comes from the crustacean's habitat, the Dungeness Spit in northwest Washington. Most of the world's Dungeness crab comes from Washington, as well as Oregon and California. It's a leggy, meaty crab that is one of my favorite varieties for its sweet and tender flesh.

This dish comes together fast. If you are experienced in the kitchen, feel free to take on a few tasks at a time. For example, while the crab is warming up, you can poach the eggs, slice the avocados and toast the sourdough English muffins.

INGREDIENTS

Hollandaise sauce
(see page 532)

1 pound jumbo lump or backfin
crab meat, picked through for
shells

Fresh avocado slices

2 tablespoons minced fresh
parsley, for garnish

10 saltine crackers, crushed

1 tablespoon Dijon mustard

1 teaspoon Worcestershire
sauce

Freshly ground black pepper to
taste

5 large eggs

Vegetable oil for pan-frying, as
needed

Water and ice, as needed

1 teaspoon white vinegar

2 English muffins, halved

Fresh chives, for garnish

DIRECTIONS

{ Serves 4 }

Make the Hollandaise sauce per the directions on
page 530. Cover and set aside.

Meanwhile, preheat the oven to 350°F.

Wrap the crab meat in foil and place it in the oven for 5
minutes to heat. Meanwhile, poach the eggs.

Poach the eggs:
First, set up an ice bath by adding 1 cup of ice and 1 cup
of water to a large bowl; set aside. In a
medium-sized saucepan, add 2 cups of water along
with the vinegar. Bring the pot to a simmer. Crack one
egg into a bowl, then gently slide the egg into the pan
of simmering water, taking care not to break up the
yolk and white. Repeat with the remaining eggs. Cook
for 3–4 minutes or until the whites begin to set and the
yolks firm up a bit. Use a slotted spoon to gently remove the eggs from the pan and place them in the ice
bath. Set aside.

Remove the crab from the oven and set aside.

Toast the English muffins:
Turn the oven to broil, then place the halved sourdough English muffins on a baking sheet and place in the
oven. (Alternatively, you can also use a toaster for this.)
Once they've turned golden brown, remove muffins
from the oven and slather on a little butter if desired;
set aside.

Make the benedict:
Place each English muffin half on a plate and spread
with a tablespoon of Hollandaise. Add a few slices of
avocado, a poached egg and equal portions of the
crab. Top with Hollandaise and a dash of cayenne pepper. Serve immediately.

Tillamook Bay Wild Sockeye Salmon Grilled Cheese

This tart and savory Pacific Coast-inspired sandwich is a decadent treat inspired by Oregon's gorgeous Tillamook Bay, a small inlet on the Pacific Ocean where wild salmon, dolphins and orca whales cohabitate. It's an important ecological area for wildlife and for private oyster cultivation.

Similar to seafood, apples are a pretty big deal in Oregon. There are roughly 24 varieties of apples grown in the state—Fuji, Gala and Granny Smith are some of the most popular. I like Granny Smith for this recipe, as its tartness works perfectly to counterbalance the richness of the salmon and cheese.

INGREDIENTS

{ Makes 2 sandwiches }

- **2 ounces Gouda cheese**, shredded

- **2 ounces Gruyère cheese**, shredded

- **4 slices sourdough bread**

- **4 tablespoons unsalted butter**, softened

- **1 large green Granny Smith apple**, cored and thinly sliced

- **1 large tomato**, sliced into 6 thin slices

- **4 ounces cooked wild sockeye salmon**, flaked

DIRECTIONS

1. Combine the shredded Gouda and Gruyère cheese in a small bowl; set aside.

2. Heat a large skillet over medium-high heat. To make the first sandwich, butter one side of a piece of bread, then place the bread butter-side down in the pan. Carefully add 1 ounce of the cheese, three slices of Granny Smith apple, three slices of tomato, 2 ounces of salmon, and another ounce of cheese.

3. To complete the sandwich, butter another slice of bread, then place the bread butter-side up on top of the sandwich in the pan. Repeat with the remaining two slices of bread and ingredients.

4. Cook the sandwich on medium-high heat for 2 minutes, then turn to low and cover with a lid. This will allow the cheese to gently melt and the bread to get toasty. Remove the lid and use a spatula to lift the sandwich and check for your ideal level of brownness. Cook a little longer if necessary. When ready, carefully flip the sandwich with the spatula, taking care not to spill the ingredients, then turn the heat back to medium for 2 minutes. Turn the heat to low, cover, and cook for 2–3 minutes. Repeat with the remaining sandwich. Cut sandwiches in half and serve immediately.

'Best Coast' Salmon Caprese Sandwich

A twist on an Italian favorite, my 'Best Coast'-inspired sandwich is a savory pescatarian version of the classic Caprese salad that's traditionally made with mozzarella cheese, fresh tomato and fresh basil. I use basil lemon butter to add richness and depth, and of course, plenty of flavorful salmon.

Cooked salmon, cold-smoked salmon slices, or Nova lox all work well for this recipe. Add a few tablespoons of scrambled eggs for a savory, satisfying brunch option.

INGREDIENTS

{ Makes 2 sandwiches }

- **4 slices sourdough bread**

- **2 tablespoons unsalted butter**, softened

- **2 tablespoons basil lemon butter (see page 536)**, softened

- **4 ounces mozzarella cheese**, sliced into 4–6 pieces, or 1 cup shredded mozzarella

- **1 large tomato**, sliced into 6 thin slices

- **4 ounces cooked wild salmon**, flaked

DIRECTIONS

1. Preheat a large skillet over medium heat.

2. To make the first sandwich, spread one side of a piece of bread with unsalted butter and the other side with the basil lemon butter.

3. Place the bread unsalted-butter-side down in the pan, then carefully add 1 ounce of the cheese, three slices of tomato and 2 ounces of the salmon, followed by another ounce of cheese. To complete the sandwich, spread unsalted butter on one side of the second piece of bread and basil lemon butter on the other side. Place the bread basil-lemon-butter-side down on top of the stacked sandwich fillings in the pan, forming a sandwich. Repeat with the remaining two slices of bread and ingredients.

4. Cook on medium-high heat for 2 minutes, then turn to low and cover with a lid. This will give the cheese time to gently melt and the bread time to get toasty. Remove the lid and use a spatula to lift the sandwich and check for your ideal level of brownness. Cook a little longer if necessary. When ready, carefully flip the sandwich with the spatula, taking care not to spill the ingredients. Turn the heat back to medium for 2 minutes then turn the heat to low, cover, and cook for 2–3 minutes. Repeat with the remaining ingredients. Cut sandwiches in half and serve immediately.

Monterey Bay Sardine Sandwich

I grew up in California eating sardines on Saltine crackers with my dad. When we were kids, Dad would open a tin and my sisters and I would gather around for a bite or two, which he'd happily share. This open-faced sandwich recipe is an ode to simpler times and demonstrates the beauty of tinned fish.

Sardines are one of the most popular varieties of tinned fish in the world, with Portugal and Morocco leading the way in production. Adding fish to a metal tin along with oil, water and spices is a centuries old method of preserving seafood at its peak of freshness.

At one point in time, Monterey Bay, California was a canning powerhouse for sardines and served as the backdrop for John Steinbeck's classic Cannery Row. According to the Cannery Row website, the onset of World War I brought on the demand for sardines, turning the city into a boomtown for production. Fish were harvested overnight from the cold, nutrient-rich waters of Monterey Canyon and the next morning, workers, mostly newly arrived immigrants, would work until the day's catch was canned. This was hard work, with long hours and limited workplace regulations, which came later.

The decline of Cannery Row's canning industry was the result of overfishing around 1950, from which it never fully recovered. It is a stark reminder of the fragility of our oceans. The area is now a popular tourist destination with restaurants, shopping and outdoor activities.

I like sourdough bread for this sandwich, which is a staple in California—think San Francisco-style. I like the combination of the savory fish with the tangy bread. Quality among brands varies widely, so buy the best available. I prefer tinned fish in olive oil. Make this open-faced sandwich your own by adding sprouts, herbs or whatever floats your boat!

INGREDIENTS

{ Serves 5 }

- **2 tablespoons basil lemon butter (see page 536)**

- **5 slices sourdough bread**, cut on the diagonal

- **1 clove garlic, halved**

- **1 large avocado**, thinly sliced

- **1 medium tomato**, thinly sliced

- **3 4-ounce tins boneless**, skinless sardines in olive oil, with oil reserved

- **2 tablespoons capers in brine**, drained

- **Rosemary sea salt (see page 552) to taste**

- **Freshly ground black pepper to taste**

- **¼ cup shaved red onion**

  Optional: chopped hard boiled egg, capers

DIRECTIONS

1. Preheat your broiler to 500°F.

2. Spread equal portions of the basil lemon butter onto each slice of bread. Rub the open end of the garlic clove and on each piece of bread.

3. Place the bread on a baking sheet and place under the broiler for a quick toast. Remove as soon as the bread turns a light golden brown. Set aside.

4. Artfully layer on the avocado, tomato, sardines and capers on one slice of toasted bread. Finish by adding rosemary sea salt and freshly ground black pepper to taste, the red onion, and a drizzle of the reserved fish oil. Top with another slice of toasted bread and serve immediately.

Brazilian Salmon Cobb Salad

WITH ORANGE DRESSING

This South American Cobb is my take on a salad I enjoyed while visiting Rio de Janeiro, Brazil years ago. The ingredients are distinctly South American with a modern twist.

Although relatively new to the region, salmon has become increasingly popular in Brazil with the advent of aquaculture. It is now a widely available fish that can be found on South American restaurant menus and family dinner tables. Salad recipes are famously customizable, so feel free to make changes to this versatile salad to suit your palate.

INGREDIENTS

SALMON:

- **4 3-ounce skin-on salmon fillets,** pin bones removed

- **1 teaspoon onion powder**

- **1 teaspoon paprika**

- **1 teaspoon oregano**

- **½ teaspoon dried ground orange peel or minced orange zest**

- **Dash freshly ground black pepper**

- **1 tablespoon avocado oil (or oil of choice)**

DRESSING:

- **½ cup olive oil**

- **1 teaspoon water**

- **1 teaspoon honey**

- **1 large orange,** juice (about ½ cup) and zest (1 tablespoon)

- **1 bunch fresh cilantro**

- **1 clove garlic**

- **½ teaspoon sea salt**

- **½ teaspoon freshly ground black pepper**

SALAD:

- **1 head romaine lettuce,** rinsed, dried and chopped

- **1 cup arugula,** rinsed and dried

- **1 small red onion,** sliced

- **1 small jicama, peeled and julienned**

- **½ cup prepared hearts of palm**

- **2 large tomatoes,** diced

- **4 hard-boiled eggs,** peeled and chopped

- **2 large ripe avocados,** peeled and diced

- **4 tablespoons feta cheese,** crumbled

- **2 cups cooked black beans,** homemade or canned

- **4 tablespoons roasted salted Brazil nuts,** crushed

DIRECTIONS

1. Preheat oven to 375°F.

2. Place the salmon on a clean surface and add a generous pinch of sea salt to each piece. Set aside and allow to rest for 10 minutes or so until moisture forms on top of the fish, which will help reduce albumin formation during cooking.

3. While the salmon is resting, make the dressing. Add the olive oil, water, honey, orange juice and zest, cilantro, garlic, sea salt and black pepper to the bowl of a food processor. Pulse to combine until smooth. Taste for seasoning and adjust as needed. Transfer to a serving bowl and set aside.

4. Combine the onion powder, paprika, oregano, dried ground orange and a few cracks of black pepper. Set aside. After the salmon has rested, blot excess moisture from the fish with a paper towel, then sprinkle the spice mixture on the flesh side of the fish. Set aside.

5. In a cast iron or oven-safe skillet, heat 1 tablespoon of avocado oil (or oil of choice) over medium-high heat. When the skillet is hot, add the fish, flesh side down, and cook for 3 minutes, then place in the oven for 5 minutes. Remove the salmon from the oven and set aside while you assemble the salad.

6. Put the salad together by artfully arranging the romaine, arugula, red onion, jicama, hearts of palm, tomatoes, hard-boiled eggs, avocado, feta cheese and black beans in individual serving bowls. Top with cooked salmon, crushed Brazil nuts, and orange dressing as desired. Serve immediately.

Thai Shrimp & Peanut Salad

Thailand is known for its gorgeous and fragrant recipes that are filled with aromatics and spices. This recipe is loosely based on a salad that I enjoy at a local Thai restaurant on occasion. Some Thai cooks use formal recipes, but most often use their sense of taste as a true test of a good dish. I'm a big fan of this style of kitchen magic.

Don't let the long list of ingredients intimidate you. Since this is a Thai-inspired salad, there are lots of fresh veggies and seasonings used that are indicative of the recipe's Southeast Asian roots. These items are accessible and can be found in most markets.

I listed the dressing ingredients separately in case you prefer to purchase the Thai Peanut dressing from the store (there are some good ones out there); if this is the case, you can omit these items from your shopping list. White shrimp is featured here, but most varieties of shrimp will work. See page 151 for tips on selecting shrimp.

INGREDIENTS

PEANUT DRESSING:

- ¼ cup creamy peanut butter
- 2 teaspoons minced fresh ginger
- 1 tablespoon toasted sesame oil
- ¼ cup tamari soy sauce
- 2 tablespoons honey
- 1 teaspoon red pepper flake
- 3 tablespoons rice wine vinegar
- 2 tablespoons orange juice
- 1 tablespoon lime juice
- Sea salt and freshly ground black pepper to taste

SALAD:

- 1 16-ounce package Asian soba noodles
- 2 cups chopped Napa cabbage
- 2 cups chopped Romaine lettuce
- 1 cup shredded carrot
- 1 large English cucumber, thinly sliced cup thinly sliced red onion
- 1 small jicama, peeled and sliced into matchsticks
- 2 large scallions, green part only, sliced
- 5 Thai basil leaves, finely chopped
- 2 tablespoons toasted sesame seeds, 2 teaspoons reserved for garnish
- ½ cup crushed salted peanuts, 3 tablespoons reserved for garnish

SHRIMP:

- 4 cups water
- 2 tablespoons sea salt
- 1 teaspoon whole black peppercorns

- 1 lemon, halved
- 1½ pounds white shrimp, peeled and deveined, halved lengthwise

DIRECTIONS

Make the dressing:

In a medium-sized bowl, combine the peanut butter, ginger, sesame oil, soy sauce, honey, red pepper flake, rice wine vinegar, orange juice and lime juice. Whisk to combine and make a creamy dressing—it should be smooth and coat the back of a spoon. Add a little water if the dressing is too thick. Taste for seasoning and add sea salt and freshly ground black pepper as needed. Cover and set aside.

Prepare the shrimp:

Add water to a medium-sized pot along with the sea salt, peppercorns and lemon. Bring to a boil, remove from heat, and add the shrimp, cover. Allow the pot to sit for 8–10 minutes. Drain the pot, place the shrimp in a bowl, and set aside in the refrigerator.

Prepare the salad:

Bring a large pot of salted water to a boil. Add soba noodles and cook according to package instructions. Transfer to a colander and rinse under cold running water; drain. Cover and refrigerate.

In a large bowl, toss the cooked, chilled shrimp with ¼ cup of the peanut dressing in a large bowl; set aside. Add the chilled soba noodles, vegetables and aromatics to the bowl and pour in the remaining dressing. Toss to combine.

To serve, divide the salad among 5–6 large bowls. Top each bowl with equal portions of the shrimp and garnish with the crushed peanuts, sesame seeds and cilantro. Serve immediately.

Tropical Grilled Scallop Sandwich

WITH SWEET PLANTAIN & AVOCADO

This recipe is a mash-up of some of my favorite tropical coastal flavors. Scallops, sweet plantain and avocado may not seem like a natural match, but they are a magical combination.

My first time enjoying a sandwich made with scallops was in Carlsbad, California at Pelly's, a small fish market just a few steps away from the Pacific Ocean. The store had a tiny restaurant on the side and sold simple, tasty entreés and seafood sandwiches, which were my favorite. This recipe is my play on this classic Carlsbad favorite!

I call for a sweet ripe plantain in this recipe and avocado mash (not guacamole). If you are new to plantains, they are the starchier cousin of bananas and must always be cooked before eating. It's important that the plantains are the right level of ripeness so that they spread properly over the sourdough bread, creating a sweet layer juxtaposed to the succulent shellfish and creamy avocado.

Plantains range from green, which are firm to the touch and can be prepared like a potato, to the very ripe and sweet. Ripe plantains are often referred to as "black" plantains because of the number of black spots that signify ripeness, along with the deep yellow color the skin turns; this is the type you'll need for this recipe.

INGREDIENTS

1 large ripe, sweet plantain

½ cup avocado oil

8 large dry sea scallops

Sea salt and freshly ground black pepper to taste

2 tablespoons ghee (clarified butter)

4 slices sourdough bread

1 tablespoon butter, at room temperature

½ teaspoon garlic powder

½ cup shredded green and purple cabbage

1 small red onion, thinly sliced

1 large ripe avocado, peeled, pitted and lightly mashed

DIRECTIONS

{ Makes 2 sandwiches }

1. Peel the plantains using a paring knife to remove the thick outer layer. Once peeled, slice the plantain into 1-inch pieces. Set aside.

2. In a large grill pan or skillet, heat the avocado oil over medium-high heat and add the plantain pieces in batches. Cook on one side for 2 minutes until lightly browned, then flip over and cook for another 2 minutes. Remove from the pan and rest on a bed of paper towels. Set aside.

3. Place the sea scallops on a clean surface and season with sea salt and freshly ground black pepper. Dust with flour on both sides and allow to rest for 1 or 2 minutes—this will help the flour adhere.

4. In the meantime, discard the oil from the skillet where the plantains were cooked and wipe the pan with paper towels. Add the ghee to the pan over high heat. When the ghee has melted, add the sea scallops in batches and cook until golden brown on one side, then flip and cook on the other side—this should only take 1 or 2 minutes. Remove from the pan and rest on a bed of paper towels. When cool, slice each scallop two-thirds of the way through, leaving a bit of a hinge.

5. In a conventional toaster or oven, lightly toast the bread and coat one side with a little butter.

6. To compose the sandwich, place a few pieces of plantain on the buttered side of a slice of bread. Using a butter knife, spread the fruit over the bread. Add a layer of scallops (flattened), a layer of shredded cabbage and a few slices of red onion. On a second piece of bread, spread a layer of avocado and put the sandwich together. Repeat with the remaining ingredients, slice the sandwiches in half, and serve immediately.

Scandinavian Seared Salmon

WITH LEMON-DILL CUCUMBER SALAD

Salmon is a popular fish along the Scandinavia peninsula where seafood is a staple; it's often smoked or cured and enjoyed for lunch or dinner alongside potatoes and lingonberries. The cuisine of this region, made up of Denmark, Norway and Sweden, is flavorful and mild.

Most varieties of salmon will work for this recipe; Atlantic salmon is a good option, but use what you have available. See page 297 for tips on selecting salmon.

The lemon-dill cucumber salad brings bright flavor and creamy flavor to savory salmon. It's meant to be eaten within 30 to 45 minutes of preparation; otherwise, the salt will release too much moisture from the cucumbers, adding excess water to the dish. Not to worry—if this happens, simply drain the moisture and carry on, but the texture will be affected.

INGREDIENTS

{ Serves 4 }

- **½ pounds center-cut salmon,** skin and pin bones removed

- **Sea salt and freshly ground black pepper to taste**

- **3 Persian or English cucumbers,** diced small

- **½ small red onion,** thinly sliced

- **1 small lemon,** juice and zest

- **1 tablespoon chopped fresh dill**

- **2 tablespoons ghee**

DIRECTIONS

1. Slice the salmon into even ¼-inch diagonal slices. Season with salt and pepper to taste and set aside.

2. To prepare the salad, add the cucumber and red onion to a medium-sized bowl along with the lemon juice, lemon zest and dill. Toss to combine. Taste for seasoning and adjust as needed. Cover and place in the refrigerator until ready to serve.

3. In a large nonstick skillet, melt the ghee over medium-high heat. When the ghee is melted, add the salmon to the pan and cook for about 1½ minutes on each side. Remove the fish from the heat and allow it to rest for 1 minute before serving.

4. To serve, divide the fish among 4 platters or bowls and artfully add a scoop of the cucumber salad. Serve immediately.

Catalina Spicy Lobster Salad

A part of the Channel Islands archipelago, Santa Catalina Island is a resort town that lies 20 miles off the coast of California. It's an easy 60-minute ferry ride from Los Angeles or Orange County. This ruggedly beautiful location is a playground for those seeking outdoor activities like hiking, horseback riding, snorkeling, SCUBA diving and lobster fishing.

This salad is inspired by my time spent in Avalon, the capital city, where I spent the day harvesting lobster traps with a local fisherman. Spiny lobsters are harvested mostly for their tail meat, and their shells make a nice broth.

I call for Tabasco sauce in this recipe—a brand of hot sauce made from Louisiana-grown tabasco peppers—which has a distinct, spicy, clean pepper flavor that works well with this dish. Feel free to use your favorite hot sauce; just be mindful of those with too many ingredients, as they can mask the flavor of the lobster. Consider serving this dish with tortilla chips, jicama tostada shells (page 420) or fresh lettuce leaves.

INGREDIENTS

{ Serves 4 }

- **1 cup plain Greek yogurt**

- **½ cup capers in brine**, drained

- **¼ cup finely diced celery**

- **1 tablespoon Dijon mustard**

- **¼ cup minced shallots**

- **½ cup thinly sliced scallions**, green part only

- **1 teaspoon of Tabasco sauce or other hot sauce of choice**

- **Sea salt and freshly ground black pepper to taste**

- **2 pounds steamed lobster meat**, roughly chopped

- **3 tablespoons fresh cilantro leaves**, for garnish

DIRECTIONS

1. In a medium-sized bowl, combine the Greek yogurt with the capers, celery, Dijon mustard, shallots, scallions, Tabasco sauce, and sea salt and freshly ground black pepper to taste. Mix thoroughly.

2. Gently fold in the lobster meat with a rubber spatula, keeping the pieces as large as possible. Taste for seasoning and adjust as needed.

3. To serve, divide the lobster mixture among 4 plates. Garnish with cilantro leaves and serve as desired.

NOLA Oyster 'Po Boy

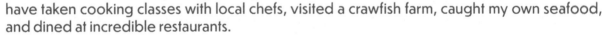

Located along the Gulf of Mexico, New Orleans, Louisiana has a diverse and world-class food scene. I have had fun exploring the region and have taken cooking classes with local chefs, visited a crawfish farm, caught my own seafood, and dined at incredible restaurants.

One item you'll find in most eateries is the 'po boy sandwich, a deliciously famous sandwich found in and around New Orleans, or NOLA as it is affectionately called. 'Po boys can be stuffed with practically anything, from fried alligator to shrimp, catfish, or in this case, oysters.

Much like oysters, the 'po boy comes from humble beginnings. Legend has it that the sandwich was created in the 1920s by two brothers—former streetcar drivers who created a simple sandwich to provide an affordable meal for workers during a citywide streetcar strike. The sandwich was composed of French bread, gravy, and spare bits of meat and was eventually dubbed the "poor boy" (later shortened to 'po boy) after the down-on-their-luck workers.

Medium-sized jarred oysters work great for this recipe, which is an ideal use for pre-shucked oysters. Dress this one up to suit your palate. Remoulade sauce, made with mayonnaise and spices, is a traditional sauce used for this sandwich, but I prefer spicy cocktail sauce.

INGREDIENTS

{ Serves 2 }

- **2 8-ounce jars oysters**, drained, or 8 large oysters, shucked

- **2 teaspoons rosemary sea salt (see page 552)**

- **1 teaspoon cayenne pepper**

- **1 teaspoon white pepper**

- **1 teaspoon dried thyme**

- **2 cups all-purpose flour**

- **½ cup cornmeal**

- **2 cups vegetable oil**, for frying

- **1 loaf French bread**, halved and partially split lengthwise

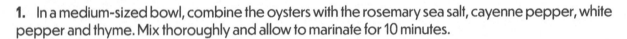

TOPPINGS SUGGESTIONS: SPICY COCKTAIL SAUCE OR REMOULADE SAUCE, TOMATO SLICES, SHREDDED LETTUCE, SHREDDED CABBAGE SLAW, SLICED RED ONION, DILL PICKLES

DIRECTIONS

1. In a medium-sized bowl, combine the oysters with the rosemary sea salt, cayenne pepper, white pepper and thyme. Mix thoroughly and allow to marinate for 10 minutes.

2. In a large brown paper bag, carefully pour in the flour and cornmeal. Add the oysters, a few at a time, to the bag and gently shake to coat them in flour—hold the bottom of the bag for extra security.

3. Remove the oysters and place on a plate or clean surface to rest for 3–5 minutes; this will help form a thin crust. Repeat with the remaining oysters.

4. Meanwhile, in a Dutch oven or heavy-bottomed skillet, heat the vegetable oil to 375°F.

5. Fry the oysters in batches until golden brown and drain them on a bed of paper towels or a cooling rack.

6. When the oysters are done, make the 'po boys: Slather two teaspoons of the spicy cocktail sauce or remoulade on the bottom half of both pieces of French bread, then layer on the tomato, lettuce, cabbage slaw, red onion, pickles and oysters as desired. Serve immediately.

Middle Eastern Grilled Barramundi

WITH TAHINI SAUCE & CUCUMBER SALATA

This is a lovely Eastern Mediterranean twist on an Australian fish, thanks to the addition of tahini paste, which is made from toasted hulled sesame seeds. Its luxurious texture and nutty flavor combined with the lemon and cumin make for a sauce that's great with grilled white fish. This recipe works wonderfully as a wrap or a salad.

Barramundi is also known as Asian sea bass or giant perch. It is cultivated in the waters surrounding Australia. Its lean, mild-tasting, white flesh pairs well with Middle Eastern flavors.

INGREDIENTS

- **4 4-ounce Barramundi fillets,** skin on

- **2 cloves garlic,** minced and separated

- **2 large lemons,** juice only

- **2 tablespoons olive oil,** separated

- **1 teaspoon sea salt**

- **1 tablespoon cumin**

- **Freshly ground black pepper to taste**

- **½ cup tahini**

- **¼ cup chopped fresh parsley,** separated

- **4 Persian or English cucumbers,** diced medium

- **6 large ripe tomatoes,** chopped

- **5 mint leaves,** chopped

- **1 teaspoon ground sumac**

- **Sea salt and freshly ground black pepper to taste**

DIRECTIONS

1. Preheat a lump charcoal grill to medium-high.

2. In a large plastic bag, add the barramundi, 1 minced garlic clove, the juice of one lemon, 1 tablespoon olive oil, sea salt, cumin, and freshly ground black pepper to taste. Shake the bag to combine the ingredients and refrigerate for 15 minutes.

3. In a small bowl, whisk together the tahini, the remaining lemon juice and 1 tablespoon of parsley. Combine thoroughly and set aside.

4. In a large bowl, combine the cucumber, tomato, remaining parsley, mint, the remaining chopped garlic clove, sumac, a pinch of sea salt and freshly ground black pepper. Taste for seasoning and adjust as needed. Cover and refrigerate until ready to use.

5. Remove the fish from the bag and blot away any excess moisture using paper towels. Place the fish securely into fish grates and add to the grill. Cook on both sides for 3–4 minutes. Remove and allow the fish to rest for 1–2 minutes.

6. To serve, divide the fish among individual plates and add a drizzle of the tahini sauce and a scoop of the cucumber salad. Serve with toasted whole wheat pita.

SERVING SUGGESTION:
TOASTED WHOLE WHEAT PITA

California Avocado Salad

Avocados are one of the only fruits that contain monounsaturated fat—the good kind of fat. There are several varieties of avocado grown in California, including Bacon, Fuerte, Gwen, Hass, Lamb Hass, Reed and Zutano. This simple California-inspired salad is easy to put together and requires very little effort yet offers a punch of flavor. It works great on its own for a light meal or as a side dish for grilled and roasted seafood. I prefer Hass for this recipe, but most varieties will work well.

For a more substantial meal, mix in some chilled grilled or steamed shrimp.

INGREDIENTS

{ Serves 2-4 }

- **2 large firm ripe avocados,** pitted and chopped

- **1 small red onion,** peeled and thinly sliced

- **2 medium Roma tomatoes,** diced medium

- **1 large lime,** juice only

- **2 tablespoons olive oil**

- **Sea salt and freshly ground black pepper to taste**

DIRECTIONS

In a medium-sized bowl, gently combine the avocado, red onion, tomato, lime juice, olive oil and a pinch of sea salt and black pepper. Taste for seasoning and adjust as needed. Cover and chill for 10 minutes before serving.

Soups, Chowders and Broths

~~~~~~~~~~~~~~~~~~~~~~

- Shikoku Island Dashi (Bonito Broth) Udon Bowl

- San Francisco Dungeness Crab Cioppino

- Pacific Coast Salmon Bone Broth

- Norwegian Halibut Bone Broth

- French Whitefish Fumet

- Maine Lobster Stock

- Japanese Awase Dashi (Dried Bonito Flake) Broth

- Central Coast Wild Salmon & Fresh Corn Chowder

Shikoku Island Dashi (Bonito Broth) Udon Bowl

Shikoku is the smallest and least populated of Japan's four main islands, coming in second to Okinawa. The island's region of Kagawa is famous for its sanuki udon, which are thick, flat, white noodles made from wheat flour. They have a dense, slightly chewy texture and can be purchased dried, fresh or precooked. You can also make your own, but there are so many quality brands on the market that it's hardly worth the effort.

Bonito is a large game fish that is often mistaken for mackerel. It is an important fish in Japanese cuisine, but it is rarely eaten as a meal; it is mostly dried, fermented and made into thin flakes. These wispy shavings are made into broth that serves as the base for many traditional dishes like miso soup and ramen. Bonito lends an unmistakable umami flavor when combined with seaweed to make a broth called dashi.

This dashi udon bowl can be easily customized with your favorite Asian-inspired ingredients—get creative!

INGREDIENTS

{ Serves 4 }

- **2 pounds refrigerated, fresh or frozen udon noodles**

- **4 cups awase dashi broth (see page 488)**

- **2 tablespoons mirin (Japanese sweet rice wine)**

- **2 tablespoons tamari soy sauce**

- **1 thumb ginger**, quartered

- **8–10 mushrooms** (a mix of enoki, shiitake, oyster, maitake or your favorite variety)

- **4 baby bok choy**, halved

- **4 soft-boiled eggs**, halved

- **4 large scallions**, green part only, sliced

- **Japanese chili flake**, as needed

SUGGESTED TOPPINGS: TEMPURA SHRIMP, TOFU, SLICED SURIMI, TEMPURA VEGETABLES, SHREDDED CARROT, DAIKON RADISH, NEGI (JAPANESE GREEN ONION)

DIRECTIONS

1. Cook the udon noodles per package instructions. Drain and set aside.

2. In a large pot, bring the awase dashi broth to a simmer. Add the mirin and soy sauce and stir to combine. Taste for seasoning and adjust as needed. Turn off the heat and add the ginger, mushrooms and baby bok choy, then cover with a lid.

3. To serve, place equal portions of the cooked udon noodles in 4 bowls along with the awase dashi broth. Top with the mushrooms, bok choy, soft boiled eggs, scallions, Japanese chili flake and other suggested toppings as desired. Enjoy immediately.

San Francisco Dungeness Crab Cioppino

WITH TAHINI SAUCE & CUCUMBER SALATA

Legend has it that the Portuguese and Italian fishers who worked along the coast of San Francisco, California in the late 1800s came together at the end of the day to create supper made from the unsold seafood of the day. The stew was named 'cioppino' after an Italian soup of the same name. What is now called 'cioppino' has since been refined into a classic seafood dish.

Two classic California ingredients, Dungeness crab and wine are the major ingredients of cioppino and should be used generously.

Adding the seafood at the end is a dance you'll have to get comfortable with. I like to start with the live shellfish so they have plenty of time to open, then the white fish, shrimp and scallops. Since the crab will likely already be cooked, it only needs time to warm and absorb the flavors of the sauce.

Like most stews, this one is fantastic on the first day of cooking, but is even better on day two, since the seafood will have had a chance to absorb all of the flavors of the dish.

INGREDIENTS

- **¼ cup olive oil**

- **2 stalks celery,** diced small

- **1 fennel bulb,** sliced

- **4 cloves garlic,** peeled and chopped

- **1 large brown onion,** peeled and chopped

- **3 sprigs fresh basil or 1 teaspoon dried basil**

- **1 teaspoon crushed red pepper flake**

- **5 sprigs fresh thyme**

- **1½ cups dry white wine (or water, if preferred)**

- **1 14-ounce can crushed tomatoes**

- **5 cups whitefish fumet (see page 490) or lobster stock (see page 492)**

- **2 bay leaves**

- **½ teaspoon honey**

- **Sea salt and freshly ground black pepper to taste**

- **1 pound littleneck clams,** sorted and purged (see page 49)

- **1 pound black mussels,** debearded

- **1 pound cod, pollock or halibut fillets,** or other firm white fish, cut into chunks

- **1 pound large white shrimp,** deveined and shells removed

- **12 large dry sea scallops**

- **2 large cooked Dungeness crabs,** cleaned, legs removed, and body split into 4 pieces

DIRECTIONS

1. In a large Dutch oven, heat the olive oil over medium-high heat. Add the celery, fennel, garlic and onion and cook until soft and fragrant, about 5–6 minutes.

2. Add the basil, crushed red pepper flake and fresh thyme. Cook for 2–3 minutes, then add the wine (or water), crushed tomatoes, fish or seafood stock, bay leaves and honey. Stir to combine, then cover the pot with the lid slightly ajar. Reduce the heat to a simmer and cook for 25 minutes.

3. When the time is up, remove the lid and taste the sauce. Adjust the seasoning with salt and pepper as needed. Be careful with the salt at this stage, as the seafood will bring a layer of brininess to the dish.

4. Turn up the heat to medium-high and add the clams and mussels. Cover fully with the lid, allowing the shellfish time to open—about 5 minutes. Next, add the white fish, making sure the chunks are submerged as much as possible in the broth, and cook for 2 minutes, followed by the shrimp, sea scallops and crab. Cover the pot for 2 minutes, then reduce the heat to a simmer. Cook for 4 minutes, then remove from the heat. Allow the pot to rest for 5 minutes.

5. To serve, ladle equal portions of the tomato sauce into bowls, then artfully arrange the seafood along with slices of crusty sourdough bread. Garnish with fresh parsley.

SERVING SUGGESTIONS: CRUSTY SOURDOUGH BREAD,
½ BUNCH FRESH PARSLEY, CHOPPED

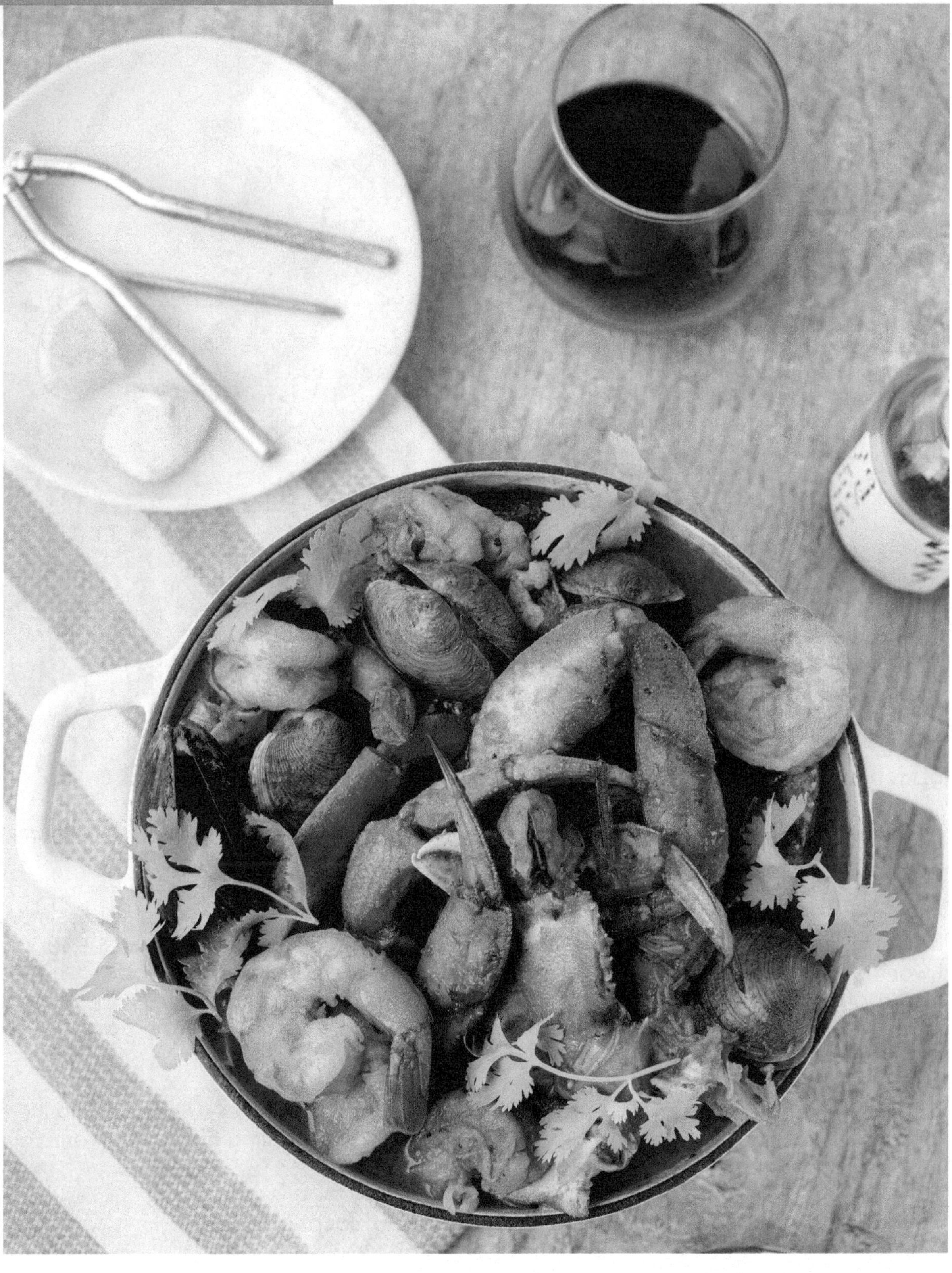

Pacific Coast Salmon Bone Broth

During our annual Christmas trip, my husband and I headed to Leavenworth, Washington. This small Bavarian-themed town is home to one of the West Coast's largest tree-lighting festivals. Christmas lights and holiday décor are passions of my husband's.

As the temperature cooled and a light rain began to fall, we tucked into a stylish restaurant called Yodelin, a storefront specializing in seafood bone broth. It was kismet.

With a menu featuring an impressive batch of soup bowls created from local wild salmon, halibut and Dungeness crab, it was hard to choose. After recommendations from the server, I went for the Asianinspired house special—the Yodelin. Filled with udon noodles, shiitake mushrooms and fresh greens, I was not disappointed. The dish was extraordinary. I have been making bone broths for several years, and the chance to experience broth prepared by another cook is a real treat.

I purchase fish bones from my favorite vendor at a local farmer's market. If you can't find them locally, you can make your own by filleting a whole fish, requesting fish bones from your fishmonger, or ordering them online.

This broth is great for sipping warm or as a base for gravy, soups or stews.

INGREDIENTS

{ Makes about 2 quarts }

- **2 tablespoons ghee**
- **2 stalks celery**, halved
- **1 small white onion**, quartered
- **2 cloves garlic**, peeled and halved
- **3 sprigs fresh thyme**
- **8 cups water**
- **1 bay leaf**
- **4 pounds salmon bones and heads**, rinsed
- **Salt and freshly ground black pepper to taste**

DIRECTIONS

1. In a large soup pot, heat the ghee over medium-high heat. When ghee is melted, add the celery, onion, garlic and thyme sprigs. Cook for 3 minutes or until the vegetables are fragrant and have softened.

2. Pour in the water, then add the bay leaf and salmon bones and heads. Simmer on low for 20 minutes, then turn off the heat. Allow the pot to cool.

3. When the liquid is cool, pick the salmon meat from the bones and transfer to a bowl; refrigerate and reserve for another dish (see salmon and corn chowder recipe page 496).

4. Strain the broth through a fine-mesh sieve until the liquid runs relatively clear and is free of large particles. Pour into a storage container and refrigerate until ready to use.

Norwegian Halibut Bone Broth

Halibut are renowned the world over for their meaty flesh and delicate flavor. They are particularly revered in Norway, where the flatfish appears in Stone Age carvings and is featured in traditional fables.

Wild halibut can be found throughout the region, but cultivated fish are likely what you'll find in local stores, high-end hotels, markets and restaurants. Norwegian halibut (a select group of Atlantic halibut) are raised in deep-sea cages in pristine fjords surrounding Averøy, Hjelmeland and Sognefjord.

To find halibut bones, you have a few options: make your own by filleting a whole Halibut, buy them from a fish market, or order them online (often called fish stock bones).

This bone broth recipe is satisfying sipped from a mug or used as the base for seafood soup, ramen or seafood gravy.

INGREDIENTS

- **2 tablespoons ghee**

- **1 small fennel bulb**, sliced

- **1 small white onion**, quartered

- **2 cloves garlic**, halved

- **8 cups (2 quarts) water**

- **1 4-inch square dried seaweed (kelp)**

- **2 pounds Norwegian halibut bones or Atlantic fish bones**

- **Sea salt and freshly ground black pepper to taste**

DIRECTIONS

1. In a large soup pot, heat the ghee over medium-high heat. When the ghee is melted, add the fennel, onion and garlic. Cook for 4 minutes or until the vegetables are fragrant and have softened.

2. Pour in the water and add the seaweed and halibut bones. Simmer on low for 10 minutes, then turn off the heat and allow the broth to cool.

3. When the liquid is cool, discard the seaweed and pick the halibut meat from the bones and place it in a bowl; refrigerate and reserve for another dish. (Halibut posole is a great option—see page 510.)

4. Strain the broth through a fine-mesh sieve until it runs relatively clear. Use immediately or store in the refrigerator until ready to use. This will keep well for 2–3 days; otherwise freeze it for up to 6 months.

Japanese Awase Dashi (Bonito) Broth

INGREDIENTS

{ Makes 4 cups }

- 5 cups filtered water
- 1 cup Bonito flakes
- 4 ounces kombu seaweed

DIRECTIONS

1. Add the filtered water to a pot along with the kombu and allow it to soak for 24 hours.

2. Place the pot with the kombu on the stove and bring to a low simmer. Remove from the heat and add the bonito flakes. Steep for 5 minutes. Strain and use the broth as desired.

Dashi refers to a group of Japanese broths made from seaweed and other ingredients. Awase dashi uses dried bonito flakes, which serve as the foundation for many broths used for dishes like miso soup.

Bonito are a small member of the tuna family and an important fish in East Asia. They can grow up to 13 pounds in size and are often mistaken for mackerel with a flavor profile that is equally as pungent. An important part of Japanese gastronomy, the fish is typically dried, smoked and fermented to make flakes, a process that gives the fish an intense umami flavor.

There are many uses for this broth—try it as a replacement for your afternoon tea, or serve it as the base for ramen, soba or udon noodle soup (see page 478) along with your favorite Japanese ingredients.

Marseille Whitefish Fumet (Stock)

Marseille is a city located in the South of France in a region called Provence-Alpes-Côte d'Azur that borders Italy and the Mediterranean Sea. It's a sprawling city known for a flagship dish called bouillabaisse, a flavorful fish stew. Along the city's Vieux Port (old port), a popular travel destination, restaurants along the waterfront work hard to entice tourists into trying their stew, all claiming to be the best and most authentic.

Truth be told, locals rarely order bouillabaisse or bourride, another regional fish stew, in restaurants. These dishes are typically made at home and every household has its rendition. The foundation of these stews is fish broth, or fumet, which is a French word that refers to a concentrated fish stock.

My version of fumet roasts the fish parts prior to simmering, which creates a richly flavored stock. The bones of turbot, halibut and sole or other saltwater whitefish are great options for this recipe.

INGREDIENTS

{ Makes about 1 quart }

- **4 pounds white saltwater fish bones and trimmings (remove gills if using a fish head)**

- **1 cup white wine**

- **4 cups water**, more as needed

- **1 shallot**, peeled and halved

- **1 large carrot**, halved

- **1 leek**, cleaned and quarteredw

- **4 cloves garlic**

- **2 stalks celery**, quartered

- **2 bay leaves**

- **4 sprigs fresh parsley**

- **3 sprigs fresh tarragon**

- **1 teaspoon sea salt or Kosher salt**

- **4 white peppercorns**

DIRECTIONS

1. Preheat oven to 400°F.

2. Rinse the fish under cold water to remove any excess blood or protein. Pat dry and place on a rimmed baking sheet and bake for 5 minutes.

3. Add the roasted fish to a large Dutch oven or a stockpot. Pour in the wine and enough water to cover the fish. Add the shallot, carrot, leek, garlic, celery, bay leaves, parsley, tarragon, sea salt and white peppercorns. Place the pot over medium heat, cover and bring to a low simmer. As the pot simmers, a film will begin to form, use a spoon or ladle to remove and discard. Continue cooking on low heat for 15 minutes and skim the fumet as needed.

4. Remove the pot from the heat and allow it to cool. Strain the fumet through a sieve into another pot. Bring the pot to a simmer for 10 minutes and continue to skim if needed. Cook until the stock reduces by one-third, then remove. Use immediately, store for up to 3 days in the refrigerator, or freeze for 3–4 months.

Maine Lobster Stock

This simple, flavorful lobster stock is made from the shells of Maine lobster, the brightly colored clawed version of the crustacean that is also known as American lobster.

The addition of tomato paste and paprika gives this dish New England flair. Creating your own stock from cracked shells is a great way to make use of the whole animal and waste nothing.

INGREDIENTS

{ Makes about 1 quart }

- **4–5 lobster shells**
- **1 tablespoon olive oil**
- **4 stalks celery**, halved
- **1 large carrot**, halved
- **1 shallot**, peeled and quartered
- **2 cloves garlic**, peeled and halved
- **1 fennel bulb**, stalks and fronds only, sliced

- **2 bay leaves**
- **5 cups water**
- **1 cup white wine**
- **4 black peppercorns**
- **2 tablespoon tomato paste**
- **½ teaspoon paprika**
- **Sea salt to taste**

DIRECTIONS

1. Preheat oven to 400°F.

2. Add the lobster shells to a rimmed baking sheet and cook for 3–4 minutes. Remove and set aside.

3. In a Dutch oven or stockpot, heat the olive oil over medium heat and add the celery, carrot, shallot, garlic, fennel and bay leaves and cook for 3–4 minutes or until fragrant. Add the lobster shells, water, wine, black peppercorns, tomato paste and paprika. Stir to combine and taste for seasoning. Simmer for 45 minutes. Turn off the heat and allow the pot to cool for 15 minutes.

4. Strain through a sieve and use immediately or freeze for up to 3–4 months.

Spicy Manhattan Clam Chowder

It's interesting that one of the most cosmopolitan cities on the planet is associated with one of the humblest seafood chowders around.

Manhattan clam chowder is the "red" version of clam chowder that uses tomatoes as its base. Rumor has it that tomatoes became popular in clam chowder in the mid-1800s with the arrival of Italian and Portuguese fishers in Rhode Island, a New England state that shares a border with New York.

This recipe is one of my go-to favorites—I typically have all the ingredients stocked in my fridge and pantry, plus it only takes 30 minutes to put together. I like lots of clams in my chowder, but feel free to adjust the amount based on your preference.

INGREDIENTS

{ Serves 4 }

- **2 tablespoons ghee or olive oil**

- **1 small Spanish or brown onion,** finely chopped

- **3 stalks celery,** diced medium

- **2 carrots,** chopped

- **2 cloves garlic, chopped**

- **1½ cups clam juice**

- **3 cups lobster stock (see page 492), halibut bone broth (see page 486) or whitefish fumet (see page 490)**

- **5 russet potatoes,** peeled and diced medium

- **1 28-ounce can crushed tomatoes**

- **1 tablespoon crushed red pepper flake**

- **4 sprigs fresh thyme**

- **Sea salt and freshly ground black pepper to taste**

- **2 pounds clam meat** (if using canned clams in juice, use two large 50-ounce cans and eliminate the 1½ cups of clam juice)

SERVING SUGGESTIONS: RUSTIC BREAD, OYSTER CRACKERS

DIRECTIONS

1. In a medium-sized Dutch oven or soup pot, heat the ghee or olive oil over medium-high heat. Add the onion, celery, carrot and garlic and sauté for 5 minutes or until fragrant.

2. Add the clam juice (if not using canned clams), seafood stock, potatoes, tomatoes, crushed red pepper flake and thyme and reduce the heat to a simmer. Cover the pot with the lid slightly ajar, bring to a boil, and cook for 8–10 minutes or until the potatoes are tender. Taste for seasoning and adjust with sea salt and freshly ground black pepper as needed.

3. Add the clam meat or the cans of clams and their broth, cover the pot fully, and cook for 10 minutes.

4. When the time is up, remove the pot from the heat and let sit for 10–15 minutes, giving the flavors time to meld. Ladle into soup bowls and serve with rustic bread or oyster crackers as desired.

Central Coast Wild Salmon & Fresh Corn Chowder

Every summer, my dad is first in line to buy a bushel of the legendary sweet corn from the Gibson Farm Market located on the Fresno State University campus. He then uses the corn as gifts and in some cases, as a bartering tool to garner visits from grandchildren. I make soup with my spoils, and this salmon and corn chowder recipe is one of my favorites.

This recipe uses the oft-overlooked salmon bones and heads. These fish parts add a distinctly delicious flavor to soup, sauces and chowders. See page 485 for my salmon broth recipe. This chowder is on the brothier side and does not include thickeners like roux or cornstarch.

I call for half-and-half in this recipe, but I occasionally swap it out for coconut milk to mix things up. Do your best to find wild fish bones, but farmed ones will do as well.

INGREDIENTS

3 pounds wild salmon bones and heads

1 bay leaf

2 cups water

3 ears fresh sweet corn

2 tablespoons ghee

1 large Spanish onion, diced small

2 stalks celery, diced small

1 quart (4 cups) salmon bone broth (see page 484)

3 large russet potatoes, diced medium

3 sprigs fresh thyme, whole

Sea salt and freshly ground black pepper to taste

2 tablespoons half-and-half

DIRECTIONS

{ Serves 6–8 }

1. Rinse the salmon bones and heads, taking care to remove any blood or organs.

2. In a medium-sized pot, add the fish along with the bay leaf and water. Bring to a boil for 3 minutes, then cover and reduce the heat to a low simmer for 5 minutes. Turn off the heat and allow the fish and liquid to cool.

3. Next, pick the cooled salmon bones and heads of any meat, placing the meat in a separate bowl. (The fish head has some pretty tender and delicious flesh called "cheeks.") Set the salmon meat aside; discard the naked bones and heads.

4. To prepare the corn, remove the corn kernels from the cobs with a paring knife and place the kernels in a bowl. When the kernels have been removed, carefully use the back end of the knife blade or another dull, firm kitchen tool to squeeze out the milky centers from the cobs into the bowl with the kernels. Discard the cobs and set the kernels aside.

5. In a large sauté pan or nonstick skillet, heat the ghee over medium-high heat. Add the onion and celery and sauté until the onion is soft and fragrant.

6. Add the strained salmon liquid along with the quart of bone broth, potatoes, thyme, and sea salt and black pepper to taste. Cover and bring to a boil. When the potatoes are soft yet firm, about 12 minutes, reduce the heat to simmer and stir in the corn, salmon and half-and-half. Stir to combine and taste for seasoning. Adjust as needed. Cook for another 5 to 8 minutes or until the potatoes reach your preferred firmness.

Thai Creamy Coconut Salmon Chowder

Soup is a common way to enjoy seafood in Southeast Asia. Savory salmon broth infused with the Thai flavors of ginger, garlic, cilantro, lemongrass and chili is delightful.

Salmon is not native to Thailand; in fact, most of this variety of fish is imported from Norway. You will find it in markets and high-end restaurants in the region. The Thai appetite for salmon is steadily increasing and cooks have found new ways to incorporate it into traditional dishes or neo Thai food. This tropically inspired chowder recipe is an example of this trend and is a nice way to bring the flavors of Thailand together with salmon.

Coconut milk is a key ingredient in Thai cooking; it serves as the base for curries and desserts. You can purchase it in most grocery stores, Asian markets or online. If you are fortunate enough to visit the country, you can buy it freshly pressed.

INGREDIENTS

{ Serves 4-6 }

- **2 tablespoons ghee**

- **1 medium brown onion**, peeled and chopped

- **2 large carrots**, diced

- **2 large stalks celery**, chopped

- **2 teaspoons white pepper**

- **2 tablespoons all-purpose flour**

- **1 tablespoon avocado oil**

- **½ cup water**

- **3 cups Pacific salmon bone broth (see page 484) or low-sodium seafood stock**

- **1½ cups coconut milk**

- **3 fresh sprigs thyme**, whole

- **1½-inch piece fresh ginger**, grated

- **1 tablespoon lemongrass paste**

- **1 bay leaf**

- **3 large russet potatoes**, peeled and diced

- **2 cups cooked salmon**, flaked

- **½ bunch fresh cilantro**, leaves only

- **Sea salt and freshly ground black pepper to taste**

DIRECTIONS

1. In a large Dutch oven or heavy-bottomed pot, heat the ghee over medium heat. Add the onion, carrot and celery and sweat the vegetables for 5 minutes until soft and fragrant.

2. Next, stir in the white pepper, flour and avocado oil, stirring constantly for about 2 minutes— make sure the flour does not brown.

3. Pour in the water, bone broth or seafood stock, coconut milk, thyme, ginger, lemongrass paste and bay leaf, and bring to a boil for 5 minutes. Add the potatoes and reduce heat to a simmer. Cook with the lid slightly ajar for 25 minutes.

4. Add the cooked salmon and cilantro and simmer for another 5 minutes. Taste for seasoning and add sea salt and freshly ground black pepper as desired. Allow the pot to sit for 5–10 minutes before serving.

Lohikeitto (Finnish) Salmon Soup

Finland is surrounded by the Baltic sea and is home to more than 150,000 lakes. With a vast coastline spanning more than 700 miles, the country has a long-held tradition of boating and sailing that remains to this day. Suffice it to say that seafood is an important part of the region's gastronomy, which celebrates an abundance of fish, including Arctic char, herring, trout and salmon.

Lohi means salmon in Finnish and keitto means soup. This warming, savory lohikeitto is popular across Scandinavia and Northwestern Russia, where the winters are brutally cold.

INGREDIENTS

{ Serves 4-6 }

- **2 tablespoons unsalted butter**

- **1 large leek**, rinsed and chopped

- **2 large carrots**, diced

- **1 quart (4 cups) salmon bone broth (see page 484)**

- **1 bay leaf**

- **1 pound large russet potatoes**, peeled and diced

- **½ teaspoon sea salt**, plus more as needed

- **½ teaspoon white pepper**, plus more as needed

- **2 pounds pink salmon**, boneless and skinless

- **1 bunch fresh dill**

- **1½ cups half-and-half**

DIRECTIONS

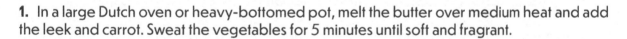

1. In a large Dutch oven or heavy-bottomed pot, melt the butter over medium heat and add the leek and carrot. Sweat the vegetables for 5 minutes until soft and fragrant.

2. Add the bone broth, bay leaf, potatoes, sea salt and white pepper. Cover the pot with a lid with the lid slightly ajar and bring to a boil for 5 minutes.

3. After 5 minutes, remove the lid and reduce heat to a simmer. Add the salmon, dill, and the half-and-half and stir to combine. Cook for another 5 minutes. Taste for seasoning and add additional salt and pepper as needed.

4. Turn off the heat and allow the pot to rest for 10 minutes before serving.

Louisiana Seafood Gumbo

Gumbo is a dish that claims West African and French roots. The dish represents the beautiful melting pot of cultures that exists along the greater Gulf Coast of the United States.

Seafood gumbo conjures up fond memories for me. It is a dish that my family makes a few times a year during Christmas and Thanksgiving. I learned the art and craft of making this luxurious soup from my aunt Joan. When "gumbo season" arrived, all of the 'tweens were given sous chef duties that ranged from chopping bell pepper, deveining shrimp and putting on the pot of rice—one year I got lucky and was assigned to roux duty.

I soon learned that the secret to making a good roux, which is by far one of the most important steps in creating an incredible gumbo, is patience. Roux adds flavor, depth and body to the dish. My seafood gumbo is lighter in flavor and color than most versions of the soup that include sausage and chicken; this is to allow the seafood to shine and not be overpowered by the roux. If you want a more gravy-like consistency to your gumbo, consider increasing the amount of roux.

INGREDIENTS

{ Serves 6–8 }

- 1 cup plus 2 tablespoons vegetable oil

- 1 cup all-purpose flour

- 1 cup chopped celery

- 1 cup chopped bell pepper

- 1 cup chopped Spanish onion

- ½ cup chopped carrot

- 3 cups lobster stock (see page 492), whitefish fumet (see page 490), or vegetable broth

- 6 cups water

- 1 bay leaf

- 1 tablespoon fresh thyme

- 2 cloves garlic, chopped

- 2 teaspoons culinary lavender

- 1 tablespoon freshly ground black pepper

- 1 tablespoon white pepper

- 1 tablespoon cayenne pepper

- 1 tablespoon paprika

- 2 tablespoons dried ground shrimp

- 1 pound mussels, scrubbed

- 1 pound hard-shell clams, scrubbed

- 2 Dungeness crabs, cleaned and broken into pieces

- 2 pounds Gulf shrimp, peeled and deveined

- 1 tablespoon gumbo filé powder (sassafras powder)

- Sea salt to taste

INGREDIENTS

- **2 pounds Gulf shrimp, peeled and deveined**

- **1 tablespoon gumbo filé powder (sassafras powder)**

- **Sea salt to taste**

SERVING SUGGESTIONS: STEAMED WHITE RICE, HOT SAUCE

DIRECTIONS

1. In a large, heavy pot over medium heat, make a roux by combining the oil and flour and cook for 10-12 minutes, stirring continuously so the flour does not burn. Continue stirring until the mix turns into a thick, peanut butter-like consistency.

2. Add the celery, bell pepper, onion and carrot, and stir until vegetables have softened, about 10 minutes. Next, add the broth or stock, water and bay leaf. Stir to incorporate, bring the pot to a boil, and allow the liquid to cook for 15 minutes.

3. Add the thyme, garlic, lavender, black pepper, white pepper, cayenne, paprika and ground shrimp to the pot. Stir to combine and bring the pot to a simmer. Cook for 10 minutes with the lid on.

4. Add the mussels and clams and bring the pot to a boil with the lid firmly on. Cook until the she-llfish have opened, about 4 minutes. Add the crab and shrimp to the pot and cook on medium for 5 minutes with the lid on, then turn off the heat. Allow the pot to rest for 10 minutes, then stir in the gumbo filé. Taste for seasoning and adjust as needed. To serve, add a scoop of rice to a large bowl and ladle on a generous portion of the soup. Add hot sauce as desired.

North African Cod & Chickpea Stew

The region referred to as North Africa is made up of seven countries and has a long Mediterranean coastline. The area is vast, and the flavors are distinct. Preserved lemons, decadent spice blends, and legumes are classic ingredients.

I make my chickpeas from scratch using dried peas. It's a simple dish to prepare; you just need a little time since the peas need to soak overnight (for best results) and cook. Making the peas from scratch allows me to make a big batch and use them for a variety of dishes. A pressure cooker will make easy work of preparing the legumes; if you choose this route, be sure to give them time to rest and absorb the flavorful liquid. In a pinch, good-quality canned chickpeas will work just as well.

This dish works interchangeably with haddock, pollock, hake and other firm white fish.

INGREDIENTS

{ Serves 4 }

- **1½ tablespoons ghee (or an oil with a high smoke point)**
- **1 large brown onion**, chopped
- **3 cloves garlic**, minced
- **1 tablespoon dried oregano**
- **2 tablespoons ground cumin**
- **1 tablespoon ground coriander**
- **1 teaspoon cayenne pepper**
- **1 tablespoon dried thyme**
- **4 cups water**
- **2 anchovy fillets in olive oil**, chopped

- **1 bay leaf**
- **2 cups cooked chickpeas** (see page 378)
- **½ preserved lemon**, minced
- **1 12-ounce can unsalted crushed tomatoes**
- **1 tablespoon harissa paste (see page 550)**, or red pepper flake to taste
- **2½ pounds white fish (cod, haddock, tilapia or halibut)**, cut into chunks
- **Sea salt and freshly ground black pepper to taste**
- **¼ cup chopped fresh cilantro**

DIRECTIONS

1. In a large Dutch oven or soup pot, heat the ghee over medium-high heat and add the onion and garlic. Sweat the veggies until tender, about 10 minutes.

2. Add the oregano, cumin, coriander, cayenne, thyme, water, anchovies, bay leaf, chickpeas, preserved lemon and crushed tomatoes. Bring to a simmer and cover for 5 minutes. Stir in the harissa or red pepper flake and add the fish. Simmer for 10 minutes or until the fish is opaque. Taste for seasoning and add salt and freshly ground black pepper as needed. Turn off the heat and allow the dish to rest for 5 minutes.

3. Serve family-style or in individual bowls and top with the fresh cilantro and with optional steamed couscous or pita bread.

Mexican Halibut Tortilla Soup

One of my favorite fairy tales is called "Stone Soup." In this classic European story, a group of hungry traveling strangers used their charm and good wit to convince an entire community of people to share bits of what they had available in their kitchens to create a meal that satisfied them all. There are many versions of this story, but this is the one that I remember.

Perhaps this is the reason that soup (including stews, chowders and broths) is one of my favorite ways to explore the food of a particular culture or part of the world. A large pot loaded with local, available ingredients and left to simmer on the stove really speaks to what a group of people find important and nourishing.

It is thought that chicken tortilla soup originates from Mexico City, Mexico, a lively and rambunctious part of the world that has brought forth some of the tastiest food around. A combination of simple, fragrant vegetables, herbs and spices along with à la carte toppings, my pescatarian version of this soup pays tribute to the classic dish, with a nod to Baja.

The foundation of this soup is halibut bone broth, a lightly flavored broth made from the collar of wild halibut, the part that runs from the clavicle to just beneath the gills. Collars are chunky and come with bones, skin and meat that is tender, flavorful and that separates easily.

Cooking with fish bones and parts is one of my favorite things. Beyond collars, I enjoy exploring other interesting cuts like wings, heads, cheeks and the skeleton. My fishmonger offers fish bones on a daily basis since they butcher and prepare fish of all types. The most common varieties I find are halibut, salmon, baqueta and salmon skin, and they range from $2 to $3 per pound.

This halibut tortilla soup is thickened with tortilla chips, whereas some versions of this soup are made with a base of black beans that thicken the soup naturally.

You can prepare the bone broth a day or two in advance, and it keeps well in the fridge. This will help cut down on overall prep time and allow you to get this meal on the table in under 30 minutes—once the broth is done the dish comes together easily. Have fun with this and host a family "soup bar" night and offer up as many optional ingredients as you'd like.

In a pinch, you can use store-bought seafood stock in place of the halibut bone broth.

INGREDIENTS

- 2 tablespoons avocado oil, or your favorite vegetable oil

- 1 medium white onion, chopped

- 2 cloves garlic, minced

- 1 tablespoon Mexican oregano

- 1 tablespoon chili powder

- 2 teaspoons cumin powder

- 1 teaspoon paprika

- 8 cups (2 quarts) halibut bone broth (see page 486)

- 1 epazote leaf

- 3 tablespoons tomato paste

- 1 serrano pepper, cut into two

- ½ cup tortilla chips, crushed

- Sea salt and black pepper to taste

- ½ bunch or ½ cup chopped fresh cilantro

- 1 cup roasted corn or 3 corn cobs cut into thirds

- 1 cup cooked halibut meat

DIRECTIONS

{ Serves 6 }

1. In a soup pot or Dutch oven, heat the oil over medium heat and add the onion and garlic and cook until fragrant. Add the oregano, chili powder, cumin and paprika and cook for 2 minutes, stirring to prevent the spices from burning.

2. Pour in the halibut bone broth and add the epazote leaf, tomato paste, serrano pepper and crushed tortilla chips. Stir to combine, then cover with a lid and cook for 5 minutes. Taste for seasoning and add sea salt and black pepper as needed.

3. Turn up the heat and add the fresh cilantro, corn and cooked halibut meat. Stir to combine, cover and cook for 5 minutes. Turn off the heat and allow the pot to rest for 5-10 minutes, giving the flavors time to meld. Taste for seasoning and serve in bowls with the optional toppings.

SERVING SUGGESTION:
SHREDDED CABBAGE, AVOCADO SLICES,
MEXICAN CHEESE BLEND, BLACK BEANS,
LIME WEDGES, SOUR CREAM, TORTILLA CHIPS

Mexican Halibut Pozole

Pozole is a Mexican stew that is made from hominy (maize kernels), spices and pork. In some parts of Mexico, the soup is cooked on Saturday afternoons, allowed to rest overnight, and enjoyed on Sunday. Soup is always better the second day in my opinion! In some homes, pozole is traditionally served on Christmas eve.

An old wive's tale suggests that this soup goes beyond nourishment and contains medicinal qualities. Similar to the American cure-all chicken soup, posole has a reputation for curing hangovers. My pescatarian version is just as flavorful with the added nutritional benefits, thanks to simmering the fish bones that supply marine collagen. It's still out for debate, but marine collagen is thought to help maintain joint and skin health with long-term use.

INGREDIENTS

- 3 tablespoons avocado oil

- **1 large white onion**, coarsely chopped

- **3 cloves garlic**, finely chopped

- **1 tablespoon ground cumin**

- **1 tablespoon ground coriander**

- **1 tablespoon chili powder**

- **2 pounds medium tomatillos**, diced

- **1 tablespoon dried oregano**

- **1 serrano pepper**, finely chopped, seeds optional

- **1 cup water**, more as needed

- **3 cups halibut bone broth (see page 486) with cooked meat (about 1 cup cooked halibut)**

- **1 15-ounce can white hominy**, rinsed

- **Sea salt and freshly ground black pepper to taste**

- **1 bunch fresh cilantro**, leaves only

DIRECTIONS

{ Serves 4-6 }

1. In a medium-sized Dutch oven or soup pot, heat the avocado oil over medium-high heat. Add the onion and sauté until soft and fragrant, about 4 minutes. Add garlic, cumin, coriander and chili powder, stirring often until fragrant, about 2 minutes.

2. Add the tomatillos, oregano and serrano pepper and stir until fragrant and the tomatillos have softened, about 3 minutes. Add the water and stir. Turn off the heat and pulse with an immersion blender until the tomatillos have broken down a bit but still have texture. If you prefer a smooth soup, continue to blend. You can also use a food processor for this and add the soup back to the pot.

3. Turn the pot to medium-high heat and pour in halibut bone broth and hominy. Stir to combine and cook for 5 minutes. The soup should be brothy; add a little water if it's too thick. Taste for seasoning and add sea salt and freshly ground black pepper as needed.

4. Reduce the heat to a simmer and add the cooked halibut and cilantro. Cover with a lid and cook for 5 minutes. Turn off the heat and allow the pot to rest for at least 15 minutes, allowing the flavors to meld.

5. To serve, ladle equal portions of the soup into bowls and garnish with lime wedges, sliced radish, cilantro, and diced avocado as desired. Serve immediately with corn or flour tortillas if desired.

SERVING SUGGESTIONS:
LIME WEDGES, SLICED RADISH, FRESH CILANTRO, DICED AVOCADO, WARM CORN OR FLOUR TORTILLAS

Djerba Harissa-Spiced Mussel Soup

Some of the Mediterranean's best beaches can be found in Tunisia. The northern coastline of the country is dotted with clear blue water, lush vegetation, and rugged cliffs, while the southern region boasts a magnificent desert landscape. Located on the Tunisian peninsula, the island of Djerba is a famous tourist spot, noted for its glowing beaches, whitewashed villages, dramatic sunsets and some of the best seafood in the country.

The town is bursting with cultural richness influenced by African, Arab, Berber and Jewish cultures, and the gastronomy reflects this ethnic mélange. Used by all, harissa is a flavorful paste made from chilis and spices. You can purchase harissa paste or make your own—try my recipe on page 550. Shellfish are not as popular as white and oily fish in North Africa, but you can find them on occasion. Feel free to use either black or New Zealand green-lipped mussels for this recipe.

INGREDIENTS

½ cup white wine

4 cups water (1 quart), separated

4 pounds fresh mussels, sorted and debearded

3 tablespoons olive oil

1 small Spanish onion, finely chopped

2 large stalks celery, finely chopped

2 large carrots, finely chopped

2 large russet potatoes, diced into ¾-inch pieces

2 tablespoons harissa paste

2 cups crushed tomatoes

1 cup fresh spinach, stems removed

Sea salt and freshly ground black pepper

DIRECTIONS

1. In a large Dutch oven or soup pot, combine the wine and 2 cups of water and heat over medium-high heat. Add the live mussels to the pot and cover tightly with a lid. Give the pot a gentle shake to help settle the shellfish and give them room to open. Cook for 4 minutes or until the mussels have opened. Turn off the heat and allow the mussels to cool.

2. Once cooled, strain the broth through a fine-mesh sieve until it runs relatively clear—two or three passes may be needed (it's important to remove all mussel shell remnants). Set the broth aside.

3. Next, pick through the mussels and place the meat in a bowl. Discard any unopened shells. Set aside. To compose the soup, heat the olive oil in the Dutch oven or soup pot over medium-high heat. Add the Spanish onion, celery and carrot and sauté until fragrant, about 3 minutes. Pour in the remaining 2 cups of water and the strained mussel broth. Reduce the heat to a simmer and cook for 5 minutes.

4. Add the potatoes to the pot and cover with the lid slightly ajar. Cook for 8–10 minutes until the potatoes have softened. Stir in the harissa paste and pour in the tomatoes. Reduce the heat and simmer uncovered for 1 minute.

5. Add the mussels and the spinach and cover with a lid. Simmer for 2 minutes—just long enough for the mussels to warm and the spinach to wilt. Taste for seasoning and add salt and freshly ground black pepper as needed. Turn off the heat and allow the pot to sit covered for 5 minutes before serving. Divide among 6 bowls and serve with toasted pita or couscous as desired.

SERVING SUGGESTIONS:
TOASTED FLATBREAD, CRUSTY FRENCH BREAD, OR STEAMED COUSCOUS

West African Fish Stew

Vibrant, colorful and rambunctious, the part of the world known as West Africa comprises 16 countries each with their own unique customs and personalities. Canvased with rocky coastlines, beautiful sandy beaches and communities that enjoy a range of diverse foods, West Africa boasts exquisite fare that is influenced by Arab and European cultures.

As one of the original farm-to-table regions, West Africa is home to many families who grow and raise their own food—cowpeas (black-eyed peas), okra, sweet potatoes, onions and hot peppers, to name a few. While there are some differences between local cuisines, there are many commonalities that can be found in this fish stew.

Stretching from Mauritania to Guinea, coastal Africa's favorite seafood varieties include mahi-mahi, mackerel, shrimp, sea bream and tilapia. Firm white fish works best for this dish, and I've selected tilapia for this recipe.

INGREDIENTS

{ Serves 4 }

- **3 tablespoons ghee**

- **2 cloves garlic**, minced

- **1 large white onion**, sliced

- **1 tablespoon ground cumin**

- **2 teaspoons ground coriander**

- **3 cups water**

- **1 15-ounce can crushed tomatoes**

- **1 heaping tablespoon peanut butter (smooth or crunchy will work)**

- **1 bay leaf**

- **1 1-inch piece fresh ginger**, sliced

- **1 13.5-ounce can coconut milk**

- **2 large sweet potatoes**, peeled and diced

- **2 whole tilapia**, dressed, cut into thirds

- **½ pound fresh okra**, sliced

- **Sea salt and freshly ground black pepper to taste**

- **½ cup fresh cilantro leaves**

- **¼ cup roasted salted peanuts**, crushed

DIRECTIONS

1. In a large soup pot or Dutch oven, heat the ghee over medium heat and add the garlic, onion, cumin and coriander and cook for 1–2 minutes or until the spices are fragrant.

2. Pour in the water and the crushed tomatoes, then add the peanut butter, bay leaf and ginger and bring to a simmer for 10 minutes. Add the coconut milk and sweet potatoes and cook for another 5 minutes. Add the fish and okra and cook, covered, for an additional 10 minutes. Add sea salt and black pepper to taste and adjust as needed. Turn off the heat and allow the pot to sit for 5–10 minutes. To serve, ladle the stew into bowls and garnish with fresh cilantro leaves and crushed peanuts as desired. Serve with coconut rice or steamed couscous, Cuban plátanos maduros or accaras, and lime wedges.

Tinned Fish Recipes

- Italian Smoked Clams and White Beans on Toast

- Pacific Coast Smoked Oyster Crostini with Ajvar

- Mediterranean Tinned Fish Oil Sauce

- Spanish Tinned Mussels with Rosemary Crackers

- Italian Seafood Piadina (Flatbread)

Italian Smoked Clams and White Beans on Toast

This simple Mediterranean-inspired dish combines tinned smoked clams and white beans, which work great together for brunch or a light supper.

Cannellini beans, also known as white kidney beans, have a natural nutty flavor and meaty texture. They are adored in Italy and throughout the Mediterranean where they are traditionally cooked in a clay pot, giving the beans a unique earthy note. Using quality smoked clams imparts a similar flavor.

INGREDIENTS

{ Serves 3-4 }

- **2 cloves garlic**, chopped

- **2 tablespoons olive oil**

- **1 15-ounce can cannellini beans**, rinsed

- **2 teaspoons dried mixed herbs (such as basil, thyme and rosemary)**

- **2 4-ounce tins smoked clams in oil**

- **1 teaspoon red pepper flake**

- **1 tablespoon lemon juice**

- **1 cup arugula or baby spinach**

- **Sea salt and freshly ground black pepper to taste**

- **3–4 slices of rustic or sourdough bread**, toasted

SERVING SUGGESTIONS: RUSTIC BREAD, OYSTER CRACKERS

DIRECTIONS

1. In a medium-sized skillet, sauté the garlic in olive oil for 30 seconds. Add the cannellini beans and mixed herbs and cook for 1 minute, stirring occasionally, until warmed through.

2. Stir in the smoked clams, red pepper flake and lemon juice, and cook for another 20 seconds. Add the arugula or baby spinach and cook until wilted. Taste for seasoning and add sea salt and freshly ground black pepper to taste. Adjust seasoning as needed.

3. Meanwhile, toast the bread—a regular toaster works great, or if you prefer, feel free to pan-toast your bread with a little butter or olive oil.

4. To serve, add equal portions of the mixture to each slice of toast. Divide toasts among individual plates and serve immediately.

Pacific Coast Smoked Oyster Crostini with Ajvar

Ilwaco is a small, sleepy fishing village in coastal Washington. Aside from luxurious B&Bs, oysters and seafood really put this small city on the map. During my most recent visit, I probably ate my body weight in raw, fried, grilled and smothered oysters, including a wonderful oyster poutine (take me back!).

Throughout the city, tinned oysters are available in shops along the main highway. I purchased as many tins as I had space for in my suitcase. Be sure to use high-quality tinned smoked oysters for this simple and underrated snack. Ajvar is a flavorful red bell pepper sauce from Serbia that can be found in specialty markets or online.

INGREDIENTS

{ Makes 2 dozen crostini }

- **1 baguette**, sliced into 24 rounds

- **2 dozen tinned smoked oysters in olive oil**, drained, oil reserved

- **3 cloves garlic**, halved

- **¼ cup ajvar sauce**

- **¼ cup chives**, chopped

DIRECTIONS

1. Heat oven to broil or 500°F.

2. Place the baguette slices on a baking sheet and brush them with the reserved oyster olive oil. Place the pan under the broiler until the bread is lightly toasted and golden brown, about 2 minutes.

3. Remove the baguette slices from the broiler. Rub each slice of bread with the sliced side of a garlic clove half. Place ½ teaspoon of ajvar sauce on each baguette slice and top with one oyster. Garnish with chopped chives and serve immediately.

Mediterranean Tinned Fish Oil Sauce

Tinned fish is an everyday treat in the Mediterranean, especially in places like Morocco, Portugal and Spain. It should be no surprise that these countries have some of the highest quality varieties around and export these morsels around the world. Sardines, tuna, squid, octopus and oysters are a few of my favorites.

Aside from the seafood, the oil in which they have been marinated is quite tasty and can be used in many ways—salad dressing, a finishing oil or a pungent dipping sauce for bread, crackers and veggies.

This is a loose recipe and I encourage you to use your intuition and taste buds as your guide.

INGREDIENTS

{ Makes about ½ cup }

- **¼ cup tinned fish oil**

- **¼ cup olive oil**

- **1 medium lemon, juice only**

- **½ teaspoon red pepper flake**

- **1 tablespoon chopped fresh mixed herbs (such as basil, oregano, thyme, rosemary, tarragon)**

- **Sea salt and freshly ground black pepper to taste**

SERVING SUGGESTIONS: SLICED BREAD, CRACKERS, VEGGIES FOR DIPPING

DIRECTIONS

1. In a small bowl, whisk together the fish oil, olive oil, lemon juice, red pepper flake and herbs. Taste for seasoning and add sea salt and black pepper to taste. Serve immediately or cover and refrigerate for up to 2 days.

Spanish
Tinned Mussels

~~~~~~~~~~~~~~~~~~~~~~~~~~~~~

WITH ROSEMARY CRACKERS

Sitting at a restaurant table overlooking the Mediterranean Sea, my husband and I enjoyed a snack very similar to this dish at one of the oceanfront bars in the Spanish beach city of Castelldefels. It's located about 20 miles from Barcelona and is a perfect place to spend a few vacation days.

I call for tinned mussels in this recipe, but you can swap them out for your favorite tinned fish. Smoked oysters, sardines, octopus in olive oil and squid in tomato sauce are nice choices— whatever floats your boat!

Making homemade crackers is pretty straightforward. It can be a rewarding experience and does not take long at all. These rosemary crackers are a wonderful addition to a charcuterie platter and make an elegant holiday gift when beautifully wrapped.

INGREDIENTS

{ Serves 4 }

- **1 cup all-purpose flour**

- **½ teaspoon sea salt**

- **1 tablespoon minced fresh rosemary leaves**

- **2 tablespoons minced black olives**

- **1 tablespoon garlic powder**

- **3 tablespoons finely grated hard Spanish cheese, like Iberico or Manchego**

- **3 tablespoons extra-virgin olive oil**

- **¼ cup half-and-half, more if needed**

- **Fleur de sel or other finishing salt, for topping**

- **3 6-ounce tins mussels in olive oil (or tinned fish of choice)**

SERVING SUGGESTIONS: SOFT CHEESE LIKE BRIE OR CAMEMBERT, FRESH FRUIT, VEGGIES

DIRECTIONS

1. Preheat oven to 400°F.

2. In a large bowl, combine the flour, sea salt, rosemary, olives, garlic powder, grated cheese and olive oil, mixing until crumbs form.

3. Add the half-and-half and mix until the dough comes together. Use your hands to form 4–5 small dough balls and set aside.

4. Lay out a sheet of parchment paper on a large clean surface. Use a rolling pin to roll out one of the pieces of dough as thin as possible—this will determine the thickness of your cracker. Use a straight or decorative pastry cutter or a sharp knife to cut the dough into ribbons. Sprinkle the dough with a little fleur de sel and repeat with the other balls of dough.

5. Bake the crackers until golden brown, about 6–8 minutes. Remove from the oven and let cool for 10 minutes. Serve alongside the tinned mussels, soft cheese, fresh fruit and veggies.

Italian Seafood Piadina (Flatbread)

Piadina is a simple yeast-free Italian flatbread that is prepared on the stovetop. It's easy to make at home, but there are so many good bakeries and commercial varieties of piadina available that I don't bother.

Piadina are quite thin, so it's important to crisp them up in the oven before adding toppings. Indian naan or a Greek-style pita will also work as a substitute in this recipe. Have fun with this dish and use your favorite seafood and veggies.

INGREDIENTS

1 tablespoons olive oil

1 tin blue mussels in olive oil, oil drained and reserved

½ pound shrimp, peeled and deveined with tails removed, halved lengthwise

1 clove garlic, minced

1 teaspoon lemon juice

Sea salt and freshly ground black pepper to taste

2 pieces of piadina or flatbread of choice (naan, Greek pita, etc.)

½ cup grated mozzarella cheese

1 large tomato, thinly sliced

1 handful black olives, sliced

1 teaspoon red pepper flake

½ cup fresh arugula

DIRECTIONS

{ Serves 2 }

1. Preheat oven to 450°F.

2. In a medium-sized skillet, heat the olive oil along with the reserved tinned mussel oil. When the oil is hot, add the shrimp, garlic and lemon juice to the pan along with a little sea salt and freshly ground black pepper to taste. Cook for 2 minutes until the shrimp just start to turn pink. Remove the shrimp from the pan and set them aside; reserve the olive oil sauce in a separate container.

3. Lay the flatbread out on a baking sheet lined with parchment paper. Brush with the reserved olive oil sauce from the pan and place in the oven for 2 minutes to crisp up the bread. Remove from the oven and set aside.

4. To serve, add equal portions of the mixture to each slice of toast. Divide toasts among individual plates and serve immediately.

5. Next, layer on your ingredients. My formula is cheese, tomato, shrimp, mussels, cheese, olives and red pepper flake.

6. Place the baking sheet in the oven and cook for 5–7 minutes, or until the cheese is melted. Remove from the oven, top with fresh arugula, slice as desired, and serve immediately.

Sauces, Salsas and Spice Blends

- Cajun Blackening Seasoning

- French Hollandaise Sauce

- Gullah Spice Blend

- Italian Basil Lemon Butter

- Poudre de Colombo (Colombo Curry Powder)

- Caribbean Pineapple Chow

- Gilroy Garlic Thyme Butter

- Carpinteria Avocado Salsa

- Mexican Avocado Crema

- Spanish Smoked Paprika Sea Salt

- Moroccan Harissa Paste

- Mediterranean Rosemary Sea Salt

- Norwegian Seaweed "Salt"

- South American Chimichurri

- Caribbean Jerk Seasoning

- California Salted Avocado

- Sunomono (Japanese Cucumber Salad)

- Hopkins Village Mango-Avocado Salsa

- St. Ann's Parish Mango Salsa

Cajun Blackening Seasoning

Legendary Louisiana chef Paul Prudhomme is attributed with popularizing Cajun cooking and the blackening cooking technique in the 1980s. If you are new to the idea of blackening, it does not imply charring or burning the fish, as so many jokes imply. It's actually the delicious effect of dry spices meeting hot oil and searing in a cast iron skillet, giving the fish a slightly dark, or blackened look. The result is a wonderful texture and rich flavor.

I like to include culinary lavender in my blackening seasoning mix to give it a minty citrus note. You can omit it if you'd like; it's great with or without, just note that a little goes a long way. This recipe easily doubles—make it my way the first time then feel free to experiment with more or less of each spice to suit your palate.

INGREDIENTS

{ Makes just over ½ cup }

- **2 tablespoons paprika**
- **1 tablespoon cayenne pepper**
- **1 tablespoon chili powder**
- **1 tablespoon onion powder**
- **1 tablespoon garlic powder**
- **1 teaspoon white pepper**
- **2 teaspoons dried oregano**
- **1 teaspoon freshly ground black pepper**
- **Pinch of culinary lavender (optional)**, crushed
- **Sea salt**, as desired

DIRECTIONS

1. Add the ingredients to the bowl of a food processor or blender and pulse 3–4 times to ensure that the mix is well combined and becomes slightly less coarse, but not turned into a powder. Alternatively, you can add the ingredients to a sealed container and shake to combine. Use immediately or store in a sealed container for 3–6 months.

French Hollandaise Sauce

Once known as Dutch Sauce, hollandaise is a classic French sauce that is used to top everything from steamed vegetables to eggs Benedict—see my Kent Island crab Benedict recipe on page 444.

My first taste of hollandaise was in an upscale breakfast restaurant in Santa Barbara, and it was delicious—the creaminess of the sauce combined with perfectly toasted bread and poached salmon is something I have been replicating for Sunday brunch with friends and family ever since.

Hollandaise is simple to make but can be fussy since it's an emulsion, which means we're mixing ingredients that don't naturally blend well—oil and water—without help. This can result in the sauce breaking or curdling if the butter is added too quickly or is too hot. Take your time with this one and you will be rewarded.

I call for an immersion blender for this recipe, but you can use any food processor you have available.

INGREDIENTS

{ Serves 4 }

- **1 cup unsalted butter, cubed**

- **3 large egg yolks**

- **1 tablespoon fresh lemon juice**

- **1 teaspoon Dijon mustard**

- **¼ teaspoon sea salt**

- **Pinch smoked paprika**

DIRECTIONS

SPECIAL EQUIPMENT: IMMERSION BLENDER

1. In a large saucepan, melt the butter on low heat.

2. While the butter is melting, add the egg yolks, lemon juice, Dijon mustard, sea salt and smoked paprika to a medium-sized bowl with a flat bottom. Using an immersion blender, pulse the ingredients to combine while drizzling in the warm melted butter until the sauce comes together—about 5–8 seconds. Use the sauce immediately or cover and refrigerate.

* To reheat the sauce, place the bowl in a pan of hot water or in a double boiler on low heat. If the sauce thickens, add a little water and whisk until smooth.

Gullah
Spice Blend

The Carolina Lowcountry region around Charleston, South Carolina and the coastal islands plays host to the Gullah-Geechee people, an African American culture that has inhabited the region for centuries. This group are the descendants of enslaved West African people who farmed the rice plantations in the region in the 1700s and brought this part of the world great fortune. Having blossomed from a dark past, this region now celebrates its rich food heritage.

Wild seafood like shrimp, crab and oysters are favorites in Lowcountry fare. Rice and grits round out most meals that are often sprinkled with a dash of this seasoning mix, a combination of sweet and savory spices that are distinct and memorable.

INGREDIENTS

{ Makes about 1½ cups }

- ¼ cup ground celery seed
- ¼ cup paprika
- ¼ cup granulated garlic
- ¼ cup granulated onion
- 2 tablespoons ground black pepper
- 2 tablespoons white pepper
- 2 tablespoons ground thyme
- 1 teaspoon ground ginger
- 1 teaspoon cinnamon
- 1 teaspoon allspice
- 1 teaspoon dry mustard
- 1 teaspoon sugar
- 2 tablespoon sea salt or kosher salt

DIRECTIONS

1. In a medium-sized bowl, combine the celery seed, paprika, granulated garlic, granulated onion, black pepper, white pepper, thyme, ginger, cinnamon, allspice, dry mustard, sugar and salt. Add to an airtight jar and use as desired. Store for up to 3 months.

Italian Basil Lemon Butter

Basil is one of the most-loved herbs in Italy and throughout the Mediterranean. It's a member of the mint family along with rosemary, lavender and sage, and has a slightly sweet flavor that pairs well with seafood. Alongside its culinary versatility, basil is celebrated for medicinal purposes. Its essential oil has been used to treat snake bites, inflammation and to help aid digestion.

This recipe is what is known as a compound butter, which is a mixture of butter and other ingredients that range in complexity, from the simple, like this basil and lemon version, to the more exotic like crab, lobster and even squid ink.

I call for European butter in this recipe because it has a higher fat content and is more flavorful than regular butter due to the culturing or fermenting process, which gives it a little tang.

Use this compound butter on grilled fish, baked seafood, vegetables, bread or baked potatoes.

INGREDIENTS

{ Makes about ½ cups }

- **1 stick unsalted European or high-fat butter (Kerrygold or Plugrá are good options),** softened

- **6 fresh sweet basil leaves,** finely minced

- **1 clove garlic,** minced

- **1 teaspoon lemon juice**

- **½ teaspoon lemon zest**

- **½ teaspoon sea salt**

DIRECTIONS

1. In a medium-sized bowl, add the softened butter, sweet basil, garlic, lemon juice, lemon zest and sea salt.

2. Use a rubber spatula to mix all of the ingredients together, occasionally mashing the mixture against the side of the bowl to crush any large bits that the knife may have missed. Use immediately, or place butter in decorative butter molds, cover with plastic wrap, and refrigerate. Alternately, you can form butter into a log and wrap tightly with plastic wrap, then refrigerate. The butter will keep for 2 weeks in the refrigerator or for 1 month in the freezer.

Poudre de Colombo

COLOMBO CURRY POWDER

On the northeast coast of South America sits the county of French Guiana, a melting pot of cultures that includes West African, Chinese, Creole, French, Native American, Indonesian and Sri Lankan, all of which are reflected in the region's gastronomy.

Seafood is the centerpiece of Guianese cooking, and the classic Colombo curry spice blend, or Poudre de Colombo, named after the capital city of Sri Lanka, is one of the most popular in the French West Indies. This fragrant curry blend made its way to the French Caribbean like other ingredients—via human migration and the blending of cultures.

French Guiana is a land where spicy curry seafood dishes sit right alongside classic French techniques. The capital city of Cayenne is where the name for the popular cayenne pepper comes from.

This curry powder stems from Indian and Sri Lankan influences that made their way to French Guiana. Like most curries and spice blends, everyone has their own version. This is mine!

INGREDIENTS

{ Makes about 1 cup }

- **2 tablespoons ground coriander**

- **2 teaspoons ground fenugreek seed**

- **1 teaspoon ground cinnamon**

- **1 teaspoon ground cumin**

- **1 teaspoon ground black pepper**

- **½ teaspoon ground allspice**

- **½ teaspoon ground ginger**

- **½ teaspoon ground turmeric**

- **4 cardamom pods**, crushed, seeds only

- **½ teaspoon dry mustard**

- **¼ teaspoon ground mace**

- **½ teaspoon cayenne pepper**

DIRECTIONS

1. In a medium-sized bowl, combine all the spices and mix well. Use immediately or store in an airtight container for 4–6 months.

Caribbean Pineapple Chow

Pineapple chow is a refreshing street food popular in Trinidad & Tobago. It's typically a combination of fruit, salt and spices served in plastic bags and enjoyed on the fly. I've created a rustic salsa version of this refreshing street food that is perfect for grilled fish, salads and tacos.

INGREDIENTS

{ Serves 4 }

- **2 cups fresh pineapple,** cut into chunks

- **1 large scallion,** sliced

- **1 small habañero pepper,** minced

- **2 limes,** juice only

- **2 cloves garlic,** minced

- **3 sprigs fresh thyme,** leaves only

- **Sea salt and freshly ground black pepper to taste**

DIRECTIONS

In a medium-sized bowl, combine the chopped pineapple, scallion, habañero pepper, lime juice, garlic, thyme, and sea salt and freshly ground black pepper to taste. Mix thoroughly. Let the mixture marinate for 10–15 minutes, then serve.

Gilroy Garlic Thyme Butter

The city of Gilroy, California is aptly nicknamed the "Garlic Capital of the World." Growing up in California about three hours from Gilroy, I was always fascinated by the annual garlic festival that had vendors who sold garlic ice cream, garlic popcorn and garlic-scented candles.

This savory butter comes in handy on so many occasions. Slather it on toast or flatbread, use it to sauté fish, or add it to rice and pasta. Explore variations of this recipe and swap out the thyme for rosemary or tarragon—get creative!

INGREDIENTS

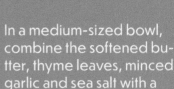

Makes ½ cup

- **1 stick unsalted butter,** softened

- **2 fresh thyme sprigs,** leaves only

- **4 cloves garlic,** minced

- **1 teaspoon sea salt**

DIRECTIONS

In a medium-sized bowl, combine the softened butter, thyme leaves, minced garlic and sea salt with a silicone spatula or a hand mixer. Transfer to a storage container and refrigerate until ready to use.

Carpinteria Avocado Salsa

Nestled between the Pacific coast and the Santa Ynez mountains is Carpinteria, a small coastal city that hosts the California Avocado Festival every year in October. There are seven varieties of avocado grown in California: Bacon, Fuerte, Gwen, Hass, Lamb Hass, Reed and Zutano. They are all tasty, but my favorite is Hass for its rich buttery flavor and tender flesh.

I like this chunky salsa with tortilla chips and with grilled and broiled fish.

INGREDIENTS

{ Serves 2–4 }

- **2 large ripe Hass avocados,** peeled, pitted, and diced into ¼-inch pieces

- **Sea salt and freshly ground black pepper to taste**

- **1 small tomato,** diced

- **¼ cup chopped fresh cilantro leaves**

- **1 small jalapeño pepper,** minced

- **2 teaspoons minced red onion**

- **2 tablespoons lime juice**

- **1 tablespoon olive oil**

DIRECTIONS

1. In a medium-sized bowl, add the avocado, sea salt and freshly ground black pepper to taste, tomato, cilantro, jalapeño and red onion. Drizzle the mixture with lime juice and olive oil and gently fold together. Take care not to mash the avocado or you'll end up with guacamole. Taste the salsa and adjust the seasoning as needed. Serve immediately or cover and refrigerate for up to 2 days.

Mexican Avocado Crema

Used as a condiment all over Central America, Mexican crema is very similar to sour cream but has a thinner consistency and more robust flavor. Combined with ripe avocado it makes for a sensational sauce for tacos, enchiladas, nachos and 'po boy sandwiches. It also works well as a dip.

Avocados are typically sold firm and underripe, yet they ripen very quickly—seemingly overnight. If you have fruit that needs to be used immediately, this is a good way to make use of them. This recipe easily doubles or triples.

INGREDIENTS

Makes about 1 ½ cups

- **1 large ripe avocado,** seeded and peeled

- **1 medium lime or 1½ tablespoons lime juice**

- **1 cup Mexican crema or sour cream**

- **½ teaspoon garlic powder**

- **½ jalapeño pepper,** seeded and minced (optional)

DIRECTIONS

Add all the ingredients to the bowl of a food processor or blender and mix until smooth. Pour into a container and serve as desired or keep in the refrigerator for up to 4 days.

Spanish Smoked Paprika Sea Salt

Often labeled as pimentón, Spanish paprika is made from peppers that are smoked and slowly dried over an oak fire for several days, giving the spice a rich, sweet, smoky flavor. It's used to add color and flavor to dishes, including cheese, and is as important to Spanish gastronomy as saffron and olive oil.

True pimentón is produced in specific regions of Spain and is tightly controlled by the Denomination of Origin (D.O.) control boards. The best Spanish smoked paprika arguably comes from Murcia in the east, and Extremadura in the western part of the country.

You can use this salt blend for finishing dishes or as an ingredient for legumes, soups, potatoes, grilled fish or steamed seafood.

INGREDIENTS

{ Makes about 1¼ cups }

- ¼ cup coarse sea salt
- 1 cup smoked paprika

DIRECTIONS

In a food processor, combine the sea salt and the smoked paprika. Pulse 5–10 times until the ingredients start to combine. Pour the mixture into a bowl and use a spoon to further incorporate. Add to an airtight container and use as desired. Keeps for 1 month or longer.

Moroccan Harissa Paste

Widely used in the African countries of Algeria, Morocco and Tunisia, harissa is a spicy chili-based sauce that is bold and flavorful.

Harissa is often used as a condiment or side dish in which to dip vegetables, bread or grilled meat, and is stirred into stews and added to couscous. It adds bright, rich flavor to almost any dish and is one of my favorite ingredients to toss into a recipe when it needs a little lift.

INGREDIENTS

{ Makes about ½ cup }

- **12 dried red chilies**
- **1 tablespoon coriander seed**
- **2 teaspoons cumin seed**
- **2 cloves garlic**
- **3 roasted red peppers**, chopped
- **1 tablespoon tomato paste**
- **1 tablespoon lemon juice**
- **½ teaspoon sea salt**
- **4–6 tablespoons olive oil**, more as needed

DIRECTIONS

1. Discard the stems and some of the seeds from the chilies and soak them in warm water for 30 minutes until softened.

2. Meanwhile, dry-fry the coriander and cumin seeds to bring out the flavor, then grind to a powder. With a large mortar and pestle, pound the garlic with the salt, add the drained chilies and pound the mixture until it is smooth. Add the red pepper, tomato paste, lemon juice, and spices and gradually add the oil, trickling it in and mixing until the sauce is well-blended and of a mayonnaise-like consistency. Alternatively, add the ingredients to a bowl of a food processor and blend until the right consistency is reached.

3. Use the harissa immediately or transfer to an airtight jar. Add more olive oil to the top of the paste to make a seal. Cover and store in the refrigerator for up to three weeks.

Mediterra-nean Rosemary Sea Salt

A native to the Mediterranean, rosemary is a robust herb that is used for culinary and medicinal purposes. It's a member of the mint family along with basil and sage and is a great addition to legume dishes like gigante beans (see page 374) or roasted potatoes.

Infused salt is a simple way to elevate the flavor of a dish. I often use this as a finishing salt for roasted fish and seafood. It also works well as part of a brine.

Citrus zest like lemon or orange can be nice additions to this recipe.

INGREDIENTS

{ Makes about ½ cup }

- ¼ cup coarse sea salt or Kosher salt (table salt is not recommended)

- ¼ cup fresh rosemary leaves

DIRECTIONS

In a food processor, combine half of the sea salt and all of the rosemary leaves. Pulse 5–10 times until the mixture starts to come together and the rosemary leaves are blended into the salt. Add the remaining sea salt and pulse a few more times; the mixture will be slightly moist. Spread on a baking tray and allow it to stand for 30 minutes, then place in an airtight jar. Keeps for 2–3 weeks.

Norwegian Seaweed "Salt"

The cold deep waters of Norway are the perfect breeding ground for sea kelp, a delicious, nutrient-dense seaweed. Sugar kelp and winged kelp are the varieties of seaweed that are commonly cultivated in the region. They both have a briny, umami flavor with a hint of sweetness. These incredibly sustainable vegetables grow in underwater forests and do not require fertilization or freshwater.

I discovered seaweed as a salt replacement during a month-long exploration of sea vegetables. Seaweed is loaded with minerals and has a divine, naturally salty flavor. You can also find this "salt" in specialty markets under the name of kelp granules or kelp flakes.

Use this recipe as a salt alternative or to finish vegetables and seafood.

INGREDIENTS

Makes about 1 cup

- **2 large dried leaves Norwegian sugar kelp or dried kombu leaves**

DIRECTIONS

In a food processor, pulse the dried seaweed 5–10 times until it turns into small flakes. Be careful not to overprocess or you'll have seaweed dust—this works for other purposes like coating fish, but in this recipe, we're looking for larger flakes. Add the seaweed salt to an airtight container and use as desired. Keeps for 1 month or longer.

South American Chimichurri

The South American countries of Argentina and Uruguay are famous for a flavorful uncooked sauce known as green chimichurri (there is also a red version). A bright earthy mix of cilantro, parsley and other simple ingredients, it's a great way to dress up roasted fish, grilled shrimp and vegetables.

I first enjoyed chimichurri at a Los Angeles restaurant called Lala's on Melrose, where house-made chimichurri was served as an appetizer alongside a sliced baguette and was replenished as needed to complement the grilled fish and veggies that would soon arrive.

INGREDIENTS

{ Makes about 1 ½ cup }

- **1 bunch fresh cilantro**

- **1 clove garlic**

- **1 bunch fresh parsley**

- **½ cup olive oil**

- **½ cup red wine vinegar**

- **1 tablespoon water, if needed**

- **½ teaspoon sea salt**

- **½ teaspoon freshly ground black pepper**

DIRECTIONS

1. In a food processor, pulse the cilantro, garlic and parsley and until chopped. Gradually add the oil, vinegar, water, sea salt and freshly ground black pepper and pulse 5–10 times until smooth. Place the mixture in a bowl, cover, and let rest for at least 30 minutes before using; this will give the flavors time to meld. After it has rested, place the sauce in an airtight jar and refrigerate until ready to use. Keeps for 4 days or more.

Caribbean Jerk Seasoning

This recipe is one of my favorite ways to bring the flavors of the Caribbean to my kitchen. There are entire chapters of books written about the origins and varieties of jerk seasoning. What I love most about jerk seasoning is how adaptable it is to a wide variety of herbs and spices; however, allspice berries and scotch bonnet pepper are essential.

There are dry spice versions of jerk and wet versions made from mostly fresh ingredients; I'm sharing my wet spice blend. This version is chunky and rustic and focuses on imparting Caribbean flavor and less on heat—but make no mistake, this blend will get your heart racing! You can swap out the Scotch bonnet for habañero pepper if needed, just know that scotch bonnets tend to be slightly sweeter in flavor than habs, but use what you can find.

To capture the true flavor of the Caribbean, I recommend cooking your seafood over natural lump charcoal made from pimento wood chips if you can find it; otherwise most natural lump charcoal should do the job (see page 131).

INGREDIENTS

{ Makes about ½ cup }

- **1 tablespoon whole dried Jamaican allspice berries**

- **1 tablespoon whole black peppercorns**

- **1 teaspoon whole cloves**

- **½ teaspoon ground cinnamon**

- **½ teaspoon ground nutmeg**

- **6 green cardamom pods**, seeds only

- **3 cloves garlic**

- **1 ½-inch piece fresh ginger root**, minced

- **½ Scotch bonnet or habañero pepper**, more or less depending on your desired heat level

- **5 sprigs fresh thyme**, leaves only

- **2 scallions**, chopped

- **2 limes**, juice and zest

- **2 tablespoons olive oil**

DIRECTIONS

1. With a mortar and pestle, pound all of the dried spices individually until ground and fragrant. You will need to remove the hull from the cardamom pods. Do this by pounding them lightly until the husk falls off, revealing the black seeds. Throw out the husks and pound the black seeds until ground and fragrant. Place spices in a small bowl and combine thoroughly.

2. Next, pound the garlic, ginger, scotch bonnet or habañero pepper, thyme and scallions with the mortar and pestle until you achieve a chunky consistency. Add these ingredients to the spice bowl along with the lime juice, lime zest and olive oil. Stir to combine. Use immediately or store in an airtight container in the refrigerator for up to 1 week.

California Salted Avocado

My parents have a small organic farm in Central California, and one of their prized fruits is avocado. Having an abundance of avocado has allowed for lots of experimentation with recipes for guacamole, smoothies, cheesecake and more. However, at the end of the day, a firm ripe avocado with a little sea salt is one of my favorites. This recipe is awesome on toast and a great addition to sandwiches or as a replacement for mayo.

INGREDIENTS

{ Serves 4 }

- **2 ripe Hass avocados**, pitted
- **1 tablespoon sea salt**
- **Lemon or lime slices**, optional

DIRECTIONS

Scoop the avocado out of the shell and add to a medium-sized bowl. Add the sea salt and use a fork to mash until combined. Add a squeeze of lemon or lime juice if desired. Serve immediately.

Sunomono

JAPANESE SPICY CUCUMBER SALAD

Cool and refreshing, this Asian cucumber salad is a favorite appetizer on the dinner tables of Japanese households and restaurants. The name Sunomono refers to a variety of vinegared vegetable salads or pickles. I first experienced this salad as part of a bento box lunch which used Japanese cucumbers, which have a firm crisp texture and no bitterness. English and Persian cucumbers are a good substitute. The cucumber can be substituted or augmented by thinly sliced radish or carrot.

INGREDIENTS

{ Serves 4 }

- **2 large Asian, English or Persian cucumbers**, thinly sliced

- **1 teaspoon sea salt**

- **1 tablespoon Korean pepper flake or sambal oelek**

- **1 scallion**, sliced

- **1 clove garlic**, minced

- **2 tablespoons rice wine vinegar**

- **1 pinch white sugar**

- **1 teaspoon sesame oil**

DIRECTIONS

1. In a medium-sized bowl, stir together the cucumber and the salt. Let the mixture sit for 20 minutes. When the time is up, drain the liquid from the bowl. Rinse the cucumber in cold water to remove excess salt and drain well.

2. In a small bowl, add the Korean pepper flake (or sambal oelek if using), scallion, garlic, rice wine vinegar, sugar and sesame oil. Mix to combine, taste for seasoning and adjust as needed. Pour the dressing over the cucumbers, cover, and refrigerate for 20–30 minutes. Serve as desired.

Hopkins Village Mango -Avocado Salsa

On my first visit to the tropical paradise known as Belize, I arrived in the middle of the balmy summer to record a few episodes of my show "Appetite for Adventure!"

As I walked along the tree-lined streets of coastal Hopkins Village with a local guide, we heard thumping sounds every so often. I got curious and asked about the noise. My guide informed me that we were walking through a grove of mango trees and what we were hearing was ripe fruit hitting the ground. With the sweet scent of mangos in the air, I looked up and saw fruit the size of my forearm swaying in the warm summer breeze. I could have stayed there forever! It's one of my favorite memories.

The sweetness of ripe mango coupled with the rich flavor of avocado is sublime in this tropical salsa. Most varieties of mango will work for this dish, but my favorite is the red variety for its firm, flavorful flesh. One of my favorite tips for this recipe is to lightly salt the mango prior to mixing with the other ingredients to give the dish a velvety texture.

When served alongside grilled or roasted seafood, this salsa tropical adds flair and texture. Served as a salsa with tortilla chips, it is beguiling and hard to resist.

INGREDIENTS

{ Serves 4 }

- **2 large ripe mangos,** peeled, pitted and chopped into ¼-inch chunks

- **½ teaspoon sea salt,** more as needed

- **¼ cup red onion,** chopped

- **1 tablespoon chopped scallion,** green part only

- **1 teaspoon minced fresh garlic**

- **¼ cup chopped fresh cilantro**

- **1 large lime,** juice and zest

- **Freshly ground black pepper to taste**

- **1 large ripe avocado,** peeled, pitted and chopped into ¼-inch chunks

DIRECTIONS

1. In a medium-sized glass bowl, stir together the mango and the salt. Cover and allow the fruit to rest for 15–20 minutes.

2. When the time is up, add the red onion, scallion, garlic and cilantro. Mix well. Add the juice and zest of the lime along with salt and freshly ground black pepper to taste. Cover with plastic wrap and refrigerate for 15 minutes to allow flavors to blend. After the mixture has chilled, add the avocado and mix gently to combine. Serve immediately or cover with plastic wrap and refrigerate. Salsa will keep for 2 days.

St. Ann's Parish Mango Salsa

The Parish of St. Ann is situated on the northern coast of the Caribbean island of Jamaica, one of the most popular travel destinations in the world. As a 5th grader, I wrote my country report on this nation simply based on the travel magazines that my adventure-loving teacher provided as a resource. The glossy photos made the place seem like a paradise with its beguiling blue water, mesmerizing views and lively culture. If I'm honest, it was also because I had a crush on Ziggy Marley, the eldest son of music legend and activist Bob Marley, who is from a small village called Nine Mile located in St. Ann.

This region is celebrated for its lush landscapes, bountiful spices and fruit trees, including mangos, and is often referred to as the "Garden Parish."

Mangos are grown all over the world and are a member of the cashew family. Like avocados, they come in many varieties. Jamaicans have roughly 20 colorful names for mangos, such as: beefy mango, cowfoot mango, bellyful mango, Julie mango and sweetie mango, to name a few. My favorite is the Julie mango, with its beautiful red-orange colored skin and juicy flesh.

With its sweet, warm and fiery flavor, this salsa is inspired by one of my favorite mango chutneys.

INGREDIENTS

{ Serves 4 }

- **2 large ripe red mangos**, peeled, pitted and chopped into ¼-inch chunks

- **½ teaspoon sea salt**, more as needed

- **¼ cup red onion**, chopped

- **¼ cup chopped fresh cilantro**

- **1 teaspoon grated ginger**

- **½ scotch bonnet pepper (optional)**

- **1 large lime**, juice and zest

DIRECTIONS

1. In a medium-sized glass bowl, combine all of the ingredients. Cover with plastic wrap and refrigerate for 15 minutes to allow flavors to blend. Serve immediately or cover with plastic wrap and refrigerate. Salsa will keep for 2 or 3 days.

Made in the USA
Coppell, TX
03 May 2023

16353814R00313